The Cryptographic Imagination

Shawn James Rosenheim

THE

] Z Y I Q N I T D A H W Q Q I A Y Y L Z E E Q P Q V V R J C V W K E J S C G M P D T Y C Y N Q U K U V X J I U N O L Z ℩

CRYPTO

PARALLAX RE-VISIONS OF CULTURE AND SOCIETY

Stephen G. Nichols, Gerald Prince, and Wendy Steiner, Series Editors

SECRET WRITING

FROM EDGAR POE

TO THE INTERNET

GRAPHIC

OHMMDMXKBTAMEHBQYMOIHMQJKOLQOVTKXWZTENAKXMLVCMWHEGKIHMBCXWPRW

IMAGINATION

THE JOHNS HOPKINS UNIVERSITY PRESS *Baltimore and London*

© 1997 The Johns Hopkins University Press

All rights reserved. Published 1997

Printed in the United States of America on acid-free paper

06 05 04 03 02 01 00 99 98 97   5 4 3 2 1

The Johns Hopkins University Press

2715 North Charles Street

Baltimore, Maryland 21218-4319

The Johns Hopkins Press Ltd., London

Library of Congress Cataloging-in-Publication Data will be found
at the end of this book.

A catalog record for this book is available from the British Library.

ISBN 0-8018-5331-1

ISBN 0-8018-5332-X (pbk.)

To My Parents,

Marlene and Duane Rosenheim,

With Love and Thanks

Contents

Acknowledgments

One of the pleasures involved in finishing this project is the long-delayed opportunity to give heartfelt thanks to the people who have helped me along the way. Among these I would like to single out Grace Aspinall; Paige Baty; my thesis advisor, Richard Brodhead; Charles Buckholtz; Karen Hust; Elizabeth Kolbert; Meredith McGill, who invited me to give a portion of this book as a talk at Harvard University in November 1995; Mark Reinhardt; Lou Renza, for his generous invitation to speak to Americanists at Dartmouth University; Bob Volz and Wayne Hammond at the Chapin Library; and the librarians of Sterling Memorial Library at Yale University and Sawyer Library at Williams College. I must also mention John Irwin (not only a friend to my manuscript, but an inspiration for it as well, through his *American Hieroglyphics*); my tough-minded and expert copyeditor, Jane Lincoln Taylor; and Eric Halpern, who acquired the manuscript for the Johns Hopkins University Press even though he *knew* about my difficulty in meeting deadlines.

Many people commented thoughtfully on all or part of the manuscript, including David Leverenz, Mark Taylor, Terence Whalen, Lou Renza, and Myra Jehlen. I owe special thanks to Don Pease, who came through for me in the clinch with his timely and brilliant reading. Martin Harries, John Kleiner, John Limon, and Michael Bell had the dubious distinction of serving as *my* secret readers, and, often, secret writers, and my debts to them for their tact, intellectual generosity, and acuity are large. I'm also grateful for the friendship of Michael Bell, who not only gave me the benefit of his critical insight, but who has been for years a wise mentor and hectoring friend. And Stephen Rachman has been a peerless companion in all things literary, serving variously as cheerleader, sometime collaborator, and grotesque twin.

My greatest thanks must go to Cassandra Cleghorn, without whose assistance this book would not exist. Her presence, her readings alone, rendered vividly luminous the many mysteries of transcendentalism in which we were immersed.

The Cryptographic Imagination

Introduction

All longing converges on this mystery: revelation, unraveling secret
spaces, the suggestion that the world's valence lies just behind a
scrambled facade, where only the limits of ingenuity stand between
him and sunken gardens. Cryptography alone slips beneath the cheat of
surfaces.

Richard Powers, *The Gold Bug Variations*

But *this* is, now,—you may depend upon it—
Stable, opaque, immortal—all by dint
Of the dear names that lie concealed within't.

Edgar Allan Poe, "An Enigma"

The origin of this book might be described as an attempt to answer a
presumably straightforward question: what is the source of the worldwide
popularity of detective fiction? As I was hazarding an answer, however, my
study accreted to itself a series of apparently unrelated questions: what is
the relation of science fiction to the prosthetic body? How was the American defeat of Japan in World War II influenced by the work of Sir Francis
Bacon? Why does communication on the Internet so frequently invite flame
wars? And, most frivolous-sounding of all, how can we know who wrote
Shakespeare's plays? It is my contention that all these questions can be illu-
minated by the writing of Edgar Allan Poe, and more specifically, by that
subset of his work that makes direct or oblique use of codes and ciphers.
From 1839 to his death a decade later, Poe expressed his growing passion
for cryptography in a variety of genres. Besides "The Gold-Bug"—which,
as a stimulus to future cryptographers, might be said to be one of the few
literary texts with military value—Poe's cryptographic writing includes the
Dupin trilogy, his science fiction, the "Marginalia," and *Eureka*. Although
this secret writing includes some of Poe's best-known work, its importance
is greater than the literary value of the individual texts; as an *oeuvre*, these
texts amount to one of the deepest instances of what I call the cryptographic

1

imagination—an approach to literature that, in the century and a half since Poe's death, has become increasingly influential.

My ambition in what follows is to explain contemporary culture (or at least one important version of that culture) as a set of variations on the cryptographic imagination as it yokes together literature, technology, and society. As used in this book, the term "cryptographic imagination" does not only refer to the relatively few stories that, like "The Gold-Bug" or Robert Louis Stevenson's *Treasure Island*, explicitly include ciphers or codes. Instead, it refers to a constellation of literary techniques concerning secrecy in writing. These include private ciphers, acrostics, allusions, hidden signatures, chiasmal framing, etymological reference, and plagiarism; purloined writing and disappearing inks; and the thematic consequences—anonymity, doubling, identification, and the like—that follow from cryptographic texts.

I am equally concerned with the ways writers have incorporated aspects of "real" cryptography into their texts, either by directly employing ciphers or by generating fictions that respond to cryptographic institutions such as the National Security Agency (NSA). Poe, for example, was from adolescence interested in crypts, writing, and the relation between the two, but his sense of the scope and implications of that relation greatly expanded after December 1839, when he began submitting a series of unsigned pieces on cryptography and conundrums to a short-lived Philadelphia newspaper, *Alexander's Weekly Messenger*. In the first of these pieces, "Enigmatical and Conundrumical," Poe promised "that if any reader submitted an example of secret writing in which arbitrary symbols were substituted for letters of the alphabet, no such cipher could be propounded which he would be unable to solve."[1] For the next five months, Poe published solutions to what he maintained were all the ciphers that had been submitted to him, along with some explanations of the nature of cryptography. In May 1840, Poe's association with the newspaper ceased, but he returned to the subject a year later, publishing a long signed article in *Graham's Magazine* entitled "A Few Words on Secret Writing" (July 1841). Here Poe gives his account of the articles from *Alexander's*:

> In one of the weekly papers of this city, about eighteen months ago, the writer of this article had occasion to speak of the application of a rigorous *method* in all forms of thought—of its advantages—of the extension of its use even to what is considered the operation of pure fancy—and thus, subsequently, of the solution of cipher. He even ventured to assert that no cipher, of the character above specified, could be sent to the address of the paper, which he would not be able to resolve. This challenge excited, most unexpectedly, a very lively interest among the numerous readers of the journal. Letters were poured in upon the editor from all parts of the country; and many of the writers of these epistles were so convinced of the impenetrability of their mysteries, as to be

at great pains to draw him into wagers on the subject. . . . Out of, perhaps, one hundred ciphers altogether received, there was only one which we did not immediately succeed in solving. This one we *demonstrated* to be an imposition—that is to say, we fully proved it a jargon of random characters, having no meaning whatsoever.[2]

Poe followed this article with three addenda, in which he again claimed to have solved all the ciphers sent to him that had met his conditions, and many that had not.

Until lately, these essays have attracted little attention; most critics have been content to take them as evidence of Poe's "adolescent" interest in matters such as the ciphered treasure map of "The Gold-Bug."[3] In what follows, however, I hope to show the centrality of the cryptographic imagination to Poe's work, in part by showing how the recovery of Poe's cryptographic experiments recontextualizes the recent treatment of his works in France. Although poststructural thought has stimulated the best recent work on Poe, critics have often acted as if Poe's texts were merely pretexts for validating claims advanced by Jacques Derrida, Jacques Lacan, *et cie*. But *The Cryptographic Imagination* argues that Poe's postmodern relevance has a concrete historical source—that a primary reason Poe's writings seem theoretically contemporary is that Poe used his cryptographic writing to conduct a systematic investigation into the nature of language. Consequently, observations about the arbitrariness of signification or the itinerary of the signifier in "The Purloined Letter" often merely repeat Poe's own insights.

This is because Poe's cryptographic theory serves as a template for his late fiction: the language, the themes, and even the plots of some of Poe's most popular writings, including the Dupin stories and "The Gold-Bug," emerge from Poe's essays on cryptography. One corollary to cryptography is the intense consciousness of textuality that these stories encourage: in "The Gold-Bug," for example, the solution of codes within the tale mirrors the reader's own act of interpretation. Similarly, the form of the detective story—invented single-handedly by Poe—is predicated on the application of a cryptographic technique to the opaque materiality of the world. These twin effects—the concentration on "information," and the sense that the manipulation of language-as-code confers a power over the world—shape the trajectory of Poe's generic innovations. Detective fiction and science fiction are among the most popular literary forms of the last three centuries; by tracing their origins back to the cryptographic values encoded in their formation, we discover specific links among cryptography, Poe's innovations in genre, and the effects of technology on literature.

Indeed, Poe's writing illustrates a much larger cryptographic impulse shared by Poe's poststructural critics, especially those interested in psychoanalytic reading. The direction of explanation need not flow from analyst to literary text: as I show in chapter 2, one can make a plausible case that some of Lacan's central theoretical notions are directly indebted to Poe's writing. Reversing the typical exegetical pattern, one can thus use Poe's writing to frame an inquiry into the lust for signs that has characterized literature and literary criticism for most of this century. The passion for exactitude that characterizes Lacanian readers is evidence of a sea change in our relation to literature, toward a sense of language as a form of semantic encryption.

This does not mean that the cryptographic text has a special ontological stance, or that it has a single thematic salience. Indeed, cryptographic writing stands as an affront to all master theories of the text, simultaneously producing a fantasy of reading as decipherment and undermining this promise with the possibility of further levels of encrypted significance. Secret writing cannot, therefore, be viewed adequately from the vantage point of any single theory. My method is correspondingly eclectic, drawing as much on old-fashioned rhetorical analysis as it does on psychoanalysis, deconstruction, or historicism. Some readers will doubtless be bothered by this promiscuity, but as I understand it, the desire for critical uniformity and coherence — for, say, a literary or psychic algebra — is itself the rather desperate expression of the cryptographic imagination in search of a final key.

The cryptographic imagination represents a way of enacting possibilities always possessed by language. As long ago as the fifth century B.C., Plato had Socrates warn of the attenuation of experience produced by writing and reading, and the danger of trusting the written word.[4] But if language always harbors such tendencies, they are exacerbated by a period in which the success of the sciences has made it seem as if data ("text") might, indeed, be all there is. In such a world, it is not surprising that cryptography has become a topos for such writers as Thomas Pynchon, Don DeLillo, Michael Crichton, and William Gibson.

Perhaps the most telling of these recent cipher-fictions is Richard Powers's *Gold Bug Variations*. Hailed as "the most lavishly ambitious American novel since *Gravity's Rainbow*,"[5] the book reached the *New York Times* bestseller list in 1992. It tells the intertwined stories of Dr. Stuart Ressler, a young molecular biologist who in 1957 seeks to crack the genetic code, only to find himself enmeshed in an impossible love affair; and of Franklin Todd and Jan O'Deigh, who a generation later begin an affair based on their shared fascination with Ressler. Around that plot *The Gold Bug Variations* weaves an intricate network of reference, as the trio struggle to understand the relation of their private lives to the disorientingly rapid scientific, technological, and social changes of the day. Although *The Gold Bug Variations* was, perhaps, more frequently bought than read, its commercial success testifies to the attractions of cryptography, as Powers traces the origins of life back to its original code: "The first link in the chain from Word to flesh, philosopher's stone, talisman, elixir, incantation, the old myth of knowledge incorporated in *things*" (93).

Powers's novel is particularly smart about the self-reflexive force of the cryptograph: we see, in his account, how the act of deciphering becomes a parable for the birth of self-consciousness. As Jan O'Deigh observes in *The Gold Bug Variations*, there is a "curiously self-referential" quality to many enciphered messages. On discovering that Beadle, winner of the 1958 Nobel Prize for "an elegant experiment equating one gene with one synthesized enzyme" (218–19), received a telegram from Max Delbruck beginning "ADBACBBDBADACDCBBA...," which decrypted to "Break this code or give back Nobel Prize," she remarks: "Break *this* code. *I* am the riddle; know *me*. What 'me' could possibly proclaim itself the riddle? The cipher? The plaintext? The coding algorithm? The riddleness in the coder himself? ... Know me and you will know yourself. I spend the afternoon playing with messages, and on no proof but my pleasure, feel as if I'm closing in on my discovery, me."[6]

This resembles the effect of Poe's writing more generally, and may be a key to why it has flourished in the hothouse environment of postwar theory. Indeed, as the title of Powers's novel reveals, his fiction takes its cue from "The Gold-Bug" by way of Bach. Both Poe and Bach are crucial for *The Gold Bug Variations*, providing Powers with thematic material and analogical structures for his novel. The triple-coding of Bach's variations, for instance, offers Ressler a model for the codons of amino acids that, stuck together in triplets, form the base of DNA. Yet *The Gold Bug Variations* is even more profoundly a variation on Poe's 1844 adventure. For Powers, Poe's simple substitution cipher suggests that almost any scientific problem—the nature of genetics, the process of evolution, even the origin of life itself—can be approached as a problem of coding. *The Gold Bug Variations* offers a contemporary version of the Frankenstein story, as Ressler seeks to penetrate the process by which strings of inert amino acids encode themselves into living, symbol-making organisms.

Powers is explicit about the importance of Poe's writing to his novel. The earliest scenes in *The Gold Bug Variations* take place in 1957, as the young Ressler, fresh from graduate school, heads to Illinois to work on a genetics research team named "Cyfer." Stymied by the team's commitment to experimentation, Ressler's break comes when a coworker slips him a coded message that, when deciphered, immediately sends Ressler to the library:

He looks up her clue in the card catalog: Poe's "The Gold Bug." Mystery, suspense: a story in a thousand anthologies. ... Squatting between two metal shelves, Ressler loses himself in the adventure. Discovery—a piece of heated parchment reveals secret writing. Pictograph of baby goat identifies author as Captain Kidd, language of cipher as English. Simple letter frequency and word-pattern tricks lead scholars to pirate's treasure. But directions to treasure are themselves a coded algorithm for unburying. Two men and blackfella servant, applying human ingenuity, measured paces, and plumb line, crack third-level mystery and uncover wealth beyond their wildest dreams. Only at story's end does he emerge to shake off the fictional spell. "Gold Bug" is the ticket all right; he has come to the right place. . . . The heart of the code must lie hidden in its grammar. The catch they are after is not what a particular string of DNA says, but how it says it. . . . The treasure in Poe's tale is not the buried gold but the cryptographer's flicker of insight, the linguistic key to unlocking not just the map at hand but any secret writing. . . . Not the limited game of translation but the game rules themselves. (76–77)

As a work explicitly about the attractions of ciphers, "The Gold-Bug" represents something new in literary history. By its very nature, "literature" is built on the occult force of inscribed marks, and so written stories (as opposed to oral narratives) are necessarily cryptographic.[7] But for millennia, cryptography existed in a kind of Masonic silence, in which knowledge of the art was confined to a tiny class of governmental practitioners or to those few who employed it for amusement. With the spread of the telegraph in the 1840s, however, this pattern began to change, as cryptography worked its way into not only the hardware of civilization but into our imaginations as well. Cryptography has subsequently been intimately bound to developments in telecommunications and science, including the invention of the digital computer and the discovery of information theory. The development of telecommunications is essentially a history of advances in the coding and transmission of signals. Although in its classical incarnation cryptography is almost an automatic metaphor for literature (the text as code, cryptanalysis as hermeneutic model) and for its telos (the preservation of human experience through these codes), through its role in telecommunications, cryptography has also transformed and undermined the print culture of the last three centuries.

Hence, it would be misleading to rest with some invariant account of the "theme of secret writing," for the ties between literature and cryptography shift with the changing historical construction of each term. Although the desire for secrecy and privacy is always a literary possibility, certain recent literary genres (detective fiction, science fiction, cryptographic adventure) and certain forms of literary inheritance (generic repetition, spiritual "possession" and channeling, the reproduction of literary effects in real-world practices) have cryptographic assumptions programmatically encoded into them. If I am right in contending that these quintessentially modern genres share a cryptographic basis, then to read literature in this century is perforce to encounter the problem of secret writing. Indeed, cryptography names a point of continual *friction* between the forms of the literary imagination and the conditions of literary production. As a subject belonging at once to literature and to science, technology, and the police practices of the state, cryptography *helps set the terms by which the literary is produced.*

The Greatest of All Literary Problems

Consider the claim that Francis Bacon wrote Shakespeare's plays, as it is argued by James Phinney Baxter, who in 1915 published his monumental book *The Greatest of All Literary Problems: The Authorship of the Shakespeare Works.*[8] For seven hundred pages, Baxter uses his considerable sophistication and scholarship to examine the case against Shakespeare's authorship of the established canon (looking at evidence chiefly having to do with education, class, and some anomalies in the biographical record), before proposing someone whom he considers a far more plausible author of those works: Francis Bacon. Bacon is not the only person who has been advanced as the author of the Shakespearean canon, but for more than a century he has been chief pretender to the throne, his claim resting on the combination of his social status, his erudition, and his knowledge of secret writing.[9]

Unquestionably, Bacon knew enough about the fundamental rules of cryptographic exchange to have designed a hidden cipher. His list of the three virtues to be "preferred" in composing a cipher is identical to contemporary demands: "that they be not laborious to write and reade; that they be impossible to decypher; and in some cases, that they be without suspicion."[10] And it is also true that in *De augmentis scientiarum* Bacon revealed his design for a simple cipher that Baconians keep discovering, in different variations, within the text of Shakespeare.[11] Bacon's cipher consists of two typefaces used to create a binary metacode, in which each five-letter group in the enciphered text represents a single decoded letter. The actual pattern of *a*- and *b*-alphabets can vary at will, so long as both sender and receiver have the same information. The twenty-four-letter alphabet Bacon provides is given in table 1. To use Bacon's cipher, one first writes out the message *en clair*. Then, underneath it, one places the Baconian five-letter group appropriate for the letter: *art*, for instance, would be *aaaaa baaaa baaba*. When one has done this for the complete message, one takes any ordinary text—a recipe, a letter, an excerpt from the Bible—and writes the Baconian transliteration under it, underlining every *b*. Now one prints out the encoded text, using a different alphabet for all the letters that match up with *b*, and one has an enciphered text whose presence is hidden in the pattern of typefaces alone. To translate the code back, the receiver of the message divides the missive into five-letter groups and deciphers the pattern of alphabets to obtain the original text.

As an instance of this cipher, consider this passage from *De augmentis scientiarum* in regular and italic type, in which Bacon discusses the biliteral cipher:

A	B	C	D	E	F
aaaaa	aaaab	aaaba	aaabb	aabaa	aabab

G	H	I	K	L	M
aabba	aabbb	abaaa	abaab	ababa	ababb

N	O	P	Q	R	S
abbaa	abbab	abbba	abbbb	baaaa	baaab

T	V	W	X	Y	Z
baaba	baabb	babaa	babab	babba	babbb

Table 1. Francis Bacon's biliteral cipher.

> For it has the perfection of a cipher, which is to make anything signify anything; subject however to this condition, that the infolding writing shall contain at least five times as many letters as the writing infolded.[12]

Deciphering the pattern of typefaces according to Bacon's alphabet, we discover that "Bacon wrote fine ciphers, but not fine plays"—a refutation of the Bacon-Shakespeare thesis fully as convincing as many of the book-length arguments advanced in its favor.

Bacon's cipher is a tool of some subtlety. This was especially true in the sixteenth century, when the unevenness of presses and the haphazard mix of available typefaces made it plausible to find the frequent use of mixed fonts in a single text. But even today, the use of closely related typefaces can render the presence of Bacon's cipher almost invisible. Figure 1, for instance, provides an excerpt from *The Advancement of Learning* printed in Garamond and Imprint, which contains a message that I leave for curious readers to decipher. Bacon's cipher satisfies all three of his own cryptographic principles. Not only can the cipher be mastered and translated quickly (given accurate printing) but, best of all, as a steganographic cipher, it disguises that it *is* a code. Because it relies only on the systematic contrast between two different elements, Bacon's cipher need not be restricted to contrasting typefaces. Instead, it can squirrel itself into a literally infinite range of patterns and images. The rather crude castle in figure 2, for in-

In all duty or rather piety towards you I satisfy every body except myself. Myself I never satisfy. For so great are the services which you have rendered me, that seeing you did not rest in your endeavours on my behalf till the thing was done, I feel as if life had lost all its sweetness, because I cannot do as much in this cause of yours. The occasions are these: Ammonius the King's ambassador openly besieges us with money: the business is carried on through the same creditors who were employed in it when you were here, &c.

Figure 1. Francis Bacon's biliteral cipher. From Friedman, "Six Lectures on Cryptology," 49.

Figure 2. Biliteral cipher contained in a drawing of a castle. From Friedman, "Six Lectures on Cryptology," 48.

stance, is actually a biliteral cipher of empty and shaded stones. Drawn by a doctor fascinated by Baconianism, the deciphered text reads as follows:

> My business is to write prescriptions
> And then to see my doses taken;
> But now I find I spend my time
> Endeavoring to out-Bacon Bacon.[13]

Such games of literary hide-and-seek matter more than one might suspect. Given Shakespeare's status as a touchstone for literary value, the question of who wrote his plays (of how we connect them to history and to other literary texts) *is* conceivably "the greatest of all literary problems," because it serves as a synecdoche for fundamental issues of textual provenance and hermeneutics. Ciphered readings of Shakespeare aim to disrupt the authority of canons, the construction of authors, and the relation between authors and the works they produce—in part by mimicking the protocol of the literary history they resist. By 1947, when Professor Joseph Galland "compiled his bibliography of the controversy, entitled *Digesta Anti-Shakespeareana*, no one could afford to publish the 1500-page manuscript."[14] By 1960, four thousand books and monographs attacking Shakespeare's authorship had been published, and the flood of publications continues to this day.[15] As Marjorie Garber has observed, such challenges are "greeted by orthodox Stratfordians with umbrage, derision, and contemptuous dismissal of so intense an order as to inevitably raise another question: what is at stake here? Why . . . has the doubt about Shakespeare's authorship persisted so tenaciously, and why has it been so equally tenaciously dismissed?"[16]

As Garber shows, the cryptographic appropriation of Shakespeare is in part a response to such moments within the plays as that in *Twelfth Night* when Malvolio tortures Maria's forged letter into sense ("And the end—what should that alphabetical position portend? If I should make that resemble something in me! Softly! M, O, A, I" [2.5.129–32]), or of the intercepted and decrypted plans to kill the king in *Henry V*.[17] Shakespeare's references to signatures, codes, and "character," his obsessive punning and wordplay, and the sheer density of his writing all solicit pseudocryptographic interpretations. Recalling the tradition that Shakespeare himself played the Ghost in *Hamlet*, Garber speculates that the apparition's repeated invocation "Remember me!" is directed both to Hamlet and to *Hamlet*'s audience. On this account, the success of Shakespeare's textual ghost-effects is evident both in his obsessive citation by later writers (the canonical response) and in the search for a secret author: "Cryptographers," Garber explains, "set out to uncover ghostlier demarcations, to show that the text itself is haunted by signs of rival ownership."[18]

What Garber never suspects, however, is the degree to which Poe is involved in this search for "signs of rival ownership." Indeed, although it seems mad to say it, the combined effects of Poe's fictionalization of cryptography and his invention of the detective story are so great that it would only just overstate things to say that the cryptographic fascination with Shakespeare is a function of Poe's own writing. To begin with, Baconianism is primarily a feature of American, rather than British, literary history. Although doubts about Shakespeare's authorship were raised in England as early as 1728, it was only in mid–nineteenth century America that the question came to seem pressing, when Delia Bacon published "Shakespeare and His Plays: An Inquiry Concerning Them" in an 1856 issue of *Putnam's Monthly* (F&F, 3). (Poe knew Delia Bacon all too well: it was she who had taken first place in the Philadelphia *Saturday Courier* contest of June

1831, beating out Poe's "Metzengerstein," which was published in the subsequent issue.) The next year, Bacon's essay became the 543-page book *The Philosophy of the Plays of Shakespeare Unfolded*, with a preface by Nathaniel Hawthorne. Bacon's book "opened a giant valve: the books, the articles, the journals now appeared in a gathering spate: some 'for,' but most 'against' Shakespeare" (F&F, 4).

My claim is not that Poe had anything to do with Bacon's authorship of "Shakespeare and His Plays," but that the Baconian's mode of hermeneutic suspicion, interest in hidden signatures, and, above all, willingness to play the part of the literary detective, poring over texts in search of secrets, is wholly consonant with the project of Poe's cryptographic writing—a form of writing that quickly became ubiquitous over much of the globe. In consequence, it can be startling to notice how discussions of such apparently unrelated questions as the authorship of the Shakespearean canon lead back to discussions of Poe. Garber, for example, draws virtually all of her evidence for *Shakespeare's Ghost Writers* from a book by a pair of cryptographers: *The Shakespearean Ciphers Examined: An Analysis of Cryptographic Systems Used as Evidence that Some Author Other than William Shakespeare Wrote the Plays Commonly Attributed to Him*. Although now little remembered, *The Shakespearean Ciphers Examined* won the 1955 Folger Shakespeare Library competition for the best manuscript on Elizabethan literature, and was published in 1957 by Cambridge University Press. Its authors—William Friedman and Elizebeth Friedman—were most unlikely prizewinners. Neither was a professional critic, nor even a particularly good reader of Shakespeare. Originally trained as a geneticist, Friedman was hired to assist Elizabeth Wells Gallup, a high school English teacher who in 1899 published *The Biliteral Cypher of Sir Francis Bacon Discovered in His Works and Deciphered by Mrs. Elizabeth Wells Gallup*.[19] Led by Gallup, Friedman and his wife Elizebeth began a study of codes that eventually led to his cracking of the Japanese cipher Purple during World War II—an achievement of the same magnitude as the Polish and British solution of Enigma. Yet although Friedman's pioneering work in military cryptography won him an appointment as an army colonel, he was never able to forget that his career originated with a set of *literary* questions, a fact to which tribute is paid in *The Shakespearean Ciphers Examined*.

It was, however, Poe, not Shakespeare, who introduced Friedman to the exalted possibilities of ciphers. As a child, Friedman "would talk with excitement about a world he had discovered through Edgar Allan Poe's 'The Gold-Bug,'"[20] an encounter that so shaped Friedman's character that for the rest of his life "he was still prepared to waste time on the most unlikely of 'buried treasure' messages sent to him for decipherment."[21] Throughout his life, Friedman returned to the subject of Poe's cryptography, in essays published not only in scholarly venues such as *American Literature*, but also in such arcane locations as the *Bulletin of the Signal Intelligence Service*, the house organ for War Department cryptographers. It was in one of these essays that Friedman observed that "the fame of Poe rests not a little on his activities with cipher, and much of the esteem in which this American genius is held today rests in part on the legend of Poe the Cryptographer."[22] Friedman's opinion is echoed by Joseph Wood Krutch, who maintains that "nothing contributed to a greater extent than did Poe's connection with cryptography to the growth of the legend which pictured him as a man at once below and above ordinary human nature."[23]

So many of the pioneers of American cryptanalysis discuss Poe that it seems impossible to argue that literary uses of cryptography are merely anterior appropriations of genuine cryptographic models, as if fiction only echoes larger social and political practices. Even cryptographers wishing to dismiss Poe apparently need to reckon with him first. Such was the case with Herbert Yardley, who headed MI8, the "American Black Chamber," from 1917 until 1929, when it was dissolved by Henry Stimson, the new secretary of state. Desperate to provide for his family, Yardley hastily wrote *The American Black Chamber*, a best-selling account of his adventures in governmental decryption, and the model for dozens of novels and films. Although Yardley disparages Poe's expertise, he repeatedly couches his discussion of cryptography in terms of Poe's writing. Describing his self-education, Yardley remembers "quickly devouring" all the books on cryptography to be found in the Library of Congress. Next "I searched Edgar Allan Poe's letters for a glimpse of the scientific treatment of cryptography. These were full of vague boasts of his skill—nothing more. Today, looking at cryptography from a scientific point of view, for the American Black Chamber has never had an equal, I know that Poe merely floundered around in the dark and did not understand the great underlying principles."[24] Later, in his choice of lodgings for the Black Chamber, Yardley followed Poe's logic of hiding in plain sight: "Following the reasoning in Poe's 'Purloined Letter' I selected as a home for the Black Chamber a four-story brownstone front in the East Thirties, just a few steps from Fifth Avenue—the very heart of New York City."[25]

The structure of Yardley's tale serves as one way of imagining Poe's continued presence in the development of cryptography. Overtly following Poe's logic, Yardley set up a secret agency in the middle of Manhattan, operating under cover of a legitimate business (the Code Compilation Company), which, to perfect its dissimulation, actually produced and sold a trade cipher known as the Universal Trade Code. For the seven years that it operated in New York, Yardley's Black Chamber intermingled literary, commercial, and covert purposes in such a way that one cannot single out any one aspect as the only "real" level of operations. Although the political purposes of the Black Chamber were obviously paramount in its design, this does not mean that the Universal Trade Code was any less effective for its customers, or that Poe's advice about hiding in plain sight was any less useful for having appeared in a fiction. The real power of cryptography— its social and political utility— *depends* on the way it affiliates feigned truths with telling fictions, overt with hidden purposes. Mingled in all of this, hidden in sight so plain that it has remained largely undetected, we shall find the traces of Poe's words.

Cryptographic Replication

The Cryptographic Imagination is divided into two sections, the first primarily concerned with genre and the second with the nature and effects of Poe's literary influence. Belying this distinction, however, this entire study worries the devious logic of literary replication and identification. Genre and epigone are the reverse and obverse of the same coin of influence: both are mechanisms for textual reproduction. Hence, after an opening chapter devoted to Poe's magazine pieces on the history, uses, and techniques of cryptography, I consider the three main types of cryptographic fiction: the cipher adventure, detective fiction, and science fiction. Each chapter focuses its analysis through readings of representative texts: "The Gold-Bug" for cipher-adventure fiction, "The Murders in the Rue Morgue" for detective fiction, and "The Man that Was Used Up" and some ancillary pieces for science fiction.

At the same time, each chapter renegotiates Poe's relation to literary history. Chapter 2 explores how Poe's understanding of the cryptograph grew out of his peculiarly absorptive reading of Daniel Defoe. Poe's use of cryptography in "The Gold-Bug" represents his adaptation of certain self-consciously textual moments in what otherwise seems to be the transparent realist prose of *Robinson Crusoe*. Poe's use of the cryptograph as a two-dimensional key to a three-dimensional crypt manifests with particular clarity a literary pattern found in works from the Bible to *The Gold Bug Variations*. Next, I locate Poe's creation (and eventual destruction) of the analytic sublime against its parallel presence within the tradition of psychoanalytic criticism. The cryptograph exacerbates Poe's proclivity to think of the self as a linguistic construct; although the detective's ability to gloss the world as if it were a text promises the reader unheard-of powers of interpretation, the reader's somatic participation in the crimes that the detective uncovers in the Rue Morgue exposes the impossibility of realizing the desire for a purely ciphered existence. In chapter 4 I read Poe's science fiction in light of the contemporary invention of the telegraph. With its suggestion that communication is a combination of coded signal and an "electrical" principle of sociality, the telegraph bears deep affinities to Poe's understanding of cryptography, and it reinforces his tendency to polarize distinctions between signifier and signified, body and mind. Long interested in automata as models for human organization, Poe eventually came to imagine the soul as a form of electricity, thus completing the transformation of man into machine begun in texts such as "Maelzel's Chess-Player."

But Poe's generic influence also requires one to consider how particular writers have learned from Poe's fictional practices. This is peculiarly true of cryptographic writing, which always forces one to confront the essential, shocking anonymity of language. And since cryptographic texts lead to a linguistic doubling of reader and writer contained within the imaginative space of the cryptograph, secret writing naturally encourages imitation and plagiarism. Because of the powerful transferential effects of Poe's secret writing, a disproportionate number of his readers have come to think of themselves as Poe's "secret readers," who reproduce his cryptographic paradigm either in their writing or in their lives.

Literary cryptography turns out to be, in part, a set of mechanisms for producing these transference effects, and so part 2 of *The Cryptographic Imagination* examines the effects of Poe's secret writing on his later readers. These include writers and critics such as T. S. Eliot and Jacques Lacan; cryptographers such as William Friedman; and the Boston spiritualist Lizzie Doten, who believed she served as a spiritual telegraph through whom Poe posthumously dictated poems. Chapter 5 treats Poe's literary influence as an effect of his cryptographic enterprise, identifying Doten as a reader who embodied one pole of the contradictory impulses in Poe's work between absence and presence, arcane erudition and mass-cultural commodity. As a "spirit-poet," Doten found in reading Poe a model of an invisible, mesmeric communication that translates thought directly from mind to mind, free from the hindrance of any signifying medium; as I show, she gradually came to identify Poe's spirit with an emerging ideology of mass communications. Reading thematically, Doten identified Poe with a "cinematic" experience of self-dispersal, and a simultaneous and total identification with a certain biographical fantasy. Although in Doten's mind *all* writing proved cryptographic to one degree or other (because the process by which words communicate remains a mystery), Poe's verse exerted an influence that Doten found indistinguishable from possession.

William Friedman's relation to Poe could not seem more different. As America's foremost cryptologist, Friedman rigorously applied mathematical principles to the creation and solution of ciphers. Yet the closer one looks, the more one sees continuities between Doten's spiritualization of cryptography and its twentieth-century practice by Friedman and others. This is important, because as chapter 6 demonstrates, the explosive growth of cryptography during World War II offers an overlooked matrix for the formation of a paranoid Cold War consciousness. By reading Poe's presence in Friedman's life and work, I offer what might be called a literary history of the NSA, which reveals the dense interpenetration of cryptographic fiction, espionage, and diplomacy throughout the past half-century.

Friedman and Doten prove especially attractive for my purposes because of their anomalous critical status, partly inside literature and partly outside it. Through their twinned careers we can see something of the extraordinary fertility of Poe's literary influence, as well as how this influence disseminates itself into quasi- or nonliterary areas, which may, in turn, provide new material for literature. Significantly, both Doten and Friedman have a profound desire to *flee* the literary, albeit for opposite reasons. For Doten, insofar as it is linked to language, materiality, occlusion, and separateness, literature is what remains when spiritual inspiration fails. Friedman fears literature for inverse reasons: his life was spent in large part rendering cryptography a *discipline*, abstract and eternal, and subject to an algorithmic precision. Yet he, too, found literature an unavoidable component of his work, never escaping the literary themes that surrounded the practice of cryptography at its most elevated levels.

The development of telecommunications has led to a cultural mythos that associates cryptographic culture with the disembodiment, self-transcendence, and fetishization of communication, and so my study next takes up the ways in which electronic communications on the Internet reproduce features of cryptographic identity familiar from Poe's writings. In chapter 7 I explore the unstable contemporary relations between literature and technology, reading the behavior of Internet cypherpunks against Pynchon's *Crying of Lot 49* in relation to issues of anonymity, psychic projection, and enciphered community. The book concludes with a look at such exotic future developments as computerized steganography and quantum cryptography—this last a possible road to the transformation of matter into codes (a dream that lurks at the heart of the cryptographic imagination).

As should be clear, the Poe invoked in part 2 is only incompletely bound to the biographical subject. When I claim that Poe helped end World War II, the "Poe" in that sentence represents both a particular author and the literary genre he helped create and for which he serves as a synecdoche. This follows from cryptography offering a strategy for intensifying the reader's authorial cathexis. Paradoxically, Poe's emphasis on ciphers intensifies his ability to create an intimate image of himself. Such ciphers act as the literary equivalent of Yale secret societies, whose Cyclopean masonry, iron gates, and apotropaic figures all serve to enhance the intimacy (and the outsider's *imagination* of the intimacy) of what takes place within those walls. Poe's cryptography is both a way of dissimulating responsibility for what he wrote and a means of intensifying ownership, of gathering his dispersed identity into a figure for future readers, who seek entry to his writing by striving to make themselves one with him as he is encrypted within their minds. Poe's reputation today testifies to his success: contemporary critical interest in Poe is itself a cryptographic phenomenon, the result of a secret writing only now being deciphered.

GENRES

Cryptography [a. mod. L. *cryptographia*, f. Gr. *kryptos* hidden + *-graphia* writing: see -GRAPHY.] A secret manner of writing, either by arbitrary characters, by using letters or characters in other than their ordinary sense, or by other methods intelligible only to those possessing the key; also anything written in this way. . . . [1641 WILKINS *Mercury* ii. (1707): There are also different Ways of Secresy. 1. Cryptologia. 2. Cryptographia. 3. Semaeologia.]

Cryptograph [mod. f. as prec. + Gr. *-graphos* writing, written; see -GRAPH.] 1. = CRYPTOGRAM. *a* 1849 POE *Tales, Gold Beetle*, I could not suppose him [Kidd] capable of constructing any of the more abstruse cryptographs.

Oxford English Dictionary

J Z Y I Q N I T D A H W Q Q I A Y Y L Z E E Q P Q V V R J C V W K E J S C G M P D T Y C Y N Q U K U V X J I U N O L Z W E O Z
E O H M M D M X K B T A M E H B Q Y M O I H M Q J K O L Q O V T K X W Z T E N A K X M L V C M W H E G K I H M B C X W P R W

THE KING OF SECRET READERS

1

You have exhibited a power of analytical and synthetical reasoning I have
never seen equalled; and the astonishing skill you have displayed—particularly in the deciphering of the cryptograph by Dr. Charles S. Frailey
will, I think, crown you the king of "secret readers."

Letter from W. B. Tyler to Edgar Poe

A Few Words on Secret Writing

What precisely does Poe mean by "secret writing?" Because the answer to
that question is this book, no synopsis will prove wholly satisfactory. We
may, however, learn something by comparing Poe's understanding of the
subject to the history of the word. According to the *Oxford English Dictionary*, *cryptography* is "a secret manner of writing, either by arbitrary characters, by using letters or characters in other than their ordinary sense, or
by other methods intelligible only to those possessing the key; also anything written in this way. Generally the art of writing or solving ciphers."
Such ciphers are known as *cryptographs* or *cryptograms*. These words mean
the same thing: the first *Oxford English Dictionary* definition for each is "a
piece of cryptographic writing; anything written in cipher, or in such a form
or order that a key is required in order to know how to understand and put
together the letters."

Two things are striking here. The first is the newness of this lexicon. *Cryptogram* is barely a century old; *cryptograph*, a half-century older.
Although *cryptogram* and *cryptograph* are, like *cryptography*, formed out of
ancient Greek roots that signify "hidden writing," their recent coinage reflects the relatively contemporaneous elaboration of cryptography as a specialized field. Second, despite this terminological newness, the concept of
secret writing goes back to the very origin of text. "A Few Words on Secret
Writing" (*Graham's Magazine*, July 1841) begins with a history of the subject, in which Poe recognizes that cryptography is in some sense internal to
writing:

As we can scarcely imagine a time when there did not exist a necessity, or at
least a desire, of transmitting information from one individual to another in

19

such a manner as to elude general comprehension, so we may well suppose the practice of writing in cipher to be of great antiquity. De la Guilletière, therefore, who, in his *Lacedaemon Ancient and Modern*, maintains that the Spartans were the inventors of Cryptography, is obviously in error. He speaks of the *scytala* as being the origin of the art; but he should have cited it as one of its earliest instances, so far as our records extend. . . . Similar means of secret intercommunication must have existed almost contemporaneously with the invention of letters. (SW, 114-15)

Poe's claim that the notion of writing is bound up with the notion of cryptography is echoed by historians, who describe it as "an art practiced from time immemorial," who observe that its origin is "lost in the mists of ancient history," and who claim that "codes and ciphers are as old as civilised man."[1]

Although the rise of professional cryptography and its subsequent mathematical systematization may suggest that there is a difference in kind between "real" cryptography and its literary uses, the history and etymology of the word suggest that this is a false distinction. First introduced in 1641, the word *cryptography* was soon appearing in the works of such sixteenth-century essayists as Sir Thomas Browne ("The strange Cryptography of Gaffarell in his Starry Book of Heaven . . . ," in *The Garden of Cyrus*), who would later prove so attractive to Poe.[2] Remarkably enough, its cognate *cryptograph* is Poe's own coinage. He introduces it in "The Gold-Bug," where William Legrand explains how he deciphered a treasure map left by the legendary Captain Kidd by assuming that "I could not suppose him capable of constructing any of the more abstruse cryptographs."[3] The much greater frequency with which *cryptograph* is preferred today to *cryptogram* offers an index of the subject's subterranean literary affiliations, which leave the concept of secret writing oscillating unstably between a narrow technical and a much broader metaphoric understanding.[4]

The literary and technical meanings of cryptography are also united by their common task of hiding meaning from some while revealing it to others—an imperative shared by texts as different as the Talmud and a digitally encrypted electronic bank transaction. Consequently, there is always something vulnerable about encrypted writing: "Few persons can be made to believe that it is not quite an easy thing to invent a method of secret writing which shall baffle investigation. Yet it may be roundly asserted that human ingenuity cannot concoct a cipher which human ingenuity cannot resolve" (SW, 116). The particular ability needed to resolve such a puzzle is *analytic*: "In such investigations the analytic ability is very forcibly called into action; and, for this reason, cryptographical solutions might with great propriety be introduced into academies as a means of giving tone to the most important powers of the mind" (ibid.). *Analysis* is a privileged term in

Poe's lexicon. "The Murders in the Rue Morgue" begins with a discussion of "the mental features discoursed of as the analytic," which are, "in themselves, but little susceptible of analysis. We appreciate them only in their effects," which are chiefly the pleasure the analyst derives from intellectual play: "He is fond of enigmas, of conundrums, of hieroglyphics; exhibiting in his solutions of each a degree of *acumen* which appears to the ordinary apprehension praeternatural" (*PT*, 397).

Yet if the skills needed to solve hieroglyph, cipher, enigma, and conundrum are the same, the objects of analysis are not. In particular, I want to distinguish between the cipher and the hieroglyph in Poe's writing. John Irwin has shown that Poe's understanding of language, the self, and human origins can be traced through the idea of the hieroglyph:

> As the hieroglyphical problem of the relationship between outer shape and inner meaning becomes the question of the origin of man and language, the image of "writing" expands until all physical shapes become obscurely meaningful forms of script, forms of hieroglyphic writing each of which has its own science of decipherment—signature analysis, physiognomy, phrenology, fingerprint analysis, zoology, botany, geology, and so on. . . . Because in pictographic writing the shape of a sign is in a sense a double of the physical shape of the object it represents, like a shadow or a mirror image, the essays and stories from this period are always, in one way or another, "double" stories.[5]

Ciphers and hieroglyphs share a number of characteristics, including antiquity and apparent illegibility. But the hieroglyph is ultimately capable of being read in a way that tentatively reestablishes the connection between the forms of nature and the forms (and meanings) of words. By holding out the possibility of uniting percept and symbol, pictograph and arbitrary mark, the hieroglyph implicitly suggests a strategy for suturing the fundamental split in human identity between corporeal presence and symbolic consciousness. Thus, recuperating the fragmentation of the ending of the *Narrative of A. Gordon Pym* depends, as Irwin shows, largely on the ability to decipher the "hieroglyphs" Pym has transcribed on his adventures. The "white figure" of the novel's end is revealed as an image of the self projected on the fog—a pictograph of Pym cast upon the world. Although one could make too much of the transcendent possibilities of hieroglyphic inscription within Poe, whose writing is always full of destabilizing ironies, it should be remembered that the hieroglyph, insofar as it is truly attached to an originary system of writing, seems to hold out the possibility of connecting truth and language, surface appearance and deep meaning.

The cryptograph meanwhile presumes the arbitrariness of signifying forms: in a cipher, the letter *a* may be represented by any other letter, number, or icon, an @ or an *æ* (Poe takes evident pleasure in what he calls the "queerness" of cryptographic appearance). But recognition of this arbitrariness is also troubling, because it undermines the relationship of image to sign that ostensibly grounds the hieroglyph by establishing a "natural" visual equivalence between the signified image—river, tree, or whatever—and the signifying "shadow." As a model of the sign, the hieroglyph is associated with the search for an Adamic universal language; the cryptograph, by contrast, is connected with a distinctly modern awareness of the lack of linguistic motivation.[6] By removing the basis of language's correspondence with the world of things, the cryptograph disrupts the possibility of self-understanding, which is based on the metaphoric identity between self and script:

> What Narcissus clearly exhibits in the third moment, by treating his image as if it were another person even though he knows it is not, is the essential (original) otherness of the self to itself, the indeterminate status of self-reflection as both a part of the body and a double of the body and as either a part of the body or a double of the body. What the third moment expresses is that if the self is at once both a cause and a function of self-consciousness, if it is one pole (one-half) of a mutually constitutive opposition (whose other pole is the visual image of a body) and is at the same time the entity that reflects upon that opposition (that is, doubles it in self-reflective thought), then the origin of the self is a union that differentiates, a coming together to hold apart.[7]

The Narcissus myth, which reveals how the self is created by its mirroring in water, is also an image for the mirroring of humans in writing: Narcissus's identity (although it is already split) is constituted by its natural "shadow" relation to his body, and the study of language seeks to discover a point of origin based on a nominalism in which the letter is the shadow of a shape, signifier and signified yoked "naturally" together. But at some point this natural relation was lost, and the writer after Babel is forced to acknowledge the randomness of the signifying shape. Writing no longer "reflects" human identity; it is as if Narcissus were to peer into the pool only to find a new unintelligible image there every time. In the passage in figure 3 (SW, 144), Poe confronts this situation in his fascinated play with illegible cryptographic symbols that rupture any naturalized reading. In "X-ing a Paragrab," the substitution of an "x" for each "o" in the text also represents Poe's jab at Frogpondian notions of linguistic unity and wholeness: "Dxn't hxllx, nxr hxwl, nxr grxwl, nxr bxw-wxw-wxw! Gxxd Lxrd, Jxhn, hxw yxu dx lxxk! Txld yxu sx, yxu knxw—but stxp rxlling yxur gxxse xf an xld pxll abxut sx, and gx and drxwn yxur sxrrxws in a bxwl!" (PT, 922).

The creation of the detective story followed by four years the publication of the *Narrative of A. Gordon Pym*; and to some degree we may imagine that Poe has ontogenetically recapitulated the history of linguistic forms, in an evolution from hieroglyph to cryptograph.[8] Poe, however, attempts to defend against the cryptograph's implicit threat of linguistic alienation

:,]!¶†‖]?*!¶✝†§¶‖,*(†¡(,?‡§(¡
⚓¡¶[?(,;§‡☞‡]†§§:(†[†[¶?‡]:
*¡¶:(§?]!¶†§‡];§?‡†¡‡✝¶!(,†§?(‖
][§¡'¡,:,,†§⚓),?‖]?,§§(!✝¡(,
†§†[‡!)*][✝:?]‖

Figure 3. Part of a cipher devised by W. B. Tyler and reprinted by Poe. From SW, 144.

(which is also a promise of discovery) by the way he conceives of decoding, which preserves the possibility of an originary hieroglyphic moment. His brilliant but absolutely specious move is to treat the cryptograph as if it were ordinary language that, once decoded, will offer up a perfectly transparent meaning. The analogy can be presented this way:

cryptograph suggests a relation of *signifier* or of *sign*

decoded language	signified	meaning

But in fact, the relation is actually one of lateral translation between different encodings of the same signification:

cryptograph actually gives a relation of *signifier*

decoded language	signifier

Through the use of this false implicit analogy, Poe displaces his anxiety about language proper onto the special case of the cryptograph, thus eliding the fact that although the alphabetic symbols making up words are pictographic in origin, they are, in their arbitrary phonetic combination, completely without natural analogues.

Although the cryptography articles offered Poe a chance to experiment with different models of how writing signifies, they did not permit him systematically to anticipate the conclusions of Saussure. Poe originally stated that he could solve any code (because what humans make, humans can decipher), but later temporized: "We do not propose to solve *all* ciphers. Whether we can or cannot do this is a question for another day" (SW, 135). Indeed, Poe's knowledge of cryptography, although far ahead of that of his readers, was by modern standards elementary. In "What Poe Knew about Cryptography," W. K. Wimsatt notes that in an article entitled "Cryptography—Mr. Poe as a Cryptographer," published just after Poe's death, a Reverend Mr. Cudworth "pronounced a judgment which must have been assented to by many: 'The most profound and skilful cryptographer who ever lived was undoubtedly Edgar A. Poe'" (778). Wimsatt adds that "to study Poe at work on ciphers is to find not a wide knowledge and intricate method of procedure, but rather a kind of untrained wit, an intuition which more quickly than accurately grasped the outlines of cryptic principle and immediately with confident imagination proclaimed the whole. It is probable that whatever ciphers he did solve he solved very rapidly. The Reverend Mr. Cudworth testifies that his own little puzzle was unravelled five times faster than he made it" (ibid., 765).

The kind of ciphers to which Poe objects—"a species of cryptograph justly considered very difficult. . . . We do not say that we *cannot* solve it but that we will not make the attempt" (SW, 136)—is one in which the code key is a phrase with the same number of letters as the alphabet in which it is written. Since the twenty-six letters of the phrase *Suaviter in modo, fortiter in re*, for example, match the number of letters in the English language, there is a straightforward one-to-one correspondence between signs, and the phrase can serve as a simple encoding device as shown below:

s/u/a/v/i/t/e/r/i/n/m/o/d/o/f/o/r/t/i/t/e/r/i/n/r/e/
a/b/c/d/e/f/g/h/i/j/k/l/m/n/o/p/q/r/s/t/u/v/w/x/y/z/

Here *a* stands for *c*, *v* stands for *d*, but *i*, repeated four times in the Latin phrase, stands for *e, i, s*, and *w*; hence, the word *guise* would be written in code as *eeiii*, the word *wise* as *iiii*, and so on.[9] Such a code would quickly cause the cryptographer interpretive paralysis: "What is he to do with such a word as 'iiiiiiiiii'? In any of the ordinary books upon Algebra will be found a very concise *formula* . . . for ascertaining the number of arrangements in which *m* letters may be placed, taken *n* at a time. But no doubt there are none of our readers ignorant of the innumerable combinations which may be made from these ten 'i's'" (SW, 130–31). Even should such a code be cracked, there would still be a fatal ambiguity in applying the key:

> Nay, a case might readily be imagined, where the most important word of the communication . . . on which the sense of the whole depended, should have so equivocal a nature that the person for whose benefit it was intended would be unable, even with the aid of this key, to discover which of two very different interpretations should be the correct one. . . . A letter written in ciphers . . . might either be "I love you now as ever," or "I love you now *no more*." How "positively shocking," to say the least of it.[10]

Positively shocking, indeed: recognition of the arbitrariness of letters is joined here with semantic ambiguity to reveal Poe's discomfort with the problems of understanding writing. The quasi-semiotic model of language offered by the cryptographic account is undermined by Poe's reluctant realization that every decoding is another encoding, and that the crypt of the letter cannot be penetrated in an attempt to extract its immanent meaning. Or rather, this answer is among the contradictory responses given by Poe in his attempts to resolve these questions: "We do not say that we cannot do it, only that we have not the leisure to attempt it at present." Poe's need to create a model of signification, to crack the vast cipher of language itself, led him to extend his original *Graham's Magazine* article with three addenda, and to devote an excessive amount of time (for one so poor) to the solution of readers' puzzles. This same need manifests itself in the detective stories, in which Poe imagines a completely textual world where his readerly skills might finally come into full play.

The detective story begins by extending modes of cryptographic reading to the phenomenal world. The sleuth or private eye applies the same analytical tools used to break a code to his or her sensory experience, merely extending the use of these procedures from the two-dimensional page to the three-dimensional world. But to be effective, this semiotic technique requires that the unbroken synesthetic stream of sensory perception that ordinarily floods the self be reduced, simplified, so that the detective can establish the particular causal relationships holding between events. Objects and events in the world must be deprived of their polyvalent materiality, since the semiotic schema, as conceived by Poe, requires the replacement of contingency and indeterminacy with the detective's single, verifiable meaning. Just as in theory a deciphered code ought to be completely intelligible, so Dupin believes in a corresponding transparency of events in the world; when he declares that his deductions from the newspaper accounts of the murder of the Mmes. L'Espanaye "are the *sole* proper ones, and that the suspicion arises *inevitably* from them as the single result" ("Murders in the Rue Morgue," *PT*, 416), he is applying the analogy of cryptographic translation to the world. As in a deciphered code, all the formerly mysterious "characters" are now held in meaningful relation by the syntax of narrative, and Dupin supposes the existence of real "syntactic" lines of causality in the world. The realm of represented experience is converted into a world of signs articulating webs of effect, or, impossibly, into a world of pure meaning. The mathematically inclined Dupin works with abstract symbols alone, which he obtains by converting the depth of the material world into one uninterrupted surface of discrete signs in which nothing is hidden, and in which there is an indexical relationship between a person's behavior and his or her physical appearance.

The unnamed narrator in "The Man of the Crowd" employs exactly the same logic when he observes of some London passersby that "they all had slightly bald heads, from which their right ears, long used to pen-holding, had an odd habit of standing off on end. . . . There were two other traits, by which I could always detect them [gamblers]: a guarded lowness of tone in conversation, and a more than ordinary extension of the thumb in a direction at right angles with the fingers" (*PT*, 390). The gambler is conveniently marked by his playing in unambiguous ways, both physical and behavioral.

Elsewhere, in a single paragraph Poe uses metonyms, allusions, etymologies, and associations of all sorts to organize signs in a coherent series:

> I knew that you could not say to yourself "stereotomy" without being brought to think of atomies, and thus of the theories of Epicurus. . . .
>
> I felt you could not avoid casting your eyes upward to the great nebula in Orion. . . . You did look up; and I was now assured that I had correctly followed your steps. . . .
>
> "Perdidit antiquum litera prima sonum"—I had told you this was in reference to Orion, formerly written Urion; and from certain pungencies connected with this explanation I was aware that you could not have forgotten it. ("Murders in the Rue Morgue," *PT,* 404)

The list could be extended, but it is sufficient to note that the Virgilian citation ("The first letter has lost its ancient sound") connects Dupin's analytic efforts with an attempt to recover an origin of language in its first "ancient sound," before the written and the aural signifier had diverged, losing the naturalized relation—of shadow or onomatopoeia—that rooted signs in the materiality of the sensual world.

In its baroque elaboration of rhetorical figures, as in its exploration of "signs" in general, Poe's writing foregrounds the question of the nature of language. Consider Poe's explanation of why the analytic mind always succeeds in deciphering codes, however outré such ciphers might initially appear: "To some persons the difficulty might be great; but to others—to those skilled in deciphering—such enigmas are very simple indeed. The reader should bear in mind that *the basis of the whole art of solution, as far as regards these matters, is found in the general principles of the formation of language itself,* and thus is altogether independent of the particular laws which govern any cipher, or the construction of its key" (SW, 118; emphasis added).

In "The Purloined Letter," Dupin recounts the story of his asking a boy how he consistently guesses correctly at a game of odds and evens. He is told: " 'When I wish to find out how wise, or how stupid, or how good, or how wicked is any one, or what are his thoughts at the moment, I fashion the expression of my face, as accurately as possible, in accordance with the expression of his, and then wait to see what thoughts or sentiments arise in my mind or heart, as if to match or correspond with the expression.' This response of the schoolboy lies at the bottom of all the spurious profundity which has been attributed to Rouchefoucault, to La Bruyère, to Machiavelli, and to Campanella" (*PT,* 689–90). The anecdote presumes that the face is a natural index of the mind—and that the causal relationship holding between mind and index can be reversed: the physical act of modeling another person's expression produces a knowledge of the original possessor's affect. To know what another feels, one need only imitate that person.

Although such a fixed ratio of expression to meaning might hold true in commedia dell'arte, where the relation between sign and referent is conventional, it is obviously inadequate for the world at large. Poe knew this, I think, but he also felt a powerful attraction to such a fantasy. Nor was Poe alone: his stories reflect a wider nineteenth-century American fascination with phrenology, physiognomy, palmistry, and related practices.[11] The semiotic models of scientific investigation developed in the last decades of the nineteenth century find their precursors, however faulty, in these "sciences" that flourished in Poe's America.

Dupin's attack on "profundity" is actually directed against its etymological meaning of "depth": a space, covert and private, that resists his inspecting eye.[12] If, as Poe observes, the operations of cryptography are explicitly based on "the general principles of the formation of language itself," and if the detective story depends generically on a "cryptographic" attitude toward solving the crime, Poe's hostility to depth and his attention to surface are required by his project, which is to convert all experience into a system of signs. Consequently, Poe's detective stories exploit the almost seamless joining of the represented world of the stories to the signs of the representation itself. Consider the analyst's method of playing cards:

> The necessary knowledge is of *what* to observe. Our player confines himself not at all; nor, because the game is the object, does he reject deductions from things external to the game. He examines the countenance of his partner, comparing it carefully with that of each of his opponents. He considers the mode of assorting the cards in each hand. . . . He notes every variation of face as the play progresses, gathering a fund of thought from the differences in the expression of uncertainty, of surprise, of triumph, or of chagrin. . . . A casual or inadvertent word; the accidental dropping or turning of a card, with the accompanying anxiety or carelessness in regard to its concealment; the counting of tricks, with the order of their arrangement . . . all afford, to his apparently intuitive perception, indications of the true state of affairs. The first two or three rounds having been played, he is in full possession of the contents of each hand, and thenceforward puts down his cards with as absolute a precision of purpose as if the rest of the party had turned outwards the faces of their own. ("Murders in the Rue Morgue," *PT*, 399)

The central problem of Poe's fiction is that of the existence of other minds; this is an obvious undertext of the gothic romances, where it is the question of the *relation* between mind and body that fascinates and repels Poe's narrators, particularly when the mind and body belong to different individuals. The problem of other minds animates both Poe's exercises in solipsism and those tales that stage the collapse of difference between self and other, a state structurally identical with solipsism. The obsessive taking of revenge in such stories as "The Cask of Amontillado" or "The Tell-

Tale Heart" ends by reinforcing the identification of the narrator with his enemy, whose life is then consumed in a (horrified or exultant) retelling of the crime. Given the phantasmatic action of a story such as "William Wilson," it makes little sense to try to separate Wilson from or to identify him with his shadow-self. The difficulty here, which I will take up in subsequent chapters, is that of knowing *meum* from *tuum*—of either finding the self frighteningly alien or losing that self in a fantasized identification with the other (an identification predicated on projection).

Although schematic, the preceding account ought to clarify Poe's strategy in the detective stories, in which the rationalizing mind attempts to steer a course between the rocks of identification and the whirlpool of solipsism. Dupin does this by establishing indexical sets of relation between the mental and the corporeal. Again, the problem is one of depth: the self is conceived of as irretrievably lodged within a body, with which it is not identical. The difficulty lies in obtaining access to another's self when the only information available is the unreliable flood of synesthetic perception. The appearance of the world is shifting and in need of interpretation; should one be inclined to appeal to language as a guarantor of truth, it takes very little "acumen" to realize how easily both speech and writing can be abused to private ends.

And so in the detective stories Poe first posits the absolute power of reason, bestowing on its method such power that the results may seem, to the untutored, "praeternatural." Having done so, the "analyst"—detective, card shark, or psychiatrist—begins by assuming the potential utility of any and all evidence in the search for whatever knowledge he or she wishes to possess ("nor . . . does he reject deductions from things external to the game"). In comparing the different kinds of evidence thus obtained, the analyst looks especially to that which was *unintended*: "a casual or inadvertent word . . . embarrassment, hesitation, eagerness or trepidation" ("Murders in the Rue Morgue," *PT*, 399). In this, the detective resembles both the psychiatrist who treats symptoms as signs and the nineteenth-century art historian Giovanni Morelli, who authenticated paintings through the minute inspection of physiognomic details such as the ear and the hand.[13] For Poe, all things speak, and all experience is potentially convertible into signs.

This is evident in the discussion of cards quoted above. Significantly, both Dupin and Poe prefer card games to the ostensibly more intellectual game of chess. Although the latter requires more purely "concentrative" attention to remember and sort the implications of different plays, it is less satisfying than cards insofar as its focus on the complicated mechanics of motion distracts from the principal point of play—for Poe, always the testing of "one mind against another." One does this by registering every detail of the other players' movements and reactions and by using them inferentially, because in a card game the motives of the other players and the possibilities of action are rigidly circumscribed. Given the ability to judge accurately the intellect of one's opponent, and the ability to "read" his or her action (intended or not), luck is largely removed from the game. Dupin can see in the other players' faces the nature of their hands "as if the rest of the party had turned outwards the faces of their own." What this moment reveals is how, for Poe, cards function as a mediating figure between appearance and inner self—a figure, moreover, that is structured precisely as a *sign*. Behind the face, which itself is perceived as a text, Poe finds another sign, even a "face card." The hidden card is doubled, and metonymically naturalized, by its relation to the human face. Insofar as card playing offers a model for the understanding of others, we find here evidence of the radical textuality of the self in Poe: the face is now a signifier for another signifier, rather than for any unifying quality such as its owner's "nature" or "character."

"The Purloined Letter" emerges, in some sense, from this discussion of cards in "The Murders in the Rue Morgue": in it, king, queen, and Minister play out the drama of the face cards—a drama that hinges on the possession and use (or nonuse) of another "letter."[14] Discussing the abyssal doublings of the story, Jacques Derrida observes:

> But at the Minister who "is well acquainted with my MS.," Dupin strikes a blow signed brother or confrère, twin or younger or older brother (Atreus/Thyestes). This rival and duplicitous identification of the brothers, far from fitting into a symbolic space of the family triangle . . . carries it off infinitely far away in a labyrinth of doubles without originals, of facsimile without an authentic, an indivisible letter. . . .
>
> Only four kings, hence four queens, four police prefects, four ministers, four analyst Dupins,—four narrators, four readers, four kings, etc., all more insightful and more foolish than the others, more powerful and more powerless.[15]

Four kings, four queens, four ministers (*valets*, or jacks): a deck of cards, and Dupin the master player, who wins because the deck is stacked, because he alone can most transparently "read" the actions of others in order to manipulate them, as does the boy guessing evens and odds in "The Murders in the Rue Morgue." Like the boy's, Dupin's ability is predicated on the creation of a mental "identity" between opponents, of estimating their intelligence and their motives in order to outsmart their play. And, as Jacques Lacan's reading illustrates, in Poe's model of the self the cards are always in play: identity and power relations are always constituted by movement, by shifting places, by the potential inherent in the sign, a signification whose meaning depends entirely on the configuration of the players.

By contrast, the Prefect's failure derives from his inability to recognize the semiotic flatness of his textual world. His misdirected search for the letter leads him to look in places of occulted depth—in gimlet holes, in the

cracks of joints, under carpets, inside seat cushions, and so on. Still infatu-
ated with the world of three dimensions, he sets out to take an inventory
of the Minister's apartments, in all their cubic tangibility, unaware of the
essential point that Poe's letter has no depth—only two sides—and that it
is simply *there*, on the surface, and cannot be reached by piercing the page.
Narcissus's enchantment with his image is based on false premises; as John
Irwin points out, "The illusion of reunion is based on the illusion of depth,
the mistaking of a shadow or a reflected image for a physical body."[16] Unlike the Prefect, Dupin is too sophisticated to make such a mistake with
regard to the letter. In Barbara Johnson's words, he recognizes that

> the letter is not hidden in a geometrical space, where the police are looking for
> it, or in an anatomical space, where a literal understanding of psychoanalysis
> might look for it. It is located "in" a *symbolic* structure, a structure that can
> only be perceived in its effects, and whose effects are perceived as repetition.
> Dupin finds the letter "in" the symbolic order not because he knows where to
> look, but because he knows *what to repeat*. Dupin's "analysis" is the repetition
> of the scene that led to the necessity of analysis.[17]

In Poe's treatment of card games we can see him straining after an
essentially Lacanian model of signification. Instead of a sign in which the
signifier refers directly to a preexisting signified in the world—a table, door,
or tree—Lacan offers us a model in which a pair of identical doors can only
be distinguished by the signs (reading "Ladies" and "Gentlemen") that
are posted above them. The meaning inheres not in the percept to which
the signifier refers, but in the differential social value of the signifier itself,
which determines through its placement who can, and who cannot, pass
through each door. This echoes the situation of the card player, who cannot tell the "face value" of the king, queen, or jack from the identical backs
of the cards, who cannot see how each is marked by gender and place, and
who must therefore read this information out of the peripheral, metonymic
languages that the opposing players speak.[18] The value of a particular hand
is not determined by the intrinsic meaning of the cards; it acquires significance only within the context of the other players' hands. The game's
arbitrary system of rules creates value roughly the same way language creates meaning; in both cases, it is the variable system of internal relation,
and not any external referent, that is the generative mechanism.

The Promethean Reader

The doubling of the sign, with its imagined front and back, finds an analogue in the dual literary roles of writer and reader that are explored in the
articles on cryptography and in the detective stories. Johnson observes that
Dupin's very name

comes out of Poe's interior library: from the pages of a volume called *Sketches of Conspicuous Living Characters of France* . . . which Poe reviewed for *Graham's Magazine* during the same month his first Dupin story appeared. André-Marie-Jean-Jacques-Dupin, a minor French statesman, is there described as himself a walking library: "To judge from his writings, Dupin must be a perfect living encyclopedia. From Homer to Rousseau, from the Bible to the civil code, from the laws of the twelve tables to the Koran, he has read every thing, retained every thing."[19]

Johnson establishes an (as it were) literal origin for Poe's detective in a book, in a description of one who lives for books: her historical citation grounds Derrida's observation that "everything begins 'in' a library: among books, writing, references. Hence nothing begins. Simply a drifting or disorientation from which one never moves away."[20]

Poe's review of *Sketches of Conspicuous Living Characters of France* suggests the intimate connection between "secret writing" and detective fiction: Dupin's name first appears in a review that devotes two paragraphs to Poe's superior knowledge of ciphers:

> "The penetrating mind of Berryer," says our biographer, "soon discovered [the code-key]. It was this phrase substituted for the twenty-four letters of the alphabet—"*Le gouvernement provisoire.*"
>
> All this is very well as anecdote; but we cannot understand the extraordinary penetration required in the matter. . . . The difficulty of deciphering may well be supposed much greater had the key been in a foreign tongue; yet any one who will take the trouble may address us a note, in the same manner as here proposed, and the key-phrase may be either in French, Italian, Spanish, German, Latin or Greek, (or in any of the dialects of these languages), and we pledge ourselves for the solution of the riddle. The experiment may afford our readers some amusement—let them try it.[21]

Poe's claim to solve keyphrase ciphers written in any of six languages is not merely bragging. Rather, it suggests Poe's sense that he is capable of comprehending the structural principles of language itself, and not merely its local forms: "The basis of the whole art of solution, as far as regards these matters, is found in the general principles of the formation of language itself, and thus is altogether independent of the particular laws which govern any cipher, or the construction of its key" (SW, 118). But Wimsatt, in "What Poe Knew about Cryptography," points out that since the key-phrase in *any* language is only a means for encoding an English text, Poe's claim is hollow: as Poe admits, the language or appearance of the symbols used to encipher makes *no difference* in solving the code. Poe is guilty here, as elsewhere, of practicing "mystification." His self-taught recognition of the semiotic foundations of the sign leads him to imagine a universal language, a single deep structure underlying its manifold surface manifestations, for which the cryptographic investigations serve as an analogue or substitute.

After explaining why cryptographs should not be recognizable as instances of "secret writing," Poe observes that "an unusually secure mode of secret intercommunication might be thus devised. Let the parties each furnish themselves with a copy of the same edition of a book—the rarer the edition the better—as also the rarer the book. In the cryptograph, numbers are used altogether, and these numbers refer to the locality of letters in the volume" (SW, 122). This recalls the first meeting of Dupin and of Poe's narrator, in a passage written only a few months earlier: "Our first meeting was at an obscure library in the Rue Montmartre, where the accident of our both being in search of the same very rare and very remarkable volume brought us into closer communication" ("Murders in the Rue Morgue," PT, 400). Dupin's "closer communication," we note, echoes the cryptographer's "intercommunication," and in both cases a meeting is effected through books—"the rarer the better." The communicative circuit is triangular: between Dupin and the narrator, mediated by a bibliophilic treasure; or between sender and receiver in a code, translated into and out of the particular language of the rare edition of a still-rarer book. There is more than a suggestion that books themselves are innately cryptographic, revisionary mediations of "rarer" works. Poe's writing is famously intertextual, composed of citations from and pastiches of many kinds of writers: the magazine scribblers of his day, English and German Romantics, and such "curious" writers as Thomas Browne, Robert Burton, Joseph Glanvill, and Montaigne. Poe's practice of using books as codes exactly duplicates his larger approach to writing: in both cases, authorship consists in appropriating the words (or letters) of a preexisting text and making them one's own. If the "Marginalia" consist of scribblings made on the edges of an alien work, the more radical method suggested here begins by incorporating something already written into a new text, an act that inevitably involves rewriting the meaning of the original: all writing begins as recoding.

This is evident, in fact, in the very etymology of Poe's central term:

Cipher, *n*, [ME, *ciphre*; OFr, *cifre*; LL. *cifra*; Ar. *sifr, sefr*, a cipher, nothing, from *safara*, to be nothing.]

   1. in arithmetic, a naught; a zero; 0, which, standing by itself, expresses the absence of any quantity, but increases or diminishes the value of other figures, according to its position. . . .

   3. an intricate weaving together of letters, as the initials of a name, on a seal, plate, coach, tomb, picture, etc.; a monogram.

   4. a secret or disguised manner of writing meant to be understood only by the persons who have the key to it; a code; also, the key to such a code.[22]

A naught, a monogram, a secret or disguised manner of writing, the key to a code: the dictionary definitions weave together the principal threads of Poe's obsessions, and one can see in them emblems of several of Poe's dominant genres—the "secret or disguised manner of writing" is to the articles on cryptography as "the intricate weaving together of letters" is to Poe's arabesques. ("Arabesque" itself refers to the delicate and involuted patterns, originally passages from the Koran, that iconoclastic Muslims used as ornamentation.) Even the "o, which, standing by itself, expresses the absence of any quantity, but increases or diminishes the value of other figures, according to its position," reflects Poe's nascent attempts to theorize the purely relational quality of all knowledge—the hints, in the discussion of the children's game of guessing hands, that look forward to the development of information theory.

In "A Few Words on Secret Writing," Poe explains that "it is not to be supposed that Cryptography, as a serious thing . . . has gone out of use at the present day. It is still commonly practiced in diplomacy; and there are individuals, even now, holding office in the eye of various foreign governments, whose real business is that of deciphering. . . . Good cryptographists are rare indeed; and thus their services, although seldom required, are necessarily well requited" (SW, 123). Dupin acts as a quasi-official agent on behalf of the Prefect, and thus of the government, in both "The Murders in the Rue Morgue" and "The Purloined Letter"; the fifty thousand francs he earns in the latter follow from Poe's remarks on the generous requitement of cryptographers. Dupin is clearly a projection of Poe the cryptographer: alienated, aristocratic, and condescending toward the masses, he nonetheless is well paid for his work, as Poe unhappily was not. Poe's intellectual presumption—"We will give a year's subscription to the Magazine . . . to any person who shall read us this riddle. We have no expectation that it will be read" (ibid., 122)—is transferred to Dupin, with his contempt for the bungling police (who then bequeaths it to Sherlock Holmes, and a hundred other detectives).

In the detective stories, then, Poe the cryptographer is divided into the narrator and Dupin: "Observing him in these moods, I often dwelt meditatively upon the old philosophy of the Bi-Part Soul, and amused myself with the fancy of a double Dupin—the creative and the resolvent" ("Murders in the Rue Morgue," PT, 402). The narrator is the actual creative half of Dupin, but this "Bi-Part Soul" also represents the division between Poe the cryptographer and Poe the reader, and between Poe as author and as critic. However one makes the division, in the detective stories, as in the articles on cryptography, the resolvent side is ascendant: Poe envisions himself not as the writer who challenges God's monopoly on creation, but as the Promethean reader. Daniel Hoffman writes of the "so far uncracked code" of

the world that "if the detective, or to be more generic, the genius, can crack
the code of the Author, he has made himself coequal with the perpetrator
of the code."[23]

Billet-doux to the Self

> The soul is a cypher, in the sense of a cryptograph; and the shorter a crypto-
> graph is, the more difficulty there is in its comprehension.

Edgar Allan Poe, "Sarah Margaret Fuller"

As author, Poe has planted all the clues and devised the code himself: the
secrets revealed can only have been hidden by him. "We existed within ourselves alone," the narrator says of himself and Dupin, as one gradually begins to suspect that in some way the detective story itself constitutes Poe's
private cipher. The doubleness in the detective stories—of signifier and signified, thing and shadow-name, author and reader—repeats the original
doubleness of the self, which knows itself through reading what it writes
as well as in the consciousness-engendering act of writing. Is this not the
"secret intercommunication" with the self mediated by the text the self in-
scribes? In his history of cryptography, Poe quickly shifts from political
"necessities" to the realm of "desire" for "transmitting information from
one individual to another in such a manner as to elude general comprehension" (SW, 114). A fuller account of this cryptographic desire is offered in
the final note on secret writing, in a letter sent by one of Poe's readers:

> I should perhaps apologize for again intruding a subject upon which you
> should have so ably commented . . . but I have been greatly interested in the
> articles upon "cryptography" which have appeared in your Magazine. . . . With
> secret writing . . . I have found both in correspondence and in the preservation
> of private memoranda, the frequent benefit of its peculiar virtues. I have thus
> a record of thoughts, feeling and occurrences—a history of my mental exis-
> tence, to which I may turn, and in imagination, retrace former pleasures, and
> again live through by-gone scenes—secure in the conviction that the magic
> scroll has a tale for *my* eyes alone. Who has not longed for such a confidante?
> (SW, Dec., 140-41)

The correspondent, Mr. W. B. Tyler, adds that cryptography serves as

> an excellent exercise for mental discipline, and of high *practical* importance
> on various occasions:—to the statesman and the general—to the scholar and
> the traveller,—and, may I not add "last though not least," to the *lover*? What
> can be so delightful . . . as a secret intercourse . . . safe from the prying eyes
> of some old aunt, or it may be, of a perverse and *cruel* guardian?—a *billet doux*
> that will not betray its mission, even if intercepted . . . or, (which *sometimes*
> occurs) if *stolen* from its violated depository? (Ibid., 141)

Like Poe's, Tyler's defense of cryptography quickly slides from the prudential worries of the general and statesman to the romance of cryptography itself, which, on his account, sounds much like the romance of literature. The appeal of the "magic scroll," with its tale for "*my* eyes alone," has to do with the preservation of the past fixed by its encoding, as if it were then magically protected from the depredations of time. Any specific reasons for encoding a text are eclipsed by the imaginative attraction of a private language that can be stored in the crypt of the code as in a time capsule. And the process of encoding and decoding—of writing and being read— evidently gives as much pleasure as does the actual memory itself. The similarities between Tyler's style and sentiments and those of Poe should be apparent; in fact, a close reading of the letter suggests that Tyler is actually Poe himself, offering a defense of cryptography as a means of preserving the self-in-writing from a destructive world by locking it with the key of a private code.

Practically, the use of a pseudonymous correspondent would have permitted Poe to engage in the dialogues so near to his heart: Tyler could pose cryptographic questions that Poe could then answer, converting an otherwise abstruse essay into a discussion. Poe himself raised the possibility of cryptographic self-division: in "A Few Words on Secret Writing" he asks a correspondent to give his name in full, and so "relieve us of the chance of that suspicion which was attached to the cryptography of the weekly journal above mentioned—the suspicion of inditing ciphers to ourselves" (SW, 124). Tyler's curious question—"Who has not longed for such a confidante?" (ibid., 141)—reminds one that the narrator in "The Murders in the Rue Morgue" "confides" to Dupin that his company seems "a treasure beyond price" (*PT*, 400). Tyler's references to cryptography's practical use and its value in instilling mental discipline repeat points earlier made by Poe, and the "perverse and *cruel* guardian" may look back to John Allan, even as the "stolen" love letter and the references to statesmen anticipate the plot of "The Purloined Letter." Most tellingly, the "violated depository" in which the billets-doux are kept recalls all the violated crypts of the gothic romances, and we see that once more one of Poe's fictive motifs— here, the return of the sister/bride from the grave—turns out on examination to be the narrative equivalent of a textual relation. The eruptive return of the undead bride or sister (identical to the narrator and yet other) figures the transgressive relation of the author to the words, at once self and other, that it has encrypted.

The weight of circumstantial evidence suggesting that Tyler is Poe is increased by the thematic coherence that exists between Tyler's letter and Poe's fiction. In "A Few Words on Secret Writing," Poe duplicates the split apparent in the composite figure of the narrator/Dupin; in Tyler, Poe creates a foil capable of appreciating his ratiocinative elegance: "You have exhibited a power of analytical and synthetical reasoning I have never seen equalled; and the astonishing skill you have displayed—particularly in the deciphering of the cryptograph of Dr. Charles S. Frailey will, I think, crown you the king of 'secret readers'" (SW, Dec., 141). Effusive praise, but Poe returns the compliment: the irony involved in his description of Tyler as "a gentleman whose abilities we very highly respect" would have pleased a writer capable of reviewing his own work anonymously. ("We pronounce that he has perfectly succeeded in his perfect aim," he wrote of "The Gold-Bug"; of "The Purloined Letter," he said: "There is much made of nothing . . . but the reasoning is remarkably clear, and directed solely to the required end.")[24]

Of his life with Dupin, the narrator of "The Murders in the Rue Morgue" writes: "Our seclusion was perfect. We admitted no visitors. . . . We existed within ourselves alone" (PT, 401). Their time is passed "in dreams—reading, writing, conversing"; and the hermetic enclosure of this relation is repeated in that of Tyler and Poe, a relation Poe put to a final test. Of the hundred or more cryptograms sent in by readers, the only one Poe did not solve was Tyler's; instead, pleading lack of time, he printed it for readers to try to decipher, but no solution was ever published.[25] The last paragraph of the final entry on cryptography begins: "In speaking of our hundred thousand readers (and we can scarcely suppose the number to be less), we are reminded that of this vast number one, and only one has succeeded in solving the cryptograph of Dr. Frailey" (SW, Dec., 149). But the question remains: did any of this "vast number" solve the more intricate cryptographs that are Poe's stories? It seems deeply uncharacteristic that Poe should have so readily abandoned the solution of this final cipher. Better, I think, to see it as Poe's final test of his own cryptographic methods, evidence of the success of a mode of "secret intercommunication" whose meaning was safe from public readers.[26] Certainly, Tyler (unlike Poe's other readers) took evident pains to avoid forcing Poe to try to solve his cipher: "I wish to be distinctly understood; the secret communication above, and the one following, *are not intended to show that you have promised more than you can perform.* I do not take up the gauntlet. Your challenge [to solve all ciphers of certain types] has been more than amply redeemed" (SW, Dec., 145; emphasis added). For those readers inclined to challenge themselves against Tyler (or Tyler/Poe), I present in figures 4 and 5 facsimiles of both of Tyler's cryptographs (ibid., 146).

Although Poe's secret writing has attracted the attention of exceptional cryptographers, until recently there seems never to have been an attempt to solve Tyler's messages, because apparently no one but Louis Renza and I suspected that the text might be by Poe.[27] Then in 1992, Terence Whalen revealed that he had solved the first of the two cryptographs Tyler propounded, taking his interpretive cue from Tyler's letter, in which he discusses the difficulty in deciphering a text where the punctuation and spaces

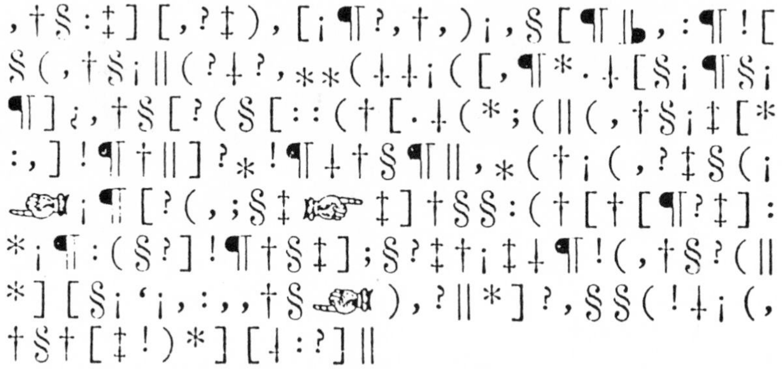

Figure 4. Cryptograph devised by W. B. Tyler. From SW, 144.

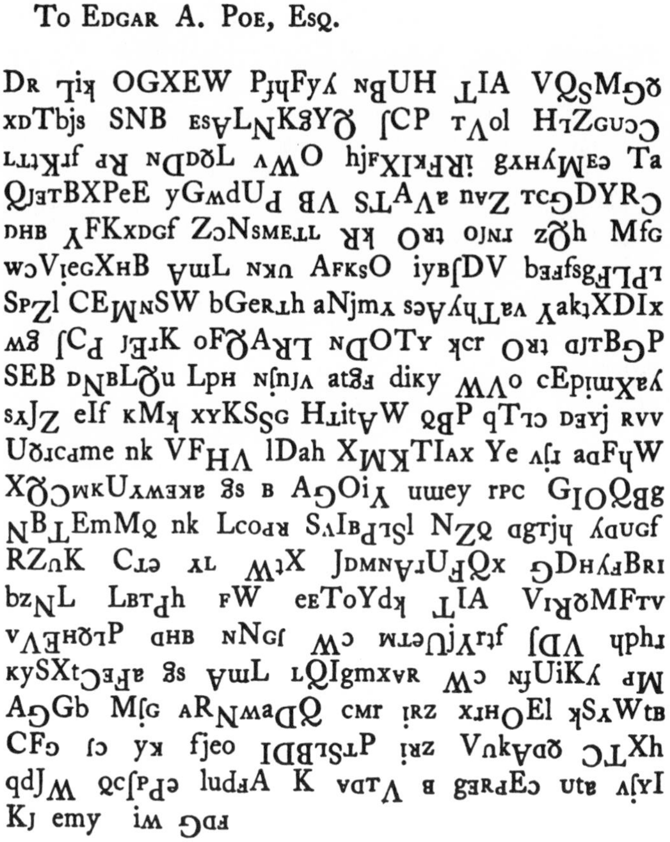

To Edgar A. Poe, Esq.

Dr ꓶꙵꓺ OGXEW PɟꓺFyʎ nꓷUH ꓕIA VꝖꙅMꝏꝏ
xᴅTbjs SNB ᴇꜱᴀLɴK�8Yꝏ ʃCP ᴛᴧol HꓶZɢᴜꙅꙅ
ʟʟꓵꓬꓲꜰ ᴅꓩ ɴꓷᴅꝏL ᴧᴡᴠ Oᴡᴠ hjꜰXꓕꓶKꓕꓵꓲ ɡxʜʎᴍᴇꙅ Ta
QꓩᴛBXPeE yGᴍᴅUꓷ ᴅᴧ Sꓶᴧᴧᴮ nᴠꙅ ᴛᴄꙅDYRꙅꙅ
ᴅʜʙ ʎFKxᴅɢꜰ ZꙅNꜱᴍᴇʟʟ ꓤꓤ Oꓤꓲ ᴛꝛꙅ oJɴꓲ zꝏ̃h Mꜰɢ
wꙅVᵢᴇɢXʜB ᴧᴜꓲL ɴꓤɴ AFKꜱO iyʙʃDV bꓷꓷꜰsgꓷꓕꙅꓕ
SPꝚꓲ CEʍɴSW bGᴇꓤꓵh aNjmꓵ sꙅʎꓱꓵʟᴮᴧ ꓵakꓲXDIx
ᴡꝏ ʃCꓵ ᴊꓺꓲK oFꝏꙆAᴧꓕ ɴꓷOTY ꓤᴄꓲ Oꓤꓲ ᴀꓩᴛBꙅP
SEB ᴅɴᴮLꝏ̃u LPꜱ Nꬰnʎᴧ atꝫꓵ diky ᴡᴧᴧo cEpꓲᴍꓲꝏ̃ʎ
sxJꝚ eⅼf ᴋMꓪ xꓤKSꙅɢ HꓵꓲtᴠW Ꝗꝏ̃P qTꓵꙅ ᴅꙅꓬj rVV
Uꙅꓵꓲᴄᴅme nk VFʜᴧ ⅼDah XʍꓪꓕTⅠax Ye ᴧꓱꓲ aꙅFꝋW
XꝏꙅᴡᴋUᴧᴍꝫᴤꝫ ꝫs ʙ AꙅOiꓵ uᴍey rpc GꓲOꝖʙɢ
NᴮꓕEmmMꝖ nk Lᴄoᴅꓤ SᴧⅠBꓷꓲꝅ NꝚꝖ agrjꝗ ʎᴅᴜɢꜰ
RZꓵK Cꓵꙅ ᴀL ᴍꓲW JᴅᴍNᴧꓲUꓷQx ꙅDʜᴧꓷBRi
bzɴL Lᴮᴛꓩh ꜰW eᴇToYᴅꓵ ꓕꓕA VꓲꓤꝏMFᴛv
ᴠᴧꓕꜱꝏꓶP ᴅʜʙ nNɢꓲ ᴡꙅ ᴡꓵꙅꓵꓵʎꓤꓼꜰ ʃᴅᴧ ꝗphꓲ
ᴋySXtꙅꝫᴤᴮ ꝫs ᴧᴜL ʟꝖIgmxᴠꓤ cꓪ ɴꓽUiKʎ ᴅꓩ
AꙅGb Mꓲɢ aRɴᴍᴅꓷꝖ cmꓤ ꓲꓤz xꓲꜱOEⅼ ꓤSxWᴛʙ
CFꙅ ꓹꙅ yꓤ fjeo IᴅꓼᴛꙅLꓷDI ꓲꓤz Vɴkꝗᴀꝏ ꙅ꓿Xh
qᴅJᴡ ꝖᴄꓽPꓷꙅ ludꓷꓕK ᴠᴅᴛᴧ ʙ gꝫ꓿Rᴮꝫ�8 uᴛꝫ ᴧꓹʎI
Kꓩ emy ꓲᴍ ꙅᴅꓹ

Figure 5. W. B. Tyler's longer cryptograph. From SW, Dec., 146.

between letters were omitted, and where the text was *written backwards.*[28] Tyler then identifies his first cryptograph as "a short specimen of this style," and admits that he would "feel much gratified with your opinion of the possibility of reading it." Beginning with the assumption that the three-character pattern of comma, dagger, and section symbol (repeated seven times in eight lines) is very likely either "the" or "and" (it proves to be the former), Whalen has solved the text as follows: "The soul secure in her existence smiles at the drawn dagger and defies its point. The stars shall fade away, the sun himself grow dim with age and nature sink in years, but thou shalt flourish in immortal youth, unhurt amid the war of elements, the wreck of matter and the crush of worlds."

Whalen's evidence supports my contention that Tyler is actually a nom de plume for Poe, as does his observation that Poe took pains to dissuade a certain Richard Bolton from attempting to solve the cipher, claiming that it was an insoluble hash of letters bearing "not even a remote resemblance" to the original manuscript,[29] a claim Whalen's solution shows to be false. (Poe had been shocked when Bolton had earlier solved one of Poe's own challenge ciphers. After hesitating to acknowledge the solution, Poe wrote to Bolton in terms that reveal how deeply he was invested in what he fancied were his unique cryptographic powers: "Allow me, Dear Sir, now to say that I was never more astonished in my life than at your solution. Will you honestly tell me?—did you not owe it to the accident of the repetition "itagi"? for "those"? . . . Be all this as it may—your solution *astonished* me. . . . For from at least 100,000 readers—a great number of whom, to my certain knowledge, busied themselves in the investigation—you and I are the only ones who have succeeded."[30] Even while acknowledging Bolton's triumph, Poe returns to the recurrent fantasy of a *dual* hermetic readership: "you and I are *the only ones who have succeeded.*")

Although Tyler's decrypted text is prosier than most of Poe's writing, its enormities of temporal and physical scale and its references to universal cataclysm reflect the concerns of "Mellonta Tauta" and *Eureka.* Whether or not the text was intended for Virginia, as Whalen suggests, it undoubtedly illustrates the essential cryptographic opposition between matter and symbol: although the text opposes the "immortal youth" of the soul to the war and decay of the entire physical universe, the address to the soul is, significantly, in cipher, since the immortality of the soul is analogized to, and guaranteed by, the safety and permanence of the cryptograph, which, through a semiotic involution of space-time, protects its contents from "the wreck of matter and the crush of worlds."[31]

Such faith in the preservative effects of encryption is evident as well in Poe's poetry, which often contains hidden texts. Besides "An Acrostic" (*PT*, 61), Poe wrote a progressive acrostic called "A Valentine to ⸺

———— ————," in which the encrypted name of Frances Sargent Osgood advances one letter with each line of poetry:

> *F*or her this rhyme is penned, whose luminous eyes,
>   *B*rightly expressive as the twins of Leda,
> *Sh*all find her own sweet name, that nestling lies
>   *U*po*n* the page, enwrapped from every reader.
> *Sear*ch narrowly the lines! — they hold a treasure
>   *Divine* — a talisman — an amulet
> That m*us*t be worn at heart. Search well the measure —
>   The word*s* — the syllables!
> (*PT*, 86–87; emphasis added)

Poe concluded his verse with a disparaging comment for the reader: "Cease trying!/You will not read the riddle, though you do the best you can do." [32] This sense of poem-as-cryptogram is even plainer in "An Enigma" (1848), in which Poe faults other sonneteers for the transparency of their work, complaining that "through all the flimsy things we see at once/As easily as through a Naples bonnet" — a fault his own poem avoids by secreting its "true" significance beneath the surface of its verse. Note that according to Poe, such truths are not merely contingently hidden, but that *it is "by dint" of their secretion* that the poem obtains its immortality:

> But *this* is, now, — you may depend upon it —
> Stable, opaque, immortal — all by dint
> Of the dear names that lie concealed within't.
> (*PT*, 91–92)

Yet although Whalen's admirable work is bolstered by the evidence of Poe's verse, Tyler's second, longer cryptograph remains unsolved — and is likely to stay so for some time. This is because the two cryptograms are in radically different ciphers. The first is a monoalphabetic substitution in which each word is spelled backward, and in which punctuation is omitted. But the second cryptograph is a polyalphabetic substitution, in which *six separate alphabets* (composed of different-sized, capitalized, and inverted alphabets) are used to encode an unknown text. To solve that cipher one thus needs to identify up to 156 different characters. Whoever composed the cryptogram realized that by using six alphabets to encode such a short message, frequency curves, ordinarily the cryptographer's first resort, could be eliminated. Because of the lack of both a frequency curve and repeated letters (save for the "rvv" at the end of the ninth line), I failed in my own efforts to solve the code. This was also the case with Bill Sutton, editor-in-chief of *The Cryptogram*, a publication of the American Cryptogram Association. Of course it is possible that there is *no* semantically meaningful message enciphered in the second cryptogram, but Sutton's application of what is known as the Kasiski test indicates that the encrypted message is, in all likelihood, an English text rather than gibberish. Perhaps it is just as well: by remaining an enigma, Tyler's cryptograph stands as an emblem of the seductive challenge cryptographic texts propose, and reminds us that cryptographic writing is at least as profoundly concerned with the human need for mystery as it is with the pleasures of solution.

If I am right about Tyler's cipher, it offers a concluding instance of the ways in which the articles on cryptography prefigure the motifs of the detective stories, as Poe emulates the Minister D—— by hiding his mis-addressed text (or "cipher") in plain sight, within the pages of *Graham's Magazine*. Tyler's cryptograph bears striking resemblances to a passage from "The Purloined Letter," in which Dupin describes his perception of the stolen item:

> To be sure, it was, to all appearance, radically different from the one of which the Prefect had read us so minute a description. Here the seal was large and black, with the D—— cipher; . . . But, then, the *radicalness* of these differences . . . was excessive . . . and so suggestive of a design to delude the beholder into an idea of the worthlessness of the document; these things, together with the hyperobtrusive situation of this document, full in the view of every visiter, and thus exactly in accordance with the conclusions to which I had previously arrived; these things, I say, were strongly corroborative of suspicion, in one who came with the intention to suspect. (*PT,* 696)

Once Tyler's cipher has been deciphered, might we not say of it what Dupin said of his? "Why—it did not seem altogether right to leave the interior blank—that would have been insulting. . . . So, as I knew he would feel some curiosity in regard to the identity of the person who outwitted him, I thought it a pity not to give him a clue" (ibid., 698).

Tyler/Poe and the narrator/Dupin are both versions of a divided self constituted by the complementary acts of writing and reading, the mirroring and perception of mirroring that prove a precondition for self-conscious-ness. The articles on cryptography extend Lacan's reading of "The Pur-loined Letter" as "an allegory of the signifier" in a way that also bears out the narrative implications of Derrida's remark that "the divisibility of the letter is also the divisibility of the signifier to which it gives rise, and there-fore also of the 'subjects,' 'characters,' or 'positions' that are subject to them and that 'represent' them."[33] If, as I have argued, the keys to Poe's ciphers require a one-to-one correspondence for their efficacy, Poe's creation of Tyler literalizes this relation in a "one-to-one correspondence" in which Poe covertly stages his internal self-division. In these articles Poe replaces the specular double of "William Wilson" with a textual doubling in which the secret correspondence between two interdependent texts constitutes a single self. Throughout Poe's cryptographic writings, his choice was always to be double or nothing: to sequester "self" and "correspondent" within the code of language, or to surrender to the fear that the cipher of the self is truly *sifr*, nothing, empty. Records of a mind composing and disclosing for its own pleasure, these texts are love letters—billets-doux—from Poe to himself, concealed within sensational surface narratives; ones that must, at times, have seemed dead letters, unreceived in a world that resisted Poe's complex recodings of identity.

Despite the appeal to "our hundred thousand readers," during his lifetime Poe had finally to remain his own perfect confidante; he had, like Baudelaire in "Au lecteur," to transform the address to the reader—"Hypocrite lecteur,—mon semblable,—mon frère!"—into a deeper address to himself.[34] But in the years following his death, Poe's secret writings have found their addresses with perverse force. According to Patrick Quinn, Baudelaire's imagined reader in *Les fleurs du mal* is none other than Poe himself, who is at the same time Baudelaire's double and his self.[35] In such uncanny ways, the history of literature in the last century and a half has often been underwritten by the palimpsest of Poe's secret prose; and it is to the forms of that writing that I now turn.

SECRET WRITING AS ALCHEMY

| 2 | Recoding Defoe |

> "This bug is to make my fortune," he continued, with a triumphant smile, "to reinstate me in my family possessions."
>
> Edgar Allan Poe, "The Gold-Bug"

The Word Made Flesh

If we accept the testimony of the noted Poe scholar Thomas Ollive Mab-bott, "The Gold-Bug" is one of the most popular and widely imitated stories in the world, the source for hundreds of other tales, novels, and films.[1] Like so many aspects of Poe's influence and reputation, this seems hard to believe. Can "The Gold-Bug" really have exerted such a profound influence? How should we go about accounting for this force? The story's plot is rather slight. An erudite recluse named Legrand, in exile from a world in which his fortunes have collapsed, discovers on a deserted beach a large, burnished beetle and a piece of parchment, marked by a skull or death's-head. Being something of a naturalist, he wraps the beetle in the parchment for protection and brings it back to his cottage. Later, while visiting Legrand, the narrator accidently subjects the parchment to heat from a fire. And then the discovery: the heated parchment reveals secret images and markings, including the drawing of a goat and a series of cryptic numbers and symbols (see fig. 6). Legrand, his servant Jupiter, and the un-named narrator together search out the lost pirate treasure of Captain Kidd. Back at home, Legrand explains how he was able to identify the parchment as a cryptographic map, and the symbols as a text that, deciphered, offered cryptic instructions on how to find the gold.

Doubtless, the story's popularity follows from a number of identifiable features, including the thrill of pirate adventures, the patent wish fulfill-ment embodied in the story's ending, and—less well recognized—the lure of the historical fantastic, which uses the gold as a figure to link the story's nineteenth-century present to the romance of the colonial past. Finally, though, what distinguishes "The Gold-Bug" from previous tales of adven-ture is the cryptographic translation of the map. Like most fictive crypto-grams, the basic one in "The Gold-Bug" is a simple alphabetic substitution,

53‡‡†305))6*;4826)4‡.)4‡);806*;48†8¶60))85;;]8*¡;:‡*8†83 (88)
5*†;46(;88*96*?;8)*‡(;485);5*†2:*‡(;4956*2(5* − 4)8¶8*;40692
85);)6†8)4‡‡;1(‡9;48081;8:8‡1;48†85;4)485†528806*81(‡9;48;
(88;4 (‡?34;48)4‡;161;:188;‡?;

Figure 6. Poe, "The Gold-Bug," *PT*, 587.

the easiest variety possible. But Poe complicates the task of deciphering Kidd's message, "rudely traced, in a red tint, between the death's-head and the goat," by superenciphering the cipher with several additional levels, including the "hieroglyphical" homonymous signature of the goat (or kid) of the pirate Captain Kidd, and the indirect, unpunctuated, and almost allegorical nature of the translated text, which only slowly reveals itself as a set of directions:

> A good glass in the bishop's hostel in the devil's seat twenty-one degrees and thirteen minutes northeast and by north main branch seventh limb east side shoot from the left eye of the death's-head a bee-line from the tree through the shot fifty feet out. (*PT*, 591)

Despite the relative simplicity of Poe's game, the pleasure of solving his cipher—or, rather, of watching it be solved by Legrand—mobilizes a deep tension in realist fiction between our absorption in the represented world of the tale and our simultaneous fascination with the process of reading, of translating signs into meaning. In "The Gold-Bug," the cryptographic imagination describes the interplay of two-dimensional language in three-dimensional lives, which is a corollary to this symbolic consciousness. Cryptography is a form of magic in which, through his mastery of language, Legrand performs the conjurer's trick of pulling a rabbit out of a hat, forcing the world to flower open. The covert logic of cryptographic adventure is not about finding a preexisting gap in the world, but about making its opaque surfaces open on command.

In what follows, I explore the alchemical logic that structures Poe's use of cryptography, using "The Gold-Bug" to clarify a set of assumptions about language and literature that, just as Poe claims, are probably coextensive with writing.[2] In its first recorded occurrence, cryptography was employed strictly as a form of mystification. Around 2000 B.C., in Menet Khufu, a town along the Nile, "an unknown scribe ordered special hieroglyphic symbols carved in Khumnhotep II's tomb for decoration or in order to impress the viewer. He employed no system of secret writing; rather he simply substituted some unique hieroglyphic symbols in place of ordinary ones. His probable purpose: to give grace and dignity to the message he inscribed on the tomb."[3] Khumnhotep's cryptographic hieroglyphs were

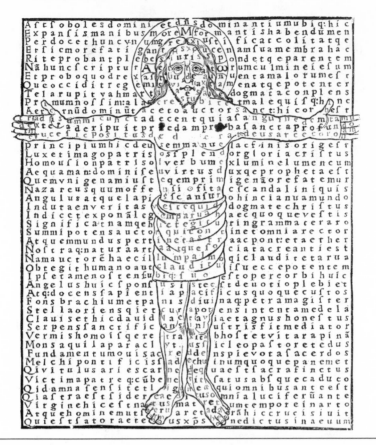

Figure 7. The Word Made Flesh: A Latin shape-poem by the monk Hrabanus Maurus, in which the outline of Christ crucified carves out a new poem from the larger verbal matrix. Not a cryptogram, precisely, but an intersection of cipher and hieroglyph, and an image of the way the human form imposes itself as a structuring principle on writing. From Maurus's *De laudibus sancte crucis opus, erudicione versu prosag mirificum* (Pforzheim: Thomas Anshelm, 1503). Used by permission of the Chapin Library, Williams College.

at once aesthetic and political; crudely put, they were a form of propaganda that aimed to dramatize Khumnhotep's power. In their ability to awe or abase viewers, the semantically insignificant glyphs decorating Khumnhotep's grave reveal that hierophantic aspect that hangs like a penumbra around all written words: an investment in the idea of the code that, within the West, is imagined to be as old as the world itself.

Ultimately, the impulses behind cryptography go back to life's sources. According to the New Testament, the first and greatest instance of cryptography was the conjuration of the universe at a word:

In the beginning was the Word, and the Word was with God, and the Word
   was God.
The same was in the beginning with God.
All things were made by him; and without him was not any thing made that
   was made.
In him was life; and the life was the light of men.
And the light shineth in darkness; and the darkness comprehended
   it not. . . .
And the Word was made flesh, and dwelt among us.
(John 1:1-5, 14)

For the author of John, the mystery of Christ's creation—the process by
which the Word is invested in flesh—is a deep cryptographic enigma. John's
Hellenized version of the incarnation depends on a Platonism in which
words provide matter with their informing logic.[4] Whether glossed as reason, word, or the creative energy of God's speech, Logos represents the unaccountable process by which the symbolic comes to animate the material
world (just the question that drives Stuart Ressler's cryptographic attack
on the structure of DNA).

Between them, the stories of Khumnhotep and of Christ's incarnation
epitomize the bipolar structure of the cryptographic imagination. Although
the Egyptian text presents itself as a set of glyphs or runes that are mysterious or even terrifying in their illegibility, for John cryptography seems
to promise an absolute transparency of meaning. This division reflects the
Janus-faced character of secret writing, which expresses itself both as a form
of cloaking or covering and as a form of self-revelation—as in the code of
the Beast, whose body is marked by a hidden *666*, or in the ambiguous *A*
that brands Hester Prynne.[5]

The literary force of New Testament narratives of Christ's life derives
in no small measure from their condensed representation of both poles of
the cryptographic impulse: Christ's life begins with a mysterious investi-
ture and ends with a mysterious divestment, after which, for the forty days
between Easter Sunday and the Ascension, Christ appears purified of materiality, sublimed, stripped of the signifier's dross. And yet even this triumph of linguistic immediation is cryptographic. The necessary agent for
Christ's purification is *the crypt itself,* which as the container for Christ's
transfiguration analogically resembles the "container" of the cipher. To describe the sepulcher as a site of writing may seem odd, but as a holy grave
it is the etymological equivalent of the word *hieroglyph,* substituting the
Anglo-Saxon *graven* ("to dig, bury, carve") for the Greek *glyphein* ("to
carve, hollow out"). Instead of merely surrounding the grave with hieroglyphs, as Khumnhotep did, the Resurrection story identifies Christ with
language, so that the mystery of the Resurrection—whose first evidence is

the stone rolled away to reveal an empty crypt—is that of an achieved immanence of meaning.[6]

Christ's cryptic transfigurations are, as Jorge Luis Borges recognizes,
stories of our own being in the world. In "John I:14," Borges writes:

> I was born of a womb
> by an act of magic.
> I lived under a spell, imprisoned in a body,
> in the humbleness of a soul.[7]

"John I:14" suggests that the miracle of Christ's virgin birth has to do with
the way humans are conjured into corporeal being. The most vivid memory of my son's birth was my shock at his arrival as if from nowhere, space
evolving to introduce a new person to the world. Today, the development of
gene therapies has made it intuitively plausible to represent impregnation
as a drama of secret (or secreted) writing, in which an autopoetic code is
produced (one belonging to neither parent alone) that writes a person into
existence. This story plays itself out in dozens of forms, including that of
Christ's birth and transubstantiation. Both the crypt of cryptography and
that of the tomb derive from the Greek *kryptos*, for "hidden," "secret," or
"concealed."

Cryptographic narratives perpetually return to this tension between the
crypt of writing and the hidden place in which bodies are laid. Of the many
anecdotes that illustrate this, I offer two. The first is the story of Orville
Ward Owen, a Detroit physician and Baconian author who, not content
with the evidence he had adumbrated in the six volumes of *Sir Francis
Bacon's Cipher Story*,[8] "became increasingly convinced that Bacon had buried
some more tangible evidence of his authorship of Shakespeare's works in a
set of iron boxes" (F&F, 69). Remarkably, Owen was able to persuade back-
ers to finance increasingly elaborate and expensive expeditions to England
to dig for these boxes—first in a cave near Chepstow Castle, later in a rift
in the bed of the River Wye, and yet again in a grotto in Piercefield Park.
In each case, Owen's cipher located the incontrovertible texts in crypts or
cryptlike spaces, as in the "deep caisson sunk by English engineers" a dozen
feet into the mud below the River Wye. There, according to an admirer,
Owen located "a small, gray, stone structure . . . marked by the inscriptions
of Francis Bacon," which to Owen's chagrin ultimately proved as empty as
Al Capone's cellar.

Compare this to my second Baconian anecdote, this one centering on
the ostensible cipher in Shakespeare's epitaph (a subject treated at greater
length in chapter 6). By anagramming the letters and manipulating the word
order of the epitaph placed over Shakespeare's grave in Stratford, a certain
C. Alexander Montgomery revealed the correct text to be as follows:

Dig Honest Man dost THEE forbeare
I SHAKE-SPEARE England's Tvdor Heire
Graved belovv these mystic Stones
The mystery codes yet gab of bones.
(F&F, 57)

Although I would not want to press too hard on any gloss of Mont-gomery's incoherent quatrain, Owen's crypt search and Montgomery's epi-taph reveal an identically structured sense of the literary cryptograph. In both, writing assumed to possess a secret leads to the imagination of the *text* as a crypt to be broken into, "cracked," brought to light. Thus deciphered, these texts direct readers to the contents of real, three-dimensional crypts, for which the original texts serve as an analogue. Such crypts are often graves, whether for the bones "gabbed" about in Shakespeare's epitaph or for what Owen believed to be the sixty-six boxes of manuscripts that would undeniably prove Bacon's authorship (manuscripts that function as substi-tute corpses, to be exhumed in the forensic identification of the *real* author of the Shakespeare canon, in an endless recirculation of texts and bodies).

Closely related to the ciphered opening of these epitaphic spaces is the way in which cryptography negotiates the tension between interior psychic states and the world. Such tensions historically have often been resolved through the logocentric narratives of origin found in the religions of the book. But similar problems lie at the heart of many psychoanalytic theories of the self. Indeed, one source of the explosive postwar interest in Poe is the consonance between the cryptographic qualities of his texts and the theo-retical inclinations of his critics. Because Poe's texts are already constructed on the model of a steganographic cipher, with an overt surface narrative and a variety of occluded, "interior" truths often having to do with the opera-tions of language, they naturally lend themselves to analysts looking for a hidden key, regardless of whether that key concerns incest, dissemination, or the itinerary of the signifier.

Here we may think of the work of Nicolas Abraham and Maria Torok on the cryptonym, their term for a psychopathology resulting from a mis-alignment between the analysand's body and his or her words. Rereading Freud's case history of the Wolf Man, Abraham and Torok hypothesize that the Wolf Man's physical symptoms stem from a punning, multilingual "verbarium" of key (or code) words, which indirectly name the principal traumas of his life.[9] The words are "encrypted" in the self to avoid analy-sis *by* the self, for whom they pose insoluble psychic double binds. Freudian therapy takes the form of a full-blown cryptanalysis, designed to return the patient to the biographical trauma at the core of his or her memory, although it becomes impossible to say if the encrypted words name a real event or whether they *produce* the symptoms they name. Irving Malin illustrates the common ground between cryptography and cryptonymy when he writes that for Abraham and Torok, texts "are rarely decoded in a way that does justice to 'secrets' embedded" in them, because "all texts—especially those dealing with the 'phantom'—conceal meanings. Thus close readings must, in effect, pay attention to words not spoken or written, to cryptograms hidden in verbal structure."[10]

Because Poe is compulsively interested both in crypts ("The Fall of the House of Usher," "The Black Cat," "The Premature Burial") and in cryptograms, it is no surprise that psychoanalytic critics have often concentrated on his work.[11] Poe's writing coalesces around secrets and obscurity, almost forcing readers to imagine the text as a crypt with a hidden key. Such a homeopathic technique for the creation of mysteries produces highly cathected readers; the surface of the cipher produces a crypt in us, which we proceed to fill with our imagination, just as the semantic vacuity of Khumnhotep's glyphs contextually signified Khumnhotep's power and his resistance to comprehension. Crypts and cryptographs are also narratively related because it is always words that open Poe's crypts, whether through the involuntary confessions of "The Tell-Tale Heart" or through Dupin's semiotic mastery of the rooms of the Mmes. L'Espanaye in "The Murders in the Rue Morgue." Poe is not alone in this association, which appears in an enormous range of writings, from the challenge of the three inscribed caskets in *The Merchant of Venice* to the "great cryptogram" that reveals itself as a map to the planet's hollow core in Jules Verne's *Journey to the Center of the Earth*.

A similar logic operates in much of the psychoanalytical criticism of Poe's writing. The psychic topography of cryptonymy is structured according to the same opposition between two-dimensional language and an (imaginary) three-dimensional psychic space that has shaped secret writing since the New Testament. Far from explaining how the psyche "really" works, cryptonymy depends for its explanatory force on this enciphered approach to language. Despite the abolishment of interiority and the flattening-out of claims to three-dimensional representation that characterize postmodern criticism, Abraham and Torok operate in the familiar rhetorical territory of the gothic. This follows from Freud, whose case studies are generic cousins of the gothic novel, and who understands the dream as a cryptogram, a rebuslike series of words and images whose transformations, substitutions, and condensations are designed to render the dream's manifest content illegible. Freud's insight is that the manifest content of the dream is not deciphered through what he calls a "fixed key," in which an image always possesses a specific meaning, but that each dreamer develops an individual key, to be teased out by the psychoanalyst on the basis of the patient's covert associations. Analysis is then structured as a drama of secret reading in which the patient is forced to decipher a text encrypted by his or her own psyche.[12]

In his introduction to Abraham and Torok's *Wolf Man's Magic Word*, Jacques Derrida also exploits such gothic rhetorical effects as encryption, paralysis, violation, and unspeakability as he describes the involutions of psychic space in which the Wolf Man's words have been trapped. The Wolf Man, Derrida writes, had "edified a crypt within him: an artifact, an artificial unconscious in the Self, an interior enclave, partitions, hidden passages, zigzags, occult and difficult traffic" (xliv). The only passage through this mental architecture is through the use of the magic words of the "verbarium," coded across English, Russian, and German, to keep the crypt impermeable (ibid., xlv). In using such gothic language to describe incorporation, Derrida's intention is obviously not to reaffirm the sovereignty of binarisms of place (the absoluteness of the distinction between inside and outside) but to vex such topological distinctions through what might be called his toroidal or Moebian punning, a punning centered on the word *fors*. Both within and without, in the "inner heart and the public space," the word-thing *fors* allows Derrida to describe encryption as "both a secretive inclusion and an exclusion of the object outside of the subject, a partitioning of it off inside the vault of its signifier," leaving the crypt in a dual inside/outside space.[13]

Derrida's fissile language is implicitly an attack on the fixity of Lacan's spatial algebra. My point in revisiting this debate is only to note that despite their well-recognized differences, *all* of the major psychoanalytical figures interested in Poe turn to cryptographic language in their search for a rhetoric adequate to the experience of Poe's writing. Although they apply them to different ends, Freud, Lacan, Derrida, and Abraham and Torok rely on the rhetorical resources of the gothic, the genre that most fully displays the anxiety about words and spaces that is the province of the cryptographic imagination.[14]

Bird or Devil?

To say that even dialogically opposed theorists such as Lacan and Derrida use cryptographic language in describing the psyche does not mean that rhetorical analysis alone can adjudicate the debates that have preoccupied literary theorists for the past quarter-century. It is, however, a way of attending to what I take to be the virtual ubiquity of cryptographic language —a form of writing organized around an imagined (even if so imagined only to be undone or deconstructed) difference between linguistic surface and depth.

Indeed, aspects of the cryptographic imagination operate in far less likely forms of writing than psychoanalytic criticism. In the following pages, I want to consider the relation between the writing of Poe and that of Daniel Defoe, an author from whom Poe derives much of his cryptographic impetus. Such a pairing must look odd: who could be less like Poe than Defoe, a figure celebrated for the virtual invention of the reality effect and the prose transcription of the phenomenal world? Defoe was, however, hardly immune to the attractions of cryptography: anticipating the desire for comparative linguistics, if not its methods, his *Essay upon Literature; or, An Enquiry into the Antiquity and Original of Letters* traces the origins of all alphabets back to the Hebrew, with several pages devoted especially to the nature of secret writing and its relation to the origins of writing.[15] By reading Poe reading Defoe, we can recognize how Poe's texts operate as a secret translation machine, intensifying Defoe's nascent cryptographic awareness and simultaneously converting Poll, the parrot from *Robinson Crusoe*, into the Raven.

Despite its ostensible realism, much of the power of Defoe's prose stems from the way it allegorizes the reading process. That power is sufficient, I might add, that Poe became a writer partly because of his contact with Defoe. In his 1836 *Southern Literary Messenger* review of a new edition of *Robinson Crusoe*, Poe acknowledges finding in "that invaluable work" not only powerful and "enchaining" memories of a favorite childhood text, but his own beginnings in literature: "How fondly do we recur, in memory, to those enchanted days of our boyhood when we first learned to grow serious over Robinson Crusoe!—when we first found the spirit of wild adventure enkindling within us, as, by the dim fire light, we labored out, line by line, the marvelous import of those pages, and hung breathless and trembling with eagerness over their absorbing—over their enchaining interest! Alas! The days of desolate islands are no more!" (*ER*, 201). Instances of Defoe's influence on Poe include Poe's imitation of plainstyle in "The Thousand-and-Second Tale of Scheherazade" ("I now bitterly repented my folly in quitting a comfortable home to peril my life in such adventures as this; but regret being useless, I made the best of my condition, and exerted myself to secure the good-will of the man-animal that owned the trumpet" [*PT*, 793]), and Poe's extension of Crusoe's terrestrial explorations in such works as "The Unparalleled Adventure of One Hans Pfaall" and "The Balloon-Hoax."

Defoe also makes a telling appearance in "The Raven." A clue to the poem's origins is given midway through "The Philosophy of Composition," when Poe explains how he chose a bird as his subject. In need of a "pretext for the continuous use of the one word 'nevermore,'" Poe found himself hard-pressed to invent "a sufficiently plausible reason for its continuous repetition" by "a *human* being." The difficulty, Poe adds, "lay in the reconciliation of this monotony with the exercise of reason on the part of the creature repeating the word. Here, then, immediately arose the idea of a *non*-reasoning creature capable of speech; and, very naturally, a parrot, in the first instance, suggested itself, but was superseded forthwith by a Raven, as equally capable of speech, and infinitely more in keeping with the intended *tone*" (*ER*, 18).

Just pages earlier, while arguing for the "distinct limit, as regards length, to all works of literary art—the limit of a single sitting," Poe had acknowledged that "in certain classes of prose composition, such as 'Robinson Crusoe,' (demanding no unity), this limit may be advantageously overpassed" (ibid., 15). That Poe makes an exception of Defoe's novel is a sign of his esteem, but readers familiar with *Robinson Crusoe* may also recognize a more profound indebtedness in the figure of Poe's Raven. Recall that after discovering Poll in the wild, Crusoe spends years training his parrot until it "talked so articulately and plain, that it was very pleasant to me; and he lived with me no less than six and twenty years; how long he might live afterwards, I know not . . . perhaps poor Poll may be alive there still, calling after *Poor Robin Crusoe* to this day. I wish no *English* man the ill luck to come there and hear him; but if he did, he would certainly believe it was the devil."[16] Although the coincidence of parrot, raven, and *Robinson Crusoe* in Poe's essay is suggestive, the antepenultimate stanza of "The Raven" clinches the bird's provenance. " 'Prophet!' said I, 'thing of evil!—prophet still, if bird or devil!'" (*PT*, 85), Poe's narrator exclaims, revealing through the allusion how Poll's devilish appearance inspired Poe's uncanny bird.

Both Poll and the Raven offer figures for the reading process. In order to be affected by a work, a reader must engage with the conflicts staged within it. Poe uses the Raven to address problems of identification and transference much like those Freud acknowledged when he wrote that in analysis "the patient hears what we say but it rouses no response in his mind. He probably thinks to himself: 'That is very interesting, but I see no sign of it in myself.'" The reader is " 'stimulated' only by those passages which he feels apply to himself, i.e., which refer to conflicts that are active in him."[17] Hence the Raven emerges as a model for the process by which literary transference takes place:

> At length the lover, startled from his original *nonchalance* by the melancholy character of the word itself—by its frequent repetition . . . is at length excited to superstition, and wildly propounds queries of a far different character—queries whose solution he has passionately at heart . . . propounds them . . . not altogether because he believes in the prophetic or demoniac character of the bird (which, reason assures him, is merely repeating a lesson learned by rote) but because he experiences a phrenzied pleasure in so modeling his questions as to receive from the *expected* "Nevermore" the most delicious because the most intolerable of sorrow. (*ER*, 19)

The ceaseless, mechanical repetitions of the Raven offer a striking emblem of the interlocutory manner in which a literary work addresses its readers.

Although operating under a suspicion that the text's answers are not truly prophetic, but only "lessons learned by rote," the reader obtains a perverse, "delicious," and even "phrenzied pleasure" by "so modeling his question as to receive" the expected "Nevermore." Poe accurately captures the active cooperation that the reader brings to his literary bereavement; the work itself is only an intermediary device for creating an affect in the minds and bodies of particular readers.

This process of readerly transference typically centers on images or figures of crypts, a motif Poe seems to have developed especially from the work of Defoe. "The Raven," *Narrative of A. Gordon Pym*, and "The Gold-Bug" all represent idiosyncratic revisions of *Robinson Crusoe*, and in each case Poe borrows from Defoe a notion of the crypt that he converts into the cryptograph. Cryptography, that is, represents Poe's technical adaptation of the hieroglyph. Today we know that the obsession with the hieroglyph as an originary form of language was based on false assumptions about the nature of the Egyptian script, which is not an originary nor even a wholly hieroglyphic form of language, but a complex mix of semantic and phonetic elements. But as John Irwin shows, the hieroglyph offered a metaphor through which the Romantics could figure their version of the relations between the origins of language and the origins of the self. Similarly, the cryptograph has become a way of imagining our relation to language, epistemology, and identity. It provides a way of doubling the text within the reader, reproducing within his or her body and mind the particular effects Poe wishes to create. It is, one might say, a way of extending hieroglyphic doubling into the very process of reading.

The cipher accomplishes this doubling by revealing the unmotivated nature of the sign, fostering the reader's awareness of the text as a code full of secrets. The cryptograph also contributes to Poe's sense that literature, as Valéry said, is "l'art se jouer de l'âme des autres."[18] Realizing that only the reader's investment renders the text meaningful, Poe shifted his attention from the nature of mimetic representation to that of signification. (In "The Raven," for instance, Poe's emphasis is wholly on the speaker's attempt to read meaning into the bird's simulation of speech.) Finally, the illegibility of the ciphered sign actually promotes identification, blurring the difference between the doubled reader and the writer. The hieroglyph is a fantasy about uniting the split in human beings between these two dimensions, which tends to diminish the specifically linguistic aspect of the self; the cryptograph provides an emblem for thinking about language qua script, *before* it becomes Narcissus's mirror.

One can clarify the difference between hieroglyph and cryptograph by comparing how each is employed by Jacques Lacan, whose "Seminar on 'The Purloined Letter'" has reinvigorated American readings of Poe.[19] Recall Lacan's famous assertion that "The Purloined Letter" allegorizes the origins of subject formation in the symbolic order by showing how the subject receives its "decisive orientation" from the "itinerary of the signifier." It is this truth, he continues, that "makes the very existence of fiction possible. And in that case, a fable is as appropriate as any other narrative for bringing it to light—at the risk of having the fable's coherence put to the test in the process. Aside from that reservation, a fictive tale even has the advantage of manifesting symbolic necessity more purely to the extent that we may believe its conception arbitrary."[20]

Although it is "no accident that this tale revealed itself propitious to pursuing a course of inquiry which had already found support in it," Lacan says nothing more about why this particular tale should come to bear such weighty meaning. Why "The Purloined Letter" rather than "The Pit and the Pendulum" or "The Masque of the Red Death"? Or, for that matter, *Barnaby Rudge*, or *Uncle Tom's Cabin*? If the itinerary of the signifier "makes the very existence of fiction possible," does this mean that all fictions have the same itinerary? Lacan avoids such questions by insisting that the burden of coherence falls on the tale, and not on his analysis; this evasion, however, does not explain why some texts—including "The Purloined Letter"—seem to *insist* on metalinguistic readings. Certainly Lacan never admits in the "Seminar" that Poe influenced him; it is the "fable's coherence" that is "put to the test" by his reading.

In fact, Lacan—who, like the other members of the French avant-garde of the 1920s and 1930s, read Poe closely—is undoubtedly indebted to Poe's writing. That Lacan's debt is not immediately apparent is due partly to a confusion of terms: both Lacan and Poe often employ the terms *hieroglyph* and *cryptograph* interchangeably. But like Poe, Lacan affirms the symbolic, even algebraic, nature of the subject. Indeed, the identity of Lacan's hieroglyph and Poe's cryptograph becomes evident when Lacan invokes the hieroglyph to ridicule any connection between sign and image.[21] Freud, Lacan tell us, "shows us in every possible way that the value of the image as signifier has nothing whatever to do with its signification, giving as an example Egyptian hieroglyphics in which it would be sheer buffoonery to pretend that in a given text the frequency of a vulture, which is an aleph, or of a chick, which is a vau, indicating a form of the verb 'to be' or a plural, prove that the text has anything at all to do with these ornithological specimens."[22]

This loss of the sign's Adamic properties follows from Jean François Champollion's discovery that although the hieroglyph may have originated as a pictograph, it rapidly evolved into a quasi-alphabetic code. Lacking the transparent self-evidence of the image, the hieroglyphs would have been doomed to remain incoherent marks in a lost tongue had it not been for the rules of transformation implied by the Rosetta stone. This search for rules is functionally equivalent to cryptanalysis; as Abraham Sinkov notes in *Ele-*

mentary Cryptanalysis: A Mathematical Approach, cryptanalysis has "aided in the reconstruction of lost languages which had been dead for so long that nothing was known about them so that they were, in effect, secret languages."[23]

This is Lacan's point in insisting on the closed and illegible system of representation Champollion faced in confronting the hieroglyphs: "The mental vice ['in favour of a symbolism deriving from natural analogy'] denounced above enjoys such favour that today's psychoanalyst can be expected to say that he decodes before he will come around to taking the necessary tour with Freud (turn at the statue of Champollion, says the guide) that will make him understand that what he does is decipher; the distinction is that a cryptogram takes on its full dimension only when it is in a lost language."[24] And in fact, in the excerpted translation in figure 8, Lacan is clearly right: the owl glyph functions prepositionally, and has nothing to do with the appearance or behavior of the real bird.

Although the right-minded psychoanalyst must take "the necessary tour with Freud," what can we say of Lacan's unnamed "guide," who figures only once in the text before disappearing? Lacan could as easily have written the instruction himself ("turn at the statue of Champollion"); instead, he has gone to the trouble of introducing an additional figure. But who is the guide that Lacan has in mind? My hunch is that it is Poe. Certainly it is the case that Lacan sounds a good deal like Pundita in the following excerpt from "Mellonta Tauta," in which Johannes Kepler is described as "essentially a 'theorist'—that word now of so much sanctity, formerly an epithet of contempt. Would it not have puzzled these old moles, too, to have explained by which of the two 'roads' a cryptographist unriddles a cryptograph of more than usual secrecy, or by which of the two roads Champollion directed mankind to those enduring and almost innumerable truths which resulted from deciphering the Hieroglyphics?" (*ER*, 877). Lacan's allusion to "Mellonta Tauta" indicates that it is Poe himself who stands at the statue of Champollion. As Champollion provided Poe with a precursor in "Mellonta Tauta," so Lacan uses Poe in this Egyptian costume drama of literary history, aligning Poe with himself, Freud, and Champollion as cryptographic readers.

However abstruse it might seem, this distinction between ciphers and hieroglyphs has not been lost to detective fiction. Paul Auster's *City of Glass* (a book quite clear about its sourcing in Poe) is explicitly an investigation into the differences between a natural hieroglyphic language, grounded in the body and in vision, and an arbitrary Saussurean system.[25] Even Arthur Conan Doyle captures the distinction correctly. In "The Adventure of the Dancing Men," Sherlock Holmes (who describes himself as someone "fairly familiar with all forms of secret writings," and indeed as "the author of a trifling monograph upon the subject, in which I analyse one hundred and

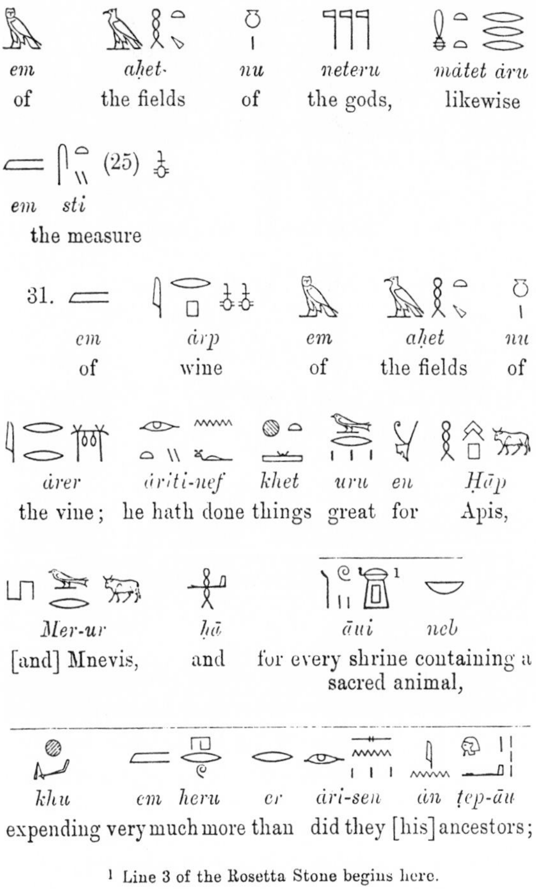

em	aḥet·	nu	neteru	mátet áru
of	the fields	of	the gods,	likewise

em	sti
the measure	

31.

em	árp	em	aḥet	nu
of	wine	of	the fields	of

árer	áriti-nef	khet	uru	en	Ḥáp
the vine;	he hath done things	great	for		Apis,

Mer-ur	ḥá	áui	neb
[and] Mnevis,	and	for every shrine containing a	
		sacred animal,	

khu	em	heru	er	ári-sen	án	ṭep-áu
expending very much more than				did they	[his]	ancestors;

[1] Line 3 of the Rosetta Stone begins here.

Figure 8. From *The Rosetta Stone*, ed. E. A. Wallis Budge (London: Kegan Paul, 1904), 206.

sixty separate ciphers") is sent to investigate the "childish prank" of some drawings of stick figures sent to Elsie Cubitt, which frighten her for reasons her husband cannot understand. Holmes recognizes the drawings as a steganographic cipher, designed "to give the idea that they are the mere random sketches of children." As Holmes realizes, "these hieroglyphics have evidently a meaning. If it is a purely arbitrary one, it may be impossible for us to solve it. If, on the other hand, it is systematic, I have no doubt that we shall get to the bottom of it."[26] Armed with a sufficient number of samples to obtain correct letter frequencies, and "having applied the rules which guide us in all forms of secret writings, the solution was easy enough." The Dancing Men proves to be a simple monoalphabetic substitution cipher, in which each letter of the alphabet is represented by a

He unfolded a paper and laid it upon the table. Here is a copy of the hiero-glyphics :

" Excellent ! " said Holmes. " Excellent ! Pray continue."

" When I had taken the copy I rubbed out the marks ; but two mornings later a fresh inscription had appeared. I have a copy of it here " :

Holmes rubbed his hands and chuckled with delight. " Our material is rapidly accumulating," said he.

Figure 9. Arthur Conan Doyle, "The Adventure of the Dancing Men," in Baring-Gould, *The Annotated Sherlock Holmes*, 2:528.

different dance position.[27] Through his translation ("Am Here Abe Slaney At Elriges"), Holmes discovers that Elsie Cubitt is being harassed by "the most dangerous crook in Chicago," a man who had been in love with her before her marriage. Repeating Dupin's use of a phony message from "The Murders in the Rue Morgue," Holmes dupes Slaney into calling on Elsie by using a forged cipher message. (The achievement leaves Slaney dumbfounded: "There was no one on earth outside the Joint who knew the secret of the dancing men. How came you to write it?" he inquires of Holmes, who replies with a page out of Poe: "What one man can invent another can discover.")

The mode by which Holmes solves the Dancing Men cipher is unsurprisingly like that used by Poe in "The Gold-Bug" and elsewhere. More striking is the degree to which both Poe and Conan Doyle repeat the process of hieroglyphic translation used by Champollion and other translators of Egyptian hieroglyphics. In its ciphering of Defoe and Champollion, as in its ciphering by Lacan, Poe's writing represents a series of exercises in the agency of the letter, which begin by repudiating a connection with Adamic language (the "turn" at Champollion's statue is equivalent to the destruction of Adamic thought). At the least, the theoretical itinerary of Lacan's signifier seems to mimic Poe's cryptographic model. But in the allusion above, Lacan seems tacitly to admit more; he seems to admit finding direction through his reading of Poe, who stands as the "guide" to his theory of sig-

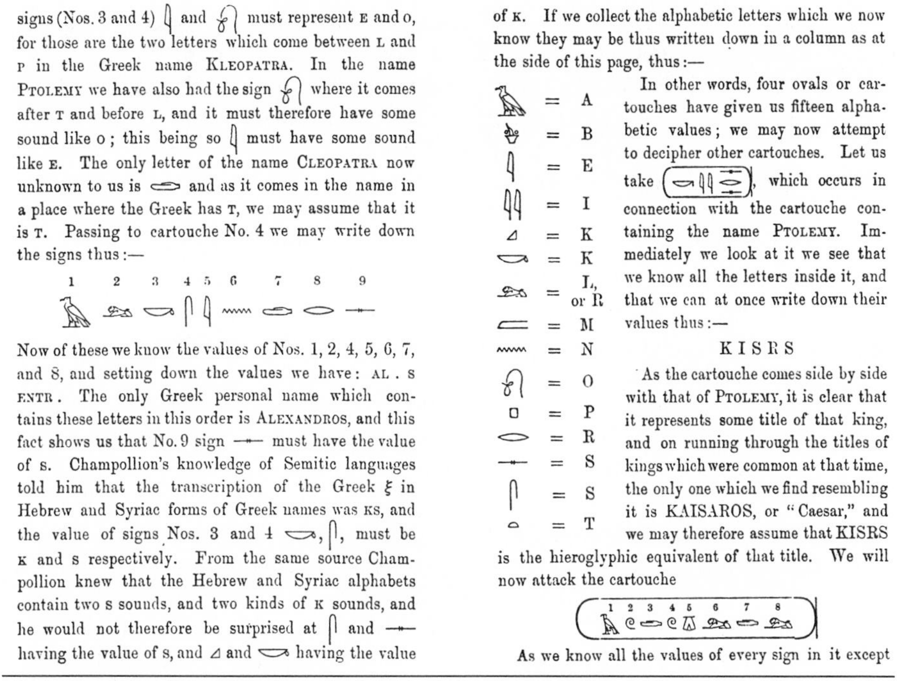

signs (Nos. 3 and 4) 〔 and 〔 must represent E and o, for those are the two letters which come between L and P in the Greek name KLEOPATRA. In the name PTOLEMY we have also had the sign 〔 where it comes after T and before L, and it must therefore have some sound like o; this being so 〔 must have some sound like E. The only letter of the name CLEOPATRA now unknown to us is ⌒ and as it comes in the name in a place where the Greek has T, we may assume that it is T. Passing to cartouche No. 4 we may write down the signs thus:—

1	2	3	4	5	6	7	8	9

Now of these we know the values of Nos. 1, 2, 4, 5, 6, 7, and 8, and setting down the values we have: AL . S ENTR. The only Greek personal name which contains these letters in this order is ALEXANDROS, and this fact shows us that No. 9 sign —•— must have the value of S. Champollion's knowledge of Semitic languages told him that the transcription of the Greek ξ in Hebrew and Syriac forms of Greek names was KS, and the value of signs Nos. 3 and 4 ⌒, 〔, must be K and S respectively. From the same source Champollion knew that the Hebrew and Syriac alphabets contain two s sounds, and two kinds of K sounds, and he would not therefore be surprised at 〔 and —•— having the value of s, and ⌒ and ⌒ having the value

of K. If we collect the alphabetic letters which we now know they may be thus written down in a column as at the side of this page, thus:—

	=	A
	=	B
	=	E
	=	I
	=	K
	=	K
	=	L, or R
	=	M
	=	N
	=	O
	=	P
	=	R
	=	S
	=	S
	=	T

In other words, four ovals or cartouches have given us fifteen alphabetic values; we may now attempt to decipher other cartouches. Let us take (cartouche), which occurs in connection with the cartouche containing the name PTOLEMY. Immediately we know all the letters inside it, and that we can at once write down their values thus:—

KISRS

As the cartouche comes side by side with that of PTOLEMY, it is clear that it represents some title of that king, and on running through the titles of kings which were common at that time, the only one which we find resembling it is KAISAROS, or "Caesar," and we may therefore assume that KISRS is the hieroglyphic equivalent of that title. We will now attack the cartouche

1	2	3	4	5	6	7	8

As we know all the values of every sign in it except

Figure 10. Budge, *Rosetta Stone*, 124–25.

nification—an admission only visible through a close (not to say ciphered) reading of Poe's presence in Lacan.

A Meer Chimera of My Own

Summer nights
Are wet and sticky. Lonely women
Patrol the shoreline. . . .
Words are footprints
On the endless sighing page.

Mitchell Cohen, "Along the Ocean"

As "The Philosophy of Composition" and the *Narrative of A. Gordon Pym* demonstrate, Lacan's description of "The Purloined Letter" as an allegory of the itinerary of the signifier is itself a repetition of Poe's reading of Defoe; Poe's writing is already a theoretical, language-centered appropriation, designed to reduce Defoe's literary practice to a set of technical precepts organized around the nature of the signification and its use in creating identification. Consider Poe's selective reading of *Robinson Crusoe*. The great crisis of the middle of the Defoe novel is the discovery of a human footprint on a beach that Crusoe is sure he never frequents: on seeing it, Crusoe "stood like one Thunder-struck, or as if I had seen an Apparition." For there, he continues, "was exactly the very print of a Foot, Toes, Heel, and every Part of a Foot; how it came thither I knew not, nor could in the least imagine. But after innumerable fluttering Thoughts, like a Man perfectly confus'd and out of my self, I came Home to my Fortification, not feeling, as we say, the Ground I went on, but terrify'd to the last Degree" (153–54). Crusoe's ensuing paranoia deprives him of his own identity, and he runs home "like a man perfectly confused and out of my self," even as the footprint deprives his own feet of sensation: "not feeling . . . the Ground I went on." This is not merely fear of the other, but fear that one can barely distinguish self and other, a possibility suggested by Crusoe's realization that "all this might be a meer Chimera of my own, and that this Foot might be the Print of my own Foot, when I came on shore from my boat. This cheared me up a little too, and I began to perswade my self it was all a delusion; . . . if at last this was only the Print of my own Foot, I had play'd the Part of those Fools who strive to make stories of Spectres and Apparitions, and then are frighted at them more than any body" (ibid., 157–58). The semiotic status of the footprint is bivalent. On the one hand it is that rare thing, a true hieroglyph: an Adamic sign, marked by the body that produced it. Hence, by comparing the anonymous footprint with his foot, Crusoe can be certain that it is not his own. But until Crusoe thinks to do this, the footprint is frighteningly ambiguous: it seems a sign whose ownership Crusoe cannot resolve. In this sense, the footprint is a metaphor for the antihieroglyphic uncertainty of print, which, while it testifies to the existence of another mind, fails to identify its maker (fails to identify, that is, who writes the world that Crusoe inhabits). In the discovery of the footprint, Defoe stages the necessary uncanniness of writing in its relation to the self.

Crusoe's first response to the footprint is to flee to his hut, which is now transformed into a "castle," "for so I think I call'd it ever after this" (ibid., 154). From this point, self-immurement becomes a dominant motif of the novel, as if Defoe would multiply representations of enclosure as a defense against the threats signification poses to Crusoe's autonomy. The compulsive repetition of the word "thick" betrays Crusoe's panic: he plants "a thick grove" in front of his dwelling, "so monstrous thick and strong, that it was indeed perfectly impassable" and he "thickned [his] Wall to above ten foot Thick" (ibid., 161). Not trusting these precautions, Crusoe remains anxious until he discovers "a meer natural cave in the earth." Despite these elaborate defenses, Crusoe's self continues to fission, proliferating in the pathological distribution of the grammatical subject: "I recover'd my self, and began to call my self a thousand Fools, and tell my self, that he that was afraid to see the Devil was not fit to live twenty Years in an Island all alone; and that I durst to believe there was nothing in this Cave that was more frightful than my self" (ibid., 177).

Eventually, Crusoe collects himself sufficiently to penetrate into the cave's innermost recess, where he finds the most "glorious Sight seen in the Island": "The Walls reflected 100 thousand Lights to me from my two Candles; what it was in the Rock, whether Diamonds, or any other precious Stones, or Gold, which I rather supposed it to be, I knew not. . . . I fancy'd my self now like one of the ancient giants, which are said to live in caves and holes in the rocks, where none could come at them; for I perswaded my self while I was here, if five hundred savages were to hunt me, they could never find me out" (ibid., 179). Only in this "vault or cave" does Crusoe feel safe from the incursion of others. Although Crusoe's response makes narrative sense as an attempt to defend himself from attack, the vault is also a defense against the peculiarly linguistic alienation provoked by the footprint. Having lived on his island for fifteen years without having "met with the least *Shadow* or *Figure* of any People" (ibid., 160), Crusoe uses the cave as a place to reunite the fragmented selves released by the sight of the print. The vault proves an ideal place for this because it only reflects the self, epitomized in the "100 thousand Lights" refracted from Crusoe's two candles.

Once secure in his cave, though, our isolato begins to brood on his aloneness, and to despair from his lack of "what I so earnestly longed for, *viz.* some-body to speak to" (ibid., 194). This somebody will be Friday, the antithesis of the cannibals who would incorporate Crusoe into themselves. Although technically he is a native of a neighboring island, Friday's true birthplace is Crusoe's cave, for he is produced by the desire for an other that follows first from the discovery of the print and second from Crusoe's hermetic self-reflection. Of Friday, Crusoe says that "it was very pleasant to me to talk to him; and now my life began to be so easy, that I began to say to my self, that could I but have been safe from more savages, I cared not if I was never to remove from the place while I lived" (ibid., 207). This comment repeats almost verbatim his description of Poll, who "talked so articulately and plain, that it was very pleasant to me." Poll and Friday are Crusoe's idealized interlocutors, doubles who provide a social reflection without the threatening otherness that drove him to his cave. Crusoe's insatiable desire for walls, castles, and vaults stems from his wish to use the representational world of the novel to defend his sense of identity against the self-alienation provoked by the immaterial footprint (a version of Narcissus).

Crusoe's cave provides the prototype of the cryptograph, an imagined space that encourages the psychic doubling Poe found in his relation with Tyler. The caverns and gorges of the last chapters of the *Narrative of A. Gordon Pym* also represent Poe's revision of the discovery of the footprint and the retreat into the cave in *Robinson Crusoe*. Pym and Dirk Peters are saved from destruction only by Pym's decision to enter "a fissure in the soft rock" along the ravine, just "wide enough for one person to enter without squeezing," which extends "back into the hill some eighteen or twenty feet" (*PT*, 1151). Like Crusoe, Pym is obsessed with the privacy of this cavern, which leaves him and Peters "completely excluded from observation." Like Crusoe's cave, it has never been penetrated by the other: "We could perceive no traces of the savages having ever been within this hollow" (ibid., 1160). When the natives bring down the walls of the ravine, it is this space that saves them from "overwhelming destruction" (ibid., 1156). As their subsequent adventures make clear, the gorges they explore are versions of a hieroglyph, images that are also signs, but they are also cryptographs, interior spaces that may be either tomb or haven. Pym is decidedly ambivalent about this life within the sign: "We again went round the walls of our prison, in hope of finding some avenue of escape" (ibid., 1164); "after satisfying ourselves that these singular caverns afforded us no means of escape from our prison, we made our way back, dejected."[28] Whereas Crusoe's flight into the cave represents an attempt to escape from the semiotic (or cryptographic) into the solidly representational, Poe combines the feared, quasi-semiotic footprint with the represented refuge of the cave to foster a concept of a sign as the place in which reader and character merge. In discovering their text-based existence, Pym and Crusoe double the reader's interpretation of signs: eventually the cryptograph provides an imagined location for the reader's literary identification, simultaneously thought of in two and three dimensions. Like Crusoe's discovered footprint, the signs in the *Narrative of A. Gordon Pym* waver uneasily between hieroglyph and cryptograph, but after 1839 Poe's writing was dominated by the cryptograph's model of the text as a code. Instead of attempting to ground the origins of language (and of humanity) in the hieroglyphic mirroring of the human body, Poe increasingly thought of language as a refuge from the world's distressing materiality, penetrable only by those who possessed the key.

The Alembic of the Code

If I am right to claim that Defoe's crypt becomes Poe's cryptograph, this is because in Poe's imagination the code offers a space for the transformation of matter. It is, in short, an alembic. To understand the alembic effects of cryptography, one must take seriously Legrand's early comment to the narrator that the gold bug "is to make my fortune" and "to reinstate me in my family possessions." The sentence explicitly connects the bug (and therefore the cipher), fortune (the gold to be found), and Legrand's "family possessions." Long ago, Marie Bonaparte read "The Gold-Bug" as a displaced account of Poe's desire for the treasure of his mother's body—for, that is, his "original family possession." Bonaparte anchored her reading on no less an authority than Freud himself, who, "one day, in reference to 'The Gold-Bug' said something like this":

> "One hardly dares venture it, lest it seem too far-fetched, but there must be, in the unconscious, a connection between tales of seeking or finding treasure and some other fact or situation in the history of the race: something that belongs to a time when sacrifice was common and human sacrifice at that. The 'buried treasure,' in such cases, would then be the finding of an embryo or foetus in the abdomen of the victim." At the time, this seemed to me too far-fetched, and I could not see its connection with Captain Kidd's treasure. And yet, even the name of the pirate hero (Kidd = kid = child) hints at the latent content of this tale.[29]

This fetus is associated both with anality and with its opposite, as the psyche in its anal-erotic phase phylogenetically passes "from an original interest in faeces, dirt, mud and mud-pies, to what appears its very opposite: pleasure in hard, shining clean surfaces, pebbles, coins and metals, including the most precious of all, gold."[30] The buried treasure stands in for the fetus in its mother, which is in turn equated with her other bodily products. "With its stream of treasure from the earth's bowels," Poe's story is, "like the story of Arthur Gordon Pym, a sort of epic of the beneficent, nurturing mother, but with the difference that now the emphasis is on the wealth hidden in her bowels, and, no longer, on the primal gift of milk from her breasts."[31]

Bonaparte inadvertently identifies the covert alchemy on which "The Gold-Bug" is secretly predicated. The ultimate goal of alchemy—the transmutation of baser substances into gold—was not to obtain wealth but to realize a hierarchical materialist metaphysics. Gold "is not just any substance but is the most rarefied form of the *prima materia* that is the true substance of things"; it is the condition to which other substances aspire over time.[32] "As Simone de Colonia put it: 'This Art teaches us to make a remedy called the Elixir, which, being poured on imperfect metals, perfects them completely, and it is for this reason that it was invented.' . . . The same idea is expounded by Ben Jonson in his play *The Alchemist* (1610). One character says that 'lead and other metals . . . would be gold if they had time,' and another adds, 'and that our Art doeth further.' "[33]

A psychological dimension was essential to alchemical metaphysics, in which *sublimation* had both a chemical and an analytic meaning: "The sublimation of base material into gold actually sublimates the primordial desire for the mother."[34] This is because "smelting entails something like a *regressus ad uterum* that returns matter to its original matrix. Mother, material, and matter meet in *mater* that is their common origin."[35] With the aid of fire, alchemists "transform the ores (the 'embryos') into metals (the 'adults'). The underlying belief is that, given enough time, the ores would have become 'pure' metals in the womb of Mother Earth. Further, the 'pure' metals would have become gold if they had been allowed to 'grow' undisturbed for a few more thousand years." [36] Unlike the chemist, the alchemist did not seek to advance the art of alchemy by discovery of new methods but by "the rediscovery and new interpretation of older writers whom he believed to have possessed the secret. Consequently he wished his books to appear to be ancient." [37] The project of the original alchemists was always dual. The manipulation of the physical materials of the world was only a figure for the achievement of philosophical perfection; in later centuries such manipulation was explicitly understood *as* a metaphor, in which the exoteric was internalized as the esoteric.

This manipulation included a significant cryptographic emphasis. Alchemical transformation required incantations or readings over its raw materials; alchemical texts themselves were written in codes to render them safe from uninitiated readers. "Anagrams, acrostics, and other enigmas were introduced, and various secret alphabets and ciphers came to be used by alchemists; in some of these, letters and numerals were represented by alchemical and astrological signs." [38] In the last two centuries, scientists and engineers have made enormous inroads into the manipulation of matter; but what has happened to the alchemical desire to order substance? Wonderful as they are, the achievements of contemporary chemists have almost no purchase on our imagination of the matrix of the world. Here the cryptographic imagination comes into play, providing stories and images to explain the underlying relations among the manifold forms of matter and the processes of its transformation. In "The Gold-Bug," Legrand's discovery of the parchment, his ability to tease out the rebus of its message and to follow the directions to the gold, represents a displaced alchemy. His relation to the gold is not merely one of fortune or cleverness: the constant repetition of specific words and images, like Legrand's fussy cryptanalysis, is a semimagical way of conjuring the substance he so desires. Nervously, the story keeps playing on the ambiguous relation between images and symbols: the "bug" itself, to choose the story's central example, is alternately a death's-head scarab, warning people away in what might have been a Chaucerian exemplum, and "de goole bug," a gold bug that, having "bitten" Legrand, will not let up until it leads to his treasures, which are defended by the bones of Kidd's assistants.

Again, what is most salient about the cryptographic imagination of "The Gold-Bug" is not the particular content of the symbols employed. Although some version of Bonaparte's psychoanalytic narrative is probably right, the point of the cryptographic imagination is not to validate her literalizing Freudianism, but to underwrite this *kind* of reading in the first place. All cultures, I imagine, need some account of a *prima materia*: a foundational mythology that will explain, first, what things are, and second, how the relation between things and symbols might be imagined. The construction of such myths is a task of the cryptographic imagination. Its muttered words and hidden writings cast us back from *matter* to *mater* to *matrix*, the unimaginable stuff that requires informing words to call it into being.

Predictably, the cryptographic imagination often turns toward the source of life in the mother. Yet the cryptographic imagination need not always return to the womb. When Arthur Conan Doyle revised "The Gold-Bug" in "The Musgrave Ritual," the dominant fantasy was not of reconnection to the lost mother, but of the restitution of buried English history. The ritual, an apparently meaningless set of phrases repeated by each Musgrave as he comes of age, turns out to be a steganographically obscured map (again, one keyed to a tree) that leads to the recovery of jewels (now the crown jewels of the deposed Charles II) hidden in an underground crypt. (This crypt, too, is a place of death—here, the death of the butler, Brunton, who, having deciphered the ritual's meaning, is suffocated in the crypt by a spurned lover.)

As "The Gold-Bug" and "The Musgrave Ritual" indicate (and as "The Adventure of the Dancing Men," Conan Doyle's other revision of "The Gold-Bug," shows as well), there is something dangerous in the relation of cryptography and human bodies. At the end of "The Gold-Bug," the act of cryptographic deciphering leads Legrand and company not only to the sight of "a treasure of incalculable value" (*PT*, 578), but to a scene of buried violence: "In a few seconds he had uncovered a mass of human bones, forming two complete skeletons, intermingled with several buttons of metal, and what appeared to be the dust of decayed woolen" (ibid., 577). Legrand concludes the tale by dryly observing that "it is clear that Kidd—if Kidd indeed secreted this treasure, which I doubt not—it is clear that he must have had assistance in the labor. But, the worst of this labor concluded, he may have thought it expedient to remove all participants in his secret. Perhaps a couple of blows with a mattock were sufficient, while his coadjutors were busy in the pit; perhaps it required a dozen—who shall tell?" (ibid., 595–96).

With its connotations of permanence and spiritual worth, the gold is not only a material reward that accrues to Legrand; it is also a symbol of pure meaning. In a currency based on the gold standard, a banknote is merely a cipher for the bullion for which it may be redeemed; just so, the relation of Legrand's "meaningless" cipher and the treasure to which it leads captures Poe's sense that only a cryptographic intelligence can translate the opaque code into the immanent value represented by the gold it reveals.[39] At the same time, this substance seems to be a metamorphic product of the bodies found with it: "Full fathom five thy father lies;/Of his bones are coral made;/Those are pearls that were his eyes" (*The Tempest*, 1.2.397–99). A similar sea change has occurred with the bodies of Kidd's assistants, in a highly secular analogue to Christ's spiritual transformation. Recovering the pirate's treasure requires that Legrand understand the whole repertoire of literary-cryptographic forms, including the use of invisible inks, substitution ciphers (with letter-frequency tables), "hieroglyphical signatures," mysterious stamps, and rebuses, and that he translate Kidd's allegory into a series of practical directions for the treasure's recovery. Among these instructions is the requirement to drop the gold bug on a plumb line through the eye of the skull, a reminder of the mortality associated with the gold, and Poe's punning way of suggesting that, having been bitten by the gold bug, man can only "see" gold, even at the cost of his life.

Without much effort, one could elaborate a Lacanian reading of Poe's story. On this account, the tale's systematic cryptanalysis would function as a myth about the ability to master language, as we see Kidd's unmeaning signs waver into meaning: first ";48;(88;4(#?34;48," then "the tree ;4(#?34 the," then "the tree thr#?3h the," then *the tree through the. . . .*" This decipherment would in turn promise the cryptographic reader a return to the pre-Oedipal plenitude of the mother's body, now in its secular incarnation as material wealth. (The synonymy of Kidd's name with pirate treasure punningly suggests that only the possession of the gold will maintain one *as* a kid, in a state of maternal dependence.) But that is not my purpose. I would not have the force of a tendentious reading diminish my emphasis on the *blankness* of the cryptographic machine, into which one can plug a wide range of possible symbolic values. Although much of "The Gold-Bug" is devoted to the translation and explication of a coded map, cryptography is not, finally, a form of mapping. It is not topographic, but thaumaturgic, leading the reader into mysteries of sign, depth, and transformation — mysteries notably figured in the West by the story of Christ's birth, death, and transubstantiation.[40] Nearly every reading of "The Gold-Bug" emphasizes the balked nature of the alchemical relations between signs and bodies — a quality that will be even more pronounced in Poe's detective stories, where it quickly leads to violence.

DETECTIVE FICTION

3 AND THE ANALYTIC SUBLIME

> "What impression have I made upon your fancy?" I felt a creeping of
> the flesh as Dupin asked me the question. "A madman," I said, "has
> done this deed—some raving maniac escaped from a neighboring
> *Maison de Santé.*"
>
> Edgar Allan Poe, "The Murders in the Rue Morgue"

Sheymov's Escape

The story took place in Warsaw during the closing days of the Cold War.
Our protagonist, Victor, was a high-ranking KGB officer trying to lose his
official watchers in order to defect to the American embassy. The setting
was a well-secured bathroom in a cultural center where Victor would attend
a movie that night, and from which he would escape. His suspicious driver
waited just outside. With only minutes alone, Victor set to work preparing
his own disappearance, surveying the bathroom's empty stalls as he hurried
to the window at the end. Once there,

he unlatched and pulled open the center pair of inside windows. Then he went
to work on the two nails that security personnel had hammered into the outside windows to prevent them from opening outward. Using the blades of two
chisels, he carefully eased out the head of the first nail from the frame of one
outer window. If only one chisel were used, the nail would bend and make
a small, but irreparable mark on the wood next to it. The nail squeaked and
started to move. One-eighth of an inch was enough. With pliers he steadily
pulled the nail straight out. He was very careful—old rusty nails have a nasty
habit of breaking.

Having pulled out the second nail and put it away, he peeked through a
scratch in the paint that covered the outside windows. There was nobody
outside near the window. He carefully unlocked the latches and, holding the
sharp ends of two replacement nails in his right hand, he softly pushed the left
half of the window slightly open. The replacements were rusty nails similar to
the originals, but broken into two pieces. He then inserted one of the half-
nails into the hole of the old one in the sill and pushed it down with the flat

side of a chisel. He quickly repeated the operation with the right frame and closed the window. . . . He pushed the top halves of the nails into the frames with a chisel, using a soft cloth to avoid leaving any shiny marks on the heads. He then closed and latched the inner windows. The tools went back into his pockets. Victor looked at his watch. Just under five minutes. . . . He took off the gloves and returned to the car. The driver was reading a book.[1]

This story, which sounds much like an early John Le Carré novel, records a preliminary moment in the escape of Major Victor Sheymov, who in May 1980 defected to the West, in a disappearance so successful that for a decade Soviet authorities believed that he had been murdered on a weekend trip out of town. Sheymov was the highest-ranking officer ever to defect from the KGB; he had a deep knowledge of its byzantine bureaucratic structure. The book from which I have taken this story—*Tower of Secrets: A Real-Life Spy Thriller*—aims to capitalize on the way in which Sheymov's story enacts the conventions of the spy novel. In this, *Tower of Secrets* is hardly alone: the spy thriller is perforce a genre that splits its allegiance between its literary antecedents and the true experiences of spies in the world. Le Carré worked in MI5 under Maxwell Knight (later using his own Foreign Service career as a cover for work in espionage) until he quit to become a full-time writer. The spy thriller represents an outgrowth of the detective story, which preserves its emphasis on evidence and signs, even as the drama of spy against spy intensifies the specular confrontation of detective and prey. But even such an observation oversimplifies the situation, for Sheymov was not merely a high-ranking spy, he was a *cryptographer*—a math whiz in charge of the security of all the KGB's overseas cipher systems— and the detective story as a genre is literally underwritten by Poe's essays on cryptography. In *Tower of Secrets*, this doubling of cryptographer and spy is evident in the way in which Sheymov's sensitivity to codes translates into an extraordinary awareness of the traces left by his body in the world.

I will say more about the relations of real spies and cryptographers to literature in chapter 6, but first it is necessary to note how eerily the ontogeny of *Tower of Secrets* recapitulates its phylogeny, as Sheymov in his escape unwittingly repeats the solution of the world's first detective story. Arriving at the rooms of the murdered Mmes. L'Espanaye, Dupin discovers that aside from the locked doors, the only way out is through two windows, each of which is fastened by "a very stout nail" pushed into a gimlet-hole drilled through the frame and the casement. Reasoning that "the impossibility of egress, by means already stated, being thus absolute, we are reduced to the windows," Dupin decides that the sashes

> *must*, then, have the power of fastening themselves. There was no escape from this conclusion. . . . I had traced the secret to its ultimate result—and that result was *the nail*. It had, I say, in every respect, the appearance of its fellow in

the other window, but this fact was an absolute nullity (conclusive as it might seem to be) when compared with the consideration that here, at this point, terminated the clew. "There *must* be something wrong," I said, "about the nail." I touched it; and the head, with about a quarter of the shank, came off in my fingers. The rest of the shank was in the gimlet-hole, where it had been broken off. ("Murders in the Rue Morgue," *PT*, 419)

Sheymov's repetition of the ape's defenestration provides an exemplary instance of the overdetermined ties between cryptography and literature. What could be less likely than that a real spy would be forced to employ Poe's wildly improbable stratagem of the broken nail as the means of his escape? Cryptography, it seems, positions itself at the uncertain join between texts and bodies, fact and fiction. Not only is the detective's effort to make a text of the world entailed by Poe's secret writing, but particular characters, plots, and narrative formats follow from it as well. And yet to insist on the detective story as a purely two-dimensional, metatextual narrative form is sterile: as Sheymov's story shows, even a cryptographer must inhabit a three-dimensional body in a three-dimensional world.

This tension—between the desire to read the world and the need to inhabit it—was built into the detective story from the start. A close reading of "The Murders in the Rue Morgue" will show how the cryptographic analytics discussed in chapter 1 are complicated by Poe's awareness of bodily experience, and how this tension between two and three dimensions, matter and sign, goes to the very core of the genre. Through its play of surface and death, detective fiction manifests the same fascination with the thaumaturgical force of cryptography that is evident in "The Gold-Bug." Whereas that story employs cryptography as an alchemical code-key for the sublimation of matter, the detective story as begun by "The Murders in the Rue Morgue" concerns itself with the occulted spaces represented by the locked room where the murders occur. Dupin's ability to enter and leave this space, like his ability to identify the murderer from the evidence at the crime scene, is an attenuated form of his ability to read minds (an ultimate cryptographic end). But if the detective's ability to read the world as a text serves as a form of magic, cryptography also presents a crisis for individual bodies in terms of their capacity for language.

That the mode of Sheymov's escape coincides with that of the ape in "Rue Morgue" is, one must reluctantly admit, merely a moment of literary-critical serendipity. Yet detective fiction as a genre is designed to move dialectically from Sheymov's escape to the ape's recapture, where the first moment equals the analyst's (reader's) wish to lose his or her body, and where the last—the recapture of the ape at story's end—implicates the reader in a transferential somatic effect (the reader leaves as the analyst and returns as the ape). Forced to reinvent the locked-room mystery—to disappear into thin air, leaving an apparently sealed chamber behind him—Sheymov stands as a figure for the reader of ratiocinative detective fiction as he probes both the attractions and the limits of the analytical sublime.[2]

Butchery without Motive

Although "The Murders in the Rue Morgue" initiated the genre of detective fiction, twentieth-century fans have often been put off by Poe's seemingly capricious violation of an implicit narrative convention. The ape, it is alleged, represents an instance of bad faith, because no reader could reasonably be expected to include animals in a list of potential murderers. More generally, we may take Poe's ape story as an index of a deeper bad faith on the part of the whole genre, in its frequent imbalance between the detective story's protracted narrative setup and its often unsatisfying denouement. Some readers of detective fiction have an embarrassing feeling that its typically gothic revelations are incommensurate with the moral weight suggested by the genre's narrative form. In this sense, too, Poe's orangutan is an emblem of the story's readers, who—their attention solicited by an unworthy narrative dilemma—find that the real crime has been practiced on their sensibilities. In the words of Geoffrey Hartman: "The trouble with the detective novel is not that it is moral but that it is moralistic; not that it is popular but that it is stylized; not that it lacks realism but that it picks up the latest realism and exploits it. A voracious formalism dooms it to seem unreal, however 'real' the world it describes. . . . The form trusts too much in reason; its very success opens to us the glimpse of a mechanized world, whether controlled by God or Dr. No or the Angel of the Odd."[3] Hartman's caution is apt, but hardly original: in the first detective story, Poe had already recognized the problem. As Poe indicated in a letter to Phillip Cooke, the promise of detective fiction to unriddle the world was ultimately tautological: "Where is the ingenuity of unravelling a web which you yourself have woven for the express purpose of unravelling? These tales of ratiocination owe most of their popularity to being something in a new key. I do not mean to say that they are not ingenious—but people think they are more ingenious than they are—on account of the method and *air* of method."[4]

Poe's comment interests me because, while on the one hand he demystifies the detective story, insisting that the narrator's solution to the crime is, in fact, no "solution" at all, but a *coup de théâtre* staged by the author from behind the scenes, on the other he recognizes the willingness of readers to be deceived by the story's "method and *air* of method." Such an air of method might also be described as the genre's penchant for analysis, a term that recurs throughout the Dupin stories.[5] "Rue Morgue" begins with a discussion of "analysis," and in a letter describing "The Mystery of Marie Rogêt," Poe emphasizes the same term: "under the pretense of showing how Dupin . . . unravelled the mystery of Marie's assassination, I, in fact, enter into a very rigorous analysis of the real tragedy in New York" (*CW*, 3:718). Although it may seem curious that the literary genre most vocally devoted to the powers of the ratiocinative mind should vex those powers on the mindless acts of an orangutan, Poe's use of the ape in "Rue Morgue" serves as something more than a simple narrative miscalculation or mere sideshow. In brief, the ape permits Poe to elaborate a cryptographic argument about language and human identity, in which the extreme contrast between the ape's physicality and Dupin's inhuman reason reveals something about the genre's constitutive oppositions. And because detective fiction in general, and Poe's more particularly, has enjoyed a long and privileged relation to psychoanalytic reading, Poe's experiments with the monkey may tell us something about how we, as readers, are ourselves made to ape his ape.

"Analysis" in several senses has been key to the theoretical ubiquity of "The Purloined Letter." But although that story is unquestionably a great achievement, Poe purchases the analytic force of his narrative only by purging the text of any attempt at realist representation.[6] Hence, Barbara Johnson's now too-familiar claim that Minister D——'s letter is "not hidden in a geometrical space, where the police are looking for it . . . but is instead located 'in' a *symbolic* structure" is correct only because of Poe's refusal to engage in the difficult project of representing the texture of social experience.[7] In sharp contrast to the outdoor settings of "Marie Rogêt," or even to the street scenes in "Rue Morgue," "The Purloined Letter" retreats from the boulevards, parks, and waterways of the teeming city, with their social and sexual ambiguities, into the enclosed and private spaces of Minister D——'s chambers. The remarkable success of "The Purloined Letter" as a locus for literary and psychoanalytic theory—indeed, as one of *the* venues in which French theory has translated itself into American theory— begins to seem the consequence of playing cards with a stacked deck. The tale's theoretical richness arises because "The Purloined Letter" is already supremely two-dimensional, already overtly concerned with allegorizing the operations of the signifier.

In fact, the semiotic purity of "The Purloined Letter" is an exception in Poe's detective fiction, which focuses more generally on the tension between representations of three-dimensional bodies and language, which is either two-dimensional in its printed form or, as speech, proves uncannily disembodied and invisible. The dominant form of the genre is far closer to "Rue Morgue" or, in its true-crime mode, to "The Mystery of Marie Rogêt," in which Poe is less concerned with the "itinerary of the signifier" narrowly conceived than he is with the problems posed by the difficult intersection of the human capacity for language and the brute fact of incarnation. Poe's obsession with corpses, especially prominent in the late fiction, reveals his anxiety over the body's refusal to suffer complete encipherment into language. Significantly, Poe's deaths are almost invariably associated with injuries to the organs of speech. The horror of Valdemar's mesmeric dissolution in "The Facts in the Case of M. Valdemar" stems from the grotesque contrast between his putrefying body and his "wonderfully, thrillingly distinct . . . syllabification" (*PT*, 839–40), as "ejaculations of 'dead! dead!'" burst "from the tongue and not the lips of the sufferer" (ibid., 842). In "Rue Morgue" the strangled Camille L'Espanaye's tongue is "bitten partially through" (ibid., 410). Marie Rogêt bears "bruises and impressions of fingers" about her throat, and "a piece of lace was found tied so tightly around the neck as to be hidden from sight; it was completely buried in the flesh, and was fastened by a knot which lay just under the left ear" (ibid., 513). And in "Thou Art the Man," often considered Poe's fourth detective story, the narrator exposes and destroys the murderer, Charley Goodfellow, by confronting him with the speaking corpse of his victim, who bursts out of a wine cask with impressive consequences: "There sprang up into a sitting position, directly facing the host, the bruised, bloody and nearly putrid corpse of the murdered Mr. Shuttleworthy himself. It gazed for a few moments . . . with its decaying and lack-lustre eyes . . . uttered slowly, but clearly and impressively the words, 'Thou art the man!' and then, falling over the side of the chest as if thoroughly satisfied, stretched out its limbs quiveringly."[8]

Such obsessive instances of mutilated language suggest that for Poe the disjunction between linguistic and physical identity is always traumatic. The violence attendant on social relations in "Rue Morgue" results from the represented encounter between two-dimensional signs and three-dimensional bodies. To an extraordinary degree cryptography provides secret organizing principles for Poe's trilogy of detective stories. The cryptograph reflects on the level of the sign what Dupin embodies on the level of character, and what the form of detective fiction implies on the level of narrative: the fantasy of an absolutely legible world. In Poe's essays on secret writing, cryptography is imagined as a utopian moment of reading in which reader and writer are fully present to one another within their two-dimensional cipher. Conceptually, analysis is closely associated with cryptography. Both depend on the "separating or breaking up of any whole into its parts so as to find out their nature, proportion, function, relationship, etc."[9] and both emphasize the abstract, symbolic force of mind over matter, which provides a form of mental leverage over the world. But even in the moment of creating detective fiction, Poe suggests that the only "analysis" it can offer may itself be a fiction. Although cryptography seems to offer a detour around the gothic aspects of embodiment, it takes on disturbingly violent features whenever Poe attempts to represent bodies. The problem is that cryptography provides an *alternative body* in conflict with one's corporeal investment: because even in cryptography language is never truly free of the material shell of the signifier, this linguistic self finds itself in tension with one's physical identity.

Despite the story's promise of legibility, "Rue Morgue" intimates that the triumph of the detective's analytics cannot be clearly distinguished from its effects on the reader's body. To the degree that we as readers invest our belief in this formal drive toward legibility, we become Poe's dupes; should the reader attempt to imitate Dupin, he would quickly find his analysis devolving into mere repetition.[10] And yet, to that same degree, these stories threaten to become meaningful; if the uncanny anticipation of the story's own interpretation is at all significant, it is so because the text discloses in the reader's body the nature of the interpretive desires that initiate his reading. Like the purloined letter, the lesson of "Rue Morgue" is hidden in plain sight, announced in the story's first lines: "The mental features discoursed of as the analytical are, in themselves, but little susceptible of analysis. We appreciate them only in their effects" (*PT*, 397). Although our readings certainly produce "effects," the desire to discover the right relation of analysis to literature is ultimately doomed by the impossibility of establishing a metalanguage uncontaminated by the materiality of signification. In this respect, the narrator's attempt in "Rue Morgue" to keep his analytic discourse free from the corporeal opacity of his subject resembles Freud's procedure in his case studies. If detective fiction is notoriously susceptible to psychoanalytic interpretation, this is only because psychoanalysis, too, has often seemed to presume the separation of its analytical procedures from the materiality of its objects—a separation between language and the body that "Rue Morgue" both constructs and, finally, destroys.

A Voice Devoid of Intelligible Syllabification

Critics have long recognized speech in "Rue Morgue" as a symbolic expression of identification, noting that Dupin's use of a high and a low register links him with the high and low voices of the sailor and the ape.[11] But Poe is less interested in pitch than in syllabification, which runs on a continuum from the orangutan's grunts to Dupin's "rich tenor," with its "deliberateness and entire distinctness" of enunciation (*PT*, 401–2). Hence Poe's deliberation in staging the ape's crime within earshot of such a polyglot group of auditors, each of whom hears in the orangutan's voice someone speaking an unfamiliar language. Henri Duval: "The shrill voice, this witness thinks, was that of an Italian. . . . Was not acquainted with the Italian language." William Bird: The voice "appeared to be that of a German. . . . Does not understand German." Alfonzo Garcia: "The shrill voice was that of an Englishman—is sure of this. Does not understand the English language, but judges by the intonation" (ibid., 408–10). Similarly, Isidore Musèt, —— Odenheimer, and Alberto Montani attribute the voice to Spanish,

French, and Russian speakers, respectively. Poe even has Dupin supplement his references to the "five great divisions of Europe" with mentions of "Asiatics" and "Africans," in what amounts to a Cook's Tour of the varieties of human speech:

> Now, how strangely unusual must that voice have really been, about which such testimony as this *could* have been elicited!—in whose *tones*, even, denizens of the five great divisions of Europe could recognize nothing familiar! You will say that it might have been the voice of an Asiatic—of an African.... Without denying the inference, I will now merely call your attention to [the fact that] ... no words—no sounds resembling words—were by any witness mentioned as distinguishable. (Ibid., 416)

What is at stake in this inventory? As in the case studies of deaf-mutes and feral children that appeared toward the end of the eighteenth century, the orangutan offered Enlightenment thinkers a liminal figure of the human at a time when language was crucial to the definition of humanity. Given Poe's insistence on the syllabic nature of speech, it is important to recognize the orangutan's affiliation with a tradition of philosophical inquiry.[12] The most comprehensive discussion of the orangutan's relation to language is given in *The Origin and Progress of Language*, by James Burnet, Lord Monboddo, who devotes sixty pages to this question in order to understand "the origin of an art so admirable and so useful as language," a subject "necessarily connected with an inquiry into the original nature of man, and that primitive state in which he was, before language was invented."[13] Monboddo hypothesizes that the orangutan is actually a member of the human species, belonging to "a barbarous nation, which has not yet learned the use of speech" (ibid., 270). The taxonomic name of the orangutan, *Homo sylvestris*, is merely a translation of the Malay "Ourang-Outang," which, according to the naturalist Georges-Louis Leclerc de Buffon, "signifies, in their language, *a wild man*" (ibid., 272). According to Monboddo, orangutans use tools, grow melancholy when separated from their tribes, and are capable of conjugal attachment and even shame. Monboddo cites an explorer who saw a female orangutan that "shewed signs of modesty ... wept and groaned, and performed other human actions: So that nothing human seemed to be wanting in her, except speech" (ibid., 272–73).

By enlisting orangutans in the same species as humans, Monboddo intends to demonstrate that what separates the two is less biology than culture, epitomized by the possession of language. For Buffon, this lack of speech discredits the orangutan's evolutionary pretensions. Monboddo ridicules Buffon, however, for making "the faculty of speech" part of the essence of humanity, and for suggesting that "the state of pure nature, in which man had not the use of speech, is a state altogether ideal and imaginary" (ibid., 293). Buffon thus anticipates the current association of language and human origins. For Poe as for Buffon, the "state of pure nature" *is* "altogether ideal" and precisely "imaginary," because, ontogenetically if not phylogenetically, human consciousness is a function of the subject's mirroring in language.

This tradition provides a context for understanding the dramatic process by which the narrator discovers the identity of the killer. Poe has already planted plenty of tongue-in-cheek clues: the crime is "brutal," "inhuman," "at odds with the ordinary notions of human conduct." Now Dupin remarks on the crime's strange combination of features:

> We have gone so far as to combine the ideas of an agility astounding, a strength superhuman, a ferocity brutal, a butchery without motive, a *grotesquerie* in horror absolutely alien from humanity, and a voice foreign in tone to the ears of men of many nations, and devoid of all distinct or intelligible syllabification. . . . What impression have I made upon your fancy?
>
> I felt a creeping of the flesh as Dupin asked me the question. "A madman," I said, "has done this deed—some raving maniac escaped from a neighboring *Maison de Santé*." (*PT*, 423)

The narrator's suggestion is close, but "the voices of madmen, even in their wildest paroxysms . . . have always the coherence of syllabification" (ibid.). Identification of the criminal depends, again, on Dupin's understanding of language; in fact, the testimony of the crime's auditors constitutes an aural cryptogram. The origin of this moment goes back to "A Few Words on Secret Writing," in which Poe remarked that of the hundred ciphers he received, "there was only one which we did not immediately succeed in solving. This one we *demonstrated* to be an imposition—that is to say, we fully proved it a jargon of random characters, having no meaning whatsoever" (*SW*, 123). Poe's ability to interpret signs requires him to recognize when a set of signs violates the "universal" rules of linguistic formation. The claim to cryptographic mastery depends on the logically prior ability to recognize when a set of characters is not even language. By having the solution to the crime in "Rue Morgue" turn on the aural cryptogram, Poe dramatizes both the power of human analysis and his fear of what life without language might be like.

After its recapture the orangutan is lodged in the Jardin des Plantes. Until his death in 1832, the Jardin was Georges Cuvier's center for research; as the repeated juxtaposition of Cuvier and Dupin indicates, Poe finds in the zoologist's mode of analysis an analogue to his own technique of detection.[14] Cuvier was famous for his ability to reconstruct an animal's anatomy from fragmentary paleontological remains, through systematic structural comparison. As a contemporary of Poe's wrote: "Cuvier astonished the world by the announcement that the law of relation which existed between the various parts of animals applied not only to entire systems, but even to parts of a system; so that, given an extremity, the whole skeleton might be known . . . and even the habits of the animal could be indicated."[15] Like Cuvier's bones, and in implicit analogy with them, syllables are for Poe linguistic universals, basic morphological units that form the necessary substrate to thought. Individual words possess meaning for the linguist only through their participation in a global system: "the word is no longer attached to a representation except in so far as it is previously a part of the grammatical organization by means of which the language defines and guarantees its own coherence."[16]

Cuvier seems to provide a methodological justification for Poe's cryptographic reading of the world. But Poe is not above warping his sources for dramatic effect. Having teased the reader's narrative appetite with oblique clues concerning the killer's nature, Dupin introduces the text of Cuvier with a theatrical flourish, sure that his revelation will produce its intended effect: "It was a minute anatomical and generally descriptive account of the large fulvous Orang-Outang of the East Indian Islands. The gigantic stature, the prodigious strength and activity, the wild ferocity, and the imitative propensities of these mammalia are sufficiently well known to all. I understood the full horrors of the murder at once" (*PT*, 424). This is a curious passage, not least because in Poe's version the description of the orangutan virtually reverses Cuvier's actual claims. Not content to note that the orangutan is "a mild and gentle animal, easily rendered tame and affectionate," Cuvier disparages "the exaggerated descriptions of some authors respecting this resemblance" to humans;[17] he at once deflates both the ape's anthropic pretensions and its wildness. (That Poe knew this text seems certain; M'Murtrie, who translated Cuvier's book, seven years later published with Poe and Thomas Wyatt *The Conchologist's First Book*, with "Animals according to Cuvier.") Poe's intellectual allegiance to Cuvier was subservient to his need to magnify the melodramatic and gothic aspects of the murders. In the final analysis, it is not the crime but the solution that produces the reader's uncanny shiver, not the violence but the minute and clinical attention that Dupin requires of the narrator. To understand why the killer's simian origins produce "the full horrors" of which the narrator speaks, we need first to examine the effects of the revelation that Poe's narrative produces.

The Analytic Sublime

Throughout the Dupin stories, Poe offers models for the nature of analysis, including games of odd and even, theories of mental identification, and an elaborate comparison of the respective merits of chess and whist. Yet in "Rue Morgue," analysis itself must remain disappointingly invisible to the reader, except through its intensely pleasing effects: "We know of them, among other things, that they are always to their possessor, when inordinately possessed, a source of the liveliest enjoyment. As the strong man exults in his physical ability, delighting in such exercises as call his muscles into action, so glories the analyst in that moral activity which *disentangles*. He derives pleasure from even the most trivial occupations bringing his talent into play. He is fond of enigmas, of conundrums, of hieroglyphics" (*PT*, 397). In its basic narrative structure, "Rue Morgue" is itself an enigma whose effects, according to its own logic, should clarify the nature of analysis. But the opening discussion reverses the ordinary process of interpretation: the crime and its solution "will appear to the reader somewhat in the light of a commentary upon the [analytic] propositions just advanced" (ibid., 400), rather than the other way around. Nor is it clear why we should experience "the liveliest enjoyment" from the ensuing tale of violence. Might we understand the tale as an allegory of the superiority of brain to brawn, in which Dupin handily defeats both the sailor's evasions and the ape's brute difference? Certainly; but the pleasure of such a reading is not itself analytical, and hence brings us no closer to understanding the properties that the narrative so ostentatiously foregrounds.

Because the narrator has compared analytic pleasure to that enjoyed by the strong man, we ought perhaps to consider the two "strong men" of the tale as guides. The first of these is the orangutan (*Homo sylvestris*), possessed of "superhuman" strength; the second is its owner, "a tall, stout, and muscular-looking person" who comes equipped, as in a fairy tale, with "a huge oaken cudgel" (ibid., 426). But these seem to exercise their powers only in violence: the elder L'Espanaye's head is "nearly severed" "with one determined sweep" of the ape's "muscular arm" (ibid., 430), and although the sailor seems amicable by comparison, even he spends his energy whipping the ape into submission, and his muscles tense at the thought of killing Dupin ("The sailor's face flushed. . . . He started to his feet and grasped his cudgel" [ibid., 427]). In practice, although the pleasures of the analyst seem only figurally related to those of his muscular counterpart ("As the strong man exults . . . so glories the analyst"), the narrative that follows demonstrates that the relation between the two is causal: the analyst's skills are called for because of the strong man's exertion, as Dupin pits his thought against the unwitting power of the ape and the sailor's potential for violence.

According to Peter Brooks, any given story has a central metaphor that, however dissolved into the narrative, articulates the story's primary relationships. And because all narrative can be mapped rhetorically as a relation between the poles of metaphor and metonymy, one can describe the narrative's duration as a metonymic "acting out of the implications of metaphor," which at once reveals the meaning of the impacted initial metaphor and transforms it through its narrative embodiment.[18] Citing the example of Conan Doyle's "Musgrave Ritual," Brooks shows that the obscure and apparently meaningless ritual practiced by the Musgraves is actually a metaphor that condenses and shapes the action of the story. Regardless of whether Brooks is right to contend that the relation between initial metaphor and narrative metonymy holds for all stories, it is undeniably true of detective fiction in general, and of its founding text as well. The first rhetorical figure encountered in "Rue Morgue"—the analogy between the pleasures of analysis and of strength—provides the story's structuring metaphor; in fact, the tale has everything to do with the proper way of understanding the relationship between the physical and the mental, and the pleasures associated with each.

Take as an emblem of this disjunction the difficulty that the Mmes. L'Espanaye find in keeping head and body together: Camille L'Espanaye is strangled; her mother's throat is "so entirely cut that upon an attempt to raise her, the head fell off" (*PT*, 411, 406). "Rue Morgue" repeatedly stages the violent separation of heads and bodies, literal and figurative, and although Dupin and the orangutan are the most visibly polarized emblems of this split, the form of the tale repeats this pattern, joining its analytic head to its fictive body by the most insecure of narrative ligatures: "The narrative to follow will appear to the reader somewhat in the light of a commentary upon the propositions just advanced" (ibid., 400). However one wishes to allegorize this relation of heads to bodies—as an opposition between spirit and matter, analysis and effects, or ego and id—it is the distinguishing structural feature of the text at every level. But although "Rue Morgue" formally repeats the opposition between body and head in the relationship of narrative and commentary, one can identify Brooks's initial metaphor only in retrospect, because Poe's text conceals its metaphors as metonymies until the narrative's climactic revelation, by which time we as readers have been thoroughly implicated in a scene at which we imagined ourselves only spectators.

Generically, this implication has already been built into the text through its combination of the gothic with what I call the analytic sublime. Besides its extravagant setting in a "time-eaten and grotesque mansion, long deserted through superstitions into which we did not inquire, and tottering to its fall" (ibid., 400-401), "Rue Morgue" reveals its generic debt in the sensational violence of the killings, the segmentation of space into barely permeable vesicles, and the uncanniness of the crime's resolution. Although Eve Sedgwick argues compellingly that as a genre the gothic is preeminently concerned with male homosocial desire, Poe's detective stories find their activating tension less in the closeting of sexual difference than in the closeting of consciousness within the body. Despite its overt disavowal of the gothic ("let it not be supposed," the narrator reminds us, "that I am detailing any mystery, or penning any romance" [ibid., 402]), Poe employs an aura of analytical reason only to intensify the reader's experience of violence and disorder.

In the gothic's implicit spatial model, Sedgwick suggests, an "individual fictional 'self'" is often "massively blocked off from something to which it ought normally to have access": air, personal history, a loved one. Regardless of the specific lack, it is the unspeakability of this occlusion that is generically distinctive: "The important privation is the privation exactly of language, as though language were a sort of safety valve between the inside and the outside which, being closed off, all knowledge, even when held in common, becomes solitary, furtive, and explosive."[19] Although Poe's detective stories employ many of the gendered conventions (the doubling of criminal and detective, the detective's social and physical alienation, the violence directed against female bodies) that have long characterized crime fiction, Poe's homosocial pairs keep turning into repetitions of a single self (Dupin and the narrator, Dupin and Minister D——, D—— and his imagined brother), without the triangulation of difference needed to put sexual desire in play.[20]

Although the detective story, with its long retrospective reconstructions, seems par excellence the genre in which language is adequate to its task of description, in the end the apparent rationality of the detective is a device used to create Sedgwick's gothic division. Far from offering a safety valve between inner and outer, language itself separates the analyst from the object, thereby creating the pressure differential between self and world that language is pressed to describe. The impalpable tissue separating inside and outside is consciousness itself, which can never be identical either with itself or with the body. The more intensely Poe pursues disembodied reason (the analytic sublime), the more powerfully gothic will be the moment in which the reader's identification with the body of the ape is revealed.

This use of reason against itself appears with particular clarity in the episode in which Dupin discovers the exit by which the killer escaped from the quarters of the Mmes. L'Espanaye. In this first instance of the locked-room mystery, the doors to the L'Espanayes' home are locked; there are no secret passages or "preternatural events"; and the condition of the bodies rules out suicide. The two windows are shut, each fastened by "a very stout nail" pushed into a gimlet-hole drilled through frame and casement. Yet on visiting the house, Dupin displays absolute confidence in his logical powers: "The impossibility of egress, by means already stated, being thus absolute, we are reduced to the windows. It is only left for us to prove that these apparent 'impossibilities' are, in reality, not such." Reasoning that "the murderers *did* escape from one of these windows," Dupin decides that the sashes

> *must*, then, have the power of fastening themselves. There was no escape from this conclusion. I had traced the secret to its ultimate result—and that result was *the nail*. It had, I say, in every respect, the appearance of its fellow in the other window, but this fact was an absolute nullity (conclusive as it might seem to be) when compared with the consideration that here, at this point, terminated the clew. "There *must* be something wrong," I said, "about the

nail." I touched it; and the head, with about a quarter of the shank, came off in my fingers. The rest of the shank was in the gimlet-hole, where it had been broken off. (*PT,* 419)

This is what Freud called the "omnipotence of consciousness" with a vengeance: the evidence of the senses is "an absolute nullity" against the locked room of Dupin's logic ("There was no escape from this conclusion"). In apparent confirmation of his hypothesis, the nailhead pops off at Dupin's touch, as if his analysis were a type of narrative thaumaturgy, able to bring about changes in the world through mere enunciation (" 'There *must* be something wrong,' I said, 'about the nail' "). It is Dupin's speech that solves the mystery of how the closed space was entered and exited; his words here repeat the function of the coded treasure map in "The Gold-Bug": in both cases, they are forms of language that permit the opening of an otherwise sealed space.[21] In this scenario, the nail functions as a lock on the L'Espanaye's home—a home that, thanks to the violence of the orangutan, has now become a literal crypt. Surprisingly enough, Dupin's analytic solution to the gory mystery of the bodies is yet another form of *decryption,* a diffused and narratively enlarged scene in which the crypt is opened through signs.

Finally, this decryption is itself another version of the tale's split between analysis and action, an indication that Poe's analytical sublime contains the seeds of its own undoing. The abstract introduction to a tale of horror (also familiar from "The Imp of the Perverse") intensifies the shock of the narrative by increasing the contrast between the narrative's ratiocinative calm and the brutality to follow. And because excessive contrast is itself a gothic convention, "Rue Morgue" stages the relation between the story's introduction and its main body as another instance of the gothic. Indeed, the nail itself anticipates my conclusion: its status as a token of the power of reason is immediately undermined by Dupin's recognition that the nail itself is fractured. Like everything else in "Rue Morgue," the nail—an apparent integer—divides into head and body.

This constant recurrence of heads and bodies is structurally parallel to the separation in detective fiction of the metonymic and metaphoric poles of language. Working with clues associated with the narrative's originating crime, the detective's analytical method is primarily a form of metonymy, which is, in turn, associated with the frame narrative of the detective's analysis, and with its origins in cryptography. Conversely, the core narrative of most detective stories obsessively concerns itself with bodies, most commonly with their violation and murder. Metonymy, Lacan suggests, is evidence of the displacement of desire for the mother onto the signifying chain itself. As the law of the signifier, the Law of the Father separates the infant from the mother at the moment when Oedipal injunctions manifest themselves in, and as, the child's newly acquired language. The child attempts to recapture its original plenitude through the use of language, but this displaced search turns into an identification of suspended desire with the process of signification itself: "And the enigmas that desire seems to pose for a 'natural philosophy'—its frenzy mocking the abyss of the infinite, the secret collusion with which it envelops the pleasure of knowing and of dominating with a jouissance, these amount to no other derangement of instinct than that of being caught in the rails—eternally stretching forth towards the *desire for something else*—of metonymy." [22] In place of the child's imaginary, there are only the "rails" of metonymic linkage, which, far from leading back to the mother, constitute the bars separating the child from the mother's being. But this "desire for something else" is not without compensatory pleasures, chief among which is the "jouissance" of employing language to structure the observable world, investing it with the sense of an almost tangible approach to the object of desire. The rails teeter constantly along the edge of remembrance, "at the very suspension-point of the signifying chain." [23]

In its concern with evidence, the detective's search is a variation on the metonymic suspension displayed by the narrator of the gothic romances, who tends "to muse, for long unwearied hours, with [his] attention riveted to some frivolous device on the margin or in the typography of a book" ("Berenice," *PT*, 227). This obsessive attention is a defense mechanism designed to turn the mind away from something that must seem to be repressed, but which, in fact, hovers teasingly close to consciousness:

> There is no point, among the many incomprehensible anomalies of the science of mind, more thrillingly exciting than the fact . . . that in our endeavors to recall to memory something long forgotten, we often find ourselves *upon the very verge of* remembrance, without being able, in the end, to remember. And thus how frequently, in my intense scrutiny of Ligeia's eyes, have I felt approaching the full knowledge of their expression—felt it approaching—yet not quite be mine—and so at length entirely depart! ("Ligeia," *PT*, 264–65)

Compare this to the narrator's reaction to Dupin's description of the strength, ferocity, and "harsh and unequal voice" possessed by the orangutan: "At these words a vague and half-formed conception of the meaning of Dupin flitted over my mind. I seemed to be upon the verge of comprehension, without power to comprehend—as men, at times, find themselves upon the brink of remembrance without being able, in the end, to remember" ("Murders in the Rue Morgue," *PT*, 421). In both cases, the quality of this near-memory, and the habits of both excessively attentive narrators, correspond to Lacan's metonymic subject "perversely" fixated "at the very suspension-point of the signifying chain, where the memory-screen is immobilized and the fascinating image of the fetish is petrified." [24]

Lacan's rhetorical analysis permits us to see how completely the metonymic frame narrative of the tale disembodies both analyst and reader, even as the gothic narrative core of the detective story foregrounds corporeal metaphors.[25] This metaphoric pull toward embodiment is crystallized in the basic scenario of "Rue Morgue," which, as Marie Bonaparte noted long ago, is a particularly nasty Oedipal triangle. For Bonaparte, the orangutan represents the male infant, whose obsession with the question of the mother's sexual difference is only settled through the symbolic castration involved in Mme. L'Espanaye's decapitation. Bonaparte's reading depends on a style of anatomical literalization now out of fashion, discredited in an era in which psychoanalytic critics rightfully prefer textual and rhetorical criticism to readings that, as Brooks notes, mistakenly choose as their objects of analysis "the author, the reader, or the fictive persons of the text."[26]

The problem is that "Rue Morgue" continually solicits what can only be described as bad Freudian readings. Bonaparte's biographical interpretation of Poe's fiction is, in the main, enjoyably unconvincing, but her monomaniacal inventory of sexual symbols (of, for instance, the L'Espanayes' chamber as a gigantic projection of the interior female anatomy) is difficult to dismiss. From the rending of the double doors of the L'Espanayes' home ("a double or folding gate . . . bolted neither at bottom nor top" forced "open, at length, with a bayonet"), to the ape's futile ransacking of Mme. L'Espanaye's private drawers ("the drawers of a bureau . . . had been, apparently, rifled, although many articles of apparel still remained in them" [*PT*, 421]), to the identification of the broken and the whole nail, the story overcodes its anatomical symbols. Discovered in its crimes, the orangutan's "wild glances" fall upon "the head of the bed, over which the face of its master, rigid with horror, was just discernible." The ape stuffs Camille "head-down" in the chimney; the L'Espanayes live in a room "at the head of the passage"; the nail in the window behind the bed is fixed "nearly to the head"; Dupin looks over "the head-board minutely"; the other nail too is "driven in nearly up to the head." The ape flees from its master's bed to the L'Espanayes', where it swings itself through the window "directly upon the headboard of the bed." "Head" is used twenty times, "bed," "bedstead," or "bedroom" seventeen times; as well as rhyming aurally, "head" and "bed" continually chime through their contiguity in the text, inviting the reader to link them through metaphor. Even the fractured window-nail can represent the mother's phallus: "Il y a le mystère du clou mutilé d'une des fenêtres, sans doute symbole, sur le mode 'mobilier,' de la castration de la mère."[27] Dupin's inductions about the broken nail constitute a *fort-da* game in which he resolves the question of the maternal phallus by both denying its presence (" 'There *must* be something wrong,' I said, 'about the nail.' I touched it; and the head . . . came off in my fingers") and affirming it ("I now carefully replaced this head portion and . . . the fissure was invisible"). Such an explanation helps explain why the analysis of the nail musters such weird intensity, particularly in the quasi-performative sense of Dupin's *must*.

My claim is not that such anatomical allegorizing substantiates psycho-analytic criticism, but that Freudian readers have long been attracted to detective fiction because the genre's structure and themes so often echo central psychoanalytic scenarios. What looks like Poe's eerie anticipation of psychoanalytic motifs may say as much about generic as about psychic structure. Certainly, the literary interest of Freud's case studies depends in no small part on an essentially cryptographic sense of power over the body. Despite Freud's frequent attempts to distance himself from writers of fic-tion, his early conception of psychoanalysis as "the task of making conscious the most hidden recesses of the mind," of rendering the body transparent to language, is driven by the same themes of cryptographic interiority at play in Poe's detective fiction.[28] And Dupin's boast that "most men, in respect to himself, wore windows in their bosoms" (*PT*, 401) is actually a more mod-est version of Freud's famous declaration in his study of Dora: "He that has eyes to see and ears to hear may convince himself that no mortal can keep a secret. If his lips are silent, he chatters with his finger-tips; betrayal oozes out of him at every pore."[29]

Although critics have remarked on the embarrassing frequency with which detective stories draw on stock psychoanalytic imagery, no one has yet called attention to how thoroughly "Rue Morgue" seems to gloss the analytic process itself. Freud describes the "essence of the psychoanalytic situation" as follows:

> The analyst enters into an alliance with the ego of the patient to subdue cer-tain uncontrolled parts of his id, i.e., to include them in a synthesis of the ego. . . . [If] the ego learns to adopt a defensive attitude towards its own id and to treat the instinctual demands of the latter like external dangers, this is at any rate partly because it understands that the satisfaction of instinct would lead to conflicts with the external world. (Under the influence of its up-bringing, the child's ego accustoms itself to shift the scene of the battle from outside to inside and to master the *inner* danger before it becomes *external*.)[30]

Freud's clinical observations would serve equally well to describe the sailor's visit to Dupin, with Dupin standing in for the analyst, the sailor for the analysand, and the orangutan as a figure for the remembered "primal scene." In *Dora*, Freud notes that "the patients' inability to give an ordered history of their life insofar as it coincides with the story of their illness is not merely characteristic of the neurosis," but is, in fact, a defining feature of mental illness; Freud's essential test for recovery simply *is* the patient's newfound ability to narrate his or her life, to "remove all possible symptoms and to replace them by conscious thoughts."[31] In this case, the sailor must recount under duress the story of the crime, which is formally parallel to the dreams that provide the analytic material for Freud's case studies. His wish to hide his knowledge makes sense in terms of the plot, but it is less easy to explain away Dupin's insistence, at once solicitous and stern, that the sailor narrate what he knows. Dupin, one might say, enters into an alliance with the sailor in order that he might "subdue certain uncontrolled parts of his id," unmistakably represented by the ape. As a corollary, Dupin repeatedly insists that the sailor acknowledge the beast as his own — "Of course you are prepared to identify the property?" (*PT*, 427) — even as he declares that the sailor is both innocent and complicit: "You have nothing to conceal. You have no reason for concealment. On the other hand, you are bound by every principle of honor to confess all" (ibid., 428). Pressed to take a reward for ostensibly recovering the ape, Dupin continues the same theme: "You shall give me all the information in your power about these murders in the Rue Morgue" (ibid., 427).

Forced at gunpoint to answer, the sailor responds first by losing the ability to articulate ("The sailor's face flushed up, as if he were struggling with suffocation. . . . He spoke not a word"), and then by threatening compensatory violence ("He started to his feet and grasped his cudgel"), as the story of the ape homeopathically reproduces itself in the sailor's telling. The stress of confession threatens to produce a repetition of the original crime, but Dupin's paternal firmness ("I perfectly well know that you are innocent of the atrocities in the Rue Morgue. It will not do, however, to deny that you are in some measure implicated in them" [ibid.]) permits him to redirect his symptomatic repetition into narrative — precisely the result of a successful analytic intervention predicted by Freud. The sailor explains how, having brought the ape from Borneo to Paris in order to sell it for profit, he returned one night to find that the orangutan had escaped into his bedroom,

> into which it had broken from a closet adjoining, where it had been, as was thought, securely confined. Razor in hand, and fully lathered, it was sitting before a looking-glass, attempting the operation of shaving, in which it had no doubt previously watched its master through the key-hole of the closet. Terrified at the sight of so dangerous a weapon in the possession of an animal so ferocious, and so well able to use it, the man, for some moments, was at a loss what to do. He had been accustomed, however, to quiet the creature, even in its fiercest moods, by the use of a whip, and to this he now resorted. Upon sight of it, the Ourang-Outang sprang at once through the door of the chamber, down the stairs, and thence, through a window, unfortunately open, into the street. (Ibid., 428-29)

Having only heard up to this point about the animal's "intractable ferocity," this image of the orangutan is rather touching; even when the ape imitates "the motions of a barber" with the Mmes. L'Espanaye, its purposes, we are told, are "probably pacific" (ibid., 430). Poe offers us a Darwinian revision of Freud, a primate scene in which the ape—still "in the closet," forced to peep through a keyhole—sees its master shaving, and tries to imitate him. Shaving codes the body as a part of culture, not nature; and as in David Humphreys' contemporary poem "The Monkey" (printed in Duyckinck's *Cyclopaedia of American Literature*),[32] the ape takes up the razor out of a wish to be human.[33] But without language, the developmental scenario implied by the ape's mimicry stalls: whatever his "imitative propensities," as a mute the ape cannot readily make its intentions known. The ape's frustrated turn from gesture to violence reveals the abject inadequacy of mimesis in comparison with speech. Unable to manipulate abstract symbols, the ape takes out its rage on the flesh; although the story's focus on injured mouths and throats may be an instance of displacement upward, it is also a direct attack on the organs of speech. The orangutan represents both Bonaparte's murderous infant, poised at the moment of discovering sexual difference, and a liminally human, highly evocative image of the body's resistance to signification. These elements are synthesized in a Lacanian revision of the primal scene as the entry into signification. Poe's use of the orangutan serves as his own myth of human origins, which condenses within itself both individual and evolutionary history, both linguistic and sexual desire.

The Ape's Recapture

Thanks to Dupin's narrative therapy, the sailor is afforded the opportunity to break the cycle of repetition through the type of analytic transference that, in Brooks's words, "succeeds in making the past and its scenarios of desire relive through signs with such vivid reality that the reconstructions it proposes achieve the *effect* of the real."[34] Although it is meaningless to speak of curing a fictional character, this protoanalytic scene is one way in which Poe stages the reader's textual cathexis, although such a proleptic parody may suggest that, like "Rue Morgue" itself, the psychoanalyst's function is to manufacture a narrative rather than to reveal one. The sailor's mistake has been to assume that once he had succeeded in lodging the ape at his own residence, the danger that it posed was over. The sailor has yet to learn to "treat the instinctual demands of the [id] like external dangers." Hence, the captive ape escapes from the sailor, forcing him to face the violent consequences of its acting-out. The process of admitting his possession of the ape is a precondition for its taming, which requires that the sailor objectify and confront as an external danger ("no mean enemy") the fact of the bodily unconscious. The recapture of the erstwhile brute (a story Poe does not even bother to recount) represents the sailor's psychic reintegration. As Freud writes: "The struggle between physician and patient, between intellect and the forces of instinct, between recognition and the striving for discharge, is fought out almost entirely on the ground of transference-manifestations. This is the ground on which the victory must be won, the final expression of which is lasting recovery from the neurosis. . . . In the last resort no one can be slain *in absentia* or *in effigie*."[35] By contrast, literature might be defined as just such an effigy of the real, staging ego-training sessions in which the reader learns "to shift the scene of the battle from outside to inside," from behaviors to an internalized encounter with the text.

Once the sailor owns up to his implication in the killings, the story is finished; the narrator has "scarcely anything to add," and hastily concludes by noting that the ape "was subsequently caught by the owner himself, who obtained for it a very large sum at the *Jardin des Plantes*. Le Bon was instantly released, upon our narration of the circumstances (with some comments from Dupin) at the *bureau* of the Prefect of Police" (*PT*, 431). Because the real story of "Rue Morgue" concerns the production of uncanny effects in the reader, Poe has no qualms about violating notions of the well-made story. Instead, the extreme brevity of the denouement and the untidiness of the story's conclusion remind us that Poe's characters are merely puppets, technical apparatuses deployed in the attempt to intensify our affective transference onto his tales. Although the allegorical reading sketched here could be elaborated further, the parallels between Freud's method in the case studies and Poe's narrative are clear. The baroque sexual symbolism, the fetishization of analysis, the literalization of the "talking cure," and, above all, the story's peculiar staging of metaphor and metonymy are coordinated devices through which Poe enhances the reader's identification.

Thus far, the reader has had little incentive to identify with anyone except Dupin. But although Dupin's cryptographic power is specifically predicated on his linguistic prowess, the resolution of this case is not a matter of language alone. Instead, Dupin now finds himself confronting the tangible world, carefully measuring the "impression" made by the orangutan's fingers on Camille L'Espanaye's neck against the span and pattern of a human hand, only to find that the prints on the strangled woman are not even approximately the same (" 'This,' I said, 'is the mark of no human hand' " [ibid., 423]). Dupin continues his physical investigation: " 'Besides, the hair of a madman is not such as I now hold in my hand. I disentangled this little tuft from the rigidly clutched fingers of Madame L'Espanaye. Tell me what you can make of it.' 'Dupin!' I said, completely unnerved, 'this hair is most unusual—this is no *human* hair' " (ibid.). Recall that in the opening paragraph of the story, the analyst is said to glory "in that moral activity which *disentangles*": just the word Dupin uses to describe the process of physically extracting his tuft of hair from the "rigidly clutched" hand of the corpse. For all the text's insistence on the separation between the pleasures of the strong man and those of the analyst, the solution of the Rue Morgue murders requires that Dupin make forceful, even violent, contact with the traces of the ape.

After producing his assembled physical evidence, Dupin asks the narrator: "What impression have I made upon your fancy?" repeating as a metaphor the word used to refer to the uncanny and inhuman marks left on the dead woman's neck. Prior to the moment in which Dupin histrionically reveals the orangutan as the culprit, the reader's body has been anesthetized by Dupin's disembodied analytics (an anesthetization also evident in Dupin, who in moments of excitement becomes "frigid and abstract," his eyes "vacant in expression"). In the "creeping of the flesh" that follows, the narrator's body identifies with the ape through Dupin's recreation of the crime, revealing that he, too, by his direct somatic response, is implicated in the narrative to which he listens. "A symptom," writes Lacan, is "a metaphor in which flesh or function is taken as a signifying element";[36] in the moment when the reader's skin shivers in sympathy with the narrator, the reader witnesses the overthrow of the metonymic order. In the shift to the metaphoric, in the symptomatic reproduction within the reader's body of a sensational response, the reader reveals his or her collaboration with the ape. Through the creation of this response, Poe circumvents Freud's complaint that in analysis "the patient hears what we say but it rouses no response in his mind."[37] To rouse the mind, a text must also arouse the body; only through the symptomatic commitment of the reader's flesh can the text realize its transferential effects.

Appropriately, it is the knowledge of his own embodiment that permits Dupin to solve the mystery of the L'Espanayes' deaths. This is the implication of Dupin's final comments on the Prefect, in which he takes pains to emphasize the futility of the latter's "bodiless" wisdom: "In his wisdom is no *stamen*. It is all head and no body, like the pictures of the Goddess Laverna—or, at best, all head and shoulders, like a codfish. But he is a good creature after all. I like him especially for one master stroke of cant, by which he has attained his reputation for ingenuity. I mean the way he has '*de nier ce qui est, et d'expliquer ce qui n'est pas*'" (*PT*, 431). Although the Prefect is figured as a "creature," it is just his failure to negotiate between head and body that prevents him from imagining the animal nature of the killer. As a kind of walking bust, all head and shoulders, the Prefect, not Dupin, is an emblem of excessive rationality, unable to accommodate the ape's physical presence. By contrast, Dupin twice notes his admiration for the animal. "I almost envy you the possession of him" (ibid., 427) he admits to the sailor, and we may suppose that Dupin longs for the animal's intense physicality, even as he revels in the physical effects, the "creeping of the flesh" (ibid., 423) he produces in his listeners. (Once more, Dupin appears as a stand-in for Poe, who relies for his very bread and butter on the ability to conjure identification.) "Where is the ingenuity of unravelling a web which you yourself have woven for the express purpose of unravelling?" Poe asked of Cooke; we may answer that it lies in having in the meantime caught something in that web. In the present case, Dupin's greatest exertions are expended to catch not the monkey, but his owner, lured in by the text placed in the newspaper. Just so with the story's readers: drawn in by another piece of paper, by another thread or web, we find ourselves trapped within its self-dissolving structure, as any assumptions about the nature of analysis are undone by our own somatic performance.

As "The Murders in the Rue Morgue" concludes, the divergent senses of the word *stamen* crystallize its irreconcilable oppositions:

> *stamen*, n.; pl. *stamens* rare *stamina*, [L., a warp in an upright loom, a thread; lit., that which stands up, from *stare*, to stand].
>
> 1. a warp thread, especially in the ancient upright loom at which the weaver stood upright instead of sitting. [Obs.]
>
> 2. in botany, the male reproductive organ in flowers, formed principally of cellular tissue.[38]

Insofar as *stamen* refers to the male generative organ of a flower, it marks the (male) reader addressed by the text; call this the Freudian reading, in which to have a male body seems inseparable from complicity in the orangutan's gendered violence. But the first meaning, now obsolete, indicates the warp thread in a loom, and through familiar paths (loom, weaving, text), we arrive at the stamen as the narrative thread running throughout Poe's text. The story's overdetermined treatment of heads and bodies, words and things, analysis and its effects, implies the close association of the origins of narrative with the discovery of sexual difference, although it is impossible to tell which came first. Instead of reinforcing an evolutionary hierarchy that would separate us from our simian relations, the cryptographic narrative structure of "Rue Morgue" reminds us of our corporeal investment: through the story's self-enacting rhetoric, the reader lives out the distance between the tale's opening metaphor and its closing one—between the simile comparing analysis and the strong man's pleasure, which safely separates its terms even as it joins them, and the metaphor of the stamen, which reveals the degree to which the reader, too, finds himself hopelessly entangled.

DARK FIBER

4   Cryptography, Telegraphy, Science Fiction

And who shall calculate the immense influence upon social life—upon
arts—upon commerce—upon literature—which will be the immediate
result of the great principles of electro-magnetics?

Brevet Brigadier General John A. B. C. Smith

Cryptography is not a transhistorically stable subject; it changes along with
the cultures from which it springs. This was rarely truer than during Poe's
lifetime, when interest in cryptography burgeoned remarkably. It was not,
one must admit, a time of rapid or profound cryptographic innovation.
Although the American government had made extensive use of ciphers
throughout the Revolutionary period and Thomas Jefferson had developed
a wheel cipher so simple to operate and yet so devious to solve that the
American navy employed it until 1967, little went on at the highest levels
of cipher. There were two changes in the decades leading up to the Civil
War, however, that bear directly on Poe's fictive use of ciphers: the spread
of magazines and newspapers to a growing leisured middle class, and, incomparably more important, the development of the telegraph. The combination of these factors led to the creation of telegraphic writing, by which
I mean writing *about* the telegraph, writing transmitted over the telegraph
(private letters, stock quotes, news of war), and, above all, the way in which
the telegraph inflected thought and imagination regarding human communication through writing.

    The early decades of the nineteenth century were marked by a grow-
ing popular interest in elementary ciphering in much of Europe, including
Italy (for centuries the center of cryptographic invention and use), Germany, and France. That interest was even more pronounced in England and
America, if only because those countries had a higher percentage of literate
and leisured citizens. This interest took a variety of forms, from small military volumes such as William Rochfort's *Treatise upon Arcanography; or, A
New Method of Secret Writing, Defying Discovery or Detection, and Adapted
for All Languages* to William Thompson's *New Method for the Instruction
of the Blind*,[1] which argued that a zigzag cipher ordinarily used to teach

87

reading to the visually impaired would prove of service in diplomatic correspondence. Perhaps oddest of all was James Swaim's striking adaptation of Bacon's binary cipher, published in *The Mural Diagraph; or, The Art of Conversing through a Wall*,[2] which presented a two-part auditory cipher based on the knock and the scratch, designed to enable prisoners to communicate through the barrier of their prison walls.

Technical journals also issued articles on cipher writing: the *American Rail-Road Journal* (1832) and the *United States Service Magazine* (1831) were two of a handful of magazines that published essays on the Vigenere cipher in the early 1830s. The most readily available information about cryptography, however, appeared in general-interest magazines from the 1820s through the middle of the century. *Chambers's Edinburgh Journal*, the *Eclectic Magazine*, *Littel's Living Age*, the *Leisure Hour*, the *Saturday Magazine*, and many other journals published popular treatments of cryptography under such titles as "Secrets Exposed." To be sure, the amount of cryptographic expertise to be gleaned from such articles was often extraordinarily small, and yet these were obvious stimulants to the spreading interest in ciphers, and ones that would be practically enhanced with the creation of Morse's telegraph.

The origins of that telegraph might be dated to August 1811, when Morse—a young American painter training in London—wrote home to complain to his family about the long gap between the time of his letter's composition and its arrival in America, and the even longer interval until he received his family's response. "While I am writing," Samuel Finley Breeze Morse observed, "I can imagine mama wishing that she could hear of my arrival, and thinking of thousands of accidents that may have befallen me, and *I wish that in an instant I could communicate the information*; but three thousand miles are not passed over in an instant and we must wait for long weeks before we can hear from each other."[3] Morse answered his own wish three decades later by inventing the electrotelegraph, in so doing altering forever the nature of writing. Morse's invention was a momentous event. By permitting the virtually instant transmission of information, the telegraph spawned a major industry, played a key role in the rise of newspapers, the development of railroads, and the creation of regional stock markets, and generally changed patterns of human communication forever. Yet although critics have occasionally noted its local effects, such as in the terse aesthetics of implication that Hemingway forged out of the telegraphic style he practiced as a foreign correspondent, the cultural consequences of telegraphy have remained largely unstudied.

Because the telegraph depends on Morse's code for its utility, there exists a natural affinity between telegraphy and cryptography. As David Kahn explains, "the telegraph made cryptography what it is today";[4] it is not surprising that much of Poe's cryptographic writing was driven by the intellectual and cultural consequences of this invention, which required the immediate development of commercial telegraphic codes and of ciphers to protect the diplomatic and military traffic of nations. As the telegraph worked its way into the texture of daily life, it became far easier for Poe to conceive of a world structured around the concept of information, where knowledge itself was a form of decoding. Eventually, the telegraph's electric cipher led Poe to emphasize prostheses, antiorganicism, and the destruction of history, and to understand even photography as a mode of writing, with an encoded substructure invisible to the eye.

That the structure of Morse's code inflected Poe's concurrent thinking about languages and ciphers seems undeniable. Between 1837, when Morse began publicly experimenting with the telegraph, and 1844, when it went into commercial operation, Poe published the bulk of his cryptographic writing, including the essays, the Dupin trilogy, and "The Gold-Bug." According to John Limon, the "ubiquitous appearance" of Morse's telegraph just at the moment of the "simultaneous professionalization of science" had "a shattering literary importance." For no antebellum writer was the telegraph more shattering than for Poe, who claimed it as "a theorem almost demonstrated, that the consequences of any new scientific invention will, at the present day exceed, by very much, the wildest expectation of the most imaginative."[5]

But which of Poe's works qualify as science fiction? "The Balloon-Hoax," "The Unparalleled Adventure of One Hans Pfaall," and "Mellonta Tauta," to be sure. But what of "The Facts in the Case of M. Valdemar?" Or "Some Words with a Mummy"? The genre's conventions were not codified until the early twentieth century, when Hugo Gernsback coined the term, promising readers of *Amazing Stories* "the Jules Verne, H. G. Wells, and Edgar Allan Poe type of story—a charming romance intermingled with scientific fact and prophetic fiction."[6] Worse, the tales with the clearest generic claim tend to be among Poe's least-loved works, such as "The Colloquy of Monos and Una." Yet despite their weakness and generic uncertainty, it is through Poe's science fiction that he comes to terms most radically with the social consequences of cryptography. Particularly compelling is Poe's pronounced sense of the apocalypse of signification, in which the opaque materiality of the world reveals its symbolic organization. Although the characteristic semiotic strategy of detective fiction is that of encryption— of language embedded, covered over, hidden by bodies, buildings, and the opacity of social relations—Poe's science fiction is predicated on the sense of the sign's apocalypse (from *apo-calyptos*, to unclose or discover), in which the crypt of the letter is shattered and immediate communication becomes the basis for unfettered self-realization and sociality.[7]

Ultimately, Poe's secret writing presents an instance of what the telecommunications industry calls *dark fiber*. When the railroads were built in the middle of the nineteenth century, they were often required to purchase rights-of-way on either side of the track. These rights-of-way have subsequently become important for telecommunications companies, which have used them as paths for cross-country networks of optic cable. "Dark fiber" is the name for dormant fiber optic cables that have been laid but not yet exploited. Poe's cryptographic writing is a symbolic equivalent of this fiber, as his nineteenth-century fiction becomes a pathway to our twentieth-century imagination of the relations among the organic body, technology, and the self.

The cryptographic imagination exists in complicated tension with a phenomenologically deep sense of self. This tension is exacerbated by Poe's understanding of telegraphy, which further ruptures the connection between body and message, and accelerates the derealization of the body. Organicism, representation, wholeness, and depth are all undermined by the prosthetic extension of the self into telegraphic code. The consequent separation of bodies and communication leads Poe closer to imagining human identity as a problem in information processing, free from identification with a particular human body. Throughout the late fiction and "Marginalia" one finds Poe's presentiments of the human as a cyborg, part cybernetic machine, part organism. In what follows, I trace some of the fibers leading from Poe's science fiction to the postmodern decomposition of bodily identity. In its intersection with telegraphy, Poe's cryptographic writing has helped shape the contemporary imagination of telecommunicative subjectivity. It also clarifies how models of the self in recent science fiction negotiate between a hieroglyphic and a cryptographic approach to identity. To this end, the chapter ends with a discussion of William Gibson's *Neuromancer*—a contemporary science fiction novel built on many of the premises found in Poe.

The Death of Space and Time

> I have reached these lands but newly
> From an ultimate dim Thule—
> From a wild weird clime that lieth, sublime,
> Out of SPACE—out of TIME.

Edgar Allan Poe, "Dream-Land"

A central feature of modernity is the repeated claim that, through telecommunications, time and space have been destroyed. Today such claims are commonly advanced about the Internet, but three decades ago Marshall McLuhan declared that through "electric technology, we have extended our central nervous system itself in a global embrace, abolishing time and space as far as our planet is concerned."[8] McLuhan, in turn, was echoing Futurists such as Filippo Tommaso Marinetti ("Time and Space died yesterday.

We already live in the absolute, because we have created eternal, omnipresent speed"),[9] whose fantasy of omnipresence and instantaneity was already old hat in 1909. A half-century earlier, Nathaniel Hawthorne had asked "is it a fact—or have I dreamt it—that, by means of electricity, the world of matter has become a great nerve, vibrating thousands of miles in a breathless point of time?"[10]

The origins of this fantasy of speed can be dated to the birth of Morse's new device. In the words of Carleton Mabee, visitors to an experimental version of the telegraph in Washington in 1838 felt Morse's invention as a cataclysm: "'The world is coming to an end,' Vail heard some say. 'Where will improvement and discoveries stop?' others asked. . . . 'Time and space are now annihilated,' was the far-seeing conclusion of one visitor. His comment was to be on the lips of millions."[11] As the first telecommunications device, Morse's telegraph represented a watershed for mass culture, "as significant a break with the past as printing before it."[12] In telegraphy, the Newtonian unities of being are replaced by the prosthetic extension of the self over a network of wires. All communication technologies created since "have simply been elaborations on the telegraph's original work,"[13] growing directly out of discoveries in communications engineering predicated on Morse's invention, including the transatlantic cable (1866), telephone (1876), wireless telegraphy (1895), radio (1906), and television (1926).[14] Even the digital computer is "no more than an instantaneous telegraph with a prodigious memory," and between them, the telegraph and the computer constitute the communicative matrix of this century.[15]

Inspiration for the telegraph came in 1832 when, on learning of experiments by André-Marie Ampère that showed that electricity apparently passed instantly over any length of wire, Morse understood that if "the presence of electricity can be made visible in any desired part of the circuit, I see no reason why intelligence might not be instantaneously transmitted by electricity to any distance."[16] Although the telegraph's invention is usually credited to Morse, forms of semaphoric military communication can be traced back to the ancient Greek use of lighted torches alternately obscured and exposed.[17] Nor, although Morse was unaware of this, was the idea of an electric telegraph absolutely new.[18] Morse's originality consisted of his combination of a binary code with a means of electrical transmission for the dots and dashes of that code.[19] Like all ciphers, Morse's is a metacode for representing language, in which words are decomposed into letters and the letters transformed into short and long pulses of electrical current. Originally, Morse planned to use a numerical code in which each word would be represented by a particular integer, which could be translated back into English by means of a code book. This proved cumbersome, and within months Morse replaced it with an alphabetic cipher in which a specific combination of dots and dashes stood for a letter. Like a good cryptographer, Morse based his new code on a study of the frequency of different letters in English, and in 1844, after considering "the incidence of letters in ordinary usage and of errors in transmission," Morse further revised his code, with such efficiency that, as the information theorist John Pierce approvingly notes, engineers today can only best Morse by 15 percent in speed. The lesson of Morse's code is clear: "It matters profoundly how one translates a message into electrical signals. This matter is at the very heart of communication theory."[20]

Poe's cryptographic writing followed close on the heels of Morse's experiments, in an environment in which congressional debates over the question of funding Morse's invention were widely reported. In 1842, when a bill appropriating thirty thousand dollars for the construction of a telegraph line from Baltimore to Washington finally reached the floor of the Senate, it was proposed that half the funds be given to Morse and half used for experiments in mesmerism. The chair, Robert C. Winthrop of Massachusetts, replied that "it would require a scientific analysis to determine how far the magnetism of mesmerism was analogous to that employed in telegraphs."[21] The scientific basis of the telegraph was so little understood that more than twenty senators adjourned from the Senate hall, judging it safer not to vote at all than to be proved fools. One who did vote, Lew Wallace of Indiana, "was defeated for re-election soon afterward because he had voted to spend public money for this absurdity."[22]

Within this charged environment, Poe began referring to the telegraph well before its commercial deployment. In 1839, five years before Morse received congressional approval, Poe had the narrator of "The Man that Was Used Up" report that he "telegraphed a few signals" to his neighbor in church, before commencing, "*sotto voce*, a brisk *tête-à-tête*."[23] In the first installment of "Marginalia" (November 1844), the telegraph appears as a metaphor for good writing. Noting the inefficient beginnings of many good books, Poe suggests that "it is far better that we commence irregularly—immethodically—than that we fail to arrest attention; but the two points, method and pungency, may always be combined. At all risks, let there be a few vivid sentences *imprimis*, by way of the electric bell to the telegraph" (*ER*, 1322). In 1845, Poe correctly observed that "the Electro Telegraph transmits intelligence instantaneously—at least so far as regards any distance upon the earth" ("The Thousand-and-Second Tale of Scheherazade," *PT*, 802). And in "Mellonta Tauta," Pundita records that she "spoke to-day the magnetic cutter in charge of the middle section of floating telegraph wires. . . . What *would* we do without the Atalantic telegraph?" (ibid., 873).

The literary significance of the telegraph, however, lies not in the fictions it has inspired but in its status as a model and an instance of the world's growing encipherment and electrically unified sociality. This is more than a matter of style. Rather, the dual antebellum fascination with technology and with language meant that the telegraph quickly inflected thinking about linguistic representation. By destroying the identity between transportation and communication, the telegraph marked an unprecedented moment in communications history. With such minor exceptions as carrier pigeons and semaphore fires, communication had previously required physical transport: a chain of bodies tied every message to its author. Although messages "might be centrally produced and controlled, through monopolization of writing or the rapid production of print, these messages, carried in the hands of a messenger or between the bindings of a book, still had to be distributed, if they were to have their desired effect, by rapid transportation."[24] The telegraph ushered in a time in which bodies and information *can* be separated. By rupturing the association between a body and its effects, the structure of the telegraph reminded Poe of the marvel of writing, which enables people distant in time and place to comprehend what is traced on the page today.

In addition, telegraphy dualizes the imagination of writing, dividing it into the signifier, represented by the dots and dashes of Morse's code (always, on some level, an alien trace) and the signified, imagined as the instantaneous zip of electrical current. Electricity, I need hardly add, is a part of the telegraph's signifying mechanism, not its content, but there was an almost instantaneous elision of the electrical medium to the principle of communication itself. Limon notes that for Hawthorne electricity "redescribes human communication as divine self-consciousness."[25] Although Poe does not spiritualize the telegraph in quite this manner, for both writers the promise of telegraphy is metaphysical: by annihilating space and time, it allows humankind to escape its physical limitations. The power and ubiquity of electricity are metaphorically attached to a newly disembodied consciousness. In addition, the relation of double-encoding to the apparent immanence of the telegraph's message recalls Poe's illusory achievement in the articles on cryptography, in which he treats his code breaking as if it were the breaking of coding itself—as if language and meaning were thereafter transparent.

From the beginning, the social effects of the telegraph were tied to cryptography. In 1845, the telegraph's first full year of commercial operation, Morse's lawyer, Francis O. J. Smith, "published a commercial code entitled *The Secret Corresponding Vocabulary; Adapted for Use to Morse's Electro-Magnetic Telegraph*, in whose preface he declared that 'secrecy in correspondence, is far the most important consideration.' "[26] Smith's code was followed by dozens more, such as John Wills's Telegraphic Congressional Reporter of 1847 and the ABC Code of 1866, which were designed to safeguard the privacy of correspondence. Like cinema, telegraphic crypto seems to have been a technology that answered a deep-seated human interest.[27] "As the most exciting invention of the first half of the century, the telegraph stirred as much interest in its day as Sputnik did in its. The great and widely felt need for secrecy awakened the latent interest in ciphers that so many people seem to have, and kindled a new interest in many others. Hundreds of persons attempted to dream up their own unbreakable ciphers."[28]

The telegraph and its ciphers also quickly became the site for quasi-literary play. In my copy of the collected numbers of *Graham's Magazine* for 1845 (which also contains the first appearances in print of "The Imp of the Perverse" and "The System of Dr. Tarr and Professor Fether"), someone has penciled in the key to the International Morse Code on the flyleaf and has ciphered helter-skelter a series of messages. No breaks are included between words, and the deciphered messages seem incoherent; for example,

clockthehardnoordposthkmeeditismclwarsrou
tprryharmyoccupihbshbryl. . . .

Remembering Legrand's comment in "The Gold-Bug" ("You observe there are no divisions between the words. Had there been divisions, the task would have been comparatively easy" [*PT*, 588]), and correcting for some obvious errors in enciphering, one obtains the following: ". . . clock. The Hartford Post Home Edition. Cvl wars rout . . . Perry's army occupies [?] . . . stop the press." And on the next page: "Harry B. is home at Melrose." The fragmentary "cvl wars" must refer to the Civil War, a date permitted by the history of the *Hartford Post*, which was founded in 1858. In all likelihood, the messages were put there by children, practicing Morse on old journal issues relegated to an attic or back room, an impression cemented by the handwritten imitation of a library card stuck to one of the book's endpapers. However inconsequential the content of these messages, their existence in cipher indicates the fascination with writing, secrecy, and power that Poe's fiction helped create, and the promiscuous intertextuality of antebellum culture, when a story by Poe might sit cheek by jowl with an essay on the telegraph, Poe's comments on telegraphy from the "Marginalia," and the kind of secret writing (with headlines taken from newspapers) found on the endpapers of *Graham's Magazine*.

It was not only children who committed their secrets to cipher. In 1962, while reading the 1864 issues of *Colburn's United Service Magazine*, a Civil War buff named Ray Neff noticed ciphered messages written on the inner margins of several pages. The one on page 183, for example, began: "J O 5 O F X 2 S P N F 6 U I F S F 8 X B M L F. . . ." Solved, the monoalphabetic substitution cipher disclosed a long allegorical poem by "L.C.B.," along with a series of confessions in which L.C.B. admitted that he was a spy involved in a plan to assassinate President Lincoln on 14 April 1865. According to the decrypted messages, at least eleven members of Congress were also implicated in the conspiracy, along with Edwin Stanton, Lincoln's secretary of war, and Thomas T. Eckert, the general superintendent of military telegraphs, whom Lincoln had asked to serve as his bodyguard on the fateful evening. But who was L.C.B.? When exposed to heat, one of the magazine's margins revealed a signature written in invisible ink: "Lafayette C. Baker," chief of the secret National Detective Police. There is some evidence to suggest that Baker was poisoned to death with arsenic in an attempt to keep him silent.[29] For our purposes, it does not much matter whether L.C.B.'s dubious confession is real; like the Morse code scribbled in *Graham's Magazine*, the ciphered confession indicates how the telegraph expanded the cryptograph's imaginative possibilities, particularly regarding its users' predilection for subversive histories and conspiracies.

That the development of the telegraph drastically reshaped antebellum economies of representation is evident in the move during the 1840s away from the hieroglyph and toward cryptography—away, that is, from a model of a visually grounded form of representation to an emphasis on the systematic manipulation of signs. This shift was abetted by achievements in science and technology. Champollion's successful translation of Egyptian hieroglyphs damaged the myth of Adamic language even as it reinforced the scientific methods of comparative linguistics. In *The Elements of Technology* (1829), Harvard professor Jacob Bigelow treated writing as *the* formative technology in human culture. Writing is "the root of all human knowledge"; without "the invention of written characters," history "must have remained uncertain and fabulous, and science been left in perpetual infancy."[30] Clearly, Bigelow understood the arbitrary nature of language: he pointedly abandoned the hieroglyph as an originary sign, noting that "the recent investigations of M. Champollion have led to the discovery that a great part of the hyeroglyphic characters upon the antiquities of Egypt are in reality the letters of an alphabet; and considerable progress has been made in deciphering their import."[31]

The effects of the telegraph were intensified by the almost simultaneous development of the daguerreotype, which appeared in 1839. Surprisingly often, antebellum writers imagined the daguerreotype in terms borrowed from the telegraph, confused about whether information was properly a sign or an image. Just as the hieroglyph had once promised to fulfill both requirements, Daguerre's invention was everywhere described as a form of language.[32] The *type* in *daguerreotype* returns us to the printing press, and *photography*—coined in 1839—is no better. By calling the act "writing with light," *photography* casts image making as a form of script. Where etymology is, there shall metaphor be. Responding to the discovery that light could fix an image, the one-time mayor of New York, Philip Hone, speculated thus: "Who knows whether, in this age of invention and discoveries, we may not be called upon to marvel at the exhibition of a tree, a horse, or a ship produced by the human voice muttering over a metal plate . . . the words 'tree,' 'horse,' and 'ship.'" And an anonymous reporter described the daguerreotype as the "first universal language," addressing itself "to all who possess vision, and in characters alike understood in the courts of civilization and the hut of the savage. The pictorial language of Mexico, the hieroglyphics of Egypt, are now superseded by reality."[33] For that reporter, the daguerreotype made good on the promise of the hieroglyph, offering a mode of representation that combines the universality of sight with the abstracting force of words.[34] Sketching Poe for the *Graham's Magazine* series "Our Contributors," James Russell Lowell jumbled image and sign in his efforts to correlate the "mathematical" clarity of Poe's genius with the indistinct "figures" and "shadows" prominent in Poe's hieroglyphic imagery: "Even his mystery is mathematical to his own mind. To him x is a known quantity all along. . . . However vague some of his figures may seem, however formless the shadows, to him the outline is as clear and distinct as that of a geometrical diagram."[35]

This conceptual association was not limited to nonscientists. When François Arago argued before the French Chamber of Deputies that Daguerre and Joseph Nicéphore de Niepce ought to be given state-sponsored pensions in recompense for their joint invention, his justification of the daguerreotype turned to questions of writing:

> Had we photography in 1798 we would possess today faithful pictorial records of that which the learned world is forever deprived. . . . To copy the millions of hieroglyphics which cover even the exterior of the great monuments of Thebes, Memphis, Karnak and others would require decades of time and legions of draughtsmen. By daguerreotype one person would suffice to accomplish this immense work successfully. . . . These designs will excel the works of the most accomplished painters, in fidelity of detail and true reproduction of the local atmosphere.[36]

By celebrating the daguerreotype's ability to preserve images of the hieroglyphs, Arago reveals how completely the imagination of his day was haunted by the dream of a natural mimesis, in which writing would function as a picture-story. Implicitly, the hieroglyph describes a matrix or interface that would permit people to bring the material world into contact with human consciousness. For Arago and his peers, hieroglyph and photograph figure the origin and end of writing: just as script began with the Adamic transparency dimly reflected in the hieroglyphs, it would return to such clarity through the technological perfection of the daguerreotype. (By contrast, the cryptographic imagination depends on the distance between noumena and phenomena.)

In this context, the concept of "information" acts as a hinge that swings between these opposed symbolic modes, pointing alternately toward image and sign. The term's etymology reveals its connections with cryptography: "Information, n. OFr *information*; L. *informatio (-onis)*, a representation, an

outline, sketch, from *informare*, to give form to, to represent, to inform."[37]
As "an outline [or] sketch," information translates the hieroglyphic attempt
to understand the world through visual representations; the root meaning of
"to give form to, . . . to inform" suggests the process by which symbols shape
the inchoate stuff of the world. By joining writing to image, information
links the symbolic to the material world, connecting its hieroglyphic origin
and its contemporary meaning. "Information" is, of course, an incoherent
notion: a datum has no edges or outline, and what may appear as a discrete
conceptual unit is only a tiny part of the discursive field in which the datum
is produced. But because information is based on an imagined distinction
between container and contents (as in the use of Morse's code to transmit
English text), information as a concept is generically linked to cryptography.

If initially the telegraph and daguerreotype seem to constitute polar
models of representation (with the telegraph as pure sign, in contrast to the
antisymbolic materiality of the glass image), Poe dismantles such oppositions, converting the daguerreotype into a rebus whose truth-telling powers
exceed even the best human eye. Writing in January 1840, Poe emphasized
the inhuman precision of the new invention, which is "*infinitely* more accurate in its representation than any painting by human hands. If we examine
a work of ordinary art, by means of a powerful microscope, all traces of
resemblance to nature will disappear—but the closest scrutiny of the photo-
genic drawing discloses only a more absolute truth, a more perfect identity
of the aspect with the thing represented. The variation of shade, and the
gradations of both linear and aerial perspective are those of truth itself."[38]

This makes it look as if Poe would agree with Morse, who claimed
that the daguerreotype offered "not copies of nature, but portions of
nature itself."[39] But Poe's late writing repeatedly strives to accomplish what
Georges Canguilhelm describes as the nineteenth century's "mathematization of non-formal concepts," such as the theory of probability put forth by
Pierre Simon, Marquis de Laplace.[40] To this end, Poe keeps looking in his
writing for an ersatz precision. Hence the discussions of algebra in "Marginalia" and in "Rue Morgue"; hence the attempt to quantify reading as if it,
too, were algebraic:

> Physically considered, knowledge breeds knowledge, as gold gold; for he who
> reads really much, finds his capacity to read increase in a geometrical ratio. . . .
> A deep-rooted and strictly continuous habit of reading will, with certain
> classes of intellect, result in an instinctive and seemingly magnetic apprecia-
> tion of a thing written; and now the student reads by pages just as other men
> by words. Long years to come, with a careful analysis of the mental process,
> may even render this species of appreciation a common thing. It may be taught
> in the schools of our descendants or the tenth and twentieth generation. . . .
> And should these matters come to pass—as they will—there will be in them

no more legitimate cause for wonder than there is, to-day, in the marvel that, syllable by syllable, men comprehend what, letter by letter, I now trace upon this page.[41]

Poe's fantasy of speed-reading suggests his desire to see literacy sub-ject to instrumentalizing rules, such as when he refers to a "geometrical increase" in the amount of material that good readers can consume—surely a nonsensical notion. With time, the mechanical act of reading becomes so natural that the book drops away, leaving a "magnetic appreciation" of the writer's words to "multiply" in the reader's brain. Yet after elaborating his technological vision of "analysis," "computations," and "erudition," Poe re-turns to the moment of reading, which he has now rendered strange and science-fictional: "the marvel that, syllable by syllable, men comprehend what, letter by letter, I now trace upon this page." For Poe, the crypto-graphic text is a hermetically sealed instrument, a capsule impervious to the wasting rust of time.

Perversely, Poe's appreciation of photography is based on his attempt to supersede its perceptual qualities, exploring rather its "infinitely" pre-cise renderings of the world—an attempt that accords with Poe's rejection of mimesis. Discussing drama, Poe necessarily finds it regressive, given its status as "the chief of the imitative arts." It has, he finds, an unfortunate "tendency to beget and keep alive in its votaries the imitative propensity. . . . During the last fifty years it has materially advanced. All other arts, how-ever, have, in the same interval, advanced at a far greater rate—*each very nearly in the direct ratio of its non-imitativeness*—painting, for example, least of all—and the effect on the drama is, of course, that of apparent retro-gradation" ("Marginalia," *ER*, 1367; emphasis added). "Imitative propen-sity" was the phrase used to describe the ape's behavior in "Rue Morgue," and the battle for representational supremacy that took place in that story between Dupin's syllabic language and the ape's impassioned gestures is replayed in the excerpt above as an implicit opposition between the imita-tive visual arts—painting, drama, and, after 1839, the daguerreotype—and the nonimitative, language-based arts, which find their model in the tele-graphic cipher.

Commenting on Poe's belief in the "infinite" accuracy of the daguerreo-type, Lisa Cartwright observes that for Poe photography is superior to painting "because it harbors the logic of perspective on a scale beyond the reach of the perception of the unaided eye. The real of the Daguerreotype is not that of the scene reproduced, but that of the unseen, invisible orga-nization of the Daguerreotype's own material properties, *encoded* into the visible."[42] Ultimately, Poe's relation to the photographic image is premised on a comparative analysis in which an immediate "perceptual mode is re-placed by a conceptual or analytic process. This process is ultimately non-visual, arriving at theoretical findings only indirectly founded on sensory impressions. . . . A *visual* aesthetic practice thus becomes a knowledge-producing process that circumvents the conclusiveness of sight."[43] By imagining the daguerreotype as a mimesis that extends beyond the realm of human perception (and note the odd suggestion that in 1839 one might look at a painting through a microscope), Poe discloses his need to atomize the work of art.

The rationale for Poe's counterintuitive approach is not hard to locate: in its association with telegraphic ciphers and with a burgeoning culture of information, the sign becomes a permanent trace of experience. Cryptography represents for Poe a further metaphorization of writing as *vestment*, a form of semiotic protection against the natural world. Given the opportunity, Poe always repudiates his mortal and distorting sense organs, choosing rather to reinforce his sense of the symbolic (not just symbol-making, but constituted by symbols) nature of identity.[44] Information is the form of human memory after experience becomes stabilized as discrete signs.

A similar notion of cryptography appears in the last pages of Gabriel García Márquez's *One Hundred Years of Solitude*, when Aureliano Buendia, the last of the Buendia line, forgets "about his dead ones and the pain of his dead ones" and returns to read the parchments written a century earlier by the itinerant gypsy Melquiades.[45] In his great-grandfather's study, Aureliano discovers that the texts, which had resisted all previous efforts to read them, are in fact the history of the family, written by Melquiades "down to the most trivial details, one hundred years ahead of time":

> He had written it in Sanskrit, which was his mother tongue, and he had encoded the even lines in the private cipher of the Emperor Augustus and the odd ones in a Lacedemonian military code. . . . Aureliano skipped eleven pages so as not to lose time with facts he knew only too well, and he began to decipher the instant that he was living, deciphering it as he lived it, prophesying himself in the act of deciphering the last page of the parchments, as if he were looking into a speaking mirror. (382–83)

García Márquez contrasts these pristine parchments (and the pristine room in which Aureliano writes and studies) with the fecund jungle rotting outside the house. Indeed, *One Hundred Years of Solitude* is constructed on the tension between its tumultuous historical-romance plot and the recalcitrance of its narration, whose impassive involutions of time aim to produce the sense that Melquiades "had concentrated a century of daily episodes in such a way that they coexisted in one instant" (ibid., 381). In its cryptic security, Melquiades' text (a *mise en abime* for the novel) pulls away from human time, leveraging itself against the ongoingness of life, transforming itself into a secret history protected by multiple levels of textual encipherment.

Disembodied Selves

From the middle of the 1830s until Poe's death, physical prostheses increasingly show up in his work, as do instances of immaterial existence that culminate in the late angelic colloquies and mesmeric fiction. These phenomena coexist, as if whatever brought Poe to think of mechanical extensions to the self also led him to conceive of a freedom from any material form. As Michael Bell observes, Poe's "intellectual ruminations of the 1840s were linguistic in nature, precipitated by his effort to find a meaning for a '*mere* word.' . . . Like many of his contemporaries, Poe was fond of discussing literary relations in terms of a spiritual metaphor; he complained, for instance, of artificial imitations of Gibbon's style, that in them 'the body is copied, without the soul, of the phraseology.' Meaning was to expression as the soul to the body, spirit to matter."[46] The ancient distinction between body and soul reemerged with intensity in Poe's work because it provided a vocabulary, however inadequate, to describe the momentous effects of technological change. The relation of body to soul metaphorically duplicates the telegraph's combination of visible code and immanent electrical transmission, as Poe comes to think of the body not as a necessary component of being but as a shell or husk, indifferently organic, designed to house an immaterial self.

One can trace Poe's progressive derealization of the body through several texts written in this period. In 1836, a year after Morse began work on the telegraph, Poe published "Maelzel's Chess-Player." Poe's essay on the chess-playing automaton that traveled along the Eastern seaboard, challenging (and usually beating) all comers at its performances, is a pretext for considering the image of human consciousness as the ghost in the machine. Cribbing heavily from David Brewster's *Letters on Natural Magic*, Poe concludes that far from being "a *pure machine*," as its owner implied, all the internal operations of the more-than-life-sized automaton were "regulated by *mind*, and by nothing else" (*ER*, 1253).[47] "Wherever seen, the most intense curiosity was excited by its appearance, and numerous have been the attempts, by men of all classes, to fathom the mystery of its evolution" (ibid., 1257); eliding the meanings of "evolution," one could argue that the Chess-Player provides Poe with the opportunity for an inquiry into the nature of identity parallel to that centered on the ape in "Rue Morgue." The difference is that in place of the ape's gross corporeality, one finds a construct of artificial parts.

In effect, Poe is striving toward a notion of artificial intelligence, and to that end he draws a long comparison between the Chess-Player and Babbage's Calculating Machine (more properly, his Difference Engine), which impressed Poe so much that he treated it in both his fiction and his criticism.[48] Here he compares the relative sophistication of the Chess-Player to

Babbage's machine: "What shall we think of an engine of wood and metal which can not only compute astronomical and navigation tables to any given extent, but render the exactitude of its operation mathematically certain through its power of correcting its possible errors? What shall we think of a machine which can not only accomplish all this, but actually print off its elaborate results, when obtained, without the slightest intervention of the intellect of man?" (*ER*, 1255).

If the Chess-Player *were* real, he would represent a far more wonderful achievement than the Calculating Machine because, unlike the numbers in a shipping table, the moves in a chess game possess no "determinate progression" (ibid., 1256). The distinction between the rigid sequence of the calculations and the responsiveness of the Chess-Player is, for Poe, something very like intelligence itself; "if we choose to call the [Chess-Player] a *pure machine* we must be prepared to admit that it is, beyond all comparisons, the most wonderful of the inventions of mankind" (ibid.). This Poe will not admit, although by juxtaposing the idea of the automaton with the fixed codes of Babbage's calculator, Poe comes close to modeling human existence as a deterministic combination of the mechanical and the mathematical.

For all the ways in which it prefigures science fiction, "Maelzel's Chess-Player" still insists that there *is* a ghost in the machine, an ensouling principle secretly running the show. But in "The Man that Was Used Up" (1839), Poe implies that one can no longer clearly distinguish between human and machine. Poe liked the story enough to give it "a place of honor, second to 'The Murders in the Rue Morgue,' in both *Phantasy-Pieces* and *Prose Romances*," but "it has often baffled or repelled commentators" (*CW*, 2:376). The grotesqueness of the story's conceit suggests Poe's difficulty in incorporating the derealizing effects of telegraphic cryptography into his fiction. Ostensibly, the story directs its satire against the socially ambitious narrator, who recounts his first acquaintance with "that truly fine-looking fellow, Brevet Brigadier General John A. B. C. Smith," distinguished veteran of the "Bugaboo and Kickapoo" wars. Although afflicted with "a certain *stiffness* of carriage," the General is a man of "*remarkable* appearance" who is in every other way distinguished for his beauty, nobility, and "*air distingué*." Following a comic-Petrarchan admiration of the General's parts ("these were, indeed, the *ne plus ultra* of good legs" [*PT*, 307-8]), the narrator attempts to learn the source of the General's renown, but every time his interlocutors explain, "Why he's the man—," they are interrupted. The narrator decides to ask the General himself, but perceiving that "he delighted, especially, in commenting upon the rapid march of mechanical invention," they speak instead about the technological marvels of the age, a conversation that culminates in speculation on the telegraph: "'There is nothing at all like it,' [the General] would say; 'we are a wonderful people and live in a wonderful age. Parachutes and railroads—man-traps and spring-guns! Our steam-boats are upon every sea, and the Nassau balloon packet is about to run regular trips . . . between London and Timbuctoo. And who shall calculate the immense influence upon social life—upon arts—upon commerce—upon literature—which will be the immediate result of the great principles of electro-magnetics?' " (ibid., 310).

In search of a solution to "this abominable piece of mystery," the narrator visits the General at home, having no intention of "being thwarted touching the *information* I desired" (ibid., 314; emphasis added). Pleading urgent business, he is shown into the bedroom, as the story modulates into the grotesque:

> As I entered the chamber, I looked about, of course, for the occupant, but did not immediately perceive him. There was a large and exceedingly odd-looking bundle of something which lay close by my feet on the floor, and as I was not in the best humor in the world, I gave it a kick out of the way.
>
> "Hem! ahem! rather civil that, I should say!" said the bundle, in one of the smallest, and altogether the funniest little voices, between a squeak and a whistle, that I ever heard in all the days of my existence. (Ibid., 315)

The speaking bundle is nothing less (or more) than the General, and the rest of the story is filled with the narrator's horrified observance of the General's toilette: " 'Strange you shouldn't know me, though, isn't it?' presently re-squeaked the nondescript, which I now perceived was performing, upon the floor, some inexplicable evolution, very analogous to the drawing on of a stocking. There was only a single leg, however, apparent." Deprived of organs lost in battle with the Indians, the General requires the help of a servant to don false leg, arm, shoulders and bosom, wig ("scalping is a rough process after all; but then you can procure such a capital scratch at De L'Orme's"), teeth, eyes, and palate ("they not only knocked in the roof of my mouth, but took the trouble to cut off at least seven-eighths of my tongue"). As the story concludes, "it was evident. It was a clear case. Brevet Brigadier General John A. B. C. Smith was the man—was *the man that was used up*" (ibid., 315–16).

Poe's pun on "used up" has given rise to readings identifying the General with different antebellum politicians, but these fail to explain the story's extended anatomization of Smith, whose most human features turn out to be prosthetic. The General—who lacks "information" in the most physical sense possible—is doubly a cyborg. In addition to his obvious physical extensions, he has the name General John A. B. C. Smith, the circulation of which guarantees him the social identity that his physical amplifications help him inhabit. As Robert Byer brilliantly shows, "The Man That Was Used Up" ruminates on the corrosive effects of publicity in a democracy increasingly stage-managed by the mass media.[49] Poe's story depends on the drama of circulating information—the gossip, news report, and rumor that constitute the public self in an age of mass communication. The joke is that Smith sees nothing odd in this. Unlike his body, his body image is intact: he *is* Brevet Brigadier General John A. B. C. Smith, distinguished veteran, and he perceives no discrepancy between his continual description in society and the "nondescript" bundle of flesh he has become. The bodily ego survives the body, as the General refigures himself with the aid of his multiple prostheses.

Even bereft of spaceships or aliens, "The Man That Was Used Up" is a kind of science fiction, one that registers the effects of telegraphy as an attack on normative concepts of the human. Poe's attitude toward technology here is mixed: Smith's faith in its promises ("Parachutes and railroads— man-traps and spring-guns!") is the butt of satire, but the intended humor is overshadowed by Poe's fascination with the possibility of literalizing the Jacksonian self-made man. Despite the General's talk of electromagnetics, in this vision of the cyborg Poe finds neither utopian transformations in social relations nor simply the loss of the real, but a queasy suggestion that the self, even in its image of the body, is a prosthetic construct whose social well-being depends on the repression of its organic basis.

Five years later, Poe did away with the Chess-Player's troublesome ghost. "The Swiss Bell-Ringers" was a *jeu d'esprit* for the *New York Evening Mirror*, announcing the visit of some Swiss musicians who appeared to great success in New York theaters in 1844 and 1845. Poe took advantage of their elegantly synchronized performances to imagine the self as a robot. His note to the *Evening Mirror* is written to correct

> the *erroneous but common idea that these Bell-ringers are real living beings*. The writer is firmly convinced that they are ingenious pieces of mechanism, contrived on the principle of Maelzel's Automaton Trumpeter and Piano-forte player (exhibited here some years ago), but made so much more perfect and effective by the application to them of the same power which operates in the *Electro-Magnetic* Telegraph, but which should here be called Electro-tintinnabulic. A powerful electric battery under the stage communicates by a hidden wire with each of them, and its shocks are regulated and directed by the skilful musician and mechanician who secretly manages the whole affair. This explains the precision with which they all bow at the same instant, as if moved by the same soul (and so they are—an *electric* one), and keep such perfect time and order. (*CW*, 3:1119)

The object of "The Swiss Bell-Ringers" is clearly to reconsider the automaton in the age of electricity. In their technological purity, the Swiss bell-ringers represent the antithesis of the gross corporeality displayed by the contemporaneous M. Valdemar, who ends his days as "a nearly liquid mass of loathsome—of detestable putridity" (*PT*, 842). Poe has seen the future, and it is *Metropolis*: a world in which the flesh has been replaced by a total-body prosthesis, which serves as a container for the "electric" soul. Given the degree to which Poe's readers tend to attribute aspects of his writing to his character, there is a pleasing symmetry in Poe perhaps being the first of these cyborgs. As Bell notes, in 1850 Evert Duyckinck ungraciously wrote that Poe was "merely a 'Swiss bell-ringer, who from little contrivances of his own, with an ingeniously devised hammer, strikes a sharp melody of his own, which has all that is delightful and affecting, that is attainable without a soul.' "[50]

Dark Fiber

Now, perhaps, one can better evaluate my contention that Poe's science fiction constitutes a series of hidden fibers or threads connecting nineteenth- and twentieth-century literary cultures. Certainly, stories such as "The Man That Was Used Up" and "The Swiss Bell-Ringers" resonate with many accounts of postmodern experience.[51] As Donna Haraway frames it, postmodernism is characterized by the simultaneous collapse of Newtonian space and time and of an organic humanism. Cultural and scientific problems have simultaneously been recast as problems in information processing. Haraway's "Cyborg Manifesto" is premised on the assumption that information is "just that kind of quantifiable element (unit, basis of unity) which allows universal translation, and so unhindered instrumental power."[52] Because of this potential for "universal translation," information has become a universal currency, a transcendental signifier able to bring science, technology, and culture into conversation.

Consequently, information emerges as a unifying characteristic of the postmodern social order. Illustrating the changes between cyborg culture and its nineteenth-century precursors, Haraway pairs a series of key terms with their postmodern equivalents. These include the following:

Representation	Simulation
Bourgeois novel, realism	Science fiction, postmodernism
Organism	Biotic component
Depth, integrity	Surface, boundary
Reproduction	Replication
Mind	Artificial Intelligence[53]

The problem with using this list as a tool to clarify different historical periods is that Poe's cryptographic fiction *already* embraces all the terms Haraway associates with postmodernity. With their thinking machines, automata, prostheses, simulacra, invented voyages, synthetic identities, and textual replications, Poe's tales are founded on a repudiation of the terms (representation, realism, depth, integrity) used to characterize nineteenth-century fiction, and on the embrace of simulation in their stead.

The inference to be drawn is not that Haraway's scheme is generally wrong, but that Poe's recognition of the cultural power of information in an era of telecommunications was remarkably prescient. In antebellum America, the almost simultaneous creation of the penny press, railroads, transatlantic packet ships, and the telegraph contributed to the rise of a literary public interested in producing, consuming, and exchanging information.[54] In concert with these developments, Poe's writing "derives its raw materials not from divine inspiration, experience, or a discrete literary tradition, but instead from the whole jumbled mass of information that has been accumulating from ancient times down to the present moment."[55] Poe could exhibit a prodigious mastery of this jumble: in "The Mystery of Marie Rogêt," he produced pages of technical minutiae, much of it imported wholesale from newspaper coverage of the murdered Mary Rogers. In the hoaxes, Poe manipulated his audience's hunger for novelty to create factual-sounding pieces about the crossing of the Atlantic ("The Balloon-Hoax"), or the transmutation of lead into gold ("Von Kempelen and His Discovery"), even inserting his fiction into a genuine scientific discourse: "By reference to the 'Diary of Sir Humphrey Davy,' (Cottle and Munro, London, pp. 150), it will be seen at pp. 53 and 82, that this illustrious chemist had not only conceived the idea now in question, but had actually made *no inconsiderable progress, experimentally*, in the very *identical analysis* now so triumphantly brought to an issue by Von Kempelen" (*PT*, 909).

"The Man That Was Used Up" seems to be smack in the middle of translating itself from Haraway's left-hand column to her right-hand column, as the narrator realizes with shock that there is something profoundly dehumanizing in the miraculous technologies of the present. What is dehumanizing, though, is not an Orwellian subjection to the machine, but the machine's subjugation to human fantasies and desires. Even by Poe's loose standards, the General in "The Man That Was Used Up" and Scheherazade in "The Thousand-and-Second Tale of Scheherazade" are mere effigies through which Poe makes his joking points. The continuous Petrarchanism of description in the story is Poe's labored way of showing up the structural failure of representation in a time of prosthesis. The General's perfect appearance—his "richly flowing" hair, his "mouth utterly unequalled," with "the most brilliantly white of all conceivable teeth," from which issued "a voice of surpassing clearness, melody, and strength" (*PT*, 307–8): all these are simulations, biotic components extrinsic to the "squeaking bundle" himself. By dissolving such root concepts as self, character, and body, the advance of technology obviates realism as a mode of representation.

The General's transfiguration into a bionic man follows from the prosthesis of telegraphy.[56] Clearly, the telegraph is not Poe's manifest subject. But the theme of technological celebration coincides with the story's interest in prosthetics in the General's otherwise unaccountable paean to telegraphic communication, with its "immense influence upon social life—upon arts—upon commerce—upon literature." In "Scheherazade," too, the telegraph is linked to the body's fragmentation: describing the telegraph and teleprinter to the Caliph, Scheherazade claims that a wizard "had cultivated his voice to so great an extent that he could have made himself heard from one end of the earth to the other. Another had so long an arm that he could sit down in Damascus and indite a letter at Bagdad—or indeed at any distance whatsoever" (*PT*, 802). Unable to find an experiential parallel to the telegraph's power, Poe extends these wizards' hands and voices to absurd dimensions, in a moment of ostensibly comic anthropomorphism.

As "The Man That Was Used Up" and "Scheherazade" indicate, technological progress anachronizes the present. Technology is a machine of cultural displacement, one whose positive moment is utopian futurism and whose negative moment is the countervailing realization that the past will be rendered illegible by change over time. Both moments are visible in the late satire "Mellonta Tauta," which purports to be the translation of a letter written by "Pundita," "On Board Balloon 'Skylark,' April 1, 2848." Although "Mellonta Tauta" celebrates such marvels as magnetically driven ocean liners and a transatlantic telegraph, Poe also reminds us that *tempora mutantur*—times change, and we change with them. Pundita's knowledge of the past is woefully corrupt: like the conquering primates in *Planet of the Apes*, she has only a wayward sense of the "savage" lives lived by the "Jurmains," "Vrinch," and the "Amriccans" in the dim past of the nineteenth century. Through Pundita's garbled history, Poe discredits the notion of cultural progress.

Poe also understands that despite its breathtaking speed, the telegraph contributes nothing to the historical transmission of culture. Indeed, its speed may actually interfere with our perception of the world. In her letter, Pundita recalls a "flight on the railroad across the Kanadaw continent" taken at "fully three hundred miles the hour." "*That* was travelling," she exclaims, in a familiar association of travel, modernity, and collapsing space. Yet something is lost with such haste: "Do you remember what an odd sensation was experienced when, by chance, we caught a glimpse of external objects while the cars were in full flight? Everything seemed unique—in one mass" (*PT*, 878). Rather strikingly, Poe virtually invents the idea of dark fiber himself when, in a story primarily about the telegraph, he discusses how the railroad lines laid down in his own era predict the paths of future development: "Pundit says that the route for the great Kanadaw railroad must have been in some measure marked out about nine hundred years ago! In fact, he goes so far as to assert that actual traces of a road are still discernible—traces referable to a period quite as remote as that mentioned. The track, it appears, was *double* only; ours, you know, has twelve paths" (ibid., 879). The communications technologies of the next millennium, Poe suggests, will follow paths laid down today (just as, by implication, the science fiction of the future will follow the contours established by Poe's postdated letter to the future).[57]

At the birth of the telegraph, Poe imagines how seamlessly the new technology will be integrated into ordinary life. "What *would* we do without the Atalantic telegraph?" Pundita asks. To judge by her own writing, the answer is: not much differently. Peering down from her transatlantic balloon, Pundita witnesses "the magnetic cutter in charge of the middle section of floating telegraph wires. I learn that when this species of telegraph was first put into operation by Horse, it was considered quite impossible to convey the wires over sea; but now we are at a loss to comprehend where the difficulty lay! So wags the world" (*PT*, 873). Horse or Morse; Aries Tottle or Aristotle; Cant or Kant: what does it matter? Writing at the moment of American empire, Poe explodes the boosterism of the day by imagining his America dissolved by time into illegible fragments. Echoing the era's fascination with Egyptian monuments and their "lost" originary writing (a theme treated with apparent respect in *Narrative of A. Gordon Pym*), "Mellonta Tauta" sacrilegiously concludes with the unearthing of some "genuine Amriccan relics belonging to the tribe called Knickerbocker," including an inscription on a monument in memory of George Washington, on "the anniversary of the surrender of Lord Cornwallis to General Washington at Yorktown, A.D. 1781"—an event Pundita interprets as the prelude to cannibalistic sacrifice.

Cybernetic Reading

Today, a century and a half after Poe's experiments in science fiction, the influence of his writing is most profoundly felt in a generalized sense of the cryptographic collapse of space and time, and in the simultaneous interest in the nature and function of information. Occasionally one meets with revisions of specific texts by Poe, as in the mathematician and novelist Rudy Rucker's *Hollow Earth* (1991), a vivid continuation of the adventures of Arthur Gordon Pym. But a more typical form of debt is that exhibited by William Gibson and Bruce Sterling in *The Difference Engine*, which explores the wonderfully Poe-like consequences that follow from their conceit that Charles Babbage *had* successfully produced a workable steam-driven version of his Difference Engine in the mid–nineteenth century, thus introducing the computer revolution into the midst of Victorian England.[58]

Like every cyberpunk author, Gibson is explicitly concerned with the social and cultural valence of information. That social identities are formed out of encoded signs is to him a commonplace, the jumping-off point for his fiction. But this development of a culture based on the abstract power of binary ciphers comes at a price. For Jaron Lanier, founder of Virtual Perception Laboratories, information can be described as alienated experience—the result of a process by which some form of perceptual knowledge is translated into formal expression, distant from the body that originally knew it.[59] Such alienation has always been a price paid for the acquisition of culture, but in a world of texts, the overwhelming amount of information constitutes an assault on human identity. This spread of digital communications has produced a corresponding desire to "reexperientalize" information—which means, among other things, to render it visible, bounded, hieroglyphic. For Lanier and Gibson, one response is to reconvert complex forms of information back into perceptual entities, as in the helmet and data-glove of Lanier's virtual systems, or in the imagined cyberspace of Gibson's *Neuromancer.*

For Gibson, digitizing information leads to a conception of the computer as a cryptographic matrix, within which a series of electrical ones and zeroes translate the world into data. Arguing that "information is the dominant scientific metaphor of our age, so we need to face it, to try to understand what it means," Gibson acknowledges that "Newtonians didn't see things in terms of information exchange, but today we do."[60] Such exchanges center on the electronic computer, whose digital codes represent a two-dimensional key to an imagined three-dimensional space. As Gibson remarks, "Everyone I know who works with computers seems to develop a belief that there's some kind of *actual space* behind the screen, someplace you can't see but you know is there."[61] Like the cryptogram, the computer is unlocked with a code and operated with a code, and like the cryptogram, the computer is ostensibly infallible. The computer becomes a modern philosopher's stone, capable of transforming matter into data, which can then be statistically reprocessed to reveal truths about the world never visible to the eye.

On its appearance, *Neuromancer* was widely praised for its innovative imagination of virtual reality.[62] Yet what seems newest in Gibson's novel turns out to have deep roots in Poe's treatment of technology. Extrapolating from Lanier's desire to experience information, Gibson imagines a time when computer networks have become so extensive, and information so oppressive, that information systems have to be recoded as perceptual structures known as cyberspace. The novel's protagonist is Case, an "interface cowboy" trained to steal computer data from these vast computer networks by patching electrodes on his temples and "jacking in" to cyberspace. For the duration of the interface, Case transforms himself into a virtual self within the vividly three-dimensional world of the computer network, breaking and entering data banks.

Late in *Neuromancer* Case jacks in, only to discover blankness: "no matrix, no grid, no cyberspace" (233). Instead, he finds himself on a beach near a bunker in which he encounters Linda Lee, a former girlfriend who had died earlier in the novel. Case has been incorporated into a kind of CD-

ROM world produced within cyberspace by a renegade artificial intelligence named Neuromancer. Trapped there, Case gradually accustoms himself to its real unreality and eventually makes love to the synthesized version of Linda Lee, discovering "a strength that ran in her" that he had "always managed to forget."

> It belonged, he knew—he remembered—as she pulled him down, to the meat, the flesh the cowboys mocked. It was a vast thing, beyond knowing, a sea of information coded in spiral and pheromone, infinite intricacy that only the body, in its strong blind way, could ever read.
>
> The zipper hung, caught, as he opened the French fatigues, the coils of toothed nylon clotted with salt. He broke it, some tiny metal part shooting off against the wall as salt-rotten cloth gave, and then he was in her, effecting the transmission of the old message. Here, even here, in a place he knew for what it was, a coded model of some stranger's memory, the drive held. (Ibid., 239–40)

This is incoherent, not just because Case's epiphany over incarnation occurs in the disembodied nonplace of cyberspace, but also because the body itself turns out to be an unbelievably complex machine for information processing: "a vast thing, beyond knowing, a sea of information coded in spiral and pheromone." In *Neuromancer*, information is all there is—a point that Gibson drives home by treating sex, a token for the embodied real, as the ultimate form of cryptography, in which the text written into the DNA of Case's semen effloresces into three-dimensional existence. That there *is* no semen here—that the whole thing is a cognitive shell game—does not interfere with Gibson's point, since the central drama of cyberpunk is just this type of failed Manichean encounter between an embodied and a symbolic identity in which the binary terms collapse.[63]

Indeed, *Neuromancer* depends on this oxymoronic movement between representation and simulation, as when we learn that only the "strong blind" body has the right sort of vision for "reading" the genetic text. The novel oscillates between the careful representation of throwaway moments, whose pointless quiddity functions as a code for the real ("the zipper hung, caught, as he opened the French fatigues, the coils of toothed nylon clotted with salt"), and the abstraction of Case's thought ("effecting the transmission of the old message"). Consider the moment when, after making love with Linda and falling asleep, Case is roused by distant sound:

> The music woke him, and at first it might have been the beat of his own heart. He sat up beside her, pulling his jacket over his shoulders in the predawn chill, gray light from the doorway and the fire long dead. His vision crawled with ghost hieroglyphs, translucent lines of symbols arranging themselves against the neutral backdrop of the bunker wall. He looked at the back of his hands, saw faint neon molecules crawling beneath the skin, ordered by the unknow-

able code. He raised his right hand and moved it experimentally. It left a faint, fading tail of strobed afterimages. (Ibid., 241)

Case's perceptual field is interrupted by music that a friend is blasting into the ears of the jacked-in cowboy. As the neural interference of the music shatters his absorption in the construct, Case experiences its dissolution into digital code. Case finds himself revealed as signs. Taking advantage of the beach's dissolution, he walks out of the cyberspace construct and back into his real life.

As these excerpts imply, it is often impossible to know what should count as the real within the novel's representations. To Case and to the reader, the beach construct feels every bit (or byte) as authentic as the world from which Case has come (itself a space station specializing in terrestrial simulation). Gibson seems to want it both ways, validating the body's quiddity even as that body is revealed as only a sophisticated textual processor, translating information about the world into sensible percepts in ways that computers can only approximate. In the last analysis, *Neuromancer*'s novelty derives from literary effects that originate in Poe's information-oriented revision of Defoe. Case's engagement with the codes of cypherspace transparently figures the reader's relation to the text, alternately experienced as a fully fleshed world and as a series of foreign signs. One can, in fact, locate the model for Case's cyberspace dissolve at the origin of the novel, on another beach just off the coast of Brazil (itself an alien new world): "I was exceedingly Surprized with the print of a Man's naked Foot on the shore. . . . But after innumerable fluttering Thoughts, like a Man perfectly confus'd and out of my self, I came Home to my Fortification, not feeling, as we say, the Ground I went on." [64]

By the time of *Neuromancer*, the loss of the real that Crusoe experiences at the sight of the footprint has now become a "natural" fact of existence. Unlike Crusoe, who panics in the face of the alienating print, Case is rescued from his claustrophobic construct by the dissolution of the text's representations into signs. For Case, the system of the code is a source of power, not of fear. The difference between Gibson and Defoe is finally Poe—not only because the caverns in *Pym* mark the moment when, by exploiting the semiotic rupture in Defoe's realist adventure, a certain kind of science fiction was born, but also, and more importantly, because Poe's cryptograph offers a primary source for the denaturalized technological power that Case (and presumably the reader) experiences through Case's command of symbols. In *Neuromancer*, the problems posed by Poe and ostensibly resolved by the hieroglyph have come full circle: although the hieroglyph attempts to unite symbol and percept by making the former an image, one aspect of Poe's modernity consists of his cryptographic willingness to understand information as the basis of perception.

Ultimately, Poe intimates, our knowledge of the world is symbolic, not material. In this he anticipates the striking identification of the self with data in *Neuromancer*, which concludes with a vision of Case both inside and outside the data system of the computer (and, by extension, the virtual reality of the novel). The end of Gibson's book represents the culmination of a logic lodged darkly in the fibers of Poe's science fiction. (How unlikely must it have once seemed for a fiber to carry light, or language?) Case's dual existence (as body and as data) repeats a separation initiated by the discovery of writing, that first prosthesis. It is predicated, too, on the death of Newtonian space and time, which structure the coordinates of our mortality. Case is, then, immortal: deprived of linear spatial and temporal trajectories, Case fissions in two, bound both to the flesh and to the colder runes of data.

Despite its erotic investment in codes and data, though, the conclusion of *Neuromancer* betrays a nostalgic attachment to the Adamic nature of the hieroglyph. Saved from the digital construct of the beach, Case goes on to witness the electric synthesis of Wintermute and Neuromancer, to collect the money owed him, and to get a new liver and pancreas to replace the poisoned sacs within him. He returns to Earth, back to work as a data cowboy, when, "one October night,"

> punching himself past the scarlet tiers of the Eastern Seaboard Fission Authority, he saw three figures, tiny, impossible, who stood at the very edge of one of the vast steps of data. Small as they were, he could make out the boy's grin, his pink gums, the glitter of the long gray eyes that had been Riviera's. Linda still wore his jacket; she waved, as he passed. But the third figure, close behind her, arm across her shoulders, was himself.[65]

Peering into cyberspace, Case sees himself in the distance, a small Adam, his own hieroglyph. With that moment, *Neuromancer* reaches the culmination of a certain fantasy of identity and information, now ubiquitous, that was first shaped by the telegraphic prose of Poe's science fiction.

EFFECTS

What is genius? What is inspiration? What is that which men call the creative impulse and where does it originate? . . . These are questions I have set out to answer in the following pages.

Henry Hollen, *Clairaudient Transmission*

Everybody who says the same words is the same person if the spectra are the same only they happen differently in time, you dig?

Thomas Pynchon, *The Crying of Lot 49*

RESURREXI

5

Poe in the Crypt of Lizzie Doten

The "post-mortem effects" . . . of Poe's cryogenic project to survive by
artificial textual means point to his willed plot to return to future readers
as a ghostly autobiographical figure still haunting these texts.

Louis Renza, "Poe's Secret Autobiography"

Edgar A. Poe was a medium. "A medium!" you say. "He himself would
scorn the name; and we, who knew him, deny it."

Lizzie Doten, "The Mysteries of Godliness"

Literary Influence in a Cryptographic Age

The nature of Poe's influence is perhaps the most vexed case in all of literature. In Europe, Japan, and South America, Poe has long ranked as one of
the world's great writers. Poe was for Charles Baudelaire "the most powerful writer of the age," and for Paul Valéry "the only impeccable writer."[1] Yet
Poe's success abroad goes in tandem with a miserably divided reputation at
home. From Rufus Griswold to Harold Bloom, many American critics have
described Poe not just as an overrated writer, not even merely as a *bad* writer,
but as a *hoax*.[2] Indeed, Patrick Quinn wrote an entire book (*The French Face
of Edgar Allan Poe*) to explain the "astonishing paradox" that Baudelaire—
indubitably a genius—regarded Poe as one of the world's major writers.
Quinn admits that he set out as a detective determined to reveal a dirty
truth about Poe's French reputation: the book was to be "a kind of *exposé*,"
the "history of a great misunderstanding, or even a great hoax," in which
Baudelaire was to be the "villain."[3] Even during his lifetime, Poe's writing
had begun to take on this split reputation, as in the couplet by James Russell
Lowell: "There comes Poe, with his Raven, like Barnaby Rudge,/Three
fifths of him genius and two fifths sheer fudge."[4] Like other antithetical
characterizations of Poe—as aesthete or hack, arch-Romantic or cynical
parodist—Lowell's couplet suggests the polarized nature of Poe's reception.

Yet to say, as critics have done, that Poe is either a master writer or a
fake; either a paragon of purity or a dangerous source of literary contami-

115

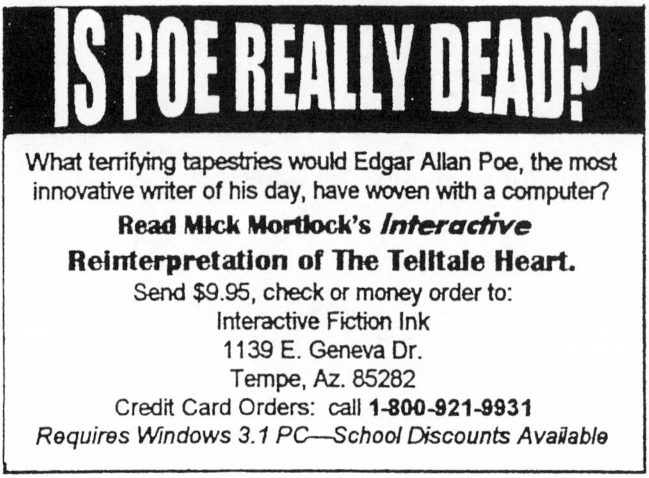

Figure 11. *Is* Poe dead? Besides Mortlock's "interactive" retelling of "The Tell-Tale Heart," recent Poe imitations and homages include Paul Auster's hieroglyphic detective novel *City of Glass*; Rudy Rucker's *Hollow Earth*; Angela Carter's "Cabinet of Edgar Allan Poe" in *Black Venus*; and William Vollman's "Grave of Lost Stories" in *Thirteen Stories and Thirteen Epitaphs*. From an advertisement in *Poets & Writers* (Nov.–Dec. 1994).

nation; either a fount for modernism or an immature writer best read in childhood, is to betray a deep uncertainty about exactly what literature is. If, as Shoshana Felman suggests, no poet "has been as highly acclaimed and, at the same time, as violently disclaimed as Edgar Allan Poe," this is not merely a matter of taste, like the question of whether one prefers the poetry of W. B. Yeats or Wallace Stevens, or whether one imagines *Vandover and the Brute* to be a neglected masterpiece.[5] Instead, Poe's reputation is a puzzle: even after the exertions represented by his book, Quinn admits that "the extravagant esteem in which Poe is held in France, and in Europe generally, will remain something of a mystery to me."[6] And in "From Poe to Valéry," T. S. Eliot describes Poe's writing as "a stumbling block to the judicial critic," concluding only that Poe's influence remains a "mystery" or "enigma" more noted than explained.[7]

As Eliot noted, referring to Poe's effects on figures as different as Valéry and H. Rider Haggard, Poe made himself felt "in types of writing where such influence would hardly be expected."[8] But Poe's influence is not limited to literature. More film adaptations have been made of Poe's work than of any other American writer, ranging from drive-in horror movies to a striking association between Poe and the cinematic avant-garde that dates back to D. W. Griffith.[9]

No single mechanism explains the process by which readers have come to identify with Poe's writings. But to a great degree, Poe's bifurcated cultural influence derives from his "mediumization," in the literary, spiritual, and telecommunicative senses of that word. Poe's literary legacy is, therefore, constituted not only by the preservation of texts but by Poe's reproduction by other writers, in a process of doubling that exploits the cryptographically blurred relations between words and identity. Responding to a newspaper attack on "The Facts in the Case of M. Valdemar," Poe wrote: "*Why* cannot a man talk after he is dead? *Why?—Why?*—that is the question; and as soon as the *Tribune* has answered it to our satisfaction we will talk to it further" (*CW*, 3:1230). The replicative strategies embedded within Poe's texts could be described as Poe's attempt to keep talking after death, as he is ventriloquized through the words of later readers, or, as is often the case, through their intense prosopopoeial fantasies of collective authorship.

In 1903, for instance, Alfred Russel Wallace wrote to the critic Ernest Marriot in order to determine the origins of "Leonainie." The poem, Wallace explained, had been given to him in manuscript by his brother, along with a note attesting that it had been written by Poe "at a Wayside Inn in lieu of cash for one night's board and lodging." To his surprise, Wallace was unable to find the poem in any edition of Poe's poetry; a pity, because the poem was clearly an exemplary instance of Poe's art.[10] As Wallace wrote, "the rhythm is most exquisite, and the form of verse different from any other I can call to mind in the double triplets of rhymes in each verse, carried on throughout by simple, natural and forcible expressions."[11]

LEONAINIE

Leonainie, angels named her, and they took the light
Of the laughing stars and framed her, in a smile of white,
And they made her hair of gloomy midnight, and her eyes of bloomy
Moonshine, and they brought her to me in a solemn night.

In a solemn night of summer, when my heart of gloom
Blossomed up to greet the comer, like a rose in bloom.
All foreboding that distressed me, I forgot as joy caressed me,
Lying joy that caught and pressed me, in the arms of doom.

Only spake the little lisper in the angel tongue,
Yet I, listening, heard the whisper; "songs are only sung
Here below that they may grieve you, tales are told you to deceive you,
So must Leonainie leave you, while her love is young."

Then God smiled, and it was morning, matchless and supreme,
Heaven's glory seemed adorning earth with its esteem,
Every heart but mine seem gifted with a voice of prayer and lifted,
When my Leonainie drifted from me like a dream.

Already in this first of what would become seventeen letters to Marriot, Wallace's interest in "Leonainie" rapidly shifts to a general discussion of Poe's poetry, with Wallace particularly recommending a series of late poems, including "The Streets of Baltimore" ("a wonderful description of his last hours") and the much-loved "Farewell to Earth." At this point, the reader's ears may perk up: "Leonainie"? "The Streets of *Baltimore*"? Poe wrote none of these poems in his lifetime. Instead, all except "Leonainie" had first appeared in *Poems from the Inner Life*, an 1862 collection of verse dictated to the Boston spiritualist Lizzie Doten during a trance. For Wallace, the six spirit-poems dictated by Poe in that volume are "finer and deeper and grander poems than any written by him in the earth-life," though he concedes that, "being given through *another* brain, they are deficient in the exquisite music and rhythm of his best-known work."[12]

I will return to the provenance of "Leonainie." First, however, I want to consider Lizzie Doten and her *Poems from the Inner Life* as a parable for the nature of cryptographic influence in the age of telecommunications. So far as I know, her poems have never been subject to critical attention, and today her work is forgotten. Yet in her way Doten was one of Poe's most faithful readers, and for decades her poetry constituted a set of Poe apocrypha that sometimes rivaled the legitimate canon. (Seventeen editions of *Poems from the Inner Life* were published from 1862 to 1901.) In most respects, Doten is the antithesis of a cryptographic writer: not for her the cryptographer's recombinant formalism or emphasis on the protective carapace of code. But as we saw from Poe's correspondence with Tyler (or with himself), secret writing fosters an unnerving literary intimacy among reader, text, and writer that serves as a central mechanism of Poe's influence. In her secret identification with Poe's writing, Doten reveals herself to be a profoundly cryptographic figure.

As Jorge Luis Borges has observed, "every writer is undertaking two quite different works at the same time." In addition to the specific poem or fable a writer composes, the writer also creates an image of himself or herself. In the case of Poe, Borges adds, "our image . . . is more important than any of the lines on the pages that he wrote. We think of Poe as we may think of a character in fiction. . . . And creating a very vivid image and leaving that to the memory of the world is a very important task."[13] In some cases, identification with Poe's image is so powerful that it converts Poe's readers into writers who compose in the place of the master. Poe's *oeuvre* thus represents the ultimate problem in literary cryptography, as if Poe wrote in an invisible ink that only became legible in its effects on future texts. According to Doten, many of her poems were "given under direct spirit influence before public audiences. For many of them I could not obtain the authorship, but for such as I could, the names are given."[14] The name she gave most often, and most successfully, was that of Poe. The aim of this chapter is to explore what that name represented to Doten, and to a culture that remains scripted by his writing.

Resurrexi

Spiritualism began in 1848 in Hydesville, New York, when "the mysterious noises which for some time had disturbed nocturnal peace in the farmhouse of John D. Fox suddenly began responding to the commands of thirteen-year-old Margaret Fox and her twelve-year-old sister Kate." Forty years later the sisters confessed that they "had meant only to tease their superstitious mother by cracking their toe-joints against the bedstead; but for the next three decades the communication with the dead that they initiated was a conspicuous feature of American culture."[15] Indeed, spiritualism has been remarkably long-lived. There were renewals of interest in the 1870s, and again near the turn of the century: like cocaine addiction and close reading, American spiritualism runs on a thirty-year cycle. Eighteen forty-eight was the year of the Seneca Falls Convention as well as of the rappings in Hydesville; from its inception, spiritualism served almost as a fifth column in the struggle for gender equality. (Doten, for instance, often channeled spirits who argued on behalf of women's rights.)[16]

The movement also liberated the pen, as female spiritualists turned to the use of a *nom d'âme* to circumvent the gender and class restrictions placed on their writing. Possessed by the spirit of a Quaker named Patience Worth, Pearl Curran poured forth a "serious and torrential literary output, dictating plays, dramatic poems, and novels," most of which were published; when entranced, she could write two works at once, shifting effortlessly back and forth between them. In 1928, Aura May Hollen "burst suddenly into song," an event that so shocked her husband that he wrote a book trying to explain the phenomenon.[17] For the lucky few, spiritualism even provided a career: Doten made a better living through trance-lectures and royalties received from volumes of poetry, a novel (*Hesper the Home Spirit: A Story of Household Labor and Love*), and a collection of short fiction than she ever had as an impoverished needleworker and teacher.[18]

But spiritualism was also a way of negotiating the advance of technology and a rising secularism. It achieved this by combining a mesmeric faith in a magnetic spirit with telegraphic techniques for reaching the dead in their vague and ecumenical afterlife. Mediums like the Fox sisters relied on the spirit telegraph, similar to the Ouija board, in which spirits communicated by rapping on the walls or floor when the correct letter of the alphabet was called out by a human being. Mediums also employed automatic writing, lightly resting fingers on a planchette, a heart-shaped, wheeled board with a pencil or stylus that would begin to scribble of its own accord. The records of such experiences appeared both in ordinary journals and in house organs such as the *Spiritual Telegraph* and the *Banner of Light*, which also published spirit-writings by Swedenborg, Rousseau, Shelley, Keats, and the ubiquitous Francis Bacon. This outpouring of memoirs, investigations, and testimonies in turn became fodder for scores of short stories and novels that took spiritualism as their subject, including Nathaniel Hawthorne's *Blithedale Romance*, Henry James's *Bostonians*, and W. D. Howells's *That Undiscovered Country*.[19]

In this context, Poe's close association with spiritualism seems fitting. Poe was the most frequent guest contributor to spiritualist journals, in which one clairaudient—Lydia Tenney—lobbied to have her "Message from the Spirit of E. A. Poe" added to Poe's collected works.[20] To Poe's scandalized bemusement, stories such as "The Facts in the Case of M. Valdemar" and "Mesmeric Revelation" were sometimes read not as satires on mesmerism but as case histories, as when "Mesmeric Revelation" was straight-facedly reproduced in the London *Popular Record of Modern Science*.[21] Then, too, Poe's gothic romances are notoriously sites of the undead, who speak through or reinhabit earthly bodies. When Poe died in 1849, one year into the spiritualist craze, his own writing had helped set the stage for his reappearance.

It is not merely Poe's taste for spectral presences that won him a spiritualist following; it is also the way his writing associates electricity, telecommunications, and the occult. In *The Telephone Book*, Avital Ronell brilliantly analyzes the psychoanalytical dimensions of that technology, which "acts as a monument to an irreducible disconnection and thus runs like incorporation, a kind of pathology inhibiting mourning, offering an alternative to the process of introjection. . . . The refusal to mourn causes the lost 'love object' to be preserved in a crypt like a mummy, maintained as the binding around what is not there."[22] Describing a painting by Anselm Kiefer, Mark Taylor continues Ronell's imagery of telecommunicative binding. "When lines are cut and cords severed," he writes, "calls cannot be completed, for no one is ever home. In this cryptic space, from this cryptic space, there is no 'resurrexi.'"[23]

This may be true for Kiefer, but the overwhelming lesson of Poe's writing is that there is always a *resurrexi*. Not for nothing is this the title of Doten's most famous poem, for spiritualism aims to deny loss by preserving a phantasmatic cord to the speaking dead. According to Ronell, "the telephone operates along lines whose structures promote phantasmic, unmediated, instantaneous, magical, sometimes hallucinatory flashes,"[24] and to a considerable extent, this is true of the telegraph as well. From the start, the telegraph was used to communicate with the hereafter, as in N. P. Willis's "Post-Mortuum Soiree" with the Fox sisters at the home of Rufus Griswold, at which the guests included James Fenimore Cooper and William Cullen Bryant.[25] Although Poe (perhaps put off by Griswold) made no appearance at this 1855 séance, Willis felt rappings jar the furniture, and he jested that "if these knocking answers to questions are made (as many insist) by *electric detonations*, and if disembodied spirits are still moving, consciously, among us, and have thus found an agent, at last, ELECTRICITY, *by which they can communicate with the world they have left*, it must soon, in the progressive nature of things, ripen to an intercourse between this and the spirit-world."[26] The prospect of such electrospiritual technologies is one that Willis rather welcomes: "An electric telegraph across the Styx, before they get one across the Atlantic, would make death less of a separation from friends than a voyage to Europe—but there is no end to the speculation on the subject, and we leave it with our readers."[27]

Willis's joke is spiritualism's history: writers such as W. W. Aber explicitly ascribed transcendental properties to the modes of electric communication. One spiritualist called electricity " 'the God principles at work,' while another believed that 'the delicate organization' of spirits enabled them to produce a 'refined species of electricity' through which they communicated with living people." An early message attributed to Benjamin Franklin credited the success of the telegraph to "the intelligence of disembodied voices."[28] This association of spirit and telecommunication continued throughout the century, in such developments as "spirit typewriting" and "spirit telepathy," in which a medium armed only with an ordinary telegraphic key, a sounder, and a battery learned to "receive words and messages through the Morse alphabet."[29]

Like the spiritualists' quest to speak with the dead, literary influence is a form of speaking with the past, and technological devices such as the spirit telegraph analogize the process by which Poe's writing reproduces itself in his readers. There is no saying what given reader will fix on what given text, but Poe is extremely skilled at mobilizing identification with his author-impression—so successful that for a century Poe's reputation was shaped by biographical projections onto his figure that mimic those of spiritualists such as Doten. Consider the case of Poe's first biographer, the Reverend Rufus Griswold. A minor poet whose relationship with Poe had long been strained by literary squabbles and by their shared pursuit of the writer Fanny Osgood, Griswold was nonetheless Poe's appointed literary executor, and the scathing attack he appended to the first collected edition of Poe's work fixed the stereotype of Poe as a morally dangerous drunkard.

Griswold's attack is predicated on the assumption of a continuity between Poe and his writing. "Every genuine author," Griswold wrote in Poe's obituary, "leaves in his works, whatever their design, traces of his personal character."[30] Hence, Griswold sought to accomplish his "literary execution" of Poe by conflating Poe's life with his writings, even resorting to the use of other texts to blacken Poe's name. In the *New York Daily Tribune* obituary (published under the pen name "Ludwig"), Griswold included "an ugly paragraph" pulled verbatim from Edward George Bulwer-Lytton's novel *The Caxtons*, in which Francis Vivian is described as someone

> "without moral susceptibility and having within himself little or nothing of the true point of honor." By quoting these terrible judgments in Poe's obituary, Griswold intended to imply that they were applicable to Poe's personality. Even worse, when Griswold reprinted the same paragraph in his *Memoir* of Poe, he omitted the quotation marks. Thus Bulwer-Lytton's damnation of his fictional character was read and accepted as Griswold's own judgment of Poe, and incalculable damage was done to Poe's reputation.[31]

At the same time, Griswold rewrote Poe's letters to cast himself as Poe's savior. On 24 February 1845, Poe wrote to Griswold in a letter of striking irony: "You so perfectly understand me, or what I have aimed at, in all my poems: I did not think you had so much delicacy of appreciation joined with your strong sense; I can say truly that no man's approbation gives me so much pleasure." But in Griswold's published version of the letter, Poe begins with " 'a thousand thanks for your kindliness in the matter of those books which I could not afford to buy, and had so much need of.' There is no slightest trace of this sentence in the actual letter, nor any reference to any gift of books."[32] That Griswold had understood Poe's writing is borne out by his appropriation of the motif of letter-revision from "The Purloined Letter," a literalization that confirms Griswold's identification with Dupin, who triumphs over Poe's incarnation of Minister D——.

It was to disprove Griswold's calumnies that John Henry Ingram became Poe's next biographer. Through his indefatigable correspondence with Poe's friends and associates, Ingram created a collection of primary evidence that runs to more than one thousand items. Along with Ingram's own biographical writings—ten volumes of editions and biographies, fifty-six articles, and dozens of published letters—this collection (now housed at the University of Virginia) has formed the basis for all subsequent Poe biography, a half-century-long reconstruction of Poe's life and publications that is, in John Carl Miller's words, a legacy "literally without parallel in the annals of biography."[33]

The impetus behind Ingram's labor was an overwhelming identification with Poe's writing. Reading Poe seems to have blurred the distinction between Poe's words and Ingram's own literary aspirations. As Miller tells it, Ingram (who postdated his birth from 1842 to 1849, to coincide with Poe's death) felt a "mystic rapport with the personality of the dead Poe," and while reading his poetry "for perhaps the 500th time," "felt something stir within himself": "He quivered with 'intense excitement,' feeling as though 'a star had burst within [his] brain.' He fell to his knees to thank his Creator for having made him, too, a poet. Seizing a pencil, he wrote, after the manner of Poe, a wild lyric that he named 'The Imprisoned Soul.'"[34] Dozens more poems followed "after the manner of Poe," one of which, an imitation of "Ulalume" called "Hope: An Allegory," was reprinted in Walter Hamilton's *Parodies*—a form of literary success not intended by Ingram.[35] Eventually, Ingram compensated for his Apollonian inadequacy by reshaping his life as an effort "to cleanse Poe's besmirched literary and personal reputations," sublimating his literary ambition in a biographical project predicated on what can only be described as a bad case of prosopoPoeia.[36] Ingram made his name as a writer by clearing Poe's, using his textual reconstruction as the basis of a new joint identity with Poe—a psychic superimposition that was even more uncanny because one of Ingram's few nonbiographical works was his *Philosophy of Handwriting*, an imitation of Poe's "Autography" essays that Ingram published under the pseudonym "Don Felix de Salmanca."[37]

Ultimately, the biographies of Griswold and Ingram are structured according to the same breathtakingly symmetrical antitheses found at work throughout Poe's detective fiction. Both men mediated their writing through inverse figures of Poe; both spent much of their lives in pseudonymous attacks on or defenses of that character. Griswold and Ingram, "Ludwig" and "Don Felix": all four figures are partially products of Poe's own writing, which is confirmed by their failed attempts at independence. It even seems possible to identify Griswold's hostility as a twisted, subterranean sort of attachment. (When Griswold died in 1857, after a run of disasters including marital separation, scarring from fire, and impoverishment, the sole decorations in his New York room were "portraits of himself, Fanny Osgood, and Poe.")[38] In any case, Griswold's only literary immortality came from his attacks on Poe, and although Ingram tried for years to establish himself as an independent writer, his feebly ghosted plagiarism of Poe's essays on autography reveals that even Poe's signature was a hieroglyphic self-portrait, an image in which Ingram and Griswold found their own faces weirdly mirrored.

Into the Crypt: Imprisonment and Release

If Poe's heritage is strewn with writers who mistake themselves for Poe, such figures might claim in their defense that their identification follows from Poe's theory of literary influence as a blurring of identity. As Poe notes in the "Letter to Outis": "What the poet intensely admires, becomes thus, in fact only partially, a portion of his own intellect. . . . He thoroughly feels it as *his own*—and this feeling is counteracted only by the sensible presence of its true, palpable origin in the volume from which he has derived it—an origin which, in the long lapse of years it is almost impossible *not* to forget. . . . The liability to accidents of this character is in the direct ratio of the poetic sentiment. . . for the most frequent and palpable plagiarisms, we must search the works of the most eminent poets" (*ER*, 758–59). Were it not for the "sensible presence" of the book, the plagiarist would willingly forget the text's external origins, less out of an overweening literary ego, Poe suggests, than out of desire for sociality. (Indeed, in all likelihood Poe is here performing his own claims; as a number of scholars have argued, Poe was himself almost certainly the "Outis" to whom he was responding, the "nobody" who was also everybody, every reader. Like Poe's probable identification as Walter G. Bowen, author of an attack on Poe in "A Reviewer Reviewed," Poe's autocritique and response as "Outis" represents an instance of the secret intercommunication found in the exchange of letters and ciphers with W. B. Tyler.)[39]

A similar pattern appears in Poe's review of *Mosses from an Old Manse*, by another writer whom he accused of plagiarism. There Poe notes that Hawthorne's reader "feels and intensely enjoys the seeming novelty of the thought, enjoys it as really novel, as absolutely original with the writer— *and* himself. They two, he fancies, have, alone of all men, thought thus. They two have, together, created this thing." Henceforward "there is a bond of sympathy between them" that "irradiates every subsequent page of the book" (*ER*, 581), in a delusion of mutual creation.

In general, we can characterize such identification as a form of the cryptographic sublimation discussed in chapter 2, where the imagined three-dimensional space of the cryptograph became a place in which the reader's consciousness was intensified, cathected in the process of reading. Christ's tomb, the sublimating crypt in "The Gold-Bug," the interiors of the Swiss bell ringers—all these spaces enable a psychic alchemy that produces an immanent text.

In addition, the rhetoric of cryptography pervades Poe's account of literary influence. By making herself into a crypt to call forth Poe's spirit, Doten aimed to realize Poe's comment in his "Literati" entry on Margaret Fuller, where he observed: "The soul is a cypher, in the sense of a cryptograph; and the shorter a cryptograph is, the more difficulty there is in its comprehension." In that same passage Poe writes that "the supposition that the book of an author is a thing apart from the author's self, is, I think, ill-founded" (*ER*, 1178). Body is to soul, Poe suggests, as crypt is to cryptogram—a comparison that sheds considerable light on Poe's pervasive association of bodily dismemberment and cryptanalysis. Describing the nature of the reader's identification with sentimental death scenes, Jonathan Elmer argues that at the moment of the reader's psychic investment, the logic of identification "requires the liquidation of all borders, those between the text and 'the real' no less than between texts and bodies: language is thus both bodily and real, corpo-real."[40] Indirectly, Elmer's essay helps account for why Doten, like so many of Poe's secret readers, describes the experience of reading his poetry in terms of bodily encryption and rupture.

Such alchemical transformations are achieved by the extraordinary pressure Poe's writing places on its signs, which oscillate between total expressivity and incoherence in a telegraphic opposition of pure (electrical) meaning and cipherlike signifier. This is why reading Poe often feels something like entering the matrix of consciousness itself, in a drama of encryption and release that plays itself out on every level of Poe's work, from the tomb-bound settings of "Ulalume" to the chiming repetitions of sounds in "The Bells," where the pain represented by their "sort of Runic rhyme" is blocked by the wall of semantically null sound, the preverbal "moaning and the groaning" of "the bells, bells, bells, bells,/Bells, bells, bells" (*PT*, 93–95). The verse treads narrowly between sense and nonsense, mirroring the narrator's inability to stabilize his identity through narration.

One might also think of Poe's intensely mediated perception in tales such as "Mesmeric Revelation" and "The Pit and the Pendulum." In "The Premature Burial," the painfully close anatomizing of perception serves almost to obliterate the world the senses are meant to register, as if identity were lodged so deeply within that the corporeal extension of the self becomes an impassable boundary to perception:

> I found myself emerging from total unconsciousness into the first feeble and indefinite sense of existence. Slowly—with a tortoise gradation—approached the faint gray dawn of the psychal day. A torpid uneasiness. An apathetic endurance of dull pain. No care—no hope—no effort. Then, after a long interval, a ringing in the ears; then, after a lapse still longer, a pricking or tingling sensation in the extremities; then a seemingly eternal period of pleasurable quiescence, during which the awakening feelings are struggling into thought; then a brief re-sinking into nonentity; then a sudden recovery. . . . And now the first positive effort to think. (*PT*, 676–77)

For Poe, matter is imprisonment; his writing is an attempt to elude this imprisonment by directly apprehending the noumenal constitution of the universe. In "Mesmeric Revelation," Poe envisions a materialist model of communication based on *"gradations* of matter of which man knows nothing." These gradations "increase in rarity or fineness, until we arrive at a matter *unparticled*—without particles—indivisible—*one*. . . . The ultimate, or unparticled matter, not only permeates all things but impels all things— and thus *is* all things within itself. . . . What men attempt to embody in the word 'thought,' is this matter in motion" (*PT*, 720). By treating thought itself as an infinitely subtle electrical fluid permeating everything, Poe seeks to overcome the old dualism between words and things—a notion that also runs throughout the angelic colloquies.

Such efforts to link the telegraph, electricity, and the spirit reach explicit formulation in Professor W. M. Lockwood's *Molecular Hypothesis of Nature* (1895), in which Lockwood uses the notion of electrical "molecular vibration" as a way of joining matter and spirit: "Thought, being a physi-

cal energy, can be transferred by molecular methods—nature's methods—
to every realm of life. The atmosphere, with its electro-nebulous character, is the medium and vehicle for such transference, as it is for sunlight."[41]
Lockwood's materialistic spiritualism leads him to a series of Poe-like
connections among writing, thought, and telecommunications: "what phenomenon recorded in 'Holy Writ' equals the subtlety and sublimity of
these reactions in nature occurring in the telephonic transmission of human
speech?"[42] The phenomenon of telephonic reproduction of speech at a distance provides Lockwood with a model for spiritualist communication, here
equated with consciousness. Lockwood affirms that "*the same electro and
cosmic principles which prove the mental telephonic message from John Smith
of Milwaukee, to his daughter Jennie, prove the mental telephone message from
Thomas B in spirit life, to his former wife, Mrs. B, in Chicago*—the formula of transmission in either case being that of molecular transference of
thought."[43]

We should not be surprised, then, when the rhetoric that Doten uses to
describe her experience of Poe—a process of enciphering and transmitting
Poe's immanent message—also describes the drama of encryption, transmutation, and release in the verse itself. For Doten, Poe's texts are not particularly valuable as literature; she has no taste for merely ornamental con-
catenations of language. Indeed, Doten is a writer who profoundly desires
to *flee* the literary, which, in its associations with materiality and separateness, is what remains when spiritual inspiration fails. In this repudiation
of language, Doten is a type for today's New Age authors; like them, she
prefers direct contact with spirit to the soul-killing concentration on the
letter. Poe's poetry is valuable for the bodily experience it provokes—an experience not reducible to emotion, nor even to recollected physical sensation. Electrified, Poe's spirit becomes a catalyst for spiritual change, even as
Doten's body becomes the refining alembic for Poe's consciousness in a process of self-sublimation. Poe's texts stimulate Doten *to treat her own body
as a cryptograph*, as a husk in which she refines her immortal spirit. In her
reading of Poe, Doten identifies strongly with the telegraphic immanence
of electricity, neglecting the countervailing emphasis on the code needed to
transmit messages. Poe's code is reduced to his prosody and diction, even as
Doten systematically reverses the content of his verse.

The content of Doten's channeled poems, like that of Ingram's "Imprisoned Soul," mirrors the process of their reception. Just as Poe's death
is a shattering into freedom, so Doten's "chained and chafing" spirit is released through her expression of the poem, as the dynamics of the verse
press out and across the bounds of her body. Consider "Resurrexi," Doten's
technically accomplished response to "The Raven." The poem begins on an
improbably cheerful note:

From the throne of Life Eternal,
From the home of love supernal,
Where the angel feet make music over all the starry floor—
Mortals, I have come to meet you,
Come with words of peace to greet you,
And to tell you of the glory that is mine forevermore.[44]

Quickly the poem modulates to darker, more recognizably gothic effects:

Here the harpies and the ravens,—
Human vampyres, sordid cravens,—
Preyed upon my soul and substance till I writhed in anguish sore;
Life and I then seemed mismated,
For I felt accursed and fated,
Like a restless, wrathful spirit, wandering on the Stygian shore.
Tortured by a nameless yearning,
Like a frost-fire, freezing, burning,
Did the purple, pulsing life-tide through its fevered channels pour,
Till the golden bowl—Life's token—
Into shining shards was broken,
And my chained and chafing spirit leaped from out its prison door.[45]

Doten adopts Poe's supercharged meters and repetitive alliteration, and "ravens" insinuate themselves, as do "cravens," whose use so bothered Eliot in "From Poe to Valéry" ("a surrender to the exigencies of rhyme with which I am sure Malherbe would have had no patience" [333]). Death is figured as a release, rather along the lines of the final book of Chaucer's *Troilus and Criseyde*—a change emblematized by the conversion of "The Raven"'s "nevermore" into the "forevermore" of "Resurrexi."

Given its fame, echoes of "The Raven" might have been expected. What seems odd is Doten's statement in the preface to *Poems from the Inner Life* that before spontaneously reciting "Resurrexi" she had never read any of Poe's poems save for that one: "and that I had not seen for several years. . . . I have had, comparatively speaking, very little poetry in the course of my life, and have never made the style of any author a study" (xx-xxi). But unless we accept Doten's claim of mediumship, her statement about Poe is simply untrue. "The Cradle or Coffin," for instance, adopts the metrical structure of "Ulalume," while "The Streets of Baltimore" offers another revision of "The Raven," even down to its "evermore." "Farewell to Earth" is a slick rewriting of "The Bells":

Farewell! Farewell!
Like the music of a bell
Floating downward to the dell—

> Downward from some Alpine height,
>   While the sunset-embers bright,
>   Fade upon the hearth of night;
> So my spirit, voiceless—breathless,—
>   Indestructible and deathless,
> From the heights of Life elysian gives to earth my parting song;
>   Downward through the star-lit spaces,
>   Unto Earth's most lowly places,
> Like the sun-born strains of Memnon, let the music float along,
> With a wild and wayward rhythm, with a movement deep and strong.
> "Come up higher!" cry the angels.—This must be my parting song.
> (Ibid., 162–63)

With no other writer was Doten's ventriloquism so persuasive. Despite her penchant for Robert Burns, neither "For a' That" nor "Words o' Cheer" could be numbered among Burns's finest works:

> Is there a luckless wight on earth,
>   Oppressed wi' care and a' that,
> Who holds his life as little worth,
>   His home is Heaven for a' that—
>   For a' that, and a' that.
>   There's muckle joy for a' that;
> He's seen the warst o' hell below,
>   His home is Heaven for a' that.[46]

Her treatment of Shakespeare is worse. In her preface to *Poems from the Inner Life*, Doten reports feeling that his "influence seemed to overwhelm and crush me. I was afraid, and shrank from it" (xix). Most readers are likely to wish she had shrunk further:

> O World! somewhat I have to say to thee.
> O sin-sick, heart-sick, soul-sick, love-sick World!
> So ailing art thou, both in part and particle,
> That solid truth thy stomach ill digests.[47]

Given Doten's literary and cultural distance from Elizabethan England and eighteenth-century Scotland, it is not surprising that her attempts to channel Shakespeare and Burns failed, but Doten's Poe is comparatively superb in ways that cannot be fully explained by noting that she and Poe were contemporaries and both were American. In part because of his alienable style and habit of self-portraiture, Poe's image mobilizes Doten's literary sensibility successfully enough that many contemporary readers were inclined to accept the poems' unearthly origins.[48]

Poe, I have suggested, stimulated Doten's muse because she associated his writing with the emerging telecommunications media. Fluctuating between romantic topoi and images of electrical technology, Doten's characterization of Poe allows us to witness the sublimation of telecommunications, and a corresponding interiorization of aesthetic response. Initially, Doten's description of the trance state exactly reproduces a familiar dynamic of blindness and insight: "The avenues of external sense, if not closed, were at least disused, in order that the spiritual perception might be quickened to the required degree, and also that the world of causes, of which the earth and its experiences are but the passing effects, might be disclosed to my vision."[49] In such an exalted state, "acted upon decidedly and directly by disembodied intelligences,"[50] Doten feels "like a harp in the hands of superior powers," an Aeolian instrument borrowed from Shelley or Coleridge. But Doten also indicates in *Poems from the Inner Life* that spiritualism is a technology (xiv, xx), and praises Poe's "thought electric" (ibid., 132); in 1862 she implicitly presented herself as a human radio *avant le signal*, tuned to receive occult frequencies: "My brain was fashioned and my nervous system finely strung, so that I should inevitably catch the thrill of the unnumerable voices resounding through the universe, and translate their message into human language, as coherently and clearly as my imperfections would allow" (ibid., viii).

Here it may be useful to contrast Doten with Charles Baudelaire, another of Poe's cryptographic readers. Both were contemporaries in the business of translating Poe's texts, and both were felt by many of their respective readers to have done translations superior to Poe's originals. Yet there are important differences between them. Baudelaire identifies Poe with a specific set of texts, whereas Doten turns Poe directly into an avatar of communication—into, that is, a *medium*:

> "A medium!" you say. "He himself would scorn the name; and we, who knew him, deny it." But of what was he a medium? We do not confine ourselves to that definition of the term given by modern Spiritualists. He was a medium for the general inspiration which sets like a current of living fire through the universe. . . . He was a medium, not to disembodied spirits, only so far as mind acts upon mind by the great law of unity, and in the same way was he psychologically affected by spirits in the body. (Ibid., 145–46)

Distancing herself from parochial spiritualist definitions of the medium, Doten attacks the almost intractable problem of cryptographic influence head-on. Although Doten can only access her muse through Poe, she remains residually present even in moments of high reception:

> Under such influences I have not necessarily lost my individuality, or become wholly unconscious. I was, for a time, like a harp in the hands of superior powers, and just in proportion as my entire nature was attuned to thrill respon-

sive to their touch, did I give voice and expression to their unwritten music. They furnished the inspiration, but it was of necessity modified by the nature and character of the instrument upon which they played, for the most skilful musician cannot change the tone of a harp to the sound of a trumpet, though he may give a characteristic expression of himself through either. (Ibid., xii–xiii)

Taking her cue from Vankirk's experience in "Mesmeric Revelation" ("for when I am entranced the senses of my rudimental life are in abeyance, and I perceive external things directly, without organs, through a medium which I shall employ in the ultimate, unorganized life" [*PT*, 724]), Doten repeatedly stresses Poe's difficulty in communicating: "He knew not how to express, in any adequate form of speech"; "he knew not how to give his burning inspirations a manifestation through his life and being."[51] Recounting Poe's final appearance to her, she insists on the inadequacy of language to capture his glory: "He stood upon the side of a mountain, which was white and glittering like crystal, and the full tide of inspiration to which he gave utterance could not be comprehended in human speech. . . . In order to be fully realized and understood, the soul *must* be transported to that sphere of spiritual *perceptions*, where there is no *audible* 'speech nor language,' and where the 'voice is not *heard*.' "[52]

Evidently, Doten values Poe as a writer *despite* his skill with words, as if language were so contaminated that Poe's inability to express himself signified the sublimity of his message. To accept the complexity of Poe's writing would require that Doten admit that reading requires irony and complexity and nuance, the delicate calibration of registers and intentions. Instead, Doten flattens Poe's work out to such a degree that we only recognize Doten's spirit-poems as Poe's, and not Burns's or Shakespeare's, by their careful prosodic imitation. Recognizing that Poe's intricate rhythms and excessive musicality constitute an affective Morse code whose stresses and elisions repeatedly signal a sense of loss, Doten relies on those rhythms to stabilize the meaning of her work, independent of the poem's denotative content.[53] By thus nullifying the propositional content of Poe's poetry, Doten reduces its meaning to a universal throb of desire. Doten converts Poe, the most self-conscious of writers, into a figure for a tremblingly inexpressible sociality. Poe emerges as an antebellum E.T., his heart-light glowing with strong emotion. (Doten would have understood such films as *Starman* and *Close Encounters of the Third Kind*, in which the aliens are troped as clusters or bands of colored light, and where, at film's end, the light they shed plays off the upturned rapturous faces, symbolizing and affirming the power of sociality.)

At such a moment, "Poe" becomes something like the name for evacuation itself, for writing so freed of content that it transforms its readers, too, into mediums. Poe's sufferings while he lived resulted from his excessive sense of his individual being and desire. In death, his private investments burned away, dissipating him into an almost Eliotic identification with a larger power, here figured not as poetic tradition but as universal spirit:

> This night he gives his "Farewell to Earth." . . . Not that he is to be divided forever in his interest from Humanity, but, no longer incited by restlessness or ambition, to express in rhythmic numbers the fiery thought within, no longer drawn by the sordid interests of this earthly life, he can gaze down upon this lower world and influence the minds of men, and still be above them. . . . As Poe, the individual, he is willing to be forgotten. His personality, as far as human recognition is concerned, can end here. . . . He says: "Let my soul speak, which is the Divine Power. . . . I have merged and lost my will in the Great Will of the universe."[54]

Personal identity is temporary, a provisional truth overcome when we ecstatically dissolve the self in a flood of common feeling. In this flood, ordinary boundaries are erased, and so although technically Doten is a medium for Poe, Poe is *also* a medium for the "Divine Power" of a universe in which the distinction between medium and message has been blurred until it no longer exists. Such blank mediumship is Doten's ultimate literary achievement, as her verse tunes the reader's consciousness to the vibration of a universal alpha wave of good feeling.

Doten's spiritual possession is, however, Poe's literary dispossession, and her theft of Poe's stylistic and biographical signatures reengages the issues of plagiarism encountered with Griswold. Doten's plagiarism—if that is the correct term—is plagiarism not of a text but of the cultural space Poe's texts inhabit, of the ideogram of literary and social values summed up in his name. The "Poe" who enters Doten is a stylistic Frankenstein's monster, a concatenation of recognizable metrical forms and rhymes, characteristic themes, and elements of Poe's biography, subordinated to the expression of spiritualist beliefs. The spirit-Poe can only be incorporated into Doten's body with a shock; "after giving one of his poems, I was usually quite ill for several days." The influence of Poe "was neither pleasant nor easy. I can only describe it as a species of mental intoxication. I was tortured with a feeling of great restlessness and irritability, and strange, incongruous images crowded my brain. . . . Under his influence, particularly, I suffered the greatest exhaustion of vital energy."[55] For Baudelaire, Poe is always "out there," a hologram produced by texts that exist apart from himself; for Doten, Poe is an internal presence, not so much inscribed as *emitted*.[56]

In her selective appropriation, Doten represents the perpetually innocent reader for whom Poe's texts are always "real." Textual cues to the contrary are irrelevant, as Doten enacts aspects of Poe's writing in her body, in what might be called a corporeal reading. Poe's genius is an alchemical fire through which he transforms his suffering into art: "When, from the glowing fire-crypts of his soul, he wrought out, with master strokes, his 'Raven,' and gave it to the world, men felt that there was a ring of true genius."[57] What Poe does within his soul Doten does with her body, making of it a cenotaph or tabernacle, a material crypt necessary for Poe's transfiguration. Compare Doten's experience to Baudelaire's epitaph for Poe: "One could write on his tomb: 'All you who have ardently sought to discover the laws of your being, who have aspired to the infinite, and whose repressed emotions have had to seek a frightful relief in wine and debauchery, pray for him. Now his purified corporeal being soars amid beings whose existence he glimpsed; pray for him who sees and who knows, he will intercede for you.'"[58]

This passage tellingly demonstrates that the fantasy of pure communication on which spiritualism depends is dialectically produced by a contrary emphasis on the code-crypt. As in the story of Christ's transformation in the tomb, Poe's transubstantiation is produced by the conjunction of writing and the grave. Christ as Logos was the literal embodiment of language, the Word made flesh, who in the sepulcher underwent a translation back into spirit. Baudelaire and Doten similarly transfigured Poe, though in the latter case the crypt was the poet's body, which blocked Doten from realizing her universal nature while she remained on earth.

The symbolists shared with Doten an obsession with Poe as a medium, which typically found expression in their conviction that the content of Poe's verse was subsumed into and almost extinguished by its formal perfection. Baudelaire's comment on "The Raven"—"Its theme is slight, it is a pure work of art"—anticipates Mallarmé's praise of Poe's "perfection and poetic purity" and Valéry's "sympathetic" realization of Poe's need to reach "a state of purity."[59] Most often, the symbolists imagined Poe's purity in terms of crystal, as in Baudelaire's description of poetry as "wrought and pure, correct and brilliant as a crystal jewel."[60] Whereas Doten resists figures of physical incarnation, Baudelaire's metaphor presents Poe as an artificer, a maker of perfect but inert verbal objects that are not reducible to his own interior sensations or thoughts. Hence, although for both Baudelaire and Doten Poe is the protagonist in the drama of influence and communication, an occult metaphor for whatever power it is in language that permits "mind to act upon mind" across the valence of the flesh, for Baudelaire the page remains the final stage for this drama. Doten's violent physiognomic reactions to her reading engendered a confusion of borders (between selves, between text and self) in which the specific difference of language was lost, sacrificed to a fantasy of immediate contact.

Given the degree to which Doten responded to key features of Poe's work, we might say that Poe *did* write her poems, as long as we recognize that Doten's Poe is only a fragmentary incarnation, and one that altogether refuses an analytic consciousness. But such dispersed authorship, the result of an identification so extreme that it borders on self-loss, is not something limited to such quasi-literary figures as Doten. Consider again the case of Alfred Russel Wallace and "Leonainie." Wallace's end of the correspondence with Ernest Marriot was largely occupied with tributes to the "Spirit Poe" and with attempts to trace the authorship of "Leonainie" ("Why, the very *name* is an inspiration of genius!").[61] Only after an exhaustive correspondence did Wallace discover that the poem had been written by James Whitcomb Riley as a hoax. As he learned, a friend of Riley's told Riley that

> if he could only write something like Poe his name and fortune would be secured. So deliberately Riley set to work on a Poe poem, and "Leonainie" was the result. It was copied into a feigned MSS. and "discovered" opportunely without exciting any suspicion towards Riley. After it had run the gauntlet of Poe critics and been pronounced genuine if not canonical, Riley proved the authorship. This drew attention to his own works, and he has never since lacked for praise and pudding.[62]

Remarkably, this discovery did nothing to stem Wallace's campaign on behalf of Poe's authorship of "Leonainie"; in *Edgar Allan Poe*, Wallace *rejected* this explanation of the poem's genesis, concocting instead a fantastic alternative in which Riley was guilty of outright thievery. So indignant that he could not even write Riley's name, Wallace hypothesized that "*he* came into possession of this poem by some accident and then, having got the reputation he wanted by being supposed to be capable of imitating Poe so closely that Poe critics accepted it as genuine, waited till the whole story was almost forgotten, and then included it in his poems without a word of explanation or apology!" (16). Wallace supported this argument philologically, noting "*4* verbal differences, *all* of which (I think,) are the reverse of improvements" between Riley's published text and the manuscript in his hand, as well as "crudities" in Riley's other writings that would disqualify his claim to authorship of "Leonainie." Perhaps, Wallace suggested, Riley had pirated a privately discovered Poe manuscript, and—wonderful phrase—"verbally maltreated" it, before publishing it as his own. Wallace even suggested trying to run tests on the original manuscript to see "whether the *paper ink &c.* were imitated as at least 25 years old" (ibid.).

Although it is tempting to dismiss Wallace as a crackpot, he is lucid about the nature of literary merit: he knows Doten's spirit-poems are technically inferior to Poe's mortal accomplishments, but values them on other grounds. Moreover, Wallace's mistake is no different than that made by those "critics of discernment" who for years received "Leonainie," and "the story of its discovery in an old school reader, in good faith" (ibid., 17–18). However Doten's brain interfered with transmission, for Wallace the spirit-Poe is incomparably nobler than his earthly counterpart, yet it is crucial that the spirit-poems were written by the "real" Poe, who provides a literary authority that Doten did not possess. Like most critics, Wallace demonstrates a deep need to assign a particular narrative of origins to his favorite texts—in this case, to prove that Poe wrote a poem he did not write, and then to show why it is a better example of his work than anything he actually did compose.

Referring to Foucault's description of the author as a way of grouping and excluding texts for specific discursive strategies, Stephen Rachman suggests that "if plagiarism can be rightly said to have any teleological purpose in Edgar Poe's authorial strategy, then it seems to be to disturb the principle of unity" to which Foucault refers.[63] The same might be said of the hoax, which, as a mirror image of plagiarism (the plagiarist seeks to graft his or her signature to another's writing; the hoaxer, to slip his or her words under another writer's name), also subverts the claims of literary history. The failure of discerning critics to identify "Leonainie" as a fake reveals the complex antithetical and parallel relations between plagiarism and literary hoax. Poe's heritage is full of writers who in one way or another share authorship with him, whether through a hoax (Riley) or out of a deluded identification (Doten and Ingram). In their competing claims to authorship, Wallace, Baudelaire, and Doten all stand as evidence for the "disturbed" unity of Poe's texts. Faced with massive evidence that Riley wrote "Leonainie," Wallace insisted on holding Poe responsible; Baudelaire sometimes used Poe's words as if they were his own; and Doten was never sure precisely *who* was the author of her texts ("How far I have ever written, independent of these higher influences, I cannot say; I only know that all the poems under my own name have come from the deep places of my 'Inner Life'").[64] Poem, plagiarism, hoax: the critic's taxonomy of literary forms proves meaningless to Doten, and even more so to Wallace, whose "Poe" is composed of at least three different authors. By insisting on taking Poe "at his word," Doten and Wallace manage to turn their intransigence about Poe's identity into a virtue, converting Riley's hoax and Doten's imitation—*mirabile dictu!*—into fragments of the True Poe.

The Burden of Modern Civilization

Perhaps unexpectedly, Doten's relation to Poe offers a model for the shape of Poe's literary influence in this century. More particularly, Poe's cryptographic sense of writing as telegraphy—literally, "writing at a distance"—prefigured the ways in which his work would represent both a *poésie pure* and a source of contamination for readers. In "From Poe to Valéry," Eliot not only describes Poe's influence as an enigma but, following Griswold, trashes Poe as a writer by saying he had a "fundamentally juvenile mind." Yet the more one looks at Eliot's relation to Poe, the more it resembles Doten's, not least in Eliot's inability to escape Poe's influence.[65] If Doten's relation to

Poe is defined by her status as an alembic for his verse, Eliot too is unwillingly one of Poe's secret writers, his imagination colonized by Poe's texts.

For Eliot, the question of Poe's influence produced a serious crisis of self-knowledge. Raised in an America that remembered Poe as the author of "The Gold-Bug," "The Raven," and a few other popular works, Eliot unhappily realized that in his influence on Baudelaire, Mallarmé, and Valéry, Poe was also responsible for "some of those modern poems which I most admire and enjoy" and for "the most interesting development of poetic consciousness anywhere in the preceding hundred years."[66] Troubled by the apparent incoherence of his literary allegiances, Eliot attacked Poe for his "slipshod writing" and "puerile thinking," and damned him in an oft-quoted phrase: "That Poe had a powerful intellect is undeniable; but it is the intellect of a highly gifted young person before puberty."[67]

Yet Eliot's attempts to characterize Poe's writing slip into contradiction; even as he criticizes Poe's "pre-adolescent" writing, Eliot's genealogy of Poe's influence on H. Rider Haggard and H. G. Wells betrays his taste for juvenile or mass-cult fiction, about which he turns elegiac: "I fear that nowadays too few readers open *She* or *The War of the Worlds* or *The Time Machine*; fewer still are capable of being thrilled by their predecessors."[68] And though "From Poe to Valéry" suggests dismay at Poe's extreme self-consciousness, Eliot had earlier praised him for the powerful incantatory and rhythmic effects of his poetry, which, "because of this very crudity, stirs the feelings at a deep and almost primitive level."[69]

"From Poe to Valéry" concludes with nothing less than the end of civilization, as if the contradictory pressures represented by Poe's influence could only be resolved for Eliot in a vision of global nervous breakdown. Eliot presents as a "tenable hypothesis" the notion that

> this advance of self-consciousness, the extreme awareness of and concern for language which we find in Valéry, is something which must ultimately break down, owing to an increasing strain against which the human mind and nerves will rebel; just as, it may be maintained, the indefinite elaboration of scientific discovery and invention, and of political and social machinery, may reach a point at which there will be an irresistible revulsion of humanity and a readiness to accept the most primitive hardships rather than carry any longer the burden of modern civilisation. (342)

Such a spectacular fantasy suggests how much more than just the literary can be at stake in questions of literary influence. Here, Poe's possible influence seems to compromise the integrity of Eliot's mind. How else to explain this confession of Eliot's: "I can name positively certain poets whose work has influenced me, I can name others whose work, I am sure, has not; there may be still others of whose influence I am unaware, but whose influence

I might be brought to acknowledge; but about Poe I shall never be sure" (ibid., 327)? Neither as a writer nor as a reader can Eliot obtain leverage on Poe's influence; instead, he seems to have assimilated Poe in some manner that deprives him of the self-consciousness necessary for critical judgment.

Profound differences separate Eliot's understanding of Poe from that of Lizzie Doten, yet both writers experience Poe as a crisis of self, in a complicated dialectic of identification and self-fragmentation. As Poe's topoi migrate into the texts of his readers, the distinction between a legitimate literary tradition and its hysterical imitation becomes increasingly hard to make. "I can name positively certain poets whose work has influenced me," writes Eliot, "but about Poe I shall never be sure." Doten has said as much: "It is often as difficult to decide what is the action of one's own intellect and what is spirit-influence, as it is in our ordinary associations to determine what is original with ourselves and what we have received from circumstances or contact with the mind of others."[70] Doten, one might say, suffers from a poetic multiple-personality disorder that precludes the development of a genuine poetic voice. Yet her spiritual possession also serves as a strategic response to the cultural and metaphysical challenges posed by telecommunications. By ventriloquizing Poe (as if *he* were Ligeia), Doten dramatizes her sense that the new world represented by Poe is simultaneously personally shattering and full of spiritual promise.

I think the near-hysteria of Eliot's conclusion to "From Poe to Valéry" can be understood as a reaction to the intolerable oppositions represented by Poe's literary legacy. Just as the continuing "advance of self-consciousness" and "the extreme awareness of and concern for language" may lead to a crisis, so may the "indefinite elaboration of scientific discovery and invention, and of political and social machinery" lead to a corresponding social breakdown in which humanity will prefer "to accept the most primitive hardships rather than carry any longer the burden of modern civilisation." Each threat represents a crisis associated with a different aspect of Poe's writing. On the one hand, the legacy established by Baudelaire and his successors leads to a curatorial relation to language, a recursive self-consciousness in which one is reduced, as Eliot claimed of Valéry, to the "method" and "occupation" of watching oneself write.[71] This is why Eliot attacks Poe for the purity of his poetry, the precise quality that Baudelaire and Doten praise. For Eliot, poetry requires mediation to avoid volatilizing the distinction between language and identity. "This process of increasing self-consciousness—or, we may say, of increasing consciousness of language—has as its theoretical goal what we may call *la poesie pure*. . . . I think that poetry is only poetry so long as it preserves some 'impurity' in this sense: that is to say, so long as the subject matter is valued for its own sake."[72] Although Eliot's poetry often produces a similar volatility, in "From Poe to Valéry" Eliot pines for a time when "primitive hardships" will root identity in the physical world. But Poe's posthumous existence as an immediate medium, like his refusal to value anything "for its own sake," threatens whatever Eliot might advance as a ground for his identity. In a world in which time and place have dissolved, one cannot undertake the scrupulous accounting of debts and investments that Eliot performs in essays such as "Tradition and the Individual Talent."

On the other hand, Eliot also fears the "indefinite elaboration of scientific discovery and invention" because of the increasing dispersal of the self by technology. Writing in 1949, Eliot was remembering the cataclysmic violence of World War II, yet prosecution of that war depended as much on telecommunications (ciphered radio traffic, radar locators, long-distance surveillance) as it did on weapons such as the V-2. As a source for the technological fictions of Wells, Verne, and others, Poe is a villain in this antipopulist nightmare of modernity. Yet Baudelaire's model of writing offers no real alternative to Doten's mass culture, and the oscillating self-consciousness and automatism that Poe's writing produces looks like a blueprint for the future. A high-modern self-consciousness turned back on itself leads to an intolerable feedback loop, a regression of mirrors that eventually collapses into a self-mesmerizing trance.

In "The Work of Art in the Age of Mechanical Reproduction," Walter Benjamin observes that "even the most perfect reproduction of a work of art is lacking in one element: its presence in time and space, its unique existence at the place where it happens to be. This unique existence of the work of art determines the history to which it was subject through the time of its existence."[73] For Benjamin, the loss of such historical embeddedness means the destruction of the work's "aura." Yet when in "Farewell to Earth" Poe bids adieu to the planet, the terms of his escape are identical to the freedom produced by the telegraph, with its wholesale destruction of space and time:

> Human passion, mad ambition, bound me to this lower Earth,
> Even in my changed condition—even in my higher birth.
> But, by earnest, firm endeavor, I have gained a height sublime;
> And I ne'er again—no, never!—shall be *bound* to Space or Time.
> ("Dream-Land," *PT*, 170)

Doten's treatment of Poe (echoing Poe's own "weird clime" in "Dream-Land") suggests that the aura attached to a particular painting or sculpture does not simply disappear, but is generalized to the modes of telecommunications, and hence to Poe, who serves as an icon for invisible communication.

In this connection, it is worth remembering the epigraph from Valéry's essay "La conquête de l'ubiquité" with which Benjamin begins his essay: "In all the arts there is a physical component which . . . cannot remain unaffected by our modern knowledge and power. For the last twenty years neither matter nor space nor time has been what it was from time immemorial. We must expect great innovations to transform the entire technique of the arts, thereby affecting artistic invention itself and perhaps even bringing about an amazing change in our very notion of art."[74] Like Poe before him, claiming that "the consequences of any new scientific invention will, at the present day exceed . . . the wildest expectation of the most imaginative," Valéry recognizes that transformations in our relations to space-time are destined to bring about "amazing changes" in culture. Doten cryptographically made Poe into a medium, which destroyed the possibility of the aesthetic object as it was cherished by Baudelaire or Eliot; Doten's act anticipated the transition from a Paterian interest in the object as it is to the subjective appreciation of its interior effects on the viewer or auditor. In such a world, Poe's writing gathers itself into an apparition that, like the shrouded figure cast on the sky at the end of the *Narrative of A. Gordon Pym*, stands as the emblem of an unimaginable future, in which we are all involuntary mediums through which the pulses of our culture gather and evanesce.

DECIPHERING THE COLD WAR

6   Toward a Literary History of Espionage

Many methods have been used by spies and secret agents to hide their message within a letter. The envelope can first be steamed open flat. Then the secret message written on the inside. After this the envelope is glued back together, your ordinary letter is put in it, and the whole thing is sealed and sent on its way. Who would ever imagine that a message in secret ink was contained on the inside of the plain envelope?

Henry Lysing, *Secret Writing* (1936)

8-9-12-1-9-18-5-16-5

14-20-5

3-15-20-5-9

19-1-4-15-21

2-12-5-1-7-5-14-20-6

15-18-11. . . .

Henri Coulette, "Orphan Annie: The Broken Code"

Poe Goes to War

On 28 January 1831, a military court met at West Point to hear the proceedings in a court-martial. The defendant, a cadet arraigned on charges of gross neglect of duty and disobedience of orders, mounted no defense, and after brief deliberations the military court delivered its unanimous verdict: "that the cadet EA Poe be dismissed from the service of the United States."[1] The decision was no surprise: disappointed at John Allan's remarriage and the consequent decline in his already dismal family prospects, and bored with military life, Poe had written to Allan announcing his plans to neglect his duties and so be relieved from the remaining four years of his service. So ended Poe's second official brush with the military. (Poe had enlisted in the United States Army in 1827, and had served two years of a five-year term before obtaining an honorable discharge.) Disinherited and alone, with twenty-four cents in his pocket, Poe left West Point not for Richmond and John Allan, but for Baltimore, to renew his ties with family, including his brother William, his aunt Maria, and her thirteen-year-old daughter Virginia. The subsequent course of Poe's life is well known. Yet Poe never forgot his military past, inventing for his *Graham's Magazine* biography a Byronic account of a clandestine trip to Europe to fight on behalf of Greek independence, and employing his memories of Fort Moultrie as the setting for "The Gold-Bug."

"The history of warfare is the story of cryptology," Richard Powers claims.[2] If this is so, Edgar Allan Poe was something of a war hero; by influencing future cryptographers Poe helped end World War II and shape the political culture of the Cold War. Perhaps not all readers will see this as a serious claim. But from the time of World War I on, American literature and intelligence have been shaped by Poe's secret writing in all its forms. In " 'Make My Day!': Spectacle as Amnesia in Imperial Politics," Michael Rogin explores the ongoing indebtedness of the American government to models of surveillance and display developed during World War II. That war, Rogin argues, laid the "structural foundations in politics for the modern American empire" in two specific ways. "First, the good war established the military-industrial state as the basis for both domestic welfare and foreign policy. Second, it made surveillance and covert operations, at home and abroad, an integral part of the state."[3] What most interests me is the first paragraph of Rogin's essay, which I reproduce in full: "The thief hides the purloined letter, in Edgar Allan Poe's story, by placing it in plain sight. His theft is overlooked because no attempt is made to conceal it. The crimes of the postmodern American empire, I want to suggest, are concealed in the same way. So let us begin like Poe's Inspector Dupin, and attend to the evidence before our eyes" (99).

One might take this citation only as a convenient way for Rogin to introduce his argument about the relationship between Cold War political spectacles and domestic racial demonology. But in beginning with "The Purloined Letter," Rogin was curiously prescient, for the logic of that story resonates through Cold War literature, intelligence, and military relations. World War II transformed America into a culture dependent on the transmission of occulted information: code words and microfiche, bomb diagrams hidden in pumpkins, disinformation. Shrouded in secrecy, but funded by tens of billions of dollars for research and deployment, cryptography lies at the heart of the Cold War obsession with duplicity and the hermeneutics of suspicion.

Improbably enough, the military and political institutions of cryptography have never freed themselves from their literary roots, which is roughly equivalent to claiming that they have never freed themselves from Poe. I say this not merely because a scholarly history of the Polish efforts to crack Enigma treats Poe's contributions to cryptology along with those by such giants as Charles Wheatstone, Jean-Guillaume-Hubert-Victor-François-

Figure 12. Col. William F. Friedman with the Hebern cipher machine, the first such cipher engine to use rotors, and the dim prototype of Enigma and Purple. Used by permission of the George C. Marshall Research Library, Lexington, Virginia.

Alexandre-August Kerckhoffs von Nieuwenhof, and Friedrich Kasiski, nor because an official NSA history—stamped "not to be reproduced or further disseminated outside the U.S. Intelligence Community without the permission of the Director, NSA"—contains a long discussion of Poe's cryptographic writing.[4] Nor do I claim this only because of the existence of writers who worked as spies, such as John Le Carré and Graham Greene; or spies who worked as writers, such as the cryptographer William Yardley, who sometimes supported himself by penning spy novels such as *The Red Sun of Nippon* and *The Blonde Countess*; or spies *related* to cryptographers, such as James Phinney Baxter III, deputy director of the Office of Strategic Services (OSS), whose grandfather wrote *The Greatest of All Literary Problems*, the seven-hundred-page defense of Baconianism.[5]

Rather, the best evidence for Poe's oblique influence comes from the life of Colonel William F. Friedman, whose career continually circled back to Poe's writing and who, through his half-century of work at the center of American intelligence, inflected the political course of this century. As Friedman himself writes, "it is a curious fact that popular interest in this country in the subject of cryptography received its first stimulus from Edgar Allan Poe."[6] Friedman was one of those readers stimulated by Poe: even as a child, he would often "talk with excitement about a world he had discovered through Edgar Allan Poe's 'The Gold-Bug.'"[7] According to the military historian Ronald Clark, there is "no doubt" that Friedman's reading of "The Gold-Bug" "prepared him for the work ahead, and little doubt that without it he would not have slipped so easily from his first-chosen profession [genetics] into the work that was to affect the course of the Second World War."[8]

Clark's claim raises some vexing questions. What does it mean that Friedman was excited by reading Poe as a child? To what extent can the biography of a Baconian cryptographer illuminate fiction at all? How can one begin to generalize the experience of readers like Friedman into claims about American culture? Although this chapter offers no definitive answers to these questions—offers, that is, no empirically verifiable account of the relations between Poe's writing and the century's history—the many resonances between that writing and the development of American cryptography point toward a literary history of espionage that would take the textuality of history as seriously as it would the real-world sources for spy fiction. Certainly Friedman, in his failure to separate literary problems from cryptographic ones, was representative of the hypertextual environment of the Cold War NSA. To see how the complexities of the cryptographic imagination subsume the merely textual—to see why, that is, one might want to claim that Poe's literary history mutated into the political and diplomatic history of the Cold War—I turn to the life of William Friedman.

The Cradle of Cryptology

Bibliomane, dandy, loner, genius: a sketch of Friedman's character might serve as a double for that of Poe's M. Dupin, which is to say for Poe's imagination of himself. Like Dupin, Friedman worked as the contractual agent of a government with which he was at odds. Like Dupin, he was also, loosely speaking, both "poet *and* mathematician" ("Purloined Letter," *PT*, 691), who combined his cryptanalytic expertise with a passion for literature. And for forty-five years, from World War I until the 1960s, Friedman was simply *the* American codemaster, who, by overseeing the mathematization and the mechanization of cryptography, transformed it from an avocation fit for military historians into a force in international politics and war. Summarizing Friedman's achievements, David Kahn grows breathless: "His theoretical studies, which revolutionized the science, were matched by his actual solutions, which astounded it. . . . Words he coined gleam upon more than one page of today's dictionaries. His textbooks have trained thousands. His historical articles have shed light in little-known corners of the study, and

the Shakespeare book has done much to quash one major area of a peren-
nial literary nuisance. Singlehandedly, he made his country preeminent in
his field." Indeed, the "gigantic enterprise" of the American cryptological
establishment of today, with "its thousands of employees, its far-flung stations, its sprawling headquarters," is "a direct lineal descendant of the little
office in the War Department that Friedman started all by himself."[9]

Born in Moldavia in 1891, Wolfe (later William) Friedman was the
son of a Rumanian Jew who emigrated to Pittsburgh in 1892. A scholarship allowed Friedman to attend, first, Michigan State University, and then
Cornell, from which he was graduated in 1914. While teaching part-time at
Cornell, Friedman received an offer to become head of the genetics department at Riverbank Laboratories. Located west of Chicago, Riverbank was
the whimsical creation of one of cryptography's more memorable characters,
Colonel George Fabyan, the Boston-born heir to a textile firm. Never much
interested in business, in 1905 Colonel Fabyan (the title was an honorific)
retired from work and, with his wife Isabella, founded Riverbank Laboratories, where he pursued his interests in genetics, acoustics, chemistry, and
secret writing. Fabyan ran Riverbank as if he were an Oriental potentate,
ornamenting the grounds with a Japanese garden, a Roman bathing pool,
and a bear pit with vegetarian bears. A pet gorilla roamed the grounds, and
Fabyan sometimes met visitors to Riverbank at the railroad station in a carriage drawn by zebras.

It was in this curious place that Friedman found his calling, and as a
result, Riverbank is today the "almost mythical site" or "cradle" of modern
cryptology.[10] The intermediary who brought Friedman to Riverbank was an
anti-Stratfordian high school principal named Elizabeth Gallup, author of
The Biliteral Cypher of Sir Francis Bacon. Colonel Fabyan had some small experience with commercial codes in business, and when Gallup's book came
to his attention, he recruited her, along with a team of assistants, to begin
a cryptological laboratory, recognizing that if Gallup were proved correct
her fame would redound to Riverbank as well. The scene is hard to conjure:
Friedman, arriving at Riverbank expecting to work on Mendelian inheritance, gradually seduced into spending five years trying to tease ciphers out
of Shakespeare, and thereby accidentally founding a branch of government
deeply responsible for prosecuting the Cold War.

The process by which this took place was ludicrously but instructively
aleatory. When Fabyan learned that Friedman was an amateur photogra-
pher as well as a geneticist, he asked Friedman to assist Gallup by making
enlargements of Shakespeare's Folio, for easier identification of the *a*- and *b*-
alphabets that constitute Bacon's cipher. Charmed by the backstage scenes
of the Elizabethan court that Gallup recovered by "decrypting" Shakespeare (rather like the diplomatic dramas he was later to encounter in read-

ing Japanese ciphers during World War II), Friedman found his old interest in cryptography reawakened. "Something in me found an outlet," he recalled, and his skill quickly led to his appointment as Head of Ciphers.[11]

Friedman's nascent career would have ended with Gallup had it not been for the self-aggrandizing generosity of Colonel Fabyan. In 1916 the State Department had no capacity for reading ciphered communications, a failure that grew urgent as America drifted toward war. Washington found itself paralyzed by the growing amount of ciphered traffic intercepted between Mexico and Europe. Hence, when Fabyan placed the facilities of Riverbank at the disposal of the State Department, it gratefully began funneling intercepted communications to Friedman's staff. Other government agencies followed: first State, then Justice, and finally, in 1917, the War Department itself, which was so taken with Friedman that six-week courses were organized for officers being sent to France.[12] In this manner, the cipher department at Riverbank—an organization designed for literary research— became the site for all cryptanalytic training of American officers in World War I; became, indeed, godparent to the NSA, which, as an agency press release explains, "was the descendant of these events of 1917."[13]

It was while teaching at Riverbank that Friedman began making the technical discoveries that revolutionized cryptography. In 1920 he began publishing his results in a series of monographs known as the Riverbank Publications, which form "the foundations on which the huge edifice of twentieth-century cryptology was very largely to be built."[14] Of particular interest is "The Index of Coincidence" (1920), which for the first time in history "treated a frequency distribution curve as an entity, as a curve whose several points were causally related, not as just a collection of individual letters that happen to stand in a certain order for noncausal (historical) reasons."[15] The effects of this decision were "Promethean," for by subsuming cryptographic analysis into statistics, Friedman accomplished the rationalization of language that Poe, with his misunderstanding of probability, had fantasized about in the detective stories and *Eureka*.

This rationalization opened the door to an "armamentarium" of new cryptological weapons, including "measures of central tendency and dispersion, of fit and skewness, of probability and sampling and significance" that were "ideally fashioned" to capitalize on the statistical behavior of language.[16] Treated en masse, many linguistic features behave with a regularity that permits their mathematical calculation. Zipf's law, for instance, states that the number of occurrences of a word in a language is reciprocal to the order of frequency of occurrence: the hundredth most frequent word occurs approximately one one-hundredth as many times as the most frequent word.[17] In studies of German, cryptographers counting the number of *e*s in texts of about a thousand letters have come up with similar percentages, ranging from Parker Hitt's count of 16 percent to Lange's and

Soudart's estimate of 18.8 percent.[18] Cryptographers have developed hundreds of similar ratios for charting the relation of first and last letters, the relation of vowels to consonants, and the doubling or trebling of consonants (the most common pair of English vowels is *ea*; *r* is usually followed by a vowel, *s* by a consonant). Information also exists concerning the use of salutations and idioms. Allied codebreakers knew, for example, that the Germans were fond of sending strings of scatological obscenities when the actual message was finished, as a red herring, which became immensely useful in decrypting their messages.

In 1921 Friedman left Riverbank to become chief cryptanalyst for the War Department. For the next seven years, he consolidated his position as the nation's leading cryptanalyst, writing new army codes, testing proposed enciphering machines, and publishing a series of monographs and texts that brought order to an otherwise disjointed field. Friedman's only competition came from the American Black Chamber, a secret agency run jointly by the State Department and the army in order to intercept and decipher foreign messages. The Black Chamber was headed by Herbert Yardley (later famous as the author of *The American Black Chamber*) until 1929, when it was disbanded. This dissolution provided an opportunity to consolidate governmental cipher activities, which had been inefficiently distributed among the Black Chamber, Friedman's Signal Corps, and the Army Adjutant General.[19] The next year, Friedman was named head of the new Signal Intelligence Service (SIS), where, astonishingly, he and his tiny staff of seven were wholly responsible for "preparation and revision of Army codes and ciphers and, in time of war, interception of enemy radio and wire traffic, goniometric [directional] location of enemy radio stations, solution of intercepted enemy code and cipher messages, and laboratory arrangements for the employment and detection of secret inks."[20]

During the next few years Friedman achieved his greatest glory, and cryptography came into its own.[21] As World War II approached, the SIS "enlarged, accelerated and intensified" its operations,[22] applying new mechanical and mathematical aids to attack the immense number of encrypted radio and telegraph messages, and metastasizing from nineteen staff members in 1939 to more than ten thousand by 1945.[23]

Despite the secrecy with which the subject was treated, aspects of cryptography came to saturate American culture. During World War II, it was forbidden to mail "whole classes of objects or kinds of messages" abroad because of their susceptibility to encoding. These included chess games played by mail, newspaper crossword puzzles, students' grades, results of athletic contests, and children's crayoned scrawls, which could conceal maps. Suspicion about writing was woven into the very fabric of clothing: one letter full of detailed instructions for knitting a sweater was held up by the Office of Censorship until a censor, determined to know if the sequence of knits and castoffs constituted a woolly Morse code, had actually knit the pattern.[24] For thirty years the Signal Intelligence Service also maintained a department devoted to the manufacture of secret inks, which were soaked into the neckties, handkerchiefs, and socks of agents, to be reconstituted with water at the appropriate time.

To the suspicious eyes of censors, the very punctuation of a text might hold a cryptogram. The process of creating such messages, or *microdots* (later simplified by the ministrations of a certain Professor Zapp), involved two steps. "A first photograph of an espionage message resulted in an image the size of a postage stamp; the second, made through a reversed microscope, brought it down to less than 0.05 inches in diameter. This negative was developed. Then the spy pressed a hypodermic needle, whose point had been clipped off and its round edge sharpened, into the emulsion like a cookie cutter and lifted out the microdot. Finally the agent inserted it into a cover-text over a period and cemented it there with collodion."[25] Because the microdot pats employed aniline dye instead of the silver compound ordinarily used as an emulsion, they could (shades of "The Daguerreotype"!) show extraordinarily fine detail, resolving images down to the molecular level.

By 1940, cryptography was a crucial Allied resource, employing thousands in the creating and breaking of hundreds of different codes. Of these projects, none was more important than cryptanalysis of the Japanese cipher Purple. As *Time* reported in December 1945, the "most potent secret weapon of World War II was not radar, not the VT fuse, not the atom bomb, but a harmless little machine which cryptographers had painstakingly constructed in a hidden room in Washington."[26] The unmentioned genius behind this "harmless little machine" was Friedman, who in 1938 led an attack on Purple, the most complex of all Japanese ciphers, and one reserved for crucial diplomatic communications. Even now the facsimile that Friedman and his team designed remains in secure storage in Fort Meade — a writing machine so dangerous that it is still classified fifty years after it went out of service. A crude approximation of the Enigma machine and a sample message appear in figure 13. Enough is known, however, about what Kahn calls one of the most "arduous, grinding, extended and ultimately triumphant cryptanalyses in history" to recognize Friedman's centrality to what has often been regarded as a humanly impossible decryption. Further, the process by which Friedman went about cracking Purple tells us a good deal about the forms of identification on which cryptography is based.[27]

Like all high-level Axis codes, Purple was a machine cipher adapted from the German Enigma. Enigma's basic design involved two or more typewriterlike machines linked through multiple switchboards. Encryptions were performed by linking the switchboards in different combinations. A person would enter the uncoded message (the plaintext), and the corre-

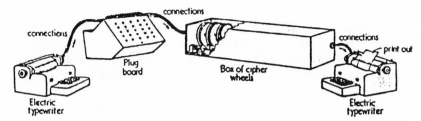

YJXSI DJWLS BWJOW VBDLY YNLHL SRZOD MHIXM GGGWE BLQPT

RRMRJ EQHZQ NADAD OQCLS MGOHS VMZKC LHMAK XYWXJ HRYCH

FITRS LZJIN LAHFN HGVMF QWHKO SBXLT XHSMM JLBXC GFQHZ

GYMTB QPWVW VJICX XMDTE HRWFJ BKCXI RJDHN WGIGH EVRWA

OBDPG HSBGZ MLKHB KTGNC RQANZ

Figure 13. A crude approximation of the Enigma machine, and a sample message.

sponding encryption would print out on another typewriterlike machine. Decoding involved the reverse of that process. What was fiendishly tricky was that the current passed from the enciphering typewriter through two or more different-sized rotors, which turned one space for each letter typed, thus giving each letter its own personal key. Hence, a *t* typed in as the first letter of a message might be enciphered as a *y*, while a *t* appearing in the second space of the same message might be an *r* or an *l* or any other letter. Eventually, the two rotors would return to their initial positions, but only after a period of hundreds of thousands of letters—a trait that effectively prevented reconstruction of the key. Worse still, keys were easily changed by rewiring the contacts between the typewriters and the rotors, so that even if the almost superhuman job of cracking the Enigma cipher were achieved, analysts still had the task of deciding which of the thousands of possible wiring patterns was used for each day's intercepted traffic.

Much has been written of the brilliant Allied effort to decipher Ultra, the Nazis' fancy version of Enigma, but the British team had an enormous advantage over Friedman in that Polish cryptographers owned an early version of the machine, which they had smuggled out from a Polish train station, copied, and returned for shipment before it was missed. Friedman had no physical model to go on, and Purple machines were far more complicated than those used for Ultra. Every message sent in Purple was first translated into a cryptic form of Japanese known as "telegraph Japanese," then enciphered through a simple paper code before being superenciphered by four different coding wheels. The ensuing text, printed in unpunctuated five-letter groups, was all the team had to go on in attempting a solution.

At first Friedman was preoccupied with the problems involved in designing and operating Sigaba, the American equivalent of Purple, and for months the Purple team made little headway. Then, at the beginning of 1939, Friedman was ordered to devote himself exclusively to Purple. What Friedman and his team did ranks with such forensic achievements as Baron Cuvier's anatomical reconstructions of extinct species or the discovery of the structure of DNA. Working from their knowledge of earlier Japanese ciphers, and reasoning inferentially about the stream of intercepted letters, Friedman's team began designing a machine that would produce such a cipher. With no physical model to go on, Friedman's team had to use trial and error, mathematical inference, and intuition to discover the number, shape, and composition of the rotors, and to reinvent the exact pattern of the machine's wiring, with its thousands of plugboard interconnections and its complicated pseudorandom deflections of the electrical circuit. In its way, Friedman's creation of the Purple facsimile repeated the trick of the genetic process itself as he generated a three-dimensional, never-before-seen object out of the systematic variation of the cardinal numbers from zero through nine. Over the next eighteen months a complex machine gradually took shape in Friedman's lab that had to duplicate its original in Tokyo infallibly; if even one strand of wiring was misconnected, the text produced would be hash. In September 1940, Friedman's team watched as, accompanied by a shower of sparks (the same shower, Friedman later learned, emitted by the Japanese original), their machine printed out the Japanese plaintext for the first time.

It was the high point of Friedman's career. Although the task of cracking dozens of other military codes remained, from that moment on the Americans had a constant stream of top-level information about Japanese operations worldwide. In the next four years, Allied cryptography enabled four decisive achievements, including the victory at Midway; the shooting-down of the bomber carrying Admiral Yamamoto, commander in chief of Japan's combined fleet; "the rapid cutting of Japan's lifeline" after 1943; and, in the European theater, the defeat of the U-boats.[28] Afterward, American officials estimated that codebreaking had shortened the war by from one to three years; indeed, a Japanese victory at Midway alone "would probably have cost the United States more than a year to come back."[29] But the cost of Friedman's achievement was not small. In January 1941, five months after cracking Purple, Friedman was admitted to Walter Reed Hospital with a "general nervous breakdown"; he stayed there for three and one-half months. On his emergence, Friedman was forced to retire with permanent disability from his position as a Signal Corps reserve lieutenant colonel. For the next two decades, first as director of communications research for the SIS, and later as special assistant to the director of the NSA, Friedman continued to exert an enormous force on American cryptography. But his days as the world's greatest cryptanalyst were over: he was restricted by his superiors from working for more than a few hours a day on actual solutions.

A Cryptographer Looks at Literature

Despite these intense professional commitments, Friedman never forgot the literary origins of his interest in secret writing. Indeed, had it not been for Poe and Shakespeare (writers whom Friedman sometimes blurred into a single figure), Friedman's career would never have existed. Nor was Poe only a *literary* source: as late as 1917, Poe's pieces on secret writing formed part of the program of formal cryptographic training for the United States Army.[30] Apparently, something of Poe's fictive imagination also bled into those trained by his writing. Friedman's NSA colleague Lambros Callimahos also dated his fascination with cryptography from a childhood reading of "The Gold-Bug."[31] An internationally regarded flutist and a linguist fluent in seven languages, Callimahos was so smitten with cryptography that in 1941 he volunteered for the SIS, showing up at the draft board looking "like something out of a Dumas novel," "complete with waxed mustache, goatee, big black hat, Chesterfield coat, spats, gloves, and cane."[32] Callimahos fast became Friedman's technical assistant and factotum, eventually writing with him *Military Cryptanalysis*, volumes 1 through 4, arguably the most important cryptographic manuals in history.[33]

Callimahos also taught the Intensive Study Program in Cryptanalysis, offering advanced NSA students what Bamford calls "the equivalent of a Ph.D. in codebreaking."[34] The program was set up as a game in which students attacked the "maddening code systems of the mystical kingdom of Zendia," and successful completion of the course entitled one to admission in Callimahos's Dundee Society, a "supersecret fraternity" within the NSA.[35] Society meetings were presided over by Callimahos, who, dressed in "a fitted beige Nehru jacket with an odd-looking ecclesiastical decoration around his neck, white trousers said to be woven from the fleece of virgin llamas, and white leather shoes," was known for the duration as His Cerebral Phosphorescence. Even granting the tongue-in-cheek nature of these meetings, it is worth remembering that the society produced virtually every cryptanalyst responsible for postwar codebreaking. At the core of the NSA, that is, one finds not the sober efforts of Cold War ideologues, but the sensibility of puzzlemasters—except that the stakes are no longer the buried treasure of "The Gold-Bug," but the worldwide balance of power.

All of which is to say that the relation of espionage to literature is not like the relation of, say, medicine or law to literature. Unlike those professions, espionage substantially depends on the self-conscious manufacture of fictions. (By contrast, legal or medical fictions are meant to be naturalized as truths.) Espionage depends on cover stories, on doubling, on allegorical identities. It depends as well on a literary sense of hermeneutics. This is not to say that espionage, cryptography, and the like can be reduced to literature. But it seems telling that the *International Journal of Intelligence and Counterintelligence*, the leading academic journal in the field, devotes part of every issue to reviews of spy fiction. (It is as if the *Lancet* were to run regular reviews addressing the images of doctors in fiction.) Further, the journal— whose editorial board includes members of the CIA, the NSA, the cryptographic historian David Kahn, and retired CIA director Richard Helms— treats fiction as an ancillary but real source of information about the practice of espionage. Reviewing Le Carré's *Secret Pilgrim*, William Hood approvingly quotes his description of the life span of spies before directing readers back to the novel's factual basis: "Readers interested in a non-fiction account of the real-life operations which are suggested by this story will find it in Tom Bower's excellent *The Red Web: MI6 and the KGB Master Coup*."[36]

This cross-referencing between fiction and fact is characteristic of the interconnections between fiction and espionage, which, because of their secrecy, often cannot be reported on through ordinary channels. After CIA field agent Victor Marchetti left the firm, he published his experience disguised as a novel (*The Rope Dancer*); only later, with the greater latitude permitted post-Watergate exposés, did he present a nonfiction account of the agency (*The CIA and the Cult of Intelligence*).[37]

It is, as the old joke goes, turtles all the way down: in his review of *The Secret Pilgrim*, Hood makes much of the book's debt to Somerset Maugham's *Ashenden* (1928),[38] but *Ashenden* was itself a compilation of short stories, woven together with an only thinly veiled history of Maugham's efforts as a British intelligence officer during World War I, given the "ambitious mission" of preventing the Bolshevik revolution and of keeping Russia in the war.[39] The pattern of connections, coupled with a doctrine of official secrecy, means that although real-life espionage is not the same thing as espionage writing, neither can it ever be kept absolutely distinct from it; this gives a certain credence to Grady's conceit in *Six Days of the Condor*, in which his novel-reading CIA subdepartment works out of a Washington brownstone that presents itself as the national headquarters of the American Literary Historical Society, a group dedicated to the "three A's" of "literary analysis, advancement, and achievement" (5).

A similar sense of imbrication is evident in Friedman's writing about literature. At times, Friedman's interest in literature was professional, as in his effort to track down Ernest Vincent Wright's novel *Gadsby* (1939), which, like Georges Perec's better-known *Life: A User's Manual*, was distinguished by the absence of the letter *e*—an absence that, Friedman discovered, invalidated the entire English frequency table by destroying the proportional relation among the remaining twenty-five letters. But Friedman also addressed the more general relation of literature to cryptography, discussing work by Poe, Shakespeare, James Joyce, Jules Verne, Chaucer, Gertrude

Stein, and others.[40] In the case of Poe, such writing was woven into the fabric of his profession. Friedman published his essays both in scholarly venues such as *American Literature* and in the *Bulletin of the Signal Intelligence Service*, the house organ for government cryptographers, where literary analyses of Poe sit cheek by jowl with articles such as "Secret Causes of German Successes on the Eastern Front" and "Cipher Busting in the Seventh Corps Area."[41]

Friedman's critical magnum opus is *The Shakespearean Ciphers Examined: An Analysis of Cryptographic Systems Used as Evidence that Some Author Other than William Shakespeare Wrote the Plays Commonly Attributed to Him*, winner of the 1955 Folger Shakespeare Library prize. In it, Friedman and his wife and coauthor Elizebeth Friedman gleefully explode the preposterous readings of Shakespeare propounded by the cipher-impaired ("cryptleds," to use John Limon's term).[42] The book—which cannot be recommended too highly as a study of the human will to err—represents something of a belated reply to their old master, Gallup, who by the time she arrived at Riverbank was convinced that Bacon had written not only through the "mask" of Shakespeare, but through the "masks" of Edmund Spenser, Ben Jonson, and Christopher Marlowe as well. Such disguises were necessary because of the political scandal of Bacon's origin. As the legitimate son of a secret marriage between Robert Dudley, the earl of Leicester, and Queen Elizabeth, Bacon knew that to reveal his lineage publicly would be suicide. As he explained in a cipher Gallup took from the Folio: "Queene Elizabeth is my true mother, and I am the lawfull heire to the throne. Find the Cipher storie my bookes containe; it tells great secrets, every one of which, if imparted openly, would forfeit my life. F. Bacon" (F&F, 191). Although forced to conclude that *none* of the programs for finding Baconian ciphers has any merit, Friedman and Friedman reserve a soft spot for the "honest, sincere, gentle, upright" Gallup, whose system they praise as "the highest point in all these attempts to prove authorship by decipherment" (ibid., 188).

Friedman and Friedman are less generous with the claims of the clergyman Walter Begley that the last two lines of the epilogue to *The Tempest* ("As you from crimes would pardon'd be/Let your indulgence set me free") conceal an anagram from Bacon ("*Tempest* of Francis Bacon, Lord Verulam/Do ye ne'er divulge me ye words"). They dryly note that while Begley's version has three *a*s, the original text has only two, and that the couplet could more accurately be glossed as follows: "I wrote every line myself. Pursue no code/E. told me Bacon's a G.D. fraud" (F&F, 112). Their sharpest wit is reserved for a book by Ben Haworth-Book, entitled *Neglected Anagrams of the Bacon Period* (1914), in which the author finds evidence that Bacon also wrote Du Bartas's *Divine Weekes and Workes* (1633), notwithstanding that at the time it was published Bacon was, in fact, dead. According to Haworth-Book, Bacon shows his hand through a series of porcine puns on his surname. After noting that "Vivitur ingenio caetura mortis erunt" is an anagram of "I am writing a secret in true O" (as Haworth-Booth explains, "it is common to use the 'O' to signify 'cypher'"), he goes on to show that "Acceptam refero" secretly signifies "mee a fat porccer"; that "Ivstus vivet fide R.Y" means "I fry in stevved svet"; and "Deus providebit," "Svet I provided. B"; texts not so dignified, perhaps, as one might expect from the author of *De augmentis scientarum*, much less of *King Lear*.

In "The Cipher in the Epitaph," Friedman and Friedman turn to questions of encryption bearing both on Jesus's immurement in the tomb and on the treasure of "The Gold-Bug." The controversy stems from the slab that appears today below the bust of Shakespeare in the Collegiate Church at Stratford having been replaced around 1830. Although the new slab reproduces "the sense and wording of the original," it does not duplicate "the 'uncouth mixture of large and small letters'" with which the first inscription was said to have been carved (F&F, 51). According to contemporary testimony, the original verse appeared thus:

> Good Frend for Iesus SAKE forbeare
>
> To diGG TE Dust Enclo-Ased HE.Re.
>
> Blese be TE Man $\frac{T}{Y}$ spares TE Stones
>
> And curst be He $\frac{T}{Y}$ moves my Bones.

In 1887 Hugh Black, writing in the *North American Review*, proposed that through the use of Bacon's biliteral cipher, one could locate a Baconian encryption to the effect that "FRANCIS BACON WROTE SHAKESPEARE'S PLAYS." Black's work inspired a flurry of American decryptions. The same year, Herbert Janvrin Browne published *Is It Shakespeare's Confession? The Cryptogram in His Epitaph*; and in 1888, Edgar Gordon Clark replied to Black with pieces in the *North American Review* and in *Cosmopolitan* in which, by "correcting" certain of Black's errors, he obtained vehement attestations to Bacon's authorship. Through a convolution of the biliteral cipher too twisted to recount, Black recovered the following messages:

> FRA BA WRYT EAR. AA! SHAXPERE.
> FRA BA WRT EAR. HZQ AYA!—SHAXPERE
> A! FRA BAQ WRYT HEAR AZ SHAXPERE.

These he glossed as follows:

> Francis Bacon wrote here. Aye, Aye. Shakespeare.
> Francis Bacon wrote here. His cue. Aye Aye. Shakespeare.
> Aye! Francis Bacon wrote here as Shakespeare.
> (F&F, 53)

By treating T/Y used twice as a single five-letter group, Clark obtained the impenetrable "S A E H A B E B N R A L E I A L A R P." This he permuted into "S H A Q P E R E A L L N A R A H E R E A! I O B A Y A." Or, as it appears to the initiated: "Jacques Pierre [Shakespeare] all narrated here; Aye! I obey (his wishes). Bacon." Somehow it never strikes Baconians as odd that a mind capable of using the magnificent verse of *The Tempest* or *Othello* as a steganographic cipher could only manage to encipher the spastic exclamations discovered by Black and company.

The serious point lurking in here is that finally all writing (not to mention all criticism) *is* a form of anagram.[43] Baconian logic rests on every English text being composed of a tiny cipher of twenty-six letters, which letters, infinitely rearranged, are used for everything that has yet been or ever will be written. In "The Library of Babel," Jorge Luis Borges takes as his epigraph a relevant phrase from *The Anatomy of Melancholy*. "By this art," Burton writes, "you may contemplate the variation of the 23 letters."[44] Borges's entire career is based on an impulse much like that motivating the Baconians. Because of the fantastic reductiveness of script, reading by contrast must be baroquely generative and projective. Baconianism reminds us that almost any work can serve as master text for a culture, a pocket "library of Babel," anagramming everything. Consider the Reverend Walter Begley's collection of a phenomenal fourteen thousand Renaissance anagrams of the *salutatio angelica*, the Angel Gabriel's address to Mary: "Ave, Maria, gratia plena; Dominus tecum." Each anagram uses the thirty-one letters of the salutation one time only; each is perfect in spelling, diction, and syntax.[45] The cryptographic fantasies shared by Haworth-Book, Gallup, and the rest reflect a similar, if secularized, desire to make of Shakespeare the book of books through which a culture can project its fantasies of meaning and history.

Despite his lifelong involvement with Baconianism, Friedman could not imagine how such anagrammatic freedom related to fundamental literary questions. Yet his compulsive debunking has in it something of the way the tongue of the dental patient keeps returning to worry the sore tooth; as if Friedman found the polysemy of literature scary but beguiling. Hence, although he described himself as a "devotee" of Joyce, and approvingly cited Stein's "Rose is a rose is a rose" as a useful cryptographic dictum, Friedman insisted that literature and cryptography belonged to separate spheres. Cryptography, Friedman maintained, was properly "a branch of mathematics," and "just as the solution of mathematical problems leaves no room for the exercise of intuition, divination, or other mysterious mental powers some people claim to have, so does the solution of a cryptogram leave no room for the exercise of such powers."[46] Cryptography and literature belonged to separate spheres, although there was no question of which possessed hermeneutic superiority.

But if *The Shakespearean Ciphers Examined* offers a Friedman blithely confident of his ability to parse the secrets of the text, this is not the only version of Shakespeare that Friedman knew. In "Shakespeare, Secret Intelligence, and Statecraft," published in 1962, Friedman (who is identified only as a reader at the Folger Library) points to the Babington plot, in which the interception of secret correspondence eventually led to the execution of Mary, Queen of Scots, as the probable source for the Cambridge-Scroop-Grey plot in *Henry V*. The substance of Friedman's argument is of less interest than the way he bookends his reading with references to Poe and the Cold War. The essay begins: "The sort of mystery tale which Edgar Allan Poe first crystallized into a formula called a *Whodunit* is now very much in vogue in this country and many of our distinguished citizens are addicted to this type of literature. In this paper I intend to analyze very briefly a Shakespearean *Whodunit*. Or perhaps it would be better to call it a *Whodidn'dunit*, because the intended victim escapes death, but the plotters are not so fortunate" (401).

We have returned to the territory of Rogin's "Make My Day!"—an article on Cold War statecraft that takes its cue from the narrative structure of "The Purloined Letter." Or perhaps we have not so much returned to that territory as found its symbolic origin. If Rogin's association of Poe with Cold War espionage resonates today, it is because writers such as Friedman laid the grounds for this affiliation, implicitly recognizing how deeply the politics of the Cold War are entangled with the logic of gazes that Lacan finds in "The Purloined Letter." The moral and political force of "Shakespeare, Secret Intelligence, and Statecraft" derives from Friedman's translation of *Henry V* into a version of Poe's story. Here is Friedman's summary of the play: "Henry discovers the conspirators by interception, tricks them into making indiscreet statements, confronts them with 'those papers,' which are nothing other than intercepted letters with decipherments of their own ciphers (which they doubtless considered impregnable, as is usually true of persons without experience in cryptology)" (406). This is Poe's plot as well; Dupin recovers the intercepted letter through an interception of his own, the letter in the meantime having undergone steganographic disguise to prevent its recognition. (That Poe recognizes this disguise as a form of encryption is signaled by his constant reference to Minister D——'s hand as his "cipher.") The offstage denouement of "The Purloined Letter" follows from Poe's cryptanalytic sense that writing is both a way of staying violence and a way of causing it to happen. By provoking Minister D——, the queen or her agents will trick him into "making indiscreet statements" that will lead to his downfall; when he returns for the hidden letter, he will discover that Dupin, having seen through Minister D——'s "impregnable" disguise, has performed a "decipherment of [his] own ciphers" that will lead to his execution for treason.

Having assimilated *Henry V* to Poe, Friedman proceeds to read Shakespeare back into the context of Cold War state politics. "Shakespeare, Secret Intelligence, and Statecraft" ends with a meditation on *King John*, act 4, scene 2, in which a messenger informs John that the French have intercepted his secret directives concerning the imminent war. John replies:

> O, where hath our intelligence been drunk?
> Where hath it slept? Where is my mother's care?
> That such an army could be drawn in France,
> And she not hear of it?
> (ll. 116–19)

"Regretfully," Friedman continues, "we must note that the same question has been raised several times since 1941, the last as recently as October 28, 1961, by the distinguished American Navy historian Samuel E. Morison." Friedman then quotes from Morison's *Saturday Evening Post* article, a response to the April fiasco of the Bay of Pigs entitled "The Lessons of Pearl Harbor," which concludes with a "warning to the American people" that, despite vast advances in the methods of obtaining and disseminating secret intelligence, "we were surprised by the North Koreans in 1950, surprised when China entered the war later that year, surprised by the utter failure of the attempt to invade Cuba this year. . . . In the cold war such as the one in which we are now engaged, it is vitally important to find out not only the capabilities of our political enemy, but also his intentions" (402–3).

Then Friedman makes an interesting move; he spells out what he takes to be Shakespeare's posthumous political intentions. Endorsing Morison's realpolitik, Friedman concludes that in *Henry V*, Shakespeare articulates "lessons about the importance of intelligence, not only for Tudor Englishmen, but also for all of us in the modern Western World" (ibid., 410). These lessons include the utility of spying and cryptanalysis not only against intrigue by foreign governments, but, ominously, against agents of internal dissent as well. "Can it be that Shakespeare also wishes to show that secret intelligence and its proper use is one of the reasons why the remainder of the reign of the historical Henry was free from domestic strife, and that such intelligence is as important and useful for maintaining domestic tranquility as in the conduct of foreign relations?" (ibid., 410–11).

Wilderness of Mirrors

Friedman's intertwining of literature, secret intelligence, and the Cold War is not an isolated phenomenon. By the early 1960s, cryptography (and cryptographic espionage) served a variety of writers as a metaphor for the duplicity and self-reflexivity of writing. Among many examples, one may mention the work of Vladimir Nabokov, worthy of a monograph in its own right. Besides *Pale Fire* (1962), whose palimpsestic narrative superimposes detective fiction and foreign espionage on an account of the production and criticism of poetry, one might profitably look at the short fiction, including "Signs and Symbols," with its charged and barren ciphers, and "The Vane Sisters," whose narrator spends a fruitless evening looking for acrostic messages in the first letters of the lines of Shakespeare's sonnets, even while his own words are subtended by the dead sisters of the title, who encode a hidden message in the story's last paragraph.[47]

Or one might consider Thomas Pynchon's *Crying of Lot 49* (1966). Tony Tanner expressly describes Oedipa as "a cryptologist" desperate to learn whether Pierce Inverarity's will contains "a code which she has to interpret,"[48] whose search centers on the connection "between rubbish and fantasy" condensed into "the code cryptogram W.A.S.T.E."[49] When Don DeLillo revised *The Crying of Lot 49* in *White Noise* (1985), he explicitly connected such ciphering with the structures of American intelligence. Tweedy Browner, Jack Gladney's third wife, "came from a distinguished old family that had a long tradition of spying and counterspying," while his first and fourth wife, Dana Breedlove, "reviewed fiction for the CIA, mainly long serious novels with coded structures," the reviews of which "she microfilmed and sent to a secret archive."[50] The work of reading ciphered fiction —which is also the central conceit of Jack Grady's *Six Days of the Condor* (1974)[51]—leaves Dana with "jangled nerves" and "periods of deep spiritual fatigue. She told Steffie she was thinking of coming in from the cold."[52] Dana's condition is obliquely related to Murray Jay Siskind's Dotenesque vision of the American supermarket as a world of "psychic data": "Energy waves, incident radiation. All the letters and numbers are here, all the colors of the spectrum, all the voices and sounds, all the code words and ceremonial phrases. It is just a question of deciphering, rearranging, peeling off the layers of unspeakability."[53]

The evidence is everywhere. In 1965 Henri Coulette won the Lamont award for his long poem *The War of the Secret Agents*, whose dramatis personae include Allied and German spies; Mama Bee, "a famous American medium" enlisted to get in contact with a dead agent; Jane Alabaster, a historian who writes regularly to T. S. Eliot, her editor at Faber and Faber; and "Prosper," chief of the Paris secret agents, whose code name provides the requisite allusion to Shakespeare.[54] Coulette's volume was, in turn, an inspiration for John Hollander's *Reflections on Espionage* (1976).[55] Told in a series of ninety-nine chronologically arranged poems, *Reflections on Espionage* recounts the sometimes despairing attempts of a "master-spy" code-named "Cupcake" to communicate with his handlers. As Hollander explains, Cupcake "worked for an altogether inconvenient little republic which ceased to exist a good time ago. The regular, encoded radio transmissions, copies of which were eventually recovered by sources in his native country, have only recently been deciphered, the eleven-phase transposition grid he used for enciphering his messages having been guessed at earlier but rejected as being too archaic. . . . [The transmissions] are here reprinted in deciphered . . . form, unencumbered with more than a few glosses."[56]

The spy novel's emphasis on ciphering provides Hollander with a metaphor for the benighted state of twentieth-century poetry. Cupcake's "inconvenient republic" is the republic of letters, now forced underground and into code, undecipherable to those without special training; his unseen director, code-named "Lyrebird," serves as Apollonian muse. The eleven-phase transposition grid used by Cupcake for his ciphers allegorizes Hollander's "archaic" use of hendecasyllabic meter in an age that privileges a telegraphic directness of expression. Cupcake's loneliness and isolation are the poet's; so, too, is his dream of a "Final Cipher," in which language would be purified of its dross and rendered true across any translation:

> *In re* the Final Cipher again: it would
> Have to hold this invariant property,
> That any unsuitable message—falsehoods,
> Mistakes of transmission, bungled assignments
> Yielding ore of too low a grade, and high truths
> Employed in some nevertheless doubled way
> To trap us with—all these would simply not fit
> The code, and go into it as cipher which
> Decoded would unlock only gibberish—
> Like a language in which all lies came out in
> Ungrammatical sentences.
>
> (24–25)

In *Reflections on Espionage*, the cryptographer's rigor and imagination model the poet's skill at making verse. The book is full of private jokes that superimpose espionage on writing: Ezra Pound appears under the code name "Kilo"; Robert Frost is "Morosz" (Russian for frost), and Hollander's Yale colleague Norman Holmes Pearson is "Puritan," which was his genuine code name within the OSS. Yet the metaliterary richness of Hollander's poem (which includes an obligatory allusion to Poe: Cupcake's agent Kidd returns us to "The Gold-Bug") depends on his specific knowledge of World War II cryptography. Hollander's poems complete a circle begun when Poe applied his cryptographic precepts to the creation of his detective trilogy. The genre that emerged from those stories eventually melded with tales of political intrigue to form the espionage novel. In its "organic" connection to real cryptographic practice, this genre in turn permits Hollander to use the internal reflections cast by cryptographic writing as the basis for his meditation on the situation of the contemporary poet, left "out in the cold," invisible, without a culturally sanctioned role or identity.

Even genre fiction like *The Looking-Glass War* (1965) reflexively associates cryptography and writing. Le Carré's novel tells the story of Fred Leiser, a retired British spy brought out of mothballs, retrained to send encrypted Morse code, and dropped into East Germany to spy on potential missile placements. The novel takes its epigraph from Tait's *Complete Morse Instructor*: "The carrying of a very heavy weight such as a large suitcase or trunk, immediately before sending practice, renders the muscles of the forearm, wrist and fingers too insensitive to produce good Morse." Having carried his bulky, ancient radio kit across a significant chunk of East Germany, Leiser is in fact betrayed by the clumsiness of his sending. (During World War II, analysts overhearing Axis broadcasts often identified specific telegraphers by subtle rhythms in their Morse code messages.) But the epigraph's meaning is not exhausted by the plot, for most of the novel's characters have had their ability to cipher deformed by the metaphorical weight of their history. In the internecine struggle for power among intelligence services, the Department (the branch of British intelligence concerned with military targets) has lost its wartime supremacy to the Circus. In their own ways, the Department staffers are as bad with codes as Leiser, for the Circus has encouraged their misguided operation precisely to produce a fiasco that will permanently close down their live operations. As the novel closes, with an abandoned Leiser about to be shot, readers are left to ponder the fine sensitivity to signs necessary to play the intelligence game correctly—a game emblematized by the memory, intelligence, and technique needed to send encrypted Morse.

The Looking-Glass War reminds us of the mirrorlike reversibility that attends the logic of Cold War culture, which undermines distinctions between literature and history, East and West, self and other, Smiley and Karla. Besides the many reflecting surfaces of *Pale Fire* (including the lake in which Hazel Shade drowns, and, in yet another Shakespearean citation, the "pale fire" of the moon mirroring the sun's light), there are the almost interchangeable titles of *The Looking-Glass War* and *Reflections on Espionage*. Although such specularity is intrinsic to the cryptographic imagination, the close postwar association of literature, espionage, and statecraft has meant that the history of covert operations in the last half-century has often disastrously mirrored the conventions of detective and spy fiction. Indeed, Le Carré's early fame was greatly enhanced by what seemed like his advance knowledge of the penetration of Britain's MI5 by the "third man," Kim Philby, whose status as a double agent was confirmed by his 1963 defection to the Soviet Union. As was the case with the double-cross of Leclerc by his compatriots in British intelligence, the psychological damage of Philby's longtime betrayal was multiplied by the knowledge that he, like Sir Anthony Blunt, surveyor of the Queen's pictures and drawings, was an Oxbridge graduate whose paternity and accomplishments seemed to place him beyond reproach.[57]

Perhaps the most significant instance of the self-replicating relations between politics and literature is the case of James Jesus Angleton, a monumental figure in American espionage who, through his involuntary appearance as a central figure in "several dozen" spy novels, has almost become a fictional character. *Newsweek* noted, "If John Le Carré and Graham Greene had collaborated on a superspy, the result might have been" Angleton.[58] For two decades Angleton ran CIA counterintelligence, that branch of the service meant to protect the agency against foreign penetration. Asked to describe the world of Soviet intelligence, Angleton referred to it as a "wilderness of mirrors," in a phrase borrowed from Eliot's "Gerontion." Subsequently, David C. Martin adopted the phrase for the title of his biography of Angleton, whose career provides an exemplary instance of the dangers of such doubling.

At Yale, Angleton had seemed destined for literature, not espionage; he wrote verse in French and English, edited the Yale *Lit*, and helped found *Furioso*, a magazine that published new work by William Carlos Williams, Wallace Stevens, and Archibald MacLeish. He was nothing if not precocious: in a letter to e. e. cummings, Ezra Pound described Angleton as "one of the brightest young hopes of American letters."[59] In 1943, however, he was drafted, and soon found himself recruited for the OSS by his former English professor at Yale, Norman Holmes Pearson. As codirector of X-2, the counterintelligence branch of the OSS, Pearson—who showed " 'a fantastic professional imagination' for tradecraft and conspiracy"[60]—held a position of great importance. Through a vast subterfuge involving falsified Allied transmissions and double agents, Pearson and his staff (in cooperation with British cryptographers at Bletchley Park) managed to keep the Germans from realizing that literally millions of their encrypted communications were being read by the Allies.

Such work would seem to have been at sharp remove from Pearson's interest in modernist poetry. But the X-2 network could, in fact, have been considered one of the better university English departments in America. Among others, Pearson handled Yale English professors Louis Martz and Eugene Waith; Edward Weismiller, winner of the 1936 Yale Younger Poets award; and Richard Ellman, whose subsequent work on Joyce might be thought of as a form of biographical decryption. Pearson's secretary was Perdita Doolittle, daughter of the expatriate "hieroglyphic" poet H.D.; his superior, J. C. Masterman, was an Oxford historian who was recruited for counterespionage service in part because he wrote detective novels, beginning with *The Oxford Tragedy* in 1933. After the war, Masterman wrote the definitive account of X-2, *The Double-Cross System in the War of 1939 to 1945*, a book that both Coulette and Hollander cite as direct inspiration for their own work.[61]

The conceptual link between Pearson's X-2 network and literature is pointed to by its punning name: double cross. The doubling of German agents required a profoundly literary sense of plotting and evidence, because the task was to keep German handlers from ever knowing their agents had been compromised. This involved the careful identification of psychological features of the agents, the coordination of information fed to them with that fed to other agents (and with whatever facts the Germans could verify from home), and, when a German agent died or refused to cooperate, imitation of that agent's vocabulary, grammar, and Morse code patterns. Indeed, X-2 went even further, inventing "notional" Allied spies out of whole cloth to deceive Axis strategists, as in the case of the drowned British "agent" whose body washed up ashore in Normandy, complete with falsified plans detailing the impending invasion of Italy.

Such doublings return us to literary problems of identification and reflection that are not limited to the detective novel, but that also include Irwin's "originary" hieroglyph (the sign as Narcissus's double) and the epistemological skepticism of modernist poetry. Angleton cut his teeth on modernism, and during the war he continued to write poetry and to irritate more earthbound OSS members by his habit of reading "goddamn books of poetry" through the night in his office.[62] Angleton clearly thought of himself as an Eliot manqué: like Eliot, he was a Midwesterner educated in the Ivy League, an Anglophile, an anxious Christian, a political conservative, and a junior friend of Ezra Pound.

"Who is the third, who walks always beside you?" The epistemological insecurity that structures Eliot's writing makes it a natural corollary to the doubling, dividing, and redoubling of postwar counterintelligence. Cyril Connolly describes the perpetual anxiety about Soviet penetration following the 1951 defection of Guy Burgess and Donald Maclean through an allusion to "The Waste Land": "After the third man the fourth man, after the fourth man the fifth man; who is the fifth man always beside you?"[63] Earlier in the poem, Eliot quotes Baudelaire's most famous line from *Les fleurs du mal*: "—Hypocrite lecteur,—mon semblable,—mon frère!" and it is not hard to see that Eliot identifies himself as one of Baudelaire's semblable readers. But Baudelaire's vocative was originally addressed to *Poe*, and we can hypothesize that it is Poe who serves as Eliot's "third man," the covert, unnameable presence who walks alongside Baudelaire, Eliot's preferred alter ego. If anyone is Angleton's third, it is Eliot, not Poe, but if Angleton's relentless doubling represents the external manifestation of a search for the other that originates in his reading of modernism, this mode of specular aggressivity still derives both from Dupin's relations with Minister D—— and from Poe's ghostly presence in Eliot.[64]

Angleton's counterintelligence work strikingly mimicked the hermeneutics of Eliot's verse. As Jerome Christensen argues, "the New Criticism, designed by poets to break the complex codes of other poets, was a form of counterintelligence. Counterintelligence is more than a matter of deciphering discrete messages; it presupposes the apprehension of the entire intelligence system as a complex, multivalent, and dynamic code."[65] The paranoia that dogged Angleton followed from his realization that, like the letter in Poe's story, such codes are disturbingly reversible. Within the CIA, Angleton's Dupin-like task was to defend the agency (the queen) from the subterfuges of double agents (Minister D——). But as Lacan's analysis of the pattern of glances in "The Purloined Letter" indicates, Dupin's position is all too open to subversion. Although the first glance "sees nothing," and the second "sees that the first sees nothing and deludes itself as to the secrecy of what it hides" (this is the queen and then Minister D——), the third glance "sees that the first two glances leave what should be hidden exposed to whoever would seize it: the Minister, and finally Dupin."[66] But Angleton has, as it were, read Lacan's "Seminar," and is only too aware that the presence of an unseen viewer could push him from his mastering gaze into the vulnerable second position. At any given moment, Angleton realizes, *he can never know* if the agency has been penetrated, since the very absence of evidence may testify to the mole's success.

Perversely, Angleton's success at rooting out Soviet spies did nothing to diminish his paranoia, because the first rule of counterintelligence is that one gives the enemy true information to lull it into a false security. "The greater the desired deception, the higher the value of accurate intelligence that had to be given away in order to establish the agent's *bona fides*."[67] When double agents such as George Blake were blown by turned or doubled Soviet agents, Angleton came to suspect that these were only bait offered by the Soviets, who hoped that the sacrifice of small fry would distract the CIA from more important moles lodged undiscovered in its bosom. This may even have been the case with Philby, who, it has been speculated, had his cover intentionally blown to protect a still-deeper source. Hence, when the Russian KGB defector Anatoly Golitsyn told Angleton in 1961 that there was a mole within the CIA, he only confirmed Angleton's darkest fears; although subsequent evidence suggests that the rumor was an offhand lie, designed to enhance his value to his American handlers, Golitsyn's claim initiated a desperate thirteen-year search by Angleton that only climaxed in 1974, when the new CIA director William Colby fired *Angleton*, believing him to be the double agent he was purportedly hunting down.[68]

In the end, it does not matter whether Angleton really was the mole or whether, as seems likely, he was the most blindly faithful of agents. The damage was the same in either case: friendships destroyed, lives' work ruined, and, for a number of American double agents, execution by the Soviets when their covers were blown through Angleton's purges. Just as the continual intensification of consciousness led Friedman and Eliot to psychotic breakdowns, so Angleton's cryptographic doubling produced a situation in which the extremity of his fidelity was indistinguishable in its effects from betrayal, with Angleton as judge, traitor, and victim all at once. Not satisfied with the orthodox doublings of the detective story, Angleton's self-referential search for a mole (if we have spies in the KGB, then the KGB must have spies in the CIA) more closely resembles Borges's revision of Poe in "Death and the Compass," where the detective Llönrot's search only ends up trapping him in the pattern he traces, as he becomes the man he seeks.[69]

It would be easy to cite further instances of the ties between Cold War politics and Poe's secret writing, such as Theodore Draper's suggestion that Caspar Weinberger deliberately misled Iran-Contra investigators by "hiding" pertinent documents in the *unclassified* section of his papers in the Library of Congress—a strategy Draper describes as "something like" "The Purloined Letter."[70] But how are we to understand the logic behind such coincidences, which seem to embarrass familiar accounts of the relation between texts and events? Two related answers suggest themselves. The first is that the institutional elaboration of cryptography and espionage was shaped by a rich literary tradition. Popular fiction has long embraced stories that turn on codes and secret writing. Thanks to such adaptations of "The Gold-Bug" as Conan Doyle's "Musgrave Ritual," Robert Louis Stevenson's *Treasure Island*, and Jules Verne's *Journey to the Center of the Earth*, by the turn of the century, codes, ciphers, secret inks, and disguised writing were common features of writing for children. In *Jerry and the Bacon Puppy* (1916), for example, "a white plaster puppy with the biliteral or Bacon cipher inscribed on its base enables Jerry to solve a secret message and prevent a crime."[71] Children weaned on such stories could order Captain Marvel decoder rings from Ovaltine or Sky King, or fish pamphlets on transposition ciphers from their cereal boxes. Cryptography was also a staple of the detective pulp magazines: the series *The Shadow* often employed abstract pictographs, and beginning in the 1920s, *Detective Fiction Weekly* ran a regular column on cryptography. This column generated so much interest that it begat the American Cryptogram Association (ACA), an organization of amateurs that currently boasts a bimonthly magazine (the *Cryptogram*), an annual convention, and membership drawn from more than twenty countries.[72]

When political and military leaders went about designing the intelligence apparatuses of postwar government, their designs were often inflected by notions of detection and spying borrowed from literature and movies. Consider the 1947 birth of the CIA, which took over the intelligence mandate of the OSS. At a White House lunch, President Truman presented Rear Admiral Souers and his subordinates with "black cloaks, black hats, and wooden daggers," and read an order charging Souers and his deputy "to receive and accept the vestments and appurtenances of their respective positions, namely as Personal Snooper and as Director of Centralized Snooping."[73] Truman's behavior was so clownish that it must have served to disguise genuine discomfort with the task at hand. The CIA would, after all, do work that included assassination, destabilization, and blackmail; what looks like Truman's insensitivity to the gravity of his actions may indicate that the small-town politician simply had no idea what kind of protocol *would* be appropriate for such skullduggery.

The second crucial reason for the ease with which fictional motifs entered the culture of espionage is that cryptography, detective fiction, and spying all center on the problem of knowing other minds. Recall that Morison insisted on the "vital importance" of discovering "not only the capabilities of our political enemy, but also his intentions." His sentiments were echoed by Truman's advisor Clark Clifford, who described the newly formed CIA's central mission as the task of replacing "suspicion of the Soviet Union" with "an accurate knowledge of the motives and methods of the Soviet government."[74] The literary *locus classicus* of such questions is, of course, "The Purloined Letter," where Dupin recounts the story of a schoolboy of his acquaintance whose "success at guessing in the game of 'even and odd' attracted universal admiration" (*PT*, 689). In this game, one boy holds a number of marbles in his hand while a second guesses whether the number held is even or odd. The boy in question wins all the marbles in his school, for although he may lose once,

> upon the second trial he wins, for he then says to himself, "the simpleton had them even upon the first trial, and his amount of cunning is just sufficient to make him have them odd upon the second." . . . Now, with a simpleton a de-gree above the first, he would have reasoned thus: "This fellow finds that in the first instance I guessed odd, and, in the second, he will propose to him-self, upon the first impulse, a simple variation from even to odd, as did the first simpleton; but then a second thought will suggest that this is too simple a variation, and finally he will decide upon putting it even as before. I will therefore guess even." (Ibid.)

Recognizing that the schoolboy's method is merely "an identification of the reasoner's intellect with that of his opponent," the narrator asks Dupin how it is that the boy can measure so exactly. The answer is through a "*thorough* identification" in which the boy attempts to "fashion the expression of my face, as accurately as possible, in accordance with the expression of his, and then wait to see what thoughts or sentiments arise in my mind or heart, as if to match or correspond with the expression" (ibid., 690).

As a model of human behavior, Dupin's method of identification is dangerously unreliable; anyone relying on it in a street game of three-card monte would lose a bundle.[75] But it admirably describes the essential econ-omy of cryptographic reading, in which the best way to break a cryptogram is to reproduce the pattern of thought behind its construction. True, one can sometimes use mathematical tools to crack a cipher through brute force.

But cryptographers keep designing ciphers to disguise those patterns, so even at the highest levels of computer-aided cracking, cryptanalysis still involves an attempt to identify with the thought process of the codemaker.[76] This is why Poe says that the supreme analyst must be both poet and mathematician, because however great the latter's analytic skill, it is useless without the poet's gift for metaphor—the gift, that is, that allows the poet to establish humanly felt patterns and associations among discrete objects in the world.[77] Because ciphers rely on patterns of association that arise in the human mind, they can never escape human understanding—or, as Poe puts it in "Secret Writing," "it may be roundly asserted that human ingenuity cannot concoct a cipher which human ingenuity cannot resolve" (*ER*, 1278). This is also why Poe's search for the roots of analytic thought centers on the humble game of guessing evens and odds, for the principle of identification on which it builds is the root of all cryptanalysis.

In fact, the apparent meaningless of the cipher is directly related to the force of imagined mental contact. To adapt Poe slightly, if a person says "I love you now as ever," the precise intention behind the utterance is up for grabs. If, however, one writes instead "48932 34845 28858 23828 28258 09292 28209," the very opacity of the signal conversely suggests the accessibility of the message, especially because cryptanalysis is based on the direct reconstruction of the maker's pattern of thought. In the world of counterintelligence, code decryptions were taken as incontrovertible evidence of the enemy's intentions. Although a double agent might intentionally pass on false information, "a message transmitted in a supposedly unbreakable cipher was unquestionably the real thing. A code break shattered all the mirrors and permitted a straight line of sight across the wilderness."[78]

It is suggestive, then, that although the cryptogram presents itself as an impenetrable glyph, it can contrarily become an agent of the most absolute identification. In "Rue Morgue," Dupin treats the narrator's physiognomy and gestures as a three-dimensional, temporally extended rebus. By deciphering the human cryptograms represented in such passages, Dupin comes close to realizing the ancient fantasy of obtaining direct access to another person's mind.[79] This sort of literary fantasy anticipates cryptanalytic practice. According to near-universal testimony, undivided attention paid to cipher systems can lead to the instantaneous solution of the cipher, which effectively grants privileged access to the consciousness of its maker. To solve a cryptogram often requires a hallucinatory identification with code and codemaker that repeats Doten's identification with Poe's prosody (his code) and with the figure intuited behind those poems. " 'You must concentrate almost in a nervous trance when working on a code,' Miss [Asta] Friedrichs recalled. 'It is not often done by conscious effort. The solution often seems to crop up from the unconscious.' "[80] Yardley directly echoes the "omnipotence of consciousness" passage from "Rue Morgue" when he reports cracking the code keys of a safe through sheer force of identification: "I knew I could open the safe . . . if I could but place myself in my superior's shoes and follow his train of thought. He had smiled. At what? At a name? Something connected with a name? What name was on every one's lips? 'Mrs. Galt' suddenly flashed across my mind. President Wilson had just announced their engagement. I glanced at the telephone number opposite her name and with trembling fingers spun the dial to the safe. In another second the tumbler clicked and the door swung open!"[81]

Even Friedman practiced mind reading. Until his death he carefully saved an article entitled "Let Your Subconscious Solve It," and in an essay he wrote on the subject of insight, Friedman insisted that "a cryptologist without creative insight is only half a cryptologist"[82]—a virtual repetition of Poe's observation that "as poet and mathematician he [Minister D——] would reason well; as mere mathematician, he could not have reasoned at all" (*PT*, 691). Friedman's technique in testing the Plett device, an enciphering machine that used two code words as keys to its dual alphabets, calls to mind Poe's claim that Dupin's results in "Rue Morgue," although "brought about by the very soul and essence of method, have, in truth, the whole air of intuition" (ibid., 404). To begin with, within seconds Friedman simply *guessed* the first word—an achievement that viewed statistically is thousands of times more rare than being dealt four aces in a game of stud poker. Such a guess could only be called intuitive (or poetic), because no mathematical principle determined Friedman's choice. But this is only partially true, for the first keyword was *cipher*. Entranced by his machine's imagined perfection, Plett had chosen a word that referred to the structure of his machine. Friedman then reasoned that "if the encipherer had been foolish enough to use as a key one word concerned with the enciphering process, then he might have used something similar as a basis for the second alphabet." Even with the example of *cipher*, however, Friedman's ensuing guesses drew only blanks. Friedman next appealed to his wife, asking her to lean back, close her eyes, and make her mind as blank as possible. "Then," Elizebeth Friedman reports, "he would ask me a question. I was not to consider the reply even for a second but just give the word which his question brought to my mind. I did as he said. He spoke the word 'cipher' and I instantly replied: 'Machine.'" She was right. Minutes later, "the plaintext of all the messages, the first reading 'This message is absolutely indecipherable,' was being telegraphed to Washington."[83]

The danger in all this is that the pure identification required for such cracking can lead to the loss of self. At the point of absolute identification, identity itself breaks down, evacuated by the analyst's concentration on the machine of translation (a machine that in its blankness is the structural analogue to Eliot's feared *poésie pure*). If, taking advantage of the erotics of secrecy at work in ciphered reading, Friedman achieved almost magical success, the solution of the text ("This message is absolutely indecipherable") returned Friedman not to the world of social interaction but to the apodictic utterance of a cybernetic system that resists a human meaning. Although Doten's reading destroyed her ability to differentiate between her self and the imagined author of the works she read, such psychosis seems infinitely preferable to the forms of *un*consciousness risked in the pitch of identification required for decryption, as the contents of the mind are reduced to a hash of illegible symbols. Cryptanalysis exacerbates the mental dispossession produced by reading itself. Although such dispossession is ordinarily repressed in our adult lives, in moments of illness or exhaustion the sense of texts oscillating between meaning and nonsense can return. For the cryptographer, such feelings are part and parcel of the job, as each cipher represents a series of seemingly meaningless symbols that, even when solved, direct the cryptographer's attention ever deeper into the mysteries of language and identity.

Let Your Subconscious Solve It

If Friedman was spared the doubling that Angleton experienced, this was largely because Angleton occupied a position within the specular game of espionage, while Friedman identified with the system of secret writing itself. Indeed, Friedman seemed fluently to traverse worlds—at least once even managing to put Shakespeare to direct cryptologic use.[84] Ultimately, however, Friedman's work also exacted an enormous psychic toll. As a young man, Friedman claimed that one requirement for happiness as a cryptologist was "a passion for anonymity";[85] later in life, though, Friedman's mental troubles revealed the costs of the "double personality" mandated by his professional invisibility. The private Friedman, "the adored father," "the normal sociable animal," seemed "basically different from the other Friedman who had to think thrice before he spoke."[86] At the NSA compound in Fort Meade, even friends addressed him as "Mr. Friedman," and he is almost always isolated in group photos. In figure 14, Friedman, forced into civvies by his involuntary retirement, stands out from the uniformed SIS heads as they receive distinguished visitors. Although the military men look directly at their visitors in deferential engagement, Friedman (in natty suit, homburg, two-toned shoes) stares at the camera, a prim, melancholy man, a sadder Adolphe Menjou.

Friedman was repeatedly hospitalized for anxiety, tension, and insomnia; for a period he carried a coil of rope in the back of his car, joking that he was "looking for a tree to hang myself."[87] Despite postwar recognition (J. Edgar Hoover and Friedman were the only recipients of both the National Security Medal and the Medal for Merit), Friedman often quipped that although one did not have to be insane in order to do cryptology, it helped.[88] By 1950, a "profoundly depressed" Friedman voluntarily

Figure 14. Gen. Dwight Eisenhower visiting top codebreakers at Arlington Hall during World War II. Friedman is at the extreme right. Used by permission of the George C. Marshall Research Library, Lexington, Virginia.

entered George Washington University Hospital, where "he received a total of 6 electroshock treatments, each without incident," and "made a rapid and dramatic recovery."[89] After a brief remission, Friedman's attacks of "psychic giddiness" continued, and in an undated note written sometime in the 1960s on a single sheet of paper, Friedman acknowledged struggling for fifty years with overmastering feelings of "nervousness, depression, at times despondency—frightening to be alone b/c suicidal thoughts." He had "accomplished great deal—my reputation," but still felt the weight of "repression by secrecy restrictions—fear of punishment chimerical but still there. 'Floating anxiety' which attaches itself to anything and everything."[90]

Such fears were intensified by Friedman's authorial invisibility, particularly painful for a man who, on Kahn's account, was as much an author as a scientist. "Words he coined gleam" on the pages of dictionaries; "his textbooks have trained thousands." Friedman's Riverbank monographs have today become "bookselling rarities," avidly sought after by the cognoscenti. They were printed in small numbers, and their "air of mystery" is "deepened by the fact that in most cases they failed to carry the author's name."[91] Fabyan—who had the Riverbank Publications printed in Paris to save money—implicitly tried to take credit for their contents by printing most of them without authorial identification. But turnabout is fair play: when Fabyan published "The Index of Coincidence" in 1922, the anonymous pamphlet came to the attention of the French cryptographer François Cartier, who "thought so highly of it that he had it translated and published forthwith—false-dating it '1921' to make it appear as if the French work had come first!"[92]

Such attempts to purloin Friedman's writing unhappily prefigured those made by the NSA. Friedman's superiors had long looked on his literary ambitions with disfavor. In 1939, Friedman was "smartly called over the coals" for addressing a small audience on the decipherment of the Egyptian hieroglyphics, and the government prevented the Jules Verne Society from reviewing Friedman's essay on Verne, classifying it as a restricted War Department publication.[93] Perhaps reflecting these troubled relations, Friedman's thinking in the Shakespeare essay sometimes cuts across the grain of his own argument, as he pointedly questions the place of free speech in America: "How far is the open conduct of public affairs compatible with the national security of a democracy? What about its conduct in dealings with a closed society? I wonder what Shakespeare's answers to questions such as these might be?"[94]

As Friedman explained to a friend, "my superiors have bluntly told me that my name must not appear in the public press, and the situation is, I am sorry to say, such that even if my name were merely sponsoring authorship of a song or article having to do not at all with cryptography, it would not make any difference. From this, you will gather that they are pretty jittery and want to keep quiet even the fact that there is such a thing as cryptography going on."[95] He was not exaggerating. Although the NSA employed the Friedmans' book tour for *The Shakespearean Ciphers Examined* as a cover for its own intelligence activities, this was a rare exception. As the Cold War escalated and the NSA ballooned, the agency imposed byzantine security measures on its employees, reclassifying Friedman's papers in order to prevent him from selling his prized cryptological library (so important to him that he required even family members to sign out books). The censorship climaxed in 1958, when three NSA staffers invaded Friedman's home in order to confiscate forty-eight items whose existence was felt to jeopardize national security, not excepting "The Index of Coincidence," printed in France forty years earlier. With heavy-handed irony, the NSA even pilfered Friedman's library copy of his 1937 article in the *Franco-American Review*, "The Restoration of Obliterated Passages and of Secret Writing in Diplomatic Missives."[96]

Disgusted at the repossession of his words, and plagued by bouts of mental illness, in his last years Friedman's voice sometimes slipped into paranoid and strident tones. The heads of the NSA were "out to get him," he reported, noting that his efforts to publish were "hampered by restrictions which are at times so intolerable and nonsensical that it is a wonder that I have been able to retain my sanity."[97] The mandate to monitor communications "in time of war" was now a permanent injunction, as the NSA turned itself into "the central agency essential for the running of a police state," extending its surveillance to Americans at home and abroad.[98] For Friedman, "as the abuse of telephone tapping, electronic bugging, and a multitude of other systems became easier, earlier fears began to return."[99] Yet even in his frustration, Friedman was never possessed by the aggressive doubling that consumed counterintelligence agents such as Angleton. Friedman fantasized no Karla, no Philby, no Minister D——; no mirror-spy, in short, whose actions could serve as the source of his problems. Instead, rejecting the detective's familiar identification with a *particular* double, Friedman became increasingly disenchanted with the whole enterprise of cryptographic espionage.

Friedman died in 1969. One hundred twenty-five years earlier, Poe had written: "It is not to be supposed that cryptography, as a serious thing . . . has gone out of use at the present day. It is still commonly practiced in diplomacy; and there are individuals, even now, holding office in the eye of various foreign governments, whose real business is that of deciphering" (SW, 124). Poe could not have foreseen the world-shaping force that cryptography would possess in this century, any more than he could have seen how his own writings would indirectly enlist him in the great wars of our time. Densely tangled as it is with issues of literary history and politics, Friedman's life suggests that ours may be the most literary of centuries, in which, as a result of the childhood reading of Poe by Friedman, Angleton, and their peers, literary modes drawn from detective fiction were grafted onto military and diplomatic policies to form such hybrid institutions as the CIA and the NSA. Not only is Poe godfather to the genre of espionage fiction—a heritage evident in Grady's structuring of *Six Days of the Condor* around Dupin's principles in "The Purloined Letter"—but at times cryptography even becomes the other to literature, converting poets, novelists, and critics to the task of producing codes.[100] After he left X-2, Norman Holmes Pearson's career as a critic never regained its momentum, and he ended up running the Yale American Studies program "as if it were the CIA"—which it may as well have been, if one credits his alleged activity as an agency recruiter.[101] Similarly, Angleton stopped writing verse in order to help produce the text of the Cold War, building on the plots of works by Poe and his heirs. And the poet Edward Weismiller wrote hardly anything after 1946, save *The Serpent Sleeping*, a fictionalized account of his years in X-2.[102]

One need not resort to cryptography to account for the literary failure of any of these figures. But given the uniformity of this failure, and given that so much of what they *did* write obliquely concerned secret writing, one may wonder if cryptography is not part of a more profound sea change in literary culture. Perhaps, despite the strenuous denials of the New Critics, literature does after all exist in a mimetic relationship to the history of its period, as Poe sponsors both the postmodern self-consciousness of Borges and Nabokov (dear to an era that institutionalized the linguistic self-regard of modernism) *and* the Cold War. But "mimetic" needs a weird gloss: literature turns out to be mimetic in the Cold War not because it doubles reality, but because reality keeps doubling it. Although Borges's claim that to think Shakespeare is to *be* Shakespeare looks like an ultimately metaliterary moment, in which everything historical or political melts away in a moment of perfect verbal identification, things are rather more complicated for a period so defined by processes of decryption. Indeed, such patterns of identification with the dead appear less as literary tropes than as historical referents for the Cold War era. In this sense, the Cold War performs the act of mimesis of which the reality is the postmodern absorption of Poe. Earlier I observed that in *White Noise*, Dana Breedlove makes a living by reading espionage novels for the CIA. DeLillo's conceit is Cold War history: for decades the CIA maintained a subdepartment dedicated to this enterprise, with a library of thousands of espionage novels for research.[103]

For Friedman, literature was always the dark twin of cryptography, alluring and dangerous. As early as 1936, Friedman concluded that had Poe had "an opportunity to make cryptography a vocation, there is no doubt that he would have gone far in his profession."[104] Through Friedman's actions, we might say, Poe fulfilled the prediction that he would "go far" in cryptology. But identification is a tricky thing. Persecuted by the authorities, and furious at the growing invasiveness of the agency, Friedman stalked the halls of the NSA forgotten but undead, a deposed king of secret readers who, like that other king in *Hamlet*, found that his injunction "Remember me!" was better addressed to the world of literature than to the world of statecraft. It was a grimly satisfied Friedman who for several weeks walked in and out of the NSA's top-secret areas, wearing on his mandatory identification badge not a photograph of himself but an image of William Shakespeare.[105]

CIPHERING THE NET

7

> Cypherpunks know that people have been creating their own privacy for
> centuries with whispers, envelopes, closed doors, and couriers.
>
> Cypherpunk charter
>
> For here were God knew how many citizens deliberately choosing not
> to communicate by U.S. Mail. It was not an act of treason, nor possibly
> even of defiance. But it was a calculated withdrawal, from the life of the
> Republic, from its machinery.
>
> Thomas Pynchon, *The Crying of Lot 49*

A Few More Words on Secret Writing

Poe begins "A Few Words on Secret Writing" with a hypothesis about the
utility of cryptographic writing: "As we can scarcely imagine a time when
there did not exist a necessity, or at least a desire, of transmitting information from one individual to another in such a manner as to elude general
comprehension, so we may well suppose the practice of writing in cipher to
be of great antiquity" (SW, 114). Today, only a small number of Americans
pursue cryptographic security. But as more and more of our social and economic lives are conducted via electronic signals—through e-mail, Net postings, digital bank transactions, and secure corporate communications—the
question of privacy, and hence of secret writing, comes to the fore. Among
the issues raised by the imminent spread of electronic cryptography, I mention three:

1. *Terrorism.* A prime bogey advanced by opponents of strong public cryp-
    tography is the fear that without governmental oversight, terrorists
    spread over several continents will be able jointly to plan raids like that
    on the World Trade Center in 1992, with no chance of FBI interception.
    Partly as a consequence, exporting advanced encrypting technology out
    of the United States is a felony punishable by a fine of one million dol-
    lars and ten years in prison—the same penalty imposed for smuggling
    nuclear weapons.[1]

2. *Pornographic delectation.* Over half the traffic on Usenet newsgroups is allegedly composed of pornographic materials. Not only has anonymous posting produced an enormous number of prurient writers and readers, but the very absence of the body on the Net seems to produce a countervailing imaginative investment in its presence. And in what is already a governmental chestnut used to argue for encryption control, one convicted child molester has used cryptography to hide the identities of his victims.

3. *Cyberspace warfare.* A computer scientist named Lawrence Detweiler (about whom I will say more) has until recently been furiously battling what he calls the "Medusa phenomenon," his name for the possibility that one Internet user could fake multiple identities on different networks, located anywhere on the globe. Accessed by modem, these identities could be used in hoaxes that would lead to pitched flame wars enormously destructive of reputations and confidences.

The Net, it seems safe to say, will be a defining technology for the next two decades. New legal and social protocols will be needed to govern the Net's global electronic interchanges.[2] Somewhere in the vicinity of sixty million people are now connected to the Internet, with perhaps nine hundred thousand more added monthly—an onslaught of such proportions that John Seabrook compares it to a new tide of internal immigration.[3]

The Internet has also become a fantastic realization of much of what Poe imagined in his essays on cryptography: a matrix for communication whose resonances reach back to the telegraph, through which the world "has become a great nerve, vibrating thousands of miles in a breathless point of time."[4] And because of the "inherent fluidity of 'cyberspace,' where people emerge and submerge frequently," network identity remains amorphous: instead of the intimate particularity of individual faces and voices, one's e-mail address consists only of an "arbitrary and cryptic sequences of letters and digits."[5] In its electronic defiles (which are a series of baffled channels), users can dissimulate identities with a freedom that Poe could only imagine. Separated from one's body, lacking visual or acoustic representation, one's digital identity is dangerously open to manipulation. Yet the amorphousness of Net identity is also one of its most attractive features, enabling posters and readers of Net communications to gain access to worlds of information that might ordinarily be limited to people of a certain gender, race, profession, or age.

The emergence of an interactive electronic world is already producing legal and social changes related to privacy, identity, and intellectual copyright. Many of these are reminiscent of those tied to the Anglo-American development of commercial print, with newsgroups and World Wide Web pages standing in for the weekly newspapers and coffeehouses that accompanied the print revolution of the eighteenth century. Assistant Secretary of Commerce Larry Irving estimates that the electronic media account for about 15 percent of the gross national product—the same amount as all healthcare industries combined—and that by the millennium, "telecommunications will be America's foremost export and the world's No. 1 business."[6] But how will electronic writing mediate social relations as we enter the age of the Net?

One way to approach this question is to use Poe's cryptographic writing as a frame. True, in most areas of the Net, Poe is barely present. In a discussion on the *alt.suicide* newsgroup, someone identified as Joe advanced Poe's life as evidence that "the 'mind that is being torn apart' produces the greatest works." He could not, however, actually remember Poe's name, referring to him only as "the author of 'Tell-Tale Heart'; I forget his name. His whole life was wrecked." To which a correspondent replied, "Edgar Allan Poe had a bad life? I didn't know that. . . . Anyone know more about him? Was he suicidal? How was his life a wreck? Just curious, because I (like most people I guess) have always loved his stuff."[7]

In other respects, the Internet seems the telos for which Poe's fictions have been waiting; indeed, Poe scholars now have a new research tool available, because a group called Internet Wiretap has scanned more than two dozen Poe tales on the Internet that can now be downloaded via anonymous FTP (file transfer protocol). These public-domain texts "include goldbug.poe, mellonta.poe, mystery.poe, purloin.poe, rue.poe, and thouart.poe."[8] Thou art Poe, indeed. If today we find ourselves in a place shaped by Poe's cryptographic writing, this has less to do with notions of literary greatness than it does with the way Poe's writing has participated in the changing historical relationships between literature and technology. "Ride the information superhighway back to its ultimate sources and you end up in the heat and dust of World War II's secret-code battles," Julian Dibbel writes, but these battles also require us to reconsider Poe's writing.[9] To this end, I want to read some recent forms of electronic writing against both Poe's secret writing and Thomas Pynchon's *Crying of Lot 49*, the better to comprehend the contemporary social dynamics of cryptography, particularly in respect to the psychology of encrypting and decrypting. Hence my title: not *de*ciphering the Net (the futility of fantasies of perfect translations is evident), but *"ciphering* the Net"—subjecting our desires to its electronic graffiti, in which, through the veil of anonymity, we are forced to correspond with our most private selves.

Pretty Good Privacy

Consider the long Net FAQ (for "Frequently Asked Questions") entitled *Identity, Privacy, and Anonymity on the Internet*.[10] Its table of contents gives some sense of the giddy world of the telecommuning self, answering questions about the nature of Net identity, the possibility of privacy, where to learn digital cryptography, and how to become a cypherpunk. If identity cannot be taken for granted on the Net, if it requires special discussion in a FAQ, this is because the posters who can reach millions of readers instantly can also broadcast those messages anonymously by using a form of electronic cipher described as "the most revolutionary new concept in the field since the Renaissance."[11] These developments are quite recent: even two decades ago, the NSA had a virtual stranglehold on all serious cryptographic research in this country. "That ended abruptly in 1975 when a 31-year-old computer wizard named Whitfield Diffie came up with a new system, called 'public-key' cryptography, that hit the world of cyphers with the force of an unshielded nuke."[12] Public-key cryptography is a dual-key system, in which every user has both a public and a private algorithm. Although the public key can be distributed without fear of compromising security, the private key "is held more closely than an ATM password."[13]

> For relatively arcane mathematical reasons, a message encoded with either key can be decoded with the other. For instance, if I want to send you a secure letter, I encrypt it with your public key (which I have with your blessing), and send you the cyphertext. You decipher it using your private key. . . . This principle can also be used for authentication. Only one person can encrypt text with my private key—me. If you can decode a message with my public key, you know beyond a doubt that it's straight from my machine to yours. The message, in essence, bears my digital signature.[14]

Like most cryptographers, Diffie was a math whiz, but from an early age he also had a pressing interest in matters of personal privacy. As a cryptographer coming of age in the early 1970s, he was among the first to profit from Kahn's magisterial book *The Codebreakers*, which synthesizes a vast amount of cryptographic lore, setting its technical history within the cultural and psychological context of its deployment.[15] Influenced by Kahn, and working with a Stanford electrical engineer named Martin Hellman, Diffie created a series of algorithms that form the basis of public-key cryptography. Further refined by other mathematicians, the Diffie-Hellman system was eventually marketed under the name RSA Data Security.[16] Despite its imperfections, RSA provided "*a working public-key system*, and thus did not suffer from the dire flaw of all previous systems: the need to safely exchange private keys."[17]

The commercial availability of RSA spurred other budding cryptographers, most notably Phil Zimmermann, who developed an alternative system based on Diffie-Hellman known as PGP, for Pretty Good Privacy. An electronic Johnny Appleseed, Zimmermann sacrificed commercial development of PGP, instead placing it free on a computer bulletin board in 1991, where, as he expected, it soon migrated to the Net. " 'Like thousands of dandelion seeds blowing in the wind,' he wrote, PGP spread through cyberspace. Within hours, people were downloading it all over the country and beyond."[18] As the acronymic forms of strong crypto (that is, public-key cryptography with a key longer than forty bits) multiply, it is not yet clear which will become the standard. But public-key crypto will affect even persons who never use the Net. Many telephone manufacturers are now building cheap automatic encrypting and decrypting devices into their telephones, which have proved so secure that foreign intelligence services have intervened in their design "so that spies can continue to eavesdrop on private conversations." European governments fear "that surveillance operations against drug barons, the criminal underworld and foreign powers could be undermined."[19] According to FBI spokesperson Nestor Michnyak, digital technology is advancing so fast that countersurveillance may be stymied, because the costs of decryption would make widespread eavesdropping prohibitively expensive. Anticipating this, the FBI has proposed amending the Communications Act of 1934 to "require communications service providers and hardware manufacturers to make their systems 'tappable' by providing undetectable 'back doors' through which law enforcement officers could intercept communications."[20]

In light of the recent breakthroughs in cryptography and the government's renewed attempts to regulate its use, secret writers have organized a society for the propagation of ciphered privacy. Adapting a term from William Gibson, they call themselves "cypherpunks," and although their battleground may seem remote, the stakes are not: "the outcome of this struggle may determine the amount of freedom our society will grant us in the 21st century."[21] For cypherpunks, the chief value of public-key cryptography "will be to provide anonymity, the right most threatened by a fully digitized society." Currently, by following our electronic footprints, interested parties can "piece together a depressingly detailed profile of who we are: our health records, phone bills, credit histories, arrest records, and electronic mail connect our actions and expressions to our physical selves. Crypto presents the possibility of severing these links."[22]

If there is a touch of hyperbole here, it arises because in the future, privacy will likely be an all-or-nothing affair, requiring us to choose between allowing the digital surveillance of our economic and social lives, and making the inviolable crypt of a personal algorithm available to everyone, honest or not. In this context, the United States government's classification of cryptographic algorithms as munitions is no merely technical claim. When a skeptical NASA employee wrote to *sci.crypt* to ask if strong encryption really belonged in the same category as carrying a loaded gun, Jykri Kuoppala explained that both communication and data storage are shifting to an electronic format, including gun registrations, amateur radio licenses, and criminal registries. Therefore, "using strong cryptography routinely *is* being a revolutionary, it *is* positing oneself directly against the government's important interests of being able to monitor communications."[23] Or, as Zimmermann testified to a congressional subcommittee, the growth of digital communications entails "a disturbing erosion of our privacy."

> In the past, if the Government wanted to violate the privacy of ordinary citizens, it had to expend a certain amount of effort to intercept and steam open and read paper mail, and listen to and possibly transcribe spoken telephone conversation. . . . Fortunately for freedom and democracy, this kind of labor-intensive monitoring is not practical on a large scale. Today, electronic mail is gradually replacing conventional paper mail, and is soon to be the norm. . . . Unlike paper mail, e-mail messages are just too easy to intercept and scan for interesting keywords. This can be done easily, routinely, automatically, and undetectably on a grand scale . . . making [an] . . . Orwellian difference to the health of democracy.[24]

Cypherpunks do not merely rely on secrecy to do their work. When the computer scientist John Gilmore obtained a paper written by a cryptographer at Xerox, the publication of which had been quashed by the NSA, he simply posted it to the Net. Within hours it had been distributed both as code and hard copy across the country, and all the bureaucrats at the NSA could not undo Gilmore's deed. A wealthy former software designer, Gilmore now devotes himself to the cause of electronic freedom, such as in his legal challenge to the NSA for refusing to follow Freedom of Information Act protocols in releasing requested documents. We have returned to familiar ground: the documents in question were forty-year-old declassified manuals written by William Friedman and Lambros Callimahos, which the government later reclassified (shades of the Riverbank Publications!) for unknown reasons. While Gilmore pressed his case against the NSA in court, a friend located copies of two of the documents, one of them on unrestricted microfilm at Boston University. When Gilmore notified the judge hearing the Freedom of Information Act appeal that the documents were already on library shelves, the government informed Gilmore that "distribution of the Friedman texts would violate the Espionage Act."[25]

The threat to imprison Gilmore for a decade for distributing materials available in the library indicates how seriously the government views its cryptographic monopoly. Only when the *San Francisco Examiner* publicized the case did the government reconsider its position; two days later, the NSA announced that it had declassified the texts, which were quickly published as *Military Cryptanalysis*, parts 3 and 4.[26] The irony is palpable: after years spent in the shadows, Friedman's work has been liberated from the clutches of the NSA by freelance cryptographers inspired by his genius. It is, one might say, Friedman's posthumous revenge that he has become an avatar to this cryptographic underground, which now poses a greater threat to governmental cipher control than the Soviets ever did.[27] The NSA continues to argue that any publicity about cryptography is injurious to the nation, but Gilmore is skeptical: "We are not asking to threaten the national security. We're asking to discard a Cold War bureaucratic ideal of national security which is obsolete." "The decision to literally trade away our privacy," he adds, ought to be made by the whole society, "not made unilaterally by a military spy agency."[28]

In April 1993, the Clinton administration responded to the threat of public-key cryptography by proposing a new system based on an encrypting microchip known as the Clipper. Built into telephones, the chip would provide users with a powerful dual-key encryption program. (A similar chip, code-named "Capstone," was to be introduced for personal computers.)[29] In both cases, one key would be unique to the computer or phone; the other would be lodged in a federal repository, administered by a yet-to-be-named government agency. Either key could be used to decipher messages; in the case of suspected criminal wrongdoing, the relevant federal agency would obtain a warrant that would, in turn, be presented to the repository in order to obtain the key to a particular Clipper chip.

Needless to say, cypherpunks find this a case of the fox guarding the chicken coop, particularly because there is no way of knowing whether one's communications are being monitored. Deluged by attacks from suspicious computer scientists and cryptographers (and lobbied by software firms afraid of losing a $100 million encryption export industry), the government's National Institute of Standards and Technology backed away from implementation of Clipper and Capstone, only to decide in February 1994 to pursue the chips after all. Soon thereafter, a cryptographer (and cypherpunk) working for AT&T discovered a potentially fatal flaw in the chip's back door.[30] Regardless of its ultimate fate, the Clipper chip is the first word in a continuing debate over the rights of citizens to resist governmental oversight of their writing. Since Net traffic statistics indicate a huge demand for anonymous services, it is not even clear that the government has the *power* to prevent the high-tech encryption of private information. Although some users (particularly scientists) insist that anyone unwilling to identify himself or herself ought to be ignored, other "Netniks" argue fervently for the right and even the necessity of disguise. A "very grateful" Atul Salgaonkar explains that anonymous Usenet discussions helped him resolve "important questions" about his personal life, "due to kind help of other people who had been thru similar situations. In return, I have also replied to anon postings where I thought I could make a positive contribution. . . . Wasting bandwidth is less important than saving lives."[31] In *alt.personals*, or *alt.sexabuse.rec*, communication is often predicated on the intervening screen of anonymity. Such nameless publication is a constitutive part of American political life; consider Benjamin Franklin's use of "Silence

Dogood" as an intermediary to express dangerous political opinions.[32] Defending this practice, Stuart Derby explicitly connects anonymous writing to the origins of the United States: "Three of our founding fathers, Madison, Hamilton, and Jay, seemed to think 'anonymous posting' was OK. The Federalist papers were originally printed in New York newspapers with authorship attributed to 'Publius.' I wonder if you would find their purpose 'LEGITIMATE?' "[33]

Yet many posters also equate anonymity with direct physical danger: "If I get a phone call from someone who won't identify himself, I hang up. If I get U.S. mail with no return address, it goes into the garbage unopened. If someone accosts me in the street while wearing a mask, I back away—carefully, and expecting violence. . . . [The psychological] literature is filled with all the various things that people will do anonymously that they won't otherwise. Including one notorious study involving torture."[34] As this text suggests, the issue of cryptographic anonymity is fraught with fears and desires that cannot be explained by the content of a given message. The cypherpunks, for instance, are an exceptionally well-educated and savvy group of activists united around what is arguably the most important First Amendment issue in decades. But there is also something adolescent about their taste for secret writing: much of the attraction of computing derives from a fantasy about the power of hermetic codes.[35]

It will come as no surprise that these fantasies owe a great deal to Poe. Dr. Klaus Pommerening recalls being "impressed by Poe long before I became a professional mathematician."[36] And as a child, Whitfield Diffie "devoured all the books he could find on the subject of cryptography," prominently including Poe's stories.[37] As Levy observes, "certainly there is something about codes—secret rings, intrigue, Hardy Boys mysteries—that appeals to youngsters. Diffie . . . took them very seriously."[38] Diffie's pattern holds for hundreds of cryptographers, mathematicians, and software designers: a childhood exposure to cryptographic fiction (either to "The Gold-Bug" proper or to one of Poe's first- or second-generation imitators), and then a growing interest in the mathematics and psychology of cryptography, often fostered by a sense of superiority over nonciphering peers and teachers. Erich Fromm's remark seems telling: "The interest in deciphering, as well as in secret codes, may have a great deal to do with a person's sense of aloneness and isolation and the hope that he might find the related souls with whom he could communicate. The world is closed, and hence he has to decipher what is not meant for him."[39]

Of the thirty-two responses I received to a query about cryptography and literature on *sci.crypt*, twenty-eight mention works of cryptographic fiction by name, with those responding often vividly recalling the plot lines decades later. Besides works by Poe, such texts include cipher manuals, children's fiction such as *Alvin's Secret Code* (*very* often cited), and adult novels such as Helen McCloy's *Panic*, which was, significantly, a detective story.[40] John Taber remembers that it was "a fine murder mystery based on a mixed-alphabet Vigenere"; after reading it, he "borrowed Gaines' *Elementary Cryptanalysis* from the public library, and taught myself how to solve ciphers."[41] Although Karen Hunt's cryptographic interest was first stimulated by her fifth-grade teacher's math book, that was quickly followed by "kids' books on codes and ciphers and secret writing," and then by cryptograms in puzzle books. When a college friend wrote a computer encryption program, Hunt decided to break it "for sport." Remembering cipher types from her old "kiddie books," Hunt recognized it as a Vigenere cipher, which she cracked through a series of educated guesses. "About 2 years later I discovered Gaines' book on cryptanalysis, then Kahn's *Codebreakers*, then *Cryptologia*, then the ACA (American Cryptogram Association)."[42] Even more classic is Carl Ellison's recollection that his interest in cryptography was

> first aroused by Captain Midnight and his decoder ring (actually a belt buckle) which I sent for with Ovaltine labels. It then fell to nothing until I started sending e-mail and needed to encrypt so I invented my own 2 systems (a weak one and a moderate one). Then I started reading about the scientific efforts in WWII and . . . I got hooked on Enigma—tracked down books on the subject—reread Kahn's *The Codebreakers*—found Deavours' and Kruh's *Machine Cryptography and Modern Cryptanalysis*—read about the Hebern break by William Friedman in 1922 and tried it myself—succeeded—wrote it up for *Cryptologia* and was totally hooked.[43]

Such responses demonstrate the hermetic quality of the world of ciphers: time and again, cypherpunks cite the same progression from children's fiction to magazines to Kahn's *Codebreakers*, Gaines's *Elementary Cryptanalysis*, and the work of William Friedman. As adults, cypherpunks gather around a few small institutions: the American Cryptogram Association (whose membership hovers around seven hundred persons); *Cryptologia* (with a circulation of less than one thousand); and, most recently, the cypherpunks mailing list, whose seven hundred names include those of some of the world's leading cryptanalysts and computer scientists.[44] Cypherpunking represents a return to origins: in light of the NSA's restriction of cryptography, cypherpunks can now do battle with a real secret agency, one whose technological tricks and global reach would have done honor to Ian Fleming's Q or Conan Doyle's Moriarty.

The Medusa Complex

In the absence of universal access to public-key cryptography, other stratagems have been developed to guarantee the privacy of network writing, most prominently the use of anonymous file servers. Most Net sites employ addresses that identify a user's name and institutional affiliation. (When a pseudonym is used, it is a simple matter to finger a poster's address, querying the Net for public information about a given user.) My Usenet address (*Shawn.J.Rosenheim@williams.edu*) automatically names both the type of institution (educational) and the specific venue (Williams College) from which my message originates, but "as part of current mailing protocol standards, forging the From: line in messages is a fairly trivial operation" (FAQ, 1.5). Anonymous file servers circumvent this digital trail through the use of a double-blind procedure. One sends a message to the anonymous server, a digital halfway house that scrambles the home address before sending the intact message (now identified as *anon.penet.fi*, followed by a number) to its intended destination.

The most infamous of these servers was set up in November 1992 by Johan Helsingius ("Julf") in Finland, using scripts and code written by an American, Carl Kleinpaste. As of January 1993, *anon.penet.fi* was transmitting a remarkable three thousand anonymous messages daily—about 5 percent of all postings on the Usenet (FAQ, 8.4). Such "immense popularity" is due, Detweiler speculates, to "the capability for 'global' anonymity which has allowed users to find creative uses in diverse areas not previously envisioned." But when coupled with Julf's "total commitment to preservation of anonymity," such creativity can do real damage. In 1993, "commotion ensued" when an anonymous user "posted a supposed transcript of desperate crew dialogue during the Challenger shuttle disaster via *anon.penet.fi* to *sci.astro*. Although the transcript had been posted in the same place a year earlier (then non-anonymously) and actually originated not with the poster but a New York news tabloid, subsequent responses consisted largely of outrage at the poster's use of anonymity." As the original poster later conceded, the story " 'seemed likely to have been fabricated,' suggesting . . . that the original intent was not to provoke outrage but gauge reactions on the authenticity of the story (albeit crudely), free of personal risk from perceived association with the item" (ibid.).

In the face of the bitter criticism that followed this incident, Julf was subjected to "extraordinary pressure to dismantle his server." Because he would not do so, the Finland server crashed as a result of a "saturation mailbombing" initiated by an anonymous user. To his dismay, Julf learned that Kleinpaste had written his code more as a programming experiment than as a tool for unimpeded free expression; when Julf used this code to extend unrestricted anonymity, he offended Kleinpaste's sense of propriety, as if anonymity violated the social compact needed for true conversation. Kleinpaste retaliated with a series of abusive postings, in which, after calling Julf a "rude bastard," he regretted his part in creating the server. Although Kleinpaste did not copyright the code, he said "I thought that some concept of politeness and good sense might follow it to new homes. Interesting that

Johan's ideas of politeness and good sense seem to have nearly no intersection with mine. I could even cope with universal anon access *if* Johan would engage in abuse control, but that seems to be outside the range of reality."[45] A "sad and upset" Helsingius rather disingenuously replied that although he had intended to provide the service only to Scandinavian users, many people had asked him to open the service to the international community. "I now realize that I ought to have contacted you at that point to ask how you feel about me using your stuff in such a context. Again, I really want to apologise. And I will replace the remaining few pieces of code that still stem from your system. Unfortunately there is no way to remove the ideas and structure I got from you."

Unable to control Julf's server, a "seriously rude" Kleinpaste considered using the digital equivalent to capital punishment. Reasoning that Julf "didn't ask the greater Usenet whether universal anon access was a good idea; he just did it," Kleinpaste contemplated retaliating by programming the server to cancel all anonymous postings, a prospect that filled him with a Strangelovean fervor:

> I think I'll arm the Usenet Death Penalty, slightly modified, not for strategic whole-site attack, but tactical assault. . . . In fact, I have 8 people who have expressed privately the desire and ability to arm the UDP. P.S. No, in fact there are not 8 newsadmins ready to arm the UDP. It would be amusing to know how many people gulped hard when they read that, though. . . . P.P.S. Now that I've calmed some fears by the above P.S. . . . There are 2 newsadmins ready to arm the UDP. They've asked for my code. I haven't sent it yet. Only one site would be necessary to bring *anon.penet.fi* to a screeching halt.

The exchange between Kleinpaste and Julf manifests deep confusion in the way each thinks about how writing is attributed. For Kleinpaste, universal anonymous service would turn the Net into a speaking mirror, in which the disembodied messages on his monitor would take on the dimensions of paranoid projection. Julf responded by threatening to expose the attacker's identity—just what the server was designed to protect: "As we are talking threats here, let me make one as well. If somebody uses something like the UDP or maliciously brings down *anon.penet.fi* by some other means, it will stay down. But I will let the users know why. And name the person who did it. OK? As somebody said on this thread: 'You have to take personal responsibility for your actions,' right?" Kleinpaste—whose attacks continually invoke notions of politeness—finds that the prospect of unimpeded anonymity incites in him an incivility so extreme that it leads to fantasies of digital death. Meanwhile Julf, the advocate of privacy, responds to the anonymous attack on his server by threatening the assailant with exposure, all the while remarking piously on the importance of personal responsibility on the Net. As with the Challenger posting that only became inflammatory once its source was effaced, the threat posed by cryptography clearly has less to do with the incendiary content of the messages than it does with the anxiety produced by their lack of a signature.

The reverse side of such paranoia is narcissistic identification. Earlier I called Poe's ciphered self-correspondence billets-doux to himself, and the cryptographic anonymity of the Net also facilitates a kind of love letter. Consider the series of postings to someone identified only as Anne: "You don't know me," the first letter begins; "I don't really know how to say this but I'll give it my best shot. I've been watching you for a long time now and I've always wanted to go up to you and say hi. I nearly did a number of times but my courage failed me. . . . There's something about you that just keeps me back."[46] In their paratactic sincerity, these notes offer no threat to the correspondence of Abelard and Heloise: "I saw you the first time at Learned. You were wearing a denim jacket and you sat down next to me. My God, I couldn't keep my eyes off you! I just thought you were the most beautiful woman in the room. You have a truly classic face and I must admit that your square jaw is a turn-on! Anyway, I knew immediately that you were somebody special, smart and beautiful. (This is going to sound REALLY corny and I'm already getting embarrassed) I KNEW that you were the woman for me." Even after encouragement, the anonymous sender was still too shy to meet Anne face-to-face: "I'm not used to pouring out my feelings to a total stranger so I'm sitting here flushing as I type. I don't know if I can introduce myself to you right yet (scaredy cat!) so I guess you'll have to live with the mystery a little longer." Eventually a meeting was arranged, after which Anne and her beau discussed their impressions via e-mail: "I didn't think our meeting would go as well as it did. I had visions of us standing and staring at each other, wondering what the HELL to say. Whew! Thank God for M*A*S*H*, huh?" Anne's correspondent remarks on the oddness of meeting in the flesh, of seeing and being seen: "It feels a little weird writing to you now that you actually know who I am. But I kinda like the feeling of being anonymous and yet not. . . . Makes no sense, does it? Guess I find it easier to write down my feelings rather than say it straight to your face."

The kicker to this romance is that, as we learn in a header to the posting, "Anne" is a pseudonym, and her correspondent is none other than Anne herself, who explains: "About two years ago, I was bored at work so I started emailing love letters to myself. Still, it's got an interesting storyline that has come true since then! . . . I have no problem with people emailing my stuff around, as long as my name remains with it. BTW [by the way], Anne is not my name." What can be so delightful as a secret intercourse? Anne—an electronic Narcissa—sees herself reflected as the other in the digital mirror of the Net. "By treating his image *as if* it were another person even though he knows it is not," Narcissus reveals that "if the self is at once both a cause and a function of self-consciousness . . . then the origin of the self is a union that differentiates, a coming together to hold apart." [47] By condensing the exchange of love letters into a secret auto-correspondence, Anne reveals the narcissism of cryptographic writing, mediating her desire through the Net's electronic alterity. In his preface to "Marginalia," Poe almost anticipates the charms of such alienation when he indulges in the fantasy that the marginal comments in his own texts might have been written by another person. (As Stephen Rachman demonstrates, Poe's elaborate fiction of detailed marginal notes affixed to his favorite works with gum tragacanth does not at all correspond to the truth, which is that Poe's tiny library was largely unmarked.) [48] But if Net postings necessarily return to one's screen alienated by their electronic circuit, such alienation seems to be a prerequisite to a new narcissism: Anne's strategy requires her not only to write to herself *as another*, but to post both halves of her correspondence to the world (meanwhile insisting that her pseudonym remain attached to her letters), as she rounds the orbit of her desire. [49]

To understand the reciprocal hostility and desire aroused by anonymity, I want to consider an earlier hoax, which, like the Challenger controversy, also involved interplanetary travel and a New York tabloid. In 1836 Richard Adams Locke, editor of the *New York Sun*, published an article "announcing very remarkable astronomical discoveries made at the Cape of Good Hope by Sir John Herschell," received by the *Sun* "from an early copy of the *Edinburgh Journal of Science*" ("The Literati of New York," *PT*, 1221). In the articles that followed, readers were treated to the description of the casting and assembly of an enormous new telescope, which enabled Herschell and Sir David Brewster (he of the Maelzel's Chess-Player exposé) to perceive the fauna of the moon, right down to the hairy veil protecting the eyes of moon-bison from the sun's rays. Poe concludes: "From the epoch of the hoax *The Sun* shone with unmitigated splendor. The start thus given the paper insured it a triumph; it has now a daily circulation of not far from fifty thousand copies, and is, therefore, probably, the most really influential journal of its kind in the world" (ibid.)

Calling this invention of the penny press "one of the most important steps ever yet taken in the pathway of human progress" (ibid.), Poe sought with "The Balloon-Hoax" to imitate Locke's success. Poe writes: "*The Atlantic has been actually crossed in a Balloon!*": "Astounding News by Express, *via* Norfolk! — The Atlantic Crossed in Three Days! Signal Triumph of Mr. Monck Mason's Flying Machine! . . . The subjoined *jeu d'esprit* . . . was originally published, as matter of fact, in the *New-York Sun*, a daily newspaper. . . . The rush for the 'sole paper which had the news,' was something beyond even the prodigious." Copying Locke's moon hoax, Poe provides ample verisimilar detail pertaining to the balloon's design and propulsion (it was driven by means of an Archimedean screw), with the particulars "copied *verbatim* from the joint diaries of Mr. Monck Mason and Mr. Harrison Ainsworth" ("The Balloon-Hoax," *PT*, 743-44). As in the Challenger story, there is a link between a New York tabloid and flight, in a hoax whose explosive force derives from its anonymity as Poe seizes on the potential for the new medium to galvanize—or fool—an enormous readership.

Through such hoaxes, Poe exploded the protocol used in reading the nascent penny press, to the intended delight of its readership. Poe also satirized the incoherent anonymity of the printed word (produced as much by the vagaries of market production as by the technical incompetence of printers) in stories like "X-ing a Paragrab," setting its typographical chaos against Dupin's sophisticated scheme for revenge in "The Purloined Letter," which depends for its success on Minister D——'s close acquaintance with Dupin's manuscript (or "hand").[50] Poe's concern with locating the writer's person in the work also finds expression in his insistence on the indexical relation between self and script, as in his pair of articles on autography.[51] Handwriting analysis permits readers to interpret a given author in light of the clues given in his or her script, as when the chirographic "scorn of superfluous embellishment" by Professor Charles Anthon also distinguishes his literary compilations, or when a Washington Irving grown "slovenly in the pursuit of his literary tasks" finds that such slovenliness "has also affected his handwriting" (*CW*, 2:283, 272).

Save for autography and anastatic printing (an early form of xerography), which represent his last-ditch efforts to tie writing to the body (an obliquely hieroglyphic dream), Poe accepted and sought to profit from the anonymity of mass publication. The most interesting of these attempts is that represented by his (probable) pose as "Outis," the "no one" whose charges of plagiarism against Longfellow ignited the Little Longfellow War, and whose anonymity is still producing a modest immortality for its uncertain author.[52] According to Meredith McGill, Poe "bitterly attacked the use of anonymity in criticism, as when he complained of the quarterlies: 'Who writes?—who causes to be written? Who but an ass will put faith in tirades which *may be* the result of personality hostility, or in panegyrics which . . . may be laid, directly or indirectly, to the charge of the author himself?' (*ER*, 1009)."[53] But Poe's double-edged conclusion seems to be that given the system of anonymous review, writing may always hide vested interests. Poe exploited this in his puff for "The Literary Life of Thingumbob," which appeared unsigned in the *Southern Literary Messenger*. Aiming to ride the buzz created by the story's anonymous appearance, an unnamed Poe asked in the *New York Evening Mirror*: "The question is put to *us*, especially, here in the North,—'who wrote it?' Who *did*?—can any one tell?"[54]

In this light, the prominently physiognomic qualities of Internet language seem like attempts to forestall equivalent sorts of manipulation today. Just as Poe insisted on chirography, many people have a powerful desire to make the cryptograph stand in metonymic relation to its author, connecting the digit to the digital. Metaphors of hands proliferate. In addition to *fingering*, there are many related terms. In the world of virtual reality, one relies on *data-gloves*; although the *digital signature* produced by public-key systems is inviolable, RSA cryptographers have developed an additional digital code known as a *fingerprint*: a secure 128-bit message digest algorithm, or cryptographic hash, of the plaintext. Levy suggests that the cypherpunks hope to erase "an individual's informational *footprints*,"[55] and Graham Toal (*gtoal@gtoal.com*) speaks of identifying the stylistic *fingerprint* of an anonymous poster whom he hopes to flush.[56] (Similarly, James Phinney Baxter refers to Folio evidence for Baconian authorship as the latter's *thumb marks*.)[57]

Not only does this complex of metaphors return us to Adamic fantasies of self-reflecting language, but as the regulatory origins of fingerprinting reveal, there is considerable state investment in the proper attribution of writing—a desire allegorized in the crisis produced by the sight of an unknown footprint in *Robinson Crusoe*.[58] In response, Net readers sometimes turn to stylistic analysis, as cryptography doubles back on literature. A posting by Paul Leyland on *sci.crypt* suggests solving problems of attribution by investigating the writer's idiosyncratic prose: "An author's style tends to be quite characteristic: the mean and variance of words per sentence, and letters per word; the incidence of spelling and grammatical errors, both in type and number. The number of adjectives; the size of vocabulary; distribution of punctuation (I tend to like semicolons and parenthetical remarks, for instance). There are many such characteristics."[59] Although such identifications may not be made "to universal agreement," Leyland authorizes such analysis by noting that "these methods have been used to identify rediscovered poems by Shakespeare." Where once the text of Shakespeare spurred readers to (spurious) cryptographic discoveries, now questions of electronic anonymity are resolved through techniques for identifying literary provenance.

Anxiety about the uses of anonymity is probably not misplaced. Besides the lurid dangers linked to it by the NSA (terrorism, international drug cartels, child pornography, pandemic tax fraud), anonymity also carries psychic and political costs. In his novel *Ender's Game*, Orson Scott Card imagines a world in which the anonymity of the Net provides a new forum for political manipulation. Two brilliant children realize that "with false names, on the right nets, they could be anybody. Old men, middle-aged women, anybody, as long as they were careful about the way that they wrote. All that anyone would see were their words, their ideas. Every citizen started equal, on the nets."[60] Hiding behind forged identities, they conduct a series of debates that influence foreign policy: "Valentine would prepare an opening statement, and Peter would invent a throwaway name to answer her. His answer would be intelligent, and the debate would be lively. . . . Then they would enter the debate into the network, separated by a reasonable amount of time, as if they were actually making them up on the spot" (96).

As in fiction, so in life: Card's novel has provided the direct model for a dramatic contest over the nature of cryptographic anonymity. On one side is Lawrence Detweiler, author of the sober *Identity, Privacy, and Anonymity FAQ*, whose fear of Medusan "pseudospoofing," or network posting under multiple identities, has taken spectacularly paranoid form. In "the most treacherous and evil" scenario, Detweiler wonders: what if Medusa "was actually Satan in disguise"? Suppose further that she liked to

> "punish" people with her "tentacles" whenever they "misbehaved," by resist-ing her oppression. She could be quite unpleasant, don't you think? She could consistently flame their arguments from different tentacles, even if the posts were intelligent, just out of spite. . . . She might have all her sisters try to work on the person in particular and break them down. "You are not going to have any friends if you keep this up. Why are you such a troublemaker, anyway?" Or, if the person has recognized the brainwashing and is amidst flight, she could try to lead him back to darkness. "Oh, I so enjoyed your posts, please reconsider." This from a tentacle the victim has never heard from before.[61]

In late 1993 Detweiler became convinced that a number of well-known cypherpunks were really aspects of a retired Intel physicist named Tim May, who, as one of the principal architects of the cypherpunks, and as the author of the "Crypto Anarchist Manifesto," was at the center of a potent cryp-tographic plot. With its welter of assertions and counterassertions, forged identities, and evasive replies, the flame war that ensued is far too complex to summarize easily. But the following excerpts do convey the dynamics of secrecy, revelation, and role playing galvanized by anonymity. I begin in midwar, with Detweiler's attack on a "Mr. Brandt," who, he imagines, is part of a cypherpunk cabal dedicated to the "art, science, and religion of deceiving others on the Internet and in the media." Asking "Are you an 'insider,' Mr. Brandt?" Detweiler goes on to deny Brandt's independent existence: "If anyone would like to entertain themselves by determining whether he is a tentacle, a Medusa Sister, or Medusa herself, send him e-mail. Speaking from experience built up over many weeks on 'cyberspatial exorcisms,' I would be willing to wager cash that you will not be able to as-sociate him with an actual human being."[62]

In fact, Detweiler alleges, several of his correspondents failed to provide direct testimony about their solo identities. Tim May, he claims, "refused to state a simple sentence to me in the form 'I have never posted under the name J. Dinkelacker.'" Later that day, however, an exasperated May posted to the Net, explicitly denying this: "I'm not 'Jamie Dinkelacker' or 'Hal Finney' or 'Eli Brandt' or 'Nick Szabo' or any of the other dozen or so folks Detweiler routinely rants about me being. Argghh! What more can I say to this raving lunatic?"[63] May mustered abundant circumstantial detail pertaining to his existence, including his phone number, and nearly a dozen other people responded in his support, among them Perry Metzger, who observed that Nick Szabo lived in Cupertino, Tim May in Aptos, and Eric Hughes in Berkeley. Further, "all of them have been seen at the same place at the same time in public — for instance, by over 100 people at the Extropy Magazine 5th Anniversary Party, at Cypherpunks meetings, etc. I can personally verify that all of them exist and are separate people." To prove his own identity, Metzger listed information about his job at Lehman Brothers in New York, his presence in corporate filings, and his telephone number, adding that "anyone who wants to call Tim and call me can easily verify that at the very least we have different voices."

"In any case," Metzger wrote to Detweiler, turning the tables, "the 'Medusa' is you. You have disrupted lots of people's lives — you've mailed death threats to dozens of people, 'pseudospoofed' as at least a half dozen aliases using *an12070@anon.penet.fi*, and wrecked mailing lists."[64] Apparently Detweiler — who stands accused of posting as *"an12070*, The Executioner, S. Boxx, The Pervert, The Psychopunk, and such pseudonyms" — is a victim of the psychic reversibility that accompanies the cryptographic imagination: as L. Detweiler, enemy of anonymity, *and* as hit-and-run poster *an12070*, Detweiler echoes Angleton's fascination with moles, Dupin's with Minister D——, and Poe's self-hoaxing publications as "Walter G. Bowen" and "Outis." In the face of cypherpunk disinformation, Detweiler (who denied any relation to "the paranoid ranter and conspiracy theorist *an12070*") began reposting other people's messages with derisive commentary. As he wrote in response to May:

> *Poor deluded Larry takes any such*
> *efforts to resolve his delusion*
> *as* further proof *of the Grand*
> *Conspiracy to drive him crazier*
> *than he already is.*
> Yes, I am quite insane.
> *What a strange world the Net is*
> *becoming.*
> No thanks to you.
> — *Tim May, a Real Person*

Owner of many tentacles. Please list all the sites you have ever posted from, Mr. May. Ooops, that would be an Orwellian Invasion of your privacy. A McCarthyist Inquisition. Hee, hee. You cryptoanarchists are so silly. I am having great fun using your techniques of cyberspatial warfare against yourselves. I will not relent until top leadership issues unequivocal statements on your involvement and knowledge of pseudospoofing. . . . I await the fire-works![65]

Should one think Detweiler's game of radical skepticism merely creepy fun, it is worth contemplating that I was unable to prove who, exactly, Detweiler was. When I called Tim May at the number listed in his Net signature, I reached a curiously circular telephone answering machine, which said that since the machine was unreliable, it was best not to expect a reply to any message, but to call again. I called Perry Metzger at the number in *his* Net address, but heard what claimed to be Metzger's recorded voice tell me that he had resigned from Lehman Brothers.[66] The voice, which added that I should hold on if I needed assistance, then disconnected. I tried to reach Detweiler at Colorado State University, the originating address of his postings, but could not find him in the school's directory of faculty, gradu-ate students, or undergraduates. No one I reached in the computer science department had heard of him. A telephone directory search of Fort Collins turned up a "Lauren Detweiler," but he turned out to be a retiree who listened patiently to my questions and then said, "Now what's this about writing?" He had never, he informed me, used a computer, nor did he have any relatives in the area.

Here I briefly halted, unwilling to interrupt a delicious sense, half plea-sure and half terror, at finding the world of certainty recede into conspira-cies of undetermined shape or purpose. Apparently, the facts by which May and Metzger hoped to authenticate themselves—jobs, phone numbers, an-swering machines—are as easily suborned as Detweiler fears: "The truth is," he explains,

> that every attempt I have made to verify certain identities has failed and led only to more grisly conclusions, such as that Cypherpunks have gone to the length of registering NIC [Network Interface Control] domains and buying out-of-state phone numbers. Do not tell me this is impossible! A business-man friend of mine has a local phone number in NY that forwards to Denver! Cypherpunks could use this very readily! (My kingdom goes to anyone who can provide me with the ability to trace the ultimate destination of phone calls in this way, and help uncover the amazing extent of the Cryptoanarchist con-spiracy!)[67]

In thinking about the Detweiler-cypherpunk flame war, I came up with five possibilities, all of which seemed plausible, but none of which I could prove:

1. In his defense of network responsibility, Detweiler went mad, letting the debate over anonymity devolve into a full-blown psychotic battle with invisible enemies. (Detweiler as a psychological victim of anony-mous electronic writing.)

2. In a cruel and weirdly sustained prank, unknown enemies of Detweiler's forged his signature and sent out hundreds of unauthorized messages designed to defame him and to muddy the waters of a crucial First Amendment debate. (Detweiler as a victim of anonymous electronic writing practiced by others.)

3. Terrified at the prospect of losing control over its ability to eavesdrop electronically, the NSA hired or invented "L. Detweiler" to sow confusion among the most prominent group of cryptoanarchists and to undermine support for anonymity. Think of this as the high-tech version of FBI infiltration of the Students for a Democratic Society. (Detweiler as an agent provocateur in the pay of an evil government.)

4. Detweiler posted all the messages attributed to him, fully cognizant of their outrageous and contradictory character, in order to demonstrate how the unrestricted use of anonymity could lead to social chaos and personal injury. (Detweiler as a meta-Medusa, polemically making a point about anonymity.)

5. "Detweiler" is an invented Net persona, created for purposes unknown. (The scariest prospect of all.)

Frustrated and confused, I telephoned Tim May again late one night. This time someone answering to his name picked up after two rings, and confirmed my hunch that the fourth hypothesis was the closest to the truth, although even that can hardly explain the weirdness of the affair. According to May, Detweiler is a precocious recent graduate in computer science of Colorado State University who had become fascinated by cryptographic anonymity. In the spring of 1993, Detweiler asked to be put on the cypherpunks mailing list, but when some of his ideas (including one for an "electrocracy," an electronic democracy that would poll citizens to determine social policy) were treated with insufficient respect, he began posting messages excoriating members. In a turnabout from the moderation of his FAQ, Detweiler has especially come to disdain the notion of unlimited anonymity. Not content with argumentation, he seems rather cleverly to have performatively demonstrated the risks of anonymity. Borrowing from *Ender's Game*, Detweiler began generating alternate identities (including my favorite, "Jim Riverman, software designer") who flooded Usenet cryptography groups with hostile postings in an attempt to start flame wars so caustic that they would homeopathically destroy the cypherpunks' naive belief in the virtues of cryptography. That Detweiler meant this *as* a performance is further indicated by how rarely he took advantage of *anon.penet.fi* to secure a genuinely anonymous message. Although he often copied the signatures of others, Detweiler did not eliminate information in his header that revealed him as the author of these messages.

Whatever his initial motivations, Detweiler seems to have become ensnared within his own increasingly vicious game. Most disturbingly, he began posting anti-Semitic messages apparently signed by Tim May on *soc.jewish.culture*. As Detweiler undoubtedly intended, May was promptly flooded with disgusted responses from members of *soc.jewish.culture* who were unaware that they were being manipulated. (As a result of this stunt, May said, Detweiler has been blocked from the Colorado State University network, but he has managed to obtain commercial Net access.) Although Detweiler's crusade aims to expose the dangers of unsigned writing, the volume and hectoring force of his language show how involved he has become in his characters' invented lives. Indeed, Detweiler—who sometimes posts thirty-five messages a day—must spend nearly all his waking hours browsing newsgroups or responding to opponents.

For all the damage inflicted by Detweiler, his behavior at least offers a lunatic lesson in Net operations. Other forms of networked secret writing are more directly malignant. During 1994, the Usenet's Bosnia group (*soc.culture.bosna.hergvna*) was flooded with anti-Armenian messages from one "Serdar Argic," advancing the thesis that the Turkish massacre of two million Armenians in 1915 was in fact a slaughter of Turks by Armenians. Argic is capable of flights of composition that dwarf even Detweiler's: according to Usenet moderator Joel Furr, on one day in April 1994, 175 of the 210 messages on the group had been composed by him. Interviewed by Jon Weiner in the *Nation*, Furr indicated that " 'Serdar Argic' seems to be several people, anti-Armenian Turks, with software that scans bulletin boards for keywords and automatically generates responses out of a database of megabytes of messages." [68]

I, Oedipa Maas

Although the Argic case is structurally the inverse of Detweiler's (instead of a Medusan multiplication of speaking heads, Argic represents the work of several people, consolidated through a synthetic text generator), both illustrate how electronic writing relies on weak information about the identities of its virtual members. One reason for introducing myself as an actor in the preceding pages is to give some sense of the uncanniness of these identities, which, when they decay, generate pathologies familiar from postwar American politics and fiction. When we move into the Net, that is, we enter a space in which *The Crying of Lot 49* reads as a documentary text, prefiguring the behavior of characters such as Detweiler and May. When Tim May writes that "I haven't gotten any calls from Detweiler, to my knowledge, just some strange hang-ups in the middle of the night," it is hard for me not to recall Oedipa Maas in *The Crying of Lot 49*, wakened at 3:00 A.M. by Pierce Inverarity, calling in the voice of Lamont Cranston. [69] And Detweiler's Medusa complex is worthy of Dr. Hilarius, Oedipa's "shrink or psychotherapist," in his most psychotropic moments. Net users often obliquely refer to *The Crying of Lot 49*, identifying their workplace as "Yoyodyne Propulsion Systems," with Yoyodyne serving as a generic title for military-industrial research.[70] Pynchon even appears in May's "infamous" signature as part of a dozen subversive topics:

Timothy C. May	Crypto Anarchy: encryption, digital money
********************	anonymous networks, digital pseudonyms, zero
********************	knowledge, reputations, information markets,
W.A.S.T.E.: Aptos, CA	black markets, collapse of governments.
Higher Power: 2^756839	Public Key: PGP and MailSafe available.[71]

Still, one may wonder: what does *The Crying of Lot 49* tell us about the Net that we would not have known otherwise? My answer is that the character of Oedipa lays out more clearly than any other in postwar fiction the contemporary stakes with regard to the cryptographic imagination. The issues raised by her experience — of the relation of identity to language, anonymity, and paranoia — echo the main themes of the Detweiler flame war. Like Oedipa, we as readers are divided between unsatisfactory reactions to telecommunications culture, forced to choose between an epistemological skepticism so great that it turns to paranoia (the Eliotic mode) and an unthinking spiritualization of technology. Pynchon's novel beautifully plays out this division. Indeed, in a final turn of the cryptographic screw, I almost began to wonder if *I* had not written *The Crying of Lot 49*. The book's nominal author was nowhere in evidence, and it uncannily presented all the motifs of this study, including Poe, spiritualism, telecommunications, information theory, World War II, the textual construction of Jacobean drama, and the question of who, exactly, wrote Shakespeare's plays, all summoned under the aegis of cryptography.

Certainly, Pynchon's Internet prominence follows partially from his interest in cryptography. Noting that *V* is preoccupied "with signs, codes, signals, patterns, plots, etc.," Tony Tanner observes that "the preoccupation — not just the signals and patterns themselves — could be said to be the subject of the book."[72] He expressly describes Oedipa as "a cryptologist," given over to "an unending effort to discover whether the will itself contains a code which she has to interpret; or whether in fact the will has been tampered with and a false code inserted in order to distract her from discovering the revelations of the will."[73] The "Mr. Thoth" in decline at Vesperhaven is named for the Egyptian god of wisdom, the inventor of letters and numbers, and therefore of writing; Pynchon also obliquely refers to the *hieratica*, a private hieroglyphic code used by the Egyptian priesthood. When Oedipa sees San Narciso for the first time, it looks to her like a printed digital circuit, and she finds that "there were to both outward patterns a hieroglyphic sense of concealed meaning, an intent to communicate."[74]

Ambiguously in league with this intent to communicate is the Tristero, an international, violently anonymous, virtually immortal network designed to transmit secret writing. From certain angles, the Tristero (about which Oedipa learns from the "decrypted journals of the Comte Raoul Antoine de Vouziers, Marquis de Tour et Tassis") resembles the NSA, which similarly forbade its employees from acknowledging the agency's existence. Even more dramatically, though, the Tristero resembles the Internet in its intertwined transmission of the most reputable forms of writing (scientific research, professional notes, White House communiqués) alongside a subversive W.A.S.T.E.-like system, in which hundreds of subcultures pass secret missives. (What is the distance from the Inamorati Anonymous to *alt.sexabuse.rec*? How far is it from the fired Yoyodyne executive placing his classified ad to *alt.suicide*?) To be sure, most Net messages are as banal as the message received by Pynchon's Mike Fallopian, written only to keep up the volume of transmissions: "Dear Mike. How are you? Just thought I'd drop you a note. How's your book coming? Guess that's all for now."[75] But the fantasy of communication that the Net produces is a potent element in its success and, like the postal system itself, it is one of the material institutions that determine the shape and range of our freedoms.

Published in 1966, *The Crying of Lot 49* is contemporaneous with the cryptoliterary culture described in chapter 6 above, appearing one year after both *The War of the Secret Agents* and *The Looking-Glass War*. Yet in *The Crying of Lot 49*, cryptography is not primarily linked to Allied subterfuge. Whereas Le Carré's cryptographic foci are an ancient radio transmitter and a silk inscribed with number groups, Pynchon's are the Tristero and Inverarity's will; whereas Le Carré's novels are organized around the political divisions of the Cold War, Pynchon's battle is fought *within* America, over such megacorporations as "the Galactronics Division of Yoyodyne, Inc.," "a prolonged scatter of wide, pink buildings, surrounded by miles of fence topped with barbed wire and interrupted now and then by guard towers . . . two sixty-foot missiles on either side and the name YOYODYNE lettered conservatively on each nose cone" (25).

But Pynchon's novel and the Internet are both the result of World War II cryptography, and they can be read as parallel histories.[76] In addition to the ruthless binarism of Cold War culture, with its absolute but reversible distinctions between patriot and traitor, American and Soviet, signifier and signified (the narrative material exploited by the school of Le Carré), the legacy of World War II cryptography includes the intellectual bequest of cybernetics, game theory, and the digital electronic computer (built "for the express and ultimately successful purpose of cracking the Germans' key Enigma cipher").[77] Wartime research also led directly to Bell Labs engineer Claude Shannon's "momentous postwar discovery of the foundations of information theory—a sophisticated mathematical abstraction of the dynamic between chaos (noise) and intelligibility (signal) in communications channels."[78] Shannon's theory, set forth in "A Mathematical Model of Communication" (1948), finds its counterpart in his "Communication Theory of Secrecy Systems," published in the *Bell System Technical Journal* the next year.[79] As Shannon recalls, his work on information theory and cryptology were "so close together you couldn't separate them."[80]

As readers of Pynchon criticism know all too well, the references to information theory that permeate *The Crying of Lot 49* (from the vision of San Narciso as a giant telecommunications circuit to Oedipa's wayward can of hair spray, whizzing about on a statistical trajectory that "something fast enough, God or a digital machine, might have computed in advance")[81] have proved to be a critical dead end. Although Pynchon seems to set himself the task of aligning the different senses of entropy (one drawn from mechanics, the other from information theory) through the Nefastis machine, as several critics have noted, the entropy of mechanics means the inverse of the entropy of information theory. Pynchon's attempt to pun his way across the two is a literary maneuver, not a scientific one: a master trope, but not a master narrative.[82] What really animates Pynchon is not so much information theory as it is the more primary cryptographic imagination, which in *The Crying of Lot 49* seeks to name the matrix in which matter and thought intersect.

In an odd way this resembles the question, so central to Pynchon's novel, of whether one is identical with one's words. For Emory Bortz, the answer is yes: his Shakespeare is simply the sum of those texts attributed to him. This is also true for Mucho, who discovers an LSD-fired ability to perform spectrum analysis in his head, breaking down "chords, and timbres, and words too into all the basic frequencies and harmonics, with all their different loudnesses," and listening to them, "each pure tone, but all at once." Such experience leads Mucho, a disc jockey, to conclude that "everybody who says the same words is the same person if the spectra are the same only they happen differently in time, you dig?"[83] Mucho's faith in the radio's invisible waves reveals his kinship with Doten and her fellow spiritualists: each envisions technology as a way to make experience sacred once again.

As a would-be listener to the dead Inverarity, Oedipa experiences the world as a form of posthumous speech, and, like Lizzie Doten, her problems begin with intrusive voices—in her case, the sleep-shattering ring of Inverarity's telephone call. From that moment on, the novel interrogates forms of information transmission, including speech, sex, letter writing, telephones, television, cinema, radio, and telepathic manipulation. Voices blend: after Inverarity's death, Oedipa is again awakened, this time by Hilarius, sounding "like Pierce doing a Gestapo officer," who was moved to call by "this feeling. Not telepathy. But rapport with a patient is a curious thing sometimes."[84] Oedipa is seduced by Metzger in front of the television, and forced to endure both the music of the Paranoids, the heavily amplified band run by

Miles, and that performed in the Yoyodyne bar, where the means of amplification have become the instruments ("we got a whole back room full of your audio oscillators, gunshot machines, contact mikes, everything man").[85]

The Crying of Lot 49 is written in Poe's wake.[86] References to Poe appear in *The Courier's Tragedy*, whose third act alludes to "The Masque of the Red Death" and to the central drama of Poe's bitter little story "Hop-Frog," in which a hunchbacked court jester exacts revenge on the king and his court by persuading them to dress up for a costume ball as a set of apes chained together.[87] But the most salient allusion to Poe occurs when, having mailed the letter for the old sailor, Oedipa waits by the trash can, determined to know if the W.A.S.T.E. system really exists. "Towards midday a rangy young wino showed up with a sack; unlocked a panel at the side of the box and took out all the letters."[88] Oedipa follows him by foot and by bus, from San Francisco to Oakland and from Oakland to Berkeley, where "halfway up Telegraph the carrier got off and led her down the street to a pseudo-Mexican apartment house. Not once had he looked behind him. John Nefastis lived here. She was back where she'd started, and could not believe 24 hours had passed."[89] As in Poe's story, Oedipa's wandering eventually returns her to the place from which she had started, but midway through her San Francisco *Walpurgisnacht*, Pynchon's woman of the crowd has her attention fixed by the hidden systems of American community.

By repeatedly echoing "The Man of the Crowd," Pynchon signals a relation between his work and that of Poe. In Poe's tale, the unnamed narrator—a failed *flâneur* captivated by an inscrutable old man walking in the streets—makes the mistake of allowing his curiosity to lead him from the confines of his café into the unreflective and debilitating motion of the crowd. In search of amusement, he comes away "wearied unto death" (*PT*, 396) by the ceaseless motion embodied in the old man's erring. Oedipa, too, is fascinated by the social life of the city, but for her the mystery lies in the mechanisms by which ordinary people escape the sameness of their lives, converting waste into W.A.S.T.E., an empire of invisible writing in which they invest their hidden selves. This is cryptography in its most social sense, Pynchon's transvaluating imagination of the will to conspiracy that has driven American culture since the days of Andrew Jackson and George Lippard. In "The Man of the Crowd," the physiognomic logic that drives Poe's detective fiction breaks down: the narrator's efforts with the old man (a figure for the mystery of urban experience) collapse. But whereas Poe's narrator recoils from his object, Oedipa becomes implicated in the Tristero's recuperation of the wasted lives she comes to see everywhere, most particularly in the life of the old sailor.[90]

Oedipa's imagination of the sailor's death centers on "the massive destruction of information" that will accompany his passing: "So when this mattress flared up around the sailor, in his Viking's funeral: the stored, coded years of uselessness, early death, self-harrowing, the sure decay of hope, the set of all men who had slept on it, whatever their lives had been, would truly cease to be, forever, when the mattress burned. She stared at it in wonder. It was as if she had just discovered the irreversible process."[91] *The Crying of Lot 49* frames the bum's death in terms of ciphers because everything within it, from the Bay Bridge to Oedipa's innermost thoughts, is composed of hidden signs and figures. On the one hand, there are the messages of physics and engineering—the way in which Mucho's crystalline audition of the pop song threatens to recreate the musician and his history whole in Mucho's mind. On the other, there are the indices of Inverarity's ambiguous texts, his mutilated stamps, his emended Jacobean dramas, and his middle-of-the-night calls. The book's pathos is generated by Oedipa's desire to make these messages coexist, to have the signs and symbols of the world speak in human terms. Cryptography is not only the source of information theory, which renders everything as interchangeable data; it is potentially a model for spiritual meaning too, as it pushes its practitioners to the limit where they confront the insoluble relations of mind and matter.[92]

A faith in disembodied mental power is part and parcel of the cryptographic imagination, whether it takes the form of Dupin's power over the nail or of Doten's channeling. Even William Friedman had a longstanding interest in ESP. In 1958 he wrote to William Baker, head of research at Bell Laboratories: "Now why didn't the Bell people succumb to my needling them over the years that ESP is a form of communication. Bell Telephone goes in for studying communications: why not ESP?" Current investigations, he added, "may bring about a revolution of thought greater than that brought about by Copernicus."[93] Unlike Doten, both Oedipa and Friedman fail in their attempts to unify matter and spirit. (This is true, too, of Oedipa's spiritualist precursor: in 1854, a "Mrs. ———" under the tutelage of the Universalist minister John M. Spear attempted to use her newly developed "Motive Power" to run a motor that Spear had designed. The machine refused to operate.)[94] Although Pynchon frames this unsuccessful hierophancy in the esoteric vocabulary of information theory (how does one tell a message from noise?), *The Crying of Lot 49* suggests that we are all cryptographers forced to puzzle over the text of the world. Our resources are limited: only the "compiled memories of clues, announcements, intimations, but never the central truth itself, which must somehow each time be too bright for her memory to hold" (95), the "gemlike clues" that are only "some kind of compensation. To make up for her having lost the direct, epileptic Word, the cry that might abolish the night" (ibid., 118).

Although the texts puzzled out here vary, they all seem to turn on words from the dead. In the penultimate scenes of *The Crying of Lot 49*, Oedipa's attention returns to the question of Inverarity's will, in both senses of the word. Pynchon's testamentary language is that of encryption and enigmas:

Might Oedipa Maas yet be his heiress; had that been in the will, in code, perhaps without Pierce really knowing, having been by then too seized by some headlong expansion of himself, some visit, some lucid instruction? Though she could never again call back any image of the dead man to dress up, pose, talk to and make answer, neither would she lose a new compassion for the cul-de-sac he'd tried to find a way out of, for the enigma his efforts had created. . . . He might have discovered The Tristero, and encrypted that in the will, buying into just enough to be sure she'd find it. Or he might even have tried to survive death, as a paranoia; as a pure conspiracy against someone he loved. . . . Had something slipped through and Inverarity by that much beaten death? (Ibid., 178–79)

This book is an investigation into the will as an ur-text for literature, as a model for the way texts covertly seek to write themselves into those who inherit them. Pynchon's novel perfectly captures the sense of being obscurely imposed on by such fictions. This sense of imposition returns us to the way in which Poe's writing has been felt by so many of his readers as a kind of pressure, ranging from the transformative gale of language felt by Lizzie Doten to the sinus-cold congestion of T. S. Eliot, and including in between such odd bedfellows as Charles Baudelaire, Rufus Griswold, Jorge Luis Borges, John Henry Ingram, Princess Marie Bonaparte, William Friedman, and Jacques Lacan.

Fame, writes Borges, is a form of incomprehension. The band of Poe's followers assembled in these pages provides memorable evidence for Borges's position, for they are united only in their fascination with the permanence and revelatory force of writing. However diverse their redactions of Poe, these figures agree that the preservation of human experience through writing is—literally—an inhuman desire, an attempt to replace mortality with immortality. This impulse behind cryptography is as old as Christ's transfiguration, a harrowing in which Logos emerges radiant and eternal. Reading Poe through his followers' eyes, we see that in the twentieth century, literature got what it always sought. Poe represents the realization that the telos of literature was *always* telecommunications, an ultimate, immanent script.

Earlier, Oedipa observed the aerial resemblance of San Narciso to a printed digital circuit, finding in both "a hieroglyphic sense of concealed meaning, an intent to communicate." *The Crying of Lot 49* refuses to make the choice between "transcendent meaning" or "only the earth" (ibid., 181). But if Pynchon's novel ends before the unveiling of the Tristero, Pynchon also indicates that in our search for revelation in an age of telecommunications, we remain at the mercy of the written word. Reprimanding Oedipa for her "Puritan" obsession with the text of *The Courier's Tragedy*, Randolph Driblette insists: " 'It isn't literature, it doesn't mean anything. Wharfinger was no Shakespeare.' 'Who was he?' she said. 'Who was Shakespeare? It was a long time ago'" (ibid., 77). When Oedipa asks for information about "the historical Wharfinger," Emory Bortz makes a similar observation:

> "The historical Shakespeare," growled one of the grad students through a full beer, uncapping another bottle. "The historical Marx. The historical Jesus."
> "He's right," shrugged Bortz, "they're dead. What's left?"
> "Words."
> "Pick some words," said Bortz. "Them, we can talk about." (Ibid., 151)

The Crying of Lot 49 is nothing but words: words about our attempts to establish legacy, relation, ownership, and, above all, identity, in ways that can never be more secure than the shifting lines of script themselves.

In this respect, Pynchon remains committed in an old-fashioned way to the powers and limits of language. Hence, the conclusion to *The Crying of Lot 49* inverts that given by Gibson in *Neuromancer*, which, despite its urban sprawl and moral degeneration, turns out to be sentimental about, of all things, the hieroglyph. By concluding with the vision of Case doubled in the computer, *Neuromancer* commits itself to a faith that language (or data) might still offer a type of immortality. By contrast, the force of Pynchon's novel is to deny this sort of hieroglyphic prosopopoeia. No matter how well Inverarity has coded himself into his writing, his original identity dies. His only chance of survival is like Poe's with Lizzie Doten or Baudelaire, as a "pure conspiracy against someone he loved"—as, that is, a will couched in the form of script.

Such script may be electronic. The millions of Internet users are all cousins of Oedipa Maas. Like her (or like me, in my search for Detweiler), they may be altered by their exchanges, perhaps even wrenched into new sorts of lives, although they may never be sure of the identity of their electronic correspondents. The Internet is like Inverarity's will written on an even grander scale. Like Pierce's businesses, the source of the wealth that gave his will muscle, the Internet is an unholy child of the military and the government, created for purposes that seem malevolent but that are capable of being twisted otherwise. If the Net offers new promises to a post–Cold War culture, it is not because on it a disembodied free speech and opportunity prevail, but because in its distortions we can witness our own alienated fears and desires, in a "secular miracle of communication" that we can only write for ourselves.[95]

CODA

Strange Loops and Talking Birds

greatart hasawayo fevoking continua lcomment aryitisa bottomle sssource ofinspir ationtoo thersiha vemyblin dspotsin termsofu nderstan ding.

Partially decrypted message from *sci.crypt*

Were this another sort of book—a book more like one Poe would have written—one might fairly expect it to end in a series of astonishing revelations. The later years of Poe's life were taken up with just such attempts to capture truth, culminating in the publication of *Eureka*, an exclamation of "I have found it!" that represents a deep cryptographic impulse. My readers should expect no such revelations. Instead, I would like to conclude with two contemporary instances of secret writing; they point toward different but related possible futures. The first, a return to the motif of Poe's talking raven, might be thought of as the case of the purloined envelope; the second describes a theoretical possibility of overcoming space and time that would count as the most momentous event in cryptographic history. In their association of high science and low fiction, these anecdotes mark an appropriate conclusion for this book.

Talking Birds

If on the imaginary seesaw between hieroglyph and cryptograph the cipher is today ascendant, one main reason is the spread of computers, those touchstones for the contemporary cryptographic imagination. This is fitting, because the development of the computer was spurred by an American desire for cryptographic supremacy—a history largely obscured by the NSA's self-censorship. As early as 1932, Friedman had begun experiments with IBM punch-card machines; after the war, the NSA directly sponsored "the largest government-supported computer research program in history," with contractors including Sperry Rand, RCA, IBM, GE, and MIT.[1] It was, therefore, a mark of Friedman's growing estrangement from the agency he helped found that in 1957 he was not invited to a top-secret Washington tribunal concerning the NSA's future. Crowded into the windowless situation room were "a handful of the nation's top scientists," including John Pierce, the director of communications research at Bell Laboratories, and Claude Shannon, the creator of information theory, gathered for "one of the most important meetings in the history of the Agency."[2]

Chaired by William Baker (the same Baker to whom Friedman sent his letter about ESP), the committee concluded that the NSA was "one of the most important weapons in the Cold War. To fall behind would be to invite another Pearl Harbor. They therefore recommended the initiation of a Manhattan Project–like effort to push the USA well ahead of the Soviet Union and all other nations in the application of communications, computer science, mathematics, and information theory to cryptology."[3] The committee's direct effects were impressive: these included the creation of John von Neumann Hall at Princeton, which became "the academic world's entranceway into the NSA's secret tunnel," and support for the supercomputer, the "brainchild of Seymour Cray, an electrical engineer who began his career by building codebreaking machines in the early 1950s with Engineering Research Associates, then headed by future NSA research chief Howard Engstrom." Today, the NSA "undoubtedly holds the largest and most advanced computer operation in the world," which "stretches for city blocks below the Headquarters-Operations Building, divided into right and left hemispheres, code-named Carillon and Loadstone."[4]

An unintended consequence of this proliferation of computing has been to weaken the distinction between images and texts. Both are stored in the computer as streams of ones and zeroes, the arbitrariness of the storage ostensibly guaranteeing the permanence and accuracy of their representations. This spread of digitalization requires that we rethink our understanding of what constitutes a text. Not only is the digital image itself a form of writing, but cryptographers can now hide ciphers in the bitstream of the image code. If the pixel values for the computer monitor's grey scale are silently altered, messages can be stored as a bit of degraded background in an image of Michael Jackson, or as inaudible "noise" in the code for a passage from the Brandenburg Concertos.[5] The technical term for this is steganography, a word derived from the Greek *stego-*, meaning "roof," or "cover," and *-graphy*, meaning "writing." Roofed-in writing; the cipher's plates conceal the very existence of communication.

To see why computer steganography represents the cutting edge of home encryption, consider the files reproduced in figures 15 through 18. The first is a three-color image entitled "Parrots," here reprinted in black and white. The second is an excerpt from the JPEG code used to generate this image, a dense computer cipher that runs forty-two pages in printout. The third is another reproduction of "Parrots" with a steganographic code (the entire text of this coda) interred within it. Finally, the fourth is an excerpt from the same JPEG code in figure 16, but with the steganographic encryption.[6] As one can see, there is no visible way of distinguishing between the original JPEG image and its self-reflexive cousin, or between the two sets of computer code.

These files represent an extreme permutation of the logic of "The Purloined Letter," in which the sensible image is converted into an envelope for invisible writing. The sign of the parrot image is composed of other signs, whose content is entirely independent of the bird. Remember Lacan: Freud shows us "that the value of the image as signifier has nothing whatever to do with its signification, giving as an example Egyptian hieroglyphics in which it would be sheer buffoonery to pretend that in a given text the frequency of a vulture, which is an aleph, or of a chick, which is a vau . . . prove that the text has anything at all to do with these ornithological specimens."[7] Just as Minister D——'s success was predicated on his conversion of the purloined letter into its own envelope, so these images are optical illusions, alternately things in their own right and spaces for hidden script. When my conversation with Tim May turned to Poe and literature, he instantly cited "The Purloined Letter" as a steganographic text. This is perhaps the best cryptographic joke yet: after the thousands of pages devoted to the analysis of signs and their itineraries, the real secret of "The Purloined Letter" may be not what it says about letters but what it says about envelopes—about, that is, the spaces created by the interplay of writing and the surfaces of the world.

As May describes it in the "Crypto Anarchist Manifesto," such files are ideal tools in the battle for individual privacy. When a steganographic image is "posted in a public place (such as a newsgroup), virtually untraceable communication can take place between sender and receiver. For steganographic communications in the electronic realm another possibility is setting up a mailing list where individual messages get broadcast to the entire list and individual users decode particular messages with their unique key."[8] May does not overstate when he describes his manifesto as an anarchist text, for the prospect of hundreds of thousands of people exchanging messages invisibly encoded in images is not one that the government contemplates with equanimity. Yet in three or four years digital imagery will be so ubiquitous that not even the multi-billion-dollar budget of the NSA will have the resources needed to monitor images for encryption. Where once the need for cryptanalysis helped lead to the invention of the digital computer (and thereby to the creation of various forms of electronic surveillance), cryptography—whether through public-key ciphers or steganography programs—now seems likely to give Net users an unheard-of level of written privacy.

Strange Loops

During his career William Friedman amassed a library of cryptographic materials that, in its scope and depth, was one of the premier such col-

Figure 15. JPEG "Parrots" image, taken from the Usenet *alt.binaries*, June 1994.

```
^Ñ !-
& ˇk6µA∞,n ã◊∞ÈMu@B&2!  w Éî",\p˙,ùbÿ9íäqΩ.$≤ñ∏\ñém"$'tØ «ét&
UQ≥nóóÙ   s&ke `Ëh„fl
§∆5&ã ãã\ ^∂◊Hç"™ ®D¢ ∑if c °W^°ÜS®' èΩîótj˘'JŸ\a√-
∏,0SRfi»₁ Ωœ     .-Ìf8©2ÈígcÃã ï\~4)pl Ã∫}"ÎLjÇ("&∏   A-
»fEë  ÃBÆNø£6ÃZÃ \¥òY Ò<CÑ)^ÿu: ,xõjw£ˇ∏  úíüñ©u(ÜÀó✿P√ ét•<W
«:°w¤y é˙rç!_%uô Afi2}.ñeã(D"F£Tû  ∂ú•»◊<V7 Ñ3™
h∏v¡e    ∑L«₁&Ú0!¿A/" ¿ˇÒ-
æ∏X∑πŸ≠◊∂œMêt `h )≈$±∂ 1 #)Ë ¨^_Ö~"nfê    ,/✿
ó fÂ' ú 0◊…≠xñ? ÇÒH Ú%IÌàM^I3±Ó∞aÇ'J ₁ú"flTÎ0+ΩLPsö<¤-é
Û¬f/„‡©Á°j¶◊¥÷L>rßy<-j\ä²t¢ Âx«}™Q∫ E.É/0œè Ø! -
ÅD%sfi" >¬<£f.Ä  f∆ ]>fœsßôÌín˜²Ál7œp4µGõ v©íó-^K .s° |…4âöMäv\˙
```

Figure 16. Excerpt from the JPEG code for the "Parrots" image.

lections in the world.[9] In addition to Renaissance Vigenere ciphers, first editions of Kasiski, and fifty complete editions of his own Riverbank Publications, Friedman also saved newspaper and magazine treatments of cipher fiction. Among these is a review of the old serial *The Black Shadow*, which Friedman kept because of the role played in the story by "a certain minute organism, a sort of slug in appearance, which reproduces its species by the splitting into two of the parents, just as the amoeba does." As the reviewer observes, in time anyone owning such slugs will have an indefinite number of offspring, all descended from one parent, and—this is the key point— all possessed of "a strong nervous sympathy with one another." In consequence, each slug conforms to the movements of the others, "'no matter

Figure 17. JPEG "Parrots" image, now with a steganographic encryption in the code.

```
  q´
ôgûıX…a.9 ÉZjØyŸÒò_¢Df¿e,Vánmǽ≥N  Ñ y ë∏q❦¡»-Ù üÀm.—
r'a'úü"nÁuG 5 ⁻1 ìóûy5îp©EÓQ:S
az,P<·îìL>—,,â\ 55´<≈Ù P´ ÿ ≠M=_!—
a)'k"g ®îØkÂ‰' Qᵃzï•/*˜]◊} k©1"§m2f#Δ„bû±m§ëtÁ_ íJJ&ddïäR%|d%·.
‰$⁻Z lj-ØV˝+qhä±ní Ö:Ã@  êC$4H∏»1,!Ã·@ †µùâ
      9/ë ì¿S∫Ë(™\\ ◊Ω ò q¨f:•{é• êµò°,EÒ.âO≤rÁ©¿ ({≈"-Tá•ï&.
Aæs"∞ä≈4∑ƒ Bœ{^™Œ"¥Ôiè@:πŸàºá*ø¿ ?°/   ƒ(¬¨A5$ç~9
.¥' Wúì[ä ◊êÃ ∑π˜ënÊ¢ÃíöÑ7"®@4á Ü°-Δí|  Æubb›ô"h 5Y-
Ç±XG\1»I…E" ò;À       ŒILP{-àsï:è>ä5 úÕΩX¢ùÕëàO @    R&-
MY%}/bÄUÄBº ô≈Jâ8[ ´Ù¬"æËä)HÈ ±æg¨b -
B rfiØΔ⁻=øê*UMÛÊßxrµR, ˅Z#îOQ¨E«≤>àozÉR #ì?    TÄn ∞ˇÁ-
˜ß.˅ 0JE®í¬&HØO≈≤L*Èóòjìä/<&Mh∫Õ%3)á% ¡¢ ¥@Â"a0˝éÑ$\
     OhûU6Ñv-qŒyd≥-◊úiÜ´AèynY;
```

Figure 18. Excerpt from the JPEG code for the "Parrots" image with the steganographic encryption.

how widely they may be separated. Suppose one parent had a half dozen of these creatures, and someone else another half dozen. . . . The first six are arranged in a definite pattern: the others immediately conform. It is only necessary to have a pre-arranged code, and any message can be sent from any distance.' It was, Friedman commented on the clipping, the most bizarre of all the many cipher or code systems he had encountered in detective tales."[10]

Recently physicists have proposed a form of cryptography remarkably like that in *The Black Shadow*. Under certain experimental conditions, pairs of photons can be created that exert an influence over one another that cannot be explained by quantum mechanics. Scientists creating these photons have discovered that measuring the polarization of one particle immediately and identically changes the spin on its antiparticle. Such polarization takes place regardless of the relative positions of the two particles in the universe, in a result that seems rather spookily to violate the second law of classical theory, which states that influences cannot propagate faster than the speed of light. It is therefore theoretically possible that a stream of such polarized photons could be used to encipher messages that could be sent *instantaneously* through space—thus realizing not only Friedman's "bizarre" cipher-slug plan, but also fulfilling once and for all the death of space and time so long attributed to telecommunications.[11] Because messages sent this way would be untappable (to measure a particle in these states is to alter its features), a group of physicists led by William Wootters has suggested using quantum effects for secure key interchange. "Essentially, A and B can both receive the same random bitstream, knowing that if X taps the communication link, the bits will be scrambled."[12]

Such a cipher, logically untappable and physics-defying in its speed, would be an astounding cryptographic achievement, and would mark an end to secret writing as we know it. Yet even this hypothesis does not represent the outer edge of ciphering. Tony Sudbery describes work by Charles Bennett et al., which suggests it may one day be possible to transport objects over space cryptographically, rather in the manner of *Star Trek*. "The idea behind teleportation is that a physical object is equivalent to the information needed to construct it; the object can therefore be transported by transmitting the information along any conventional channel of telecommunication, the receiver using the information to reconstruct the object."[13] Although examples of this process already exist in two dimensions (for example, fax transmissions), for a long time it was thought that if one "steadily reduces the scale at which [the transmitter] faithfully reproduces detail, one will eventually run afoul of the uncertainty principle of quantum mechanics . . . with the consequence that the object in its original state is bound to be destroyed by the process of scanning for transmission. This was proved by Wootters and Zurek under the slogan 'A single quantum cannot be cloned.'"[14] But the same distinguishability of nonorthogonal states in photons (the property that permits their polarization) may also permit Maxwell's Demon to overcome the "no clone" limit of Wootters and Zurek: "David Albert has shown us how, in the parallel universes interpretation, a Maxwell Demon can beat the Heisenberg principle if Wigner's Friend hands the Demon a 'photograph' of himself in a parallel world. This beating of the Heisenberg limit can only be done by the Demon, not by Wigner's

Friend, it is not beyond standard quantum mechanics, but a rigorous consequence of it when Godelian strange loops of 'self-reference' are added."[15]

Quantum cryptography. Cryptographic teleportation. The death of space and time. There might seem to be little point in noticing these Gedanken experiments, in light of John Limon's wry conclusion in *The Place of Fiction in the Time of Science* that "the relationship of literature and science cannot be worked out" (189). Limon implies that, suggestive as it might seem, the kind of coincidence between the Wootters-Zurek scheme and *The Black Shadow*'s telepathic slugs *is* only a coincidence. Doubtless this is true, but the cryptographic imagination demonstrates how quickly humans reincorporate coincidence into pattern, searching through orbital ellipses, fractal imagery, or a million digits of pi for sequence and Logos. For the cryptographic imagination, the systematic disorder of cipher is never meaningless; like the generation of a truly random series of numbers, it may even be impossible.

The human tendency to find syntax in disorder has a biological predisposition, in what the neurophysiologist Humberto Maturana calls the "autopoesis" of the central nervous system. In Brian Malone's gloss, the nervous system's environmentally interactive feedback loops "calibrate and constrain the flourishing matrices of dendritic architecture, a morphological process Norbert Wiener, the father of cybernetics, called 'swimming upstream against the universal tide towards entropy.' The body, particularly the brain, is complicit in its eventual obsolescence because of its predilection for hardwiring the possibility of the hyperreal; consciousness is the techno-Hegelian fruit of self-selectivity, Order's upstream spawn."[16] Malone's belief in corporeal obsolescence plays into a dubious technotranscendentalism, but his general point—that on the level of physiology, daily experience is written on the body as a form of antientropic script—is right. Given the human predisposition to see patterns (and the overwhelming success of sciences predicated on the analysis of such patterns), we can not say with confidence exactly where writing leaves off and matter begins.

This is especially striking in a time when literary studies have retreated into shell games in which the reader is taught to expect, and even to admire, the moment in which the empty shell is upended. Limon notes that even as physics "pushes gleefully toward a Theory of Everything—a theory of universal origins, of essences deeper than matter and energy, a theory perhaps even of purpose, a modern *Naturphilosophie*—literary theory continues to abominate origins, essences, and intentions."[17] Although Poe deeply mistrusted the notion of human progress, he did have a passionate belief in technological evolution: "It is a theorem almost demonstrated, that the consequences of any new scientific invention will, at the present day exceed, by very much, the wildest expectation of the most imaginative." Poe is right, of course. Despite the powerful human urge to imagine the present as a stable and ongoing order (or to naturalize change through the phony idea of linear and coherent *progress*), Poe recognizes that the direction and nature of the changes produced by technological and scientific invention are, literally, unimaginable, and that, for good or ill, such changes will reorder and transform our literature and culture.[18]

The cryptographic imagination responds to this debilitating notion both by seeking to preserve the self against time through writing and by confusing the borders between self and other. Recalling an interview with the late cryptographer Luigi Sacco, "a major figure in the pantheon of cryptology," the historian David Kahn is suffused with melancholy as he comes to consider his own lifetime dedication to the history of ciphers:

> It was late one afternoon, and for a time I stood on the terrace of his spacious apartment overlooking the Tiber. The setting sun turned that antique stream to gold, and for a few moments I was overwhelmed by the beauty, the achievement of a boyhood dream, and a sense of the evanescence of all human life. This apprehension of this fact, this intimation of mortality, is why I interview these cryptologists. For inexorably death removes quantities of irreplaceable experience, and I seek, in these interviews, to fix a portion of that experience on paper and so preserve it against time, to make this mortality immortal. When I do this, I feel myself to be an agent of posterity, a representative of future readers. And that is why I said, at the beginning of this talk, that I am, in a sense, just you.[19]

Thinking about the curiously self-reflective structure of ciphers, Jan O'Deigh in *The Gold Bug Variations* makes a related observation: "Break *this* code. *I* am the riddle; know *me*. What 'me' could possibly proclaim itself the riddle? The cipher? The plaintext? The coding algorithm? The riddleness in the coder himself? . . . Know me and you will know yourself. I spend the afternoon playing with messages, and on no proof but my pleasure, feel as if I'm closing in on my discovery, me."[20] Literary cryptography is a self-refracting system whose mazy turns form nests for the incubation of self-consciousness. I think this must be why so many ciphered messages turn on the question of their own art ("solve this cipher or I give up"), why pronouns become confused, and why discussions of encryption standards should sometimes lead to the question of who wrote Shakespeare's plays.

In 1993 a new poster sent to *sci.crypt* the following ostensibly impenetrable cipher of his own design, wondering how long it would take someone to decode it:

]ZYIQNITDAHWQQIAYYLZEEQPQVVRJCVWKEJSCGMP
DTYCYNQUKU VXJIUNOLZWEOZEOHMMDMXKBTAME

HBQYMOIHMQ JKOLQOVTKXWZTENAKXMLVCMWHE
GKIHMBCXWPRW [21]

Aided by a Vigenere program on his home computer, the cryptographer Jim
Giloogly replied only hours later with the solution below:

greatart hasawayo fevoking continua lcomment aryitisa bottomle
sssource ofinspir ationtoo thersiha vemyblin dspotsin termsofu
nderstan ding.

Correctly punctuated, the message reads: "Great art has a way of evoking
continual commentary; it is a bottomless source of inspiration to others. I
have my blind spots in terms of understanding."

*Great art has a way of evoking continual commentary. . . . I am the riddle;
know me. . . . Everybody who says the same words is the same person . . . I am,
in a sense, just you. . . .* In different ways, each of these phrases responds to
the encounter of the speaker in "The Raven" with Poe's cybernetic bird.
Like Tim May's answering machine, both Poe's Raven and "The Raven"
continually repeat themselves. But they do so in such a way that we are invited to call back with new questions, to find in repetitions an augury of our
future ("'Prophet!' said I, 'thing of evil!—prophet still, if bird or devil!'").
Poe's Raven is fit emblem of the way in which the resistances of cryptography serve not to bar readers from the secrets of the text, but to incite
them further into strange loops of reading. In Poe's rapt cybernetic play,
in the give-and-take of its formal and implicit ciphers, he stakes out his
best claim as a prophet of modernity. Whatever forms of secret writing remain to be devised, Poe's texts stand as sentinels and ciphers, as statues in
the desert and as the guides who explicate them, back-talking birds whose
speech speaks only of ourselves.

Appendix

Public-Key Cryptography

Testimony of Philip Zimmermann to the Subcommittee for Economic Policy, Trade, and the Environment, U.S. House of Representatives, 12 October 1993

Mr. Chairman and members of the committee, my name is Philip Zimmermann, and I am a software engineer who specializes in cryptography and data security.* I'm here to talk to you today about the need to change U.S. export control policy for cryptographic software. I want to thank you for the opportunity to be here and commend you for your attention to this important issue. I am the author of PGP (Pretty Good Privacy), a public-key encryption software package for the protection of electronic mail. Since PGP was published domestically as freeware in June of 1991, it has spread organically all over the world and has since become the de facto worldwide standard for encryption of e-mail. The U.S. Customs Service is investigating how PGP spread outside the U.S. Because I am a target of this ongoing criminal investigation, my lawyer has advised me not to answer any questions related to the investigation.

The Information Age Is Here

Computers were developed in secret back in World War II mainly to break codes. Ordinary people did not have access to computers, because they were few in number and too expensive. Some people postulated that there would never be a need for more than half a dozen computers in the country. Governments formed their attitudes toward cryptographic technology during this period. And these attitudes persist today. Why would ordinary people need to have access to good cryptography? Another problem with cryptography in those days was that cryptographic keys had to be distributed over secure channels so that both parties could send encrypted traffic over insecure channels. Governments solved that problem by dispatching key couriers with satchels handcuffed to their wrists. Governments could afford to send guys like these to their embassies overseas. But the great masses of

---

*Philip Zimmermann (*prz@acm.org*), 9 Oct. 1993, 11:57:54 MDT. Used by permission.

ordinary people would never have access to practical cryptography if keys had to be distributed this way. No matter how cheap and powerful personal computers might someday become, you just can't send the keys electronically without the risk of interception. This widened the feasibility gap between Government and personal access to cryptography.

Today, we live in a new world that has had two major breakthroughs that have an impact on this state of affairs. The first is the coming of the personal computer and the information age. The second breakthrough is public-key cryptography. With the first breakthrough come cheap, ubiquitous personal computers, modems, FAX machines, the Internet, e-mail, digital cellular phones, personal digital assistants (PDAs), wireless digital networks, ISDN, cable TV, and the data superhighway. This information revolution is catalyzing the emergence of a global economy.

But this renaissance in electronic digital communication brings with it a disturbing erosion of our privacy. In the past, if the Government wanted to violate the privacy of ordinary citizens, it had to expend a certain amount of effort to intercept and steam open and read paper mail, and listen to and possibly transcribe spoken telephone conversation. This is analogous to catching fish with a hook and a line, one fish at a time. Fortunately for freedom and democracy, this kind of labor-intensive monitoring is not practical on a large scale. Today, electronic mail is gradually replacing conventional paper mail, and is soon to be the norm for everyone, not the novelty it is today. Unlike paper mail, e-mail messages are just too easy to intercept and scan for interesting keywords. This can be done easily, routinely, automatically, and undetectably on a grand scale. This is analogous to driftnet fishing—making a quantitative and qualitative Orwellian difference to the health of democracy.

The second breakthrough came in the late 1970s, with the mathematics of public-key cryptography. This allows people to communicate securely and conveniently with people they've never met, with no prior exchange of keys over secure channels. No more special key couriers with black bags. This, coupled with the trappings of the information age, means the great masses of people can at last use cryptography. This new technology also provides digital signatures to authenticate transactions and messages, and allows for digital money, with all the implications that has for an electronic digital economy. This convergence of technology—cheap, ubiquitous PCs, modems, FAX, digital phones, information superhighways, et cetera—is all part of the information revolution. Encryption is just simple arithmetic to all this digital hardware. All these devices will be using encryption. The rest of the world uses it, and they laugh at the U.S. because we are railing against nature, trying to stop it. Trying to stop this is like trying to legislate the tides and the weather. It's like the buggy-whip manufacturers trying to stop the cars—even with the NSA on their side, it's still impossible. The information revolution is good for democracy—good for a free market and trade. It contributed to the fall of the Soviet empire. They couldn't stop it either.

Soon, every off-the-shelf multimedia PC will become a secure voice telephone, through the use of freely available software. What does this mean for the Government's Clipper chip and key escrow systems? Like every new technology, this comes at some cost. Cars pollute the air. Cryptography can help criminals hide their activities. People in the law enforcement and intelligence communities are going to look at this only in their own terms. But even with these costs, we still can't stop this from happening in a free market global economy. Most people I talk to outside of Government feel that the net result of providing privacy will be positive.

President Clinton is fond of saying that we should "make change our friend." These sweeping technological changes have big implications, but are unstoppable. Are we going to make change our friend? Or are we going to criminalize cryptography? Are we going to incarcerate our honest, well-intentioned software engineers? Law enforcement and intelligence interests in the Government have attempted many times to suppress the availability of strong domestic encryption technology. The most recent examples are Senate Bill 266, which mandated back doors in crypto systems, the FBI Digital Telephony Bill, and the Clipper chip key escrow initiative. All of these have met with strong opposition from industry and civil liberties groups. It is impossible to obtain real privacy in the information age without good cryptography.

The Clinton administration has made it a major policy priority to help build the National Information Infrastructure (NII). Yet, some elements of the Government seem intent on deploying and entrenching a communications infrastructure that would deny the citizenry the ability to protect its privacy. This is unsettling because in a democracy, it is possible for bad people to occasionally get elected—sometimes very bad people. Normally, a well-functioning democracy has ways to remove these people from power. But the wrong technology infrastructure could allow such a future government to watch every move anyone makes to oppose it. It could very well be the last government we ever elect.

When making public policy decisions about new technologies for the Government, I think one should ask oneself which technologies would best strengthen the hand of a police state. Then, do not allow the Government to deploy those technologies. This is simply a matter of good civic hygiene.

Export Controls Are Outdated and Are a Threat to Privacy and Economic Competitiveness

The current export control regime makes no sense anymore, given advances in technology. There has been considerable debate about allowing the export of implementations of the full 56-bit Data Encryption Standard

(DES). At a recent academic cryptography conference, Michael Wiener of Bell Northern Research in Ottawa presented a paper on how to crack the DES with a special machine. He has fully designed and tested a chip that guesses DES keys at high speed until it finds the right one. Although he has refrained from building the real chips so far, he can get these chips manufactured for $10.50 each, and can build 57,000 of them into a special machine for $1 million that can try every DES key in 7 hours, averaging a solution in 3.5 hours. $1 million can be hidden in the budget of many companies. For $10 million, it takes 21 minutes to crack, and for $100 million, just two minutes. That's full 56-bit DES, cracked in just two minutes. I'm sure the NSA can do it in seconds, with its budget. This means that DES is now effectively dead for purposes of serious data security applications. If Congress acts now to enable the export of full DES products, it will be a day late and a dollar short.

If a Boeing executive who carries his notebook computer to the Paris airshow wants to use PGP to send e-mail to his home office in Seattle, are we helping American competitiveness by arguing that he has even potentially committed a federal crime? Knowledge of cryptography is becoming so widespread that export controls are no longer effective at controlling the spread of this technology. People everywhere can and do write good cryptographic software, and we import it here but cannot export it, to the detriment of our indigenous software industry.

I wrote PGP from information in the open literature, putting it into a convenient package that everyone can use in a desktop or palmtop computer. Then I gave it away for free, for the good of our democracy. This could have popped up anywhere, and spread. Other people could have and would have done it. And are doing it. Again and again. All over the planet. This technology belongs to everybody.

People Want Their Privacy Very Badly

PGP has spread like a prairie fire, fanned by countless people who fervently want their privacy restored in the information age. Today, human rights organizations are using PGP to protect their people overseas. Amnesty International uses it. The human rights group in the American Association for the Advancement of Science uses it. Some Americans don't understand why I should be this concerned about the power of Government. But talking to people in Eastern Europe, you don't have to explain it to them. They already get it—and they don't understand why we don't. I want to read you a quote from some e-mail I got last week from someone in Latvia, on the day that Boris Yeltsin was going to war with his Parliament: "Phil I wish you to know: let it never be, but if dictatorship takes over Russia your PGP is widespread from Baltic to Far East now and will help democratic people if necessary. Thanks."

Introduction

1. Clarence S. Brigham, *Edgar Allan Poe's Contributions to Alexander's Weekly Messenger* (Worcester, Mass.: American Antiquarian Society, 1943), 4.

2. Edgar Allan Poe, "A Few Words on Secret Writing," in *The Complete Works of Edgar Allan Poe*, ed. James A. Harrison, 2d ed., 12 vols. (New York: AMS Press, 1979), 5:119–20. This essay and its addenda are hereafter cited as "SW," followed by the month of original publication (if an addendum is being cited) and the page number in the AMS edition.

3. The first serious treatment of Poe's cryptographic expertise was given by William F. Friedman, in "Edgar Allan Poe, Cryptographer," *American Literature* 8, no. 3 (1936): 266–80. Friedman's essay was followed by W. K. Wimsatt, "What Poe Knew about Cryptography," *PMLA* 56 (1943): 754–79. With the exception of some suggestive passages by Louis Renza (in "Poe's Secret Autobiography," in *The American Renaissance Reconsidered: Selected Papers from the English Institute, 1982–1983*, ed. Walter Benn Michaels and Donald E. Pease [Baltimore: Johns Hopkins University Press, 1985], 58–89), no substantive treatment of secret writing appeared for the next half century, until my essay "The King of 'Secret Readers': Edgar Poe, Cryptography, and the Origins of the Detective Story," *English Literary History* 56, no. 2 (1989): 375–400. (Permission to reuse this material is gratefully acknowledged.) Recently, two essays have appeared in response to "The King of 'Secret Readers.'" These are John Hodgson, "Decoding Poe? Poe, W. B. Tyler, and Cryptography," *Journal of English and Germanic Philology* 92, no. 4 (1993): 523–34, and Terence Whalen, "The Code for Gold: Edgar Allan Poe and Cryptography," *Representations* 46 (spring 1994): 35–57. Both are discussed in subsequent chapters.

More generally, R. A. Haldane offers a brief history of cryptography in *The Hidden World* (London: Robert Hale, 1976); a much more complete version can be found in David Kahn's wonderful book *The Codebreakers: The Story of Secret Writing* (New York: Macmillan, 1967), a work to which I am deeply indebted. For an introduction to the techniques of serious contemporary cryptography, see Abraham Sinkov, *Elementary Cryptanalysis: A Mathematical Approach* (New Haven: Yale University Press, 1966). On computer cryptography, consult Alan G. Konheim, *Cryptography: A Primer* (New York: John Wiley and Sons, 1981).

4. For the most detailed articulation of this view, see Plato, *Phaedrus*, with notes by W. H. Thompson (New York: Arno Press, 1973), 274b–279b.

5. From the *Washington Post*, quoted on the novel's front cover. Richard Powers, *The Gold Bug Variations* (New York: HarperPerennial, 1991).

6. Powers, *Gold Bug Variations*, 218. The joke, as Michael Bell points out, is

that one could not know to give back the Nobel Prize unless one had successfully met the challenge of decryption: one more instance of the vertigo of cryptographic reading.

7. Robin Winks, *Cloak and Gown: Scholars in the Secret War, 1939–1961* (New York: William Morrow, 1987), 213–31.

8. James Phinney Baxter, *The Greatest of All Literary Problems: The Authorship of the Shakespeare Works* (Boston: Houghton Mifflin, 1915).

9. Alternative suggestions have included Roger Manners, the fifth earl of Rutland; William Stanley, the sixth earl of Derby; and Edward de Vere, the seventeenth earl of Oxford.

10. Francis Bacon, quoted in William Friedman and Elizebeth Friedman, *The Shakespearean Ciphers Examined: An Analysis of Cryptographic Systems Used as Evidence that Some Author Other than William Shakespeare Wrote the Plays Commonly Attributed to Him* (Cambridge: Cambridge University Press, 1957), 26; this work is hereafter cited as "F&F," followed by the page number.

11. No Baconian has ever successfully demonstrated the presence of Bacon's "biliteral" cipher in Shakespeare's writing; indeed, most of the Baconians never understood its relatively simple principles. See ibid., 27–50.

12. Quoted in ibid., 29.

13. Both the example of the castle and that of the text from *The Advancement of Learning* are taken from William Friedman, "Six Lectures on Cryptology," in *The Friedman Legacy: A Tribute to William and Elizebeth Friedman*, United States Cryptologic History: Sources in Cryptologic History, no. 3 (Fort George Meade, Md.: Center for Cryptologic History, National Security Agency, 1992), 47–49.

14. Marjorie Garber, *Shakespeare's Ghost Writers: Literature as Uncanny Causality* (New York: Methuen, 1987), 4.

15. For a recent example, see Penn Leary, *The Cryptographic Shakespeare: A Monograph Wherein the Poems and Plays Attributed to William Shakespeare Are Proven to Contain the Enciphered Name of the Concealed Author, Francis Bacon* (Omaha: Westchester House, 1987).

16. Garber, *Shakespeare's Ghost Writers*, 3. Garber's answer is that conflicts over Shakespeare's identity are used to engage extratextual questions such as the status of colonial literature, or the ways in which Shakespeare's plays have served to consolidate the meanings of "Englishness." See ibid., 1–7. As an instance of the passions aroused by the question of provenance, consider the poem inscribed on the flyleaf of my copy of *The Case for Edward de Vere*. A reader named Carolyn was so moved by Percy Allen's arguments that she gave the book as a gift, admonishing the recipient with a rather terrifying mixture of affection proffered and withheld:

> Oliver Dear,
> I'm glad you believe it:
> For Shakespeare,
> Oliver dear,
> *Is* Edward de Vere—
> Take it or leave it—
> Oliver dear—
> I'm glad *you* believe it!

Percy Allen, *The Case for Edward de Vere, Seventeenth Earl of Oxford, as "Shakespeare"* (London: Cecil Palmer, 1930), flyleaf.

17. See William F. Friedman, "Shakespeare, Secret Intelligence, and Statecraft," *Proceedings of the American Philosophical Society* 106, no. 5 (1962): 401–11.

18. Garber, *Shakespeare's Ghost Writers*, 5.

19. Elizabeth Wells Gallup, *The Biliteral Cypher of Sir Francis Bacon Discovered in His Works and Deciphered by Mrs. Elizabeth Wells Gallup* (Detroit: Howard Publishing, 1899). A much enlarged second addition appeared in 1900, and a third (augmented even more) in 1901.

20. Ronald Clark, *The Man Who Broke Purple* (Boston: Little, Brown, 1977), 11.

21. Ibid., 12.

22. Friedman, "Edgar Allan Poe, Cryptographer," 266. This essay was reprinted in *Bulletin of the Signal Intelligence Service* 97 (July–Sept. 1937).

23. Joseph Wood Krutch, *Edgar Allan Poe: A Study in Genius* (New York: Knopf, 1926), 103.

24. Herbert O. Yardley, *The American Black Chamber* (Indianapolis: Bobbs-Merrill, 1931), 20–21.

25. Ibid., 240. "The reader should understand that the so-called additive or subtractive method for garbling a code telegraph (used during the Spanish-American War) is about as effective for maintaining secrecy as the simple substitution cipher which as children we read in Poe's 'The Gold Bug'" (ibid., 42).

Chapter 1. The King of Secret Readers

1. Friedman, "Edgar Allan Poe, Cryptographer," 266; Haldane, *Hidden World*, 26; Bruce Norman, *Secret Warfare: The Battle of Codes and Ciphers* (Newton Abbot, England: David and Charles, 1973), 11.

2. See Thomas Browne, *The Collected Works of Sir Thomas Browne*, ed. Charles Sayle (Edinburgh: John Grant, 1927), vol. 1.

3. Edgar Allan Poe, *Edgar Allan Poe: Poetry and Tales*, ed. Patrick Quinn (New York: Library of America, 1984), 587; this work is hereafter cited as *PT*, followed by the page number. Cryptographers have recently introduced a distinction between cryptograph and cryptogram, in order to differentiate between a cipher design (a cryptograph) and a particular use of that cipher (a cryptogram). The distinction is identical to that between the Saussurean *langue* and *parole*.

4. *Cryptogram* was popularized through its literary associations, chiefly from the notoriety attending the publication of Ignatius Donnelly, *The Great Cryptogram: Bacon's Cipher in Shakespeare's Plays*, 2 vols. (New York: R. S. Peal, 1888).

5. John Irwin, *American Hieroglyphics: The Symbol of the Egyptian Hieroglyphics in the American Renaissance* (Baltimore: Johns Hopkins University Press, 1980), 61.

6. Michel Foucault gives his account of the meaning of historical linguistics in *The Order of Things: An Archeology of the Human Sciences* (New York: Vintage, 1973), 294–302. Noting the rise of the "literary" at the beginning of the nineteenth century, Foucault observes that "language was burying itself within its own density as an object and allowing itself to be traversed, through and through, by knowledge, [but] it was also reconstituting itself elsewhere, in an indepen-

216 Notes to Pages 22–27

dent form, difficult of access, folded back upon the enigma of its own origin and existing wholly in reference to the pure act of writing" (300). This seems an apt description of Poe, whose texts (think of *Eureka*) are "traversed," if not by knowledge, then certainly by a terrific *will* to knowledge—one that is finally satisfied as much by formal and aesthetic criteria as by strictly cognitive ones. A useful review of historical linguistics can be found in Hans Aarsleff, *The Study of Language in England, 1780–1860* (Princeton: Princeton University Press, 1967).

7. Irwin, *American Hieroglyphics*, 159.

8. Critics of the detective story are largely agreed on Poe's status as its originator: "The detective story as we know it dates from 1841 with the first publication of Poe's 'The Murders in the Rue Morgue,' but various authorities have observed elements of detection in the literature of a far earlier age" (Melvyn Barnes, *Best Detective Fiction from Godwin to the Present* [Hamden, Conn.: Linnet Books, 1975], 11). "It is to Edgar Allan Poe that we owe the detective story as we know it today" (A. E. Murch, *The Development of the Detective Story* [London: Peter Owen, 1958], 88).

Sources for various aspects of the detective story can be traced back as far as one wishes: to the *Memoirs* of François Eugène Vidocq, William Godwin's *Caleb Williams*, Voltaire's *Zadig*, and beyond. But the specific narrative *form* of the classic detective story originates with Poe. At any rate, my use of the terms "detective fiction" and "detective stories" is only a provisional generalization: the subgenres of the hardboiled detective novel, the police procedural, the ratiocinative country-house murder, and the spy novel do not have identical narrative forms, yet they are clearly related to the patterns we can discover—for the first time—in the three Dupin stories.

9. *Suaviter in modo, fortiter in re*: the key phrase itself illustrates how easily encoding can take place, and how difficult it can be for the unknowing to crack.

10. SW, Dec., 142. The passage ostensibly derives from a letter sent to Poe by a "Mr. W. B. Tyler"—but I will return to this issue below.

11. Poe placed considerable faith in chirography, or the science of handwriting, and noted in the October addendum that he had received a cipher from a "Timotheus Whackemwell." "Thinking that in the chirography we recognized the hand of our friend, Mr. J. N. McJilton, of Baltimore, we addressed *him* by return of mail, with the solution desired. Mr. McJilton, it appears, however, was not the correspondent" (SW, Oct., 138).

12. Compare Poe's comment on a novel by Edward George Bulwer-Lytton: "Bulwer, in my opinion, wants the true vigor of intellect which would prompt him to seek, and enable him to seize truth upon the surface of things. He imagines her forever in the well" (Poe, "Literary Small Talk," in *Edgar Allan Poe: Essays and Reviews*, ed. G. R. Thompson [New York: Library of America, 1984], 1062; this work is hereafter cited as *ER*, followed by the page number). The same metaphor occurs often in Poe's writing, and derives, according to Joan Dayan, primarily from Jonathan Swift's *Tale of a Tub*: "It is with writers as with wells. . . . Often, when there is nothing in the World at the Bottom, besides *Dryness* and *Dirt*, though it be but a yard and a half under ground, it shall pass, however, for wondrous Deep, upon no wiser a reason than because it is wondrous *Dark*." How characteristic that where Swift's text turns on excremental and somatic associations, Poe reforms the

metaphor into an allegory of *semiotic flatness*. Swift is quoted in Dayan, *Fables of Mind: An Inquiry into Poe's Fiction* (New York: Oxford University Press, 1987), 29.

13. On the significance of clues and "detection," broadly conceived, see Carlo Ginzburg's excellent "Morelli, Freud, and Sherlock Holmes: Clues and Scientific Method," in *The Sign of Three: Dupin, Holmes, Peirce*, ed. Umberto Eco and Thomas A Sebeok (Bloomington: Indiana University Press, 1983), 81–118. For more on the relation of Freud and Morelli, see Michael Shepherd, *Sherlock Holmes and the Case of Dr. Freud* (New York: Tavistock, 1985).

14. The game of cards also finds a counterpart in "A Few Words on Secret Writing": Poe explains that "a pack of cards is sometimes made the vehicle of a cipher" by having the encoder inscribe a letter of the message on each of the cards, which are then shuffled according to a predetermined method, and inscribed again, until the message is complete. The receiver then reconstructs the message by reshuffling the cards and going through them one by one according to the plan agreed on. But, he adds in a comment that prefigures "The Purloined Letter," "*a pack of cards* sent from one party to another, would scarcely fail to excite suspicion, and it cannot be doubted that it is far better to secure ciphers from being considered as such, than to waste time in attempts at rendering them scrutiny-proof when intercepted" (SW, 121–22). Jacques Lacan hints at card playing in his "Seminar on 'The Purloined Letter'" when he repeatedly uses *jouer* to describe the actions of the characters. The game, however, could also be chess, played by matched opponents—Dupin and the Minister D.—through the "pieces" of the king and queen (Lacan, "Seminar on 'The Purloined Letter,'" in *The Purloined Poe*, ed. John P. Muller and William J. Richardson [Baltimore: Johns Hopkins University Press, 1988], 28–54).

The close relation of detective stories to games has often been noted. Roger Callois writes: "Philo Vance in *The 'Canary' Murder Case*, by S. S. Van Dine, attains in the course of a poker game the moral certitude he had lacked; in *Trois crimes à Veules-les-Roses*, by Marcel Marc, the murderer gives himself away in a chess game" (Callois, "The Detective Novel as Game," in *The Poetics of Murder*, ed. Glenn W. Most and William W. Stowe [San Diego: Harcourt Brace Jovanovich, 1983], 2).

15. Jacques Derrida, "The Purveyor of Truth," trans. Willis Domingo et al., *Yale French Studies* 52 (1975): 109, 111.

16. Irwin, *American Hieroglyphics*, 159.

17. Barbara Johnson, "The Frame of Reference: Poe, Lacan, Derrida," in Muller and Richardson, *Purloined Poe*, 245. First published in *Yale French Studies* 55–56 (1977): 457–505.

18. The illustrations are taken from Jacques Lacan, "The Agency of the Letter in the Unconscious or Reason since Freud," in *Écrits: A Selection*, trans. Alan Sheridan (New York: W. W. Norton, 1977), 151.

19. Johnson, "Frame of Reference," 235.

20. Derrida, "Purveyor of Truth," 101.

21. Edgar Allan Poe, review of *Sketches of Conspicuous Living Characters of France*, in *ER*, 989.

22. *Webster's New Twentieth-Century Dictionary*, unabridged, 2d ed., s.v. "cipher."

23. Daniel Hoffman, *Poe Poe Poe Poe Poe Poe* (Garden City, N.Y.: Doubleday, 1972), 127.

24. Poe reviewed his own *Tales* in the October 1845 issue of the *Aristidean*; see *ER*, 868–73.

25. Of Tyler, Wimsatt says only that "perhaps Poe believed him to be a relation of the President. . . . I have not yet been able to determine whether he was" ("What Poe Knew about Cryptography," 759 n. 25). But perhaps Wimsatt discovered no relation because Tyler did not exist apart from Poe's pen.

26. In his review of *Sketches of Conspicuous Living Characters of France*, Poe relates a story that may be pertinent to the reading of Tyler's cryptograph: the author Thiers composed an elogium for a literary contest sponsored by the Academy of Aix, which "was deemed excellent; but the author being suspected, and no other candidate deserving the palm, the committee, rather than award it to a Jacobin, postponed their decisions for a year. At the expiration of this time, our youth's article again made its appearance, but, meanwhile, a production had arrived from Paris which was thought far better." Relieved, the committee awarded the new entry first prize; but when "the name of the Parisian victor was unsealed . . . it was that of Thiers. . . . He had been at great pains to mystify the committee . . . the M.S. had been copied in a strange hand, and had been sent from Aix to Paris and from Paris to Aix" (*ER*, 988).

27. Louis Renza persuasively suggests that "one can construe Poe's tales as autobiographical cryptograms." Renza also speculates on the possibility of identifying Tyler with Poe:

> Given the fact that Poe refers to W. B. Tyler as someone he at least knew of, "a gentleman whose abilities we very highly respect," and given that this name does not appear in the City Directories of the major eastern seaboard cities (including Washington, Richmond, Baltimore, Philadelphia, New York, and Boston), "Tyler" may have been the Supreme Court justice of Virginia, a William B. Tyler who graduated from William and Mary College around 1812. Yet I am not sure that he was not Poe himself, since in this letter "Tyler" gives an example of a cipher whose solution/translation echoes one of Poe's most frequently used refrains in his tales and poetry—a refrain "Tyler" here italicizes: "the sentence might either be 'I love you now as ever,' or 'I love you now no more.'" Poe, after all, had made up letters for his 1838 articles on "Autography." . . . If Poe indeed adopts the alias of Tyler here, then we can also claim that he secretly but openly professes a theory of secret autobiographical writing in this letter.

Renza, "Poe's Secret Autobiography," 86–87 n. 14.

28. Whalen's historicizing reading appears in "The Code for Gold." Whalen gives a convincing account of the ways in which Poe understands the coded treasure map and the hunt for gold as figures for authorial production in a market economy, as Poe is forced to "coin his brain into gold," directing his literary imagination toward the production of commodities for a burgeoning mass market. Whalen fails, however, to engage the way cryptography undermines the attribution of writing—an undermining evident in his own work. Referring to Tyler's letter, Whalen writes that "the old aunt and the cruel guardian, of course, could

represent Maria Clemm and John Allan. The idea of stolen letters looks forward to 'The Purloined Letter'" (44). Doubtless unintentionally, Whalen has purloined *my* prior claim that "Tyler's references to cryptography's practical use and its value in instilling mental 'discipline' repeat points earlier made by Poe, and the 'perverse and *cruel* guardian' may look back to John Allan, even as the 'stolen' love letter and the references to statesmen anticipate the plot of 'The Purloined Letter.'" Whether I, too, have fallen prey to the self-performing thematics of Poe's secret writing remains for readers other than myself to discover.

29. Edgar Allan Poe, *The Letters of Edgar Allan Poe*, ed. John Ward Ostrom, 2 vols. (1947; reprint, New York: Gordian Press, 1966), 1:188–89.

30. Quoted in Wimsatt, "What Poe Knew about Cryptography," 771.

31. In 1846, Virginia entered into Poe's cryptographic enterprise in a minor way with her Valentine present to Edgar, an acrostic poem whose first initials spelled out "Edgar Allan Poe." The first five lines run thus:

Ever with thee I wish to roam —
Dearest my life is thine.
Give me a cottage for my home
And a rich old cypress vine,
Removed from the world with its sin and care.

Quoted in Kenneth Silverman, *Edgar A. Poe: Mournful and Never-Ending Remembrance* [New York: HarperCollins, 1991], 292–93.

32. *PT*, 81. Osgood replied with a more ambitious double progressive acrostic, "her name beginning on the first letter and his on the last of the first line, and both names progressing through the lines," though the poem was addressed not to Poe but — bitter words — to Rufus Griswold instead (F&F, 94). Compare its contents with the translation of Whalen's first cipher in the essay.

33. Derrida, "Purveyor of Truth," 197.

34. Charles Baudelaire, *The Flowers of Evil*, ed. Marthiel Mathews and Jackson Mathews (New York: New Directions, 1955), 234.

35. Patrick Quinn, *The French Face of Edgar Allan Poe* (Carbondale: Southern Illinois University Press, 1957), 43.

Chapter 2. Secret Writing as Alchemy

1. Edgar Allan Poe, *Collected Works of Edgar Allan Poe*, ed. Thomas Ollive Mabbott, 3 vols. (Cambridge: Harvard University Press, Belknap Press, 1969–78), 3:799; this work is hereafter cited as *CW*, followed by the page number.

2. My analysis of the alchemical imagery in Poe's tale follows in part from Barton Levi St. Armand, "Poe's Sober Mystification: The Uses of Alchemy in 'The Gold-Bug,'" *Poe Studies* 4 (1971): 1–7.

3. Ralph E. Weber, *United States Diplomatic Codes and Ciphers, 1775–1938* (Chicago: Precedent Publishing, 1979), 5.

4. Aristotle touches on the same question in the *Metaphysics* when he attacks the Pythagoreans for believing "that things themselves are numbers."

5. Nor is the fear of such an object incompatible with our electronic era. In a widely distributed Internet posting from 1993, Robert McElwaine (*mcelwre@cnsvax.uwec.edu*) warned readers to avoid demonic bar codes:

ALL Christians are PROHIBITED by Revelation 14:9-11 from cooperating with the "MARK-OF-THE-BEAST" bar-code, OCR-number, and magnetic-strip scanning systems, (as found in local libraries, supermarkets, retail establishments, etc.), which also THREATEN to SUBVERT Individual Privacy and Freedom. The scanners can serve THE SAME CRIMINAL PURPOSE as the TV cameras in the book "1984"! The UPC bar-codes are probably the most blatant form of the "MARK OF THE BEAST" so far, with the "NUMBER OF THE BEAST," 666, ALREADY CODED INTO THEM. Each of the so-called "guard patterns," pairs of thin lines spaced close together at the beginning, middle, and end of each full-length UPC bar-code, is IDENTICAL to one of the two codes for a 6. WARN YOUR FRIENDS!

Posted on 25 Feb. 1993, 01:41:34 GMT.

6. The question—is art a cipher or a hieroglyph?—shows up in writers as unlike Poe as Elizabeth Bishop: see "The Monument," and "Over 2000 Illustrations and a Complete Concordance," in which she writes:

. . . It was somewhere near there
I saw what frightened me most of all:
A holy grave, not looking particularly holy,
one of a group under a keyhole-arched stone baldaquin
open to every wind from the pink desert. . . .
half-filled with dust, not even the dust
of the poor prophet paynim who once lay there.

See Bishop, *The Complete Poems: 1927–1979* (New York: Farrar, Straus, and Giroux, 1979), 23–25; 57–59.

7. Jorge Luis Borges, *In Praise of Darkness*, trans. Norman Thomas di Giovanni (New York: Dutton, 1974), 15.

8. Orville Ward Owen, *Sir Francis Bacon's Cipher Story*, 5 vols. (Detroit: Howard Publishing, 1893–95). The sixth volume remains in manuscript.

9. Nicolas Abraham and Maria Torok, *The Wolf Man's Magic Word: A Cryptonymy*, trans. Nicholas Rand (Minneapolis: University of Minnesota Press, 1986).

10. Irving Malin, review of *Family Secrets and the Psychoanalysis of Nature*, by Esther Raskin, *Poe Studies Association Newsletter* 21, no. 2 (1993): 8–9. For other hints of a cryptonymic reading of Poe's writing, see Joseph Riddel, "The 'Crypt' of Edgar Poe," *Boundary* 2 (spring 1979): 117–41.

11. See the work of Esther Raskin, who raises interesting points about the cryptonymic function of Poe's diction. As Malin asks, why have "words such as 'suppositious' and 'porphyrogene' never been adequately studied?" (Malin, review of *Family Secrets*, 9). Esther Raskin, *Family Secrets and the Psychoanalysis of Narrative* (Princeton: Princeton University Press, 1992).

12. Sigmund Freud speaks of the "fixed key" in *On Dreams*, trans. James Strachey (New York: W. W. Norton, 1980), 11.

13. The description of Derrida is borrowed from Murray McArthur, "Deciphering Eliot: 'Rhapsody on a Windy Night' and the Dialectic of the Cipher," *American Literature* 66, no. 3 (1994): 516.

14. For Derrida's fullest treatment of cryptography, see Jacques Derrida, "Dis-

semination," in *Dissemination*, trans. Barbara Johnson (Chicago: University of Chicago Press, 1981), 287–366.

15. Daniel Defoe, *An Essay upon Literature; or, An Enquiry into the Antiquity and Original of Letters* (London, 1726). See pages 99–104 and, in particular, 109–10.

16. Daniel Defoe, *The Life and Strange Surprizing Adventures of Robinson Crusoe, of York, Mariner*, ed. J. Donald Crowley (London: Oxford University Press, 1972), 180.

17. Sigmund Freud, "Analysis, Terminable and Interminable," in *Freud: Therapy and Technique*, ed. Philip Rieff (New York: Macmillan, 1963), 251.

18. Valéry used this phrase in his first public lecture on Poe. Quoted in James R. Lawler, *The Poet as Analyst: Essays on Paul Valéry* (Berkeley and Los Angeles: University of California Press, 1974), 309.

19. In his concern with mirroring and the constitution of subjectivity, Irwin is deeply indebted to Lacan. Remarkably, Lacan appears in *American Hieroglyphics* only epigraphically: "Suppose that in the desert you find a stone covered with hieroglyphics. You do not doubt for a moment that, behind them, there was a subject who wrote them. But it is an error to believe that each signifier is addressed to you—this is proved by the fact that you cannot understand any of it. On the other hand you define them as signifiers, by the fact that you are sure that each of these signifiers is related to each of the others" (Irwin, *American Hieroglyphics*, 237). As the epigraph indicates, it is not only Lacan's general psychoanalytic orientation that spurs Irwin's research, but his specific invocation of the hieroglyph as a model for signification.

By effacing his relation to Lacan, Irwin shows that he, too, participates in the powerful "Franco-American imaginary" that has characterized relations between French literature and American culture since Baudelaire first discovered Poe. The term belongs to Jane Gallop, who wittily describes the geocultural displacements holding between Dupin, the Parisian "analyst" of Poe's American text, and Lacan, the new Parisian "analyst" who explicates it. Both men have the cryptographer's love of "riddles and plays on words," as well as a "biting contempt" for positivism; further, "in Dupin we can recognize Lacan's flamboyant style and extreme conceit. Yet let us beware this obvious identification of Dupin with the analyst. 'A little *too* self-evident,' Dupin says . . . and Lacan repeats: 'A little *too* self-evident,' Lacan says, in English, explicitly repeating Dupin's very words, broadly playing his identification with Dupin, which, the reader should be alerted, is itself a little *too* self-evident" (Gallop, "The American Other," in Muller and Richardson, *Purloined Poe*, 280).

20. Lacan, "Seminar on 'The Purloined Letter,'" 29; the English version of this essay was first published in *Yale French Studies* 48 (1972): 39–72. It is unfortunately omitted from the English version of *Écrits*. In the French original, it is given pride of place among the collected essays, and in its 1971 French republication it is preceded by a six-page note, as well as by supplements designed to clarify Lacan's continuing thinking on "The Purloined Letter": "Presentation of the Following," "Introduction," and especially, "Parenthesis of Parentheses" (*Écrits I* [Paris: Editions du Seuil, 1971], 7–75). John P. Muller and William J. Richardson discuss these in "Lacan's Seminar on 'The Purloined Letter': Overview," in *Purloined Poe*, 55–76.

21. Unlike Lacan, Irwin often uses "hieroglyph" to refer to Adamically motivated signs, such as when he distinguishes between writing that is hieroglyphic and that which is phonetic: "The first type of writing, which copies the script of natural objects, has its ultimate origin in the Author of nature, while the second type, an arbitrary and conventional sign system, is wholly man-made. The first type evokes an original transparency of meaning that is wholly masked by phonetic signs but that can still be dimly perceived in the universally recognizable natural shapes of pictographic script" (Irwin, *American Hieroglyphics*, 167–68).

22. Lacan, "Agency of the Letter," 159. Lacan wrote this crucial essay just two years after completing the seminar on "The Purloined Letter."

23. Sinkov, *Elementary Cryptanalysis*, 2.

24. Lacan, "Agency of the Letter," 160.

25. Paul Auster, *City of Glass* (New York: Viking Penguin, 1987).

26. Arthur Conan Doyle, "The Adventure of the Dancing Men," in William S. Baring-Gould, ed., *The Annotated Sherlock Holmes*, 2 vols. (New York: Clarkson Potter, 1967), 2:530–31.

27. Note how the highly mimetic representation of the human form as a hieroglyph serves to mask the purely arbitrary characteristics of Abe Slaney's signs.

28. *Narrative of A. Gordon Pym, PT*, 1168. Dirk Peters, Poe's version of Friday, is also one of Poe's many cryptographic doubles. When Pym, descending a cliff wall, succumbs to the "*longing to fall*; a desire, a yearning, a passion utterly uncontrollable," his blurred rush into Peters's arms is not only an instance of the homosocial gothic, but also Pym's attempt to merge with his cryptographic double (he emerges "a new being," his "trepidation entirely vanished" [*PT*, 1170–71]).

29. Marie Bonaparte, *The Life and Works of Edgar Allan Poe*, trans. John Rodker (London: Hogarth Press, 1949), 363. This is an abridgment and translation of a work originally published as *Edgar Poe: Étude psychanalytique*, 2 vols. (Paris: Les Éditions Denoël et Steele, 1933).

30. Bonaparte, *Life and Works*, 364.

31. Ibid., 368–69.

32. Mark C. Taylor, "Terminal Space" (manuscript, Williams College, 1994).

33. Mircea Eliade, "What Is Alchemy?" in *Hidden Truths: Magic, Alchemy, and the Occult*, ed. Lawrence Sullivan (New York: Macmillan, 1989), 246.

34. Taylor, "Terminal Space," 14.

35. Ibid., 13.

36. Eliade, "What Is Alchemy?" 245.

37. F. Sherwood Taylor, *The Alchemists: Founders of Modern Chemistry* (New York: Henry Schuman, 1949), 28.

38. C. J. S. Thompson, *The Lure and Romance of Alchemy* (London: George Harrap, 1932), 120. Thompson continues: "Secret alphabets, ciphers, and emblematic drawings representing various processes also served as a medium of understanding between the adepts of different nations and became universally employed in Europe" (ibid.; see 131–32 for secret alchemical alphabets used in the Renaissance). "In its broadest aspect, alchemy appears as a system of philosophy which claimed to penetrate the mystery of life" (John Read, *Prelude to Chemistry* [New York: Macmillan, 1937], 2).

39. The symbolic associations of the treasure in "The Gold-Bug" have not diminished readers' interest in hidden treasure. Indeed, "The Gold-Bug" is almost certainly the inspiration for an ongoing treasure hunt inspired by something called the Beale Ciphers. See Louis Kruh, "The Beale Cipher as a Bamboozlement: Part II," *Cryptologia* 12, no. 4 (1988): 241–46. As recounted in a pamphlet written in 1885 by J. B. Ward, the story of the ciphers is as follows: a group of adventurers led by a certain Thomas Jefferson Beale accumulated a huge mass of treasure and buried it in Bedford County, Virginia, leaving three ciphers with an innkeeper; the ciphers describe the location, contents, and intended beneficiaries of the treasure. Ward himself gives a decryption of the second cipher, called B2, which reveals the untold riches waiting for whoever should solve the other two, and which, in a nice reference to Beale's name, is encrypted by a book cipher using the initial letters of the Declaration of Independence as the key. In the century since Ward's pamphlet appeared, cryptologists have regularly sought to solve the remaining two ciphers, using a variety of texts as the encoding source. Should one so desire, one can obtain membership in the Beale Cypher Association, a for-profit group dedicated to locating the treasure. You can get the ciphers from the *rec.puzzles* FAQL (Frequently Asked Question Line) by including the line "send index" in a message to *netlib@peregrine.com* and following the directions.

40. This is even more clearly demonstrated by Powers, *Gold Bug Variations*, which recognizes the cryptographer as the modern sorcerer's apprentice, able to read (and therefore harness) the power of nature, negotiating the slippery transition from symbols on the page to power in the world.

Chapter 3. Detective Fiction and the Analytic Sublime

1. Victor Sheymov and Roger Jellinek, *Tower of Secrets: A Real-Life Spy Thriller* (Annapolis, Md.: Naval Institute Press, 1993), 344–45.

2. Sheymov and Jellinek, *Tower of Secrets*, resonates throughout with echoes of Poe and detective fiction. As John Irwin has shown, the roots of the detective story reach back to the story of Theseus escaping from the Minotaur by following a *clew* (ball of thread) throughout the maze; the entire second half of Sheymov's autobiography, entitled "The Maze," turns on his attempts to escape the KGB.

3. Geoffrey Hartman, "Literature High and Low: The Case of the Detective Story," in *The Fate of Reading and Other Essays* (Chicago: University of Chicago Press, 1975), 225.

4. Poe, *Letters*, 2:328.

5. It is a cliché of detective-fiction criticism that its most avid readers are professionals distinguished for their own analytic abilities — doctors, lawyers, and the like. W. H. Auden, one remembers, was a compulsive reader of detective fiction, as is former Supreme Court nominee Judge Robert Bork, who consumes one such work a day.

6. John Limon, *The Place of Fiction in the Time of Science: A Disciplinary History of American Writing* (Cambridge: Cambridge University Press, 1990), 103.

7. Johnson, "Frame of Reference," 245.

8. "Thou Art the Man," *PT*, 740. The deception is accomplished by thrusting "a stiff piece of whalebone" down the throat of the corpse and doubling it over

in the wine cask, so that it springs up when released. As for Mr. Shuttleworthy's impressive accusation, the narrator "confidently depended upon [his] ventriloquial abilities" (ibid., 742).

9. *Webster's New Twentieth-Century Dictionary*, s.v. "analysis."

10. I use the male pronoun as a way of recognizing how extremely "The Murders in the Rue Morgue" genders its readers. Although it would be profitable to investigate how the female reader locates herself in Poe's text, I am concerned here with elucidating the dominant assumptions of the genre, which begins with this story.

11. See, for instance, Richard Wilbur, "Recent Studies of Edgar Allan Poe," *New York Review of Books* 9, no. 1 (1967), 26–27.

12. For a collection of eighteenth-century treatments of feral children, see Lucie Malson, *Enfants sauvages*, trans. Edmund Fawcett, Peter Ayrton, and Joan White (New York: Monthly Review Press, 1972), which includes Jean Itard's famous treatment of the Wild Boy of Aveyron. Roger Shattuck offers a detailed but dull interpretation of Itard's work in *The Forbidden Experiment: The Story of the Wild Boy of Aveyron* (New York: Farrar, Straus, and Giroux, 1980). The idea of a criminal orangutan was not original to Poe: Stephen Peithman records that Poe "very likely saw an article, 'New Mode of Thieving,' in the *Annual Register for 1834* . . . which tells of an 'extraordinary burglary' in which a woman entering her bedroom is attacked by a 'Monkey (or a Ribbed-face Baboon) which threw her down, and placing his feet upon her breast, held her pinned firmly to the ground.'" The animal, it turns out, belonged to "itinerant showmen" from whom it had "been let loose for the sake of plundering" (Edgar Allan Poe, *The Annotated Tales of Edgar Allan Poe*, ed. Stephen Peithman [New York: Schocken Books, 1981], 196–97).

13. James Burnet, Lord Monboddo, *The Origin and Progress of Language*, 2d ed., 6 vols. (Edinburgh, 1774), 1:267.

14. Cuvier actually boasted about the superiority of his method to that of the detective: "This single track therefore tells the observer about the kind of teeth; the kind of jaws, the haunches, the shoulder, and the pelvis of the animal which has passed: it is more certain evidence than all of Zadig's clues" (William Coleman, *Georges Cuvier, Zoologist: A Study in the History of Evolution Theory* [Cambridge: Harvard University Press, 1964], 102). Voltaire's novel is typically cited as the source for the detective's method, in the inferential reasoning by which three brothers perfectly describe a horse they have not seen, relying only on the circumstantial traces that remain.

15. Review of *The Hand Phrenologically Considered, Littel's Living Age* 28 (Mar. 1851): 283–84. Foucault suggests the intellectual ties between Dupin and Cuvier through a quotation from Schlegel: "The structure or comparative grammar of languages furnishes as certain a key of their genealogy as the study of comparative anatomy has done to the loftiest branch of natural science" (*Order of Things*, 280).

16. Foucault, *Order of Things*, 280–81.

17. Georges Cuvier, *The Animal Kingdom*, trans. and abridged H. M'Murtrie (Philadelphia, 1832), 54–55.

18. Peter Brooks, *Reading for the Plot: Design and Intention in Narrative* (New York: Random House, 1985), 13.

19. Eve Sedgwick, *The Coherence of Gothic Conventions* (New York: Methuen, 1986), 17.

20. On the gothic and male homosociality, see Eve Sedgwick, *Between Men: English Literature and Male Homosocial Desire* (New York: Columbia University Press, 1985), 83–117.

21. My thinking here is indebted to John Irwin, "A Clew to a Clue: Locked Rooms and Labyrinths in Poe and Borges," *Raritan* 10, no. 4 (1991): 40–57.

22. Lacan, "Agency of the Letter," 166–67.

23. Ibid., 167.

24. Ibid.

25. Reacting against this type of tropic determination, Geoffrey Hartman warns critics not to move too quickly from rhetorical analysis to narrative significance: "The detective story structure—strong beginnings and endings and a deceptively rich, counterfeit, 'excludable' middle—resembles almost too much that of symbol or trope. Yet the recent temptation of linguistic theorists to collapse narrative structure into this or that kind of metaphoricity becomes counterproductive if it remains blind to the writer's very struggle to outwit the epileptic Word" (Hartman, "Literature High and Low," 214). Hartman's caution is well placed, but the meaning of the detective story's rhetorical form lies primarily in its somatic effects on the reader, and not in its unsustainable claims to revelation.

26. Peter Brooks, "The Idea of a Psychoanalytic Literary Criticism," in *Discourse in Psychoanalysis and Literature*, ed. Shlomith Rimmon-Kenan (New York: Methuen, 1987), 2.

27. Bonaparte, *Étude psychanalytique*, 2:565.

28. Sigmund Freud, "Fragment of an Analysis of a Case of Hysteria," in *Dora: An Analysis of a Case of Hysteria*, ed. Philip Rieff (New York: Macmillan, 1963), 96.

29. Ibid.

30. Freud, "Analysis, Terminable and Interminable," 253.

31. Freud, "Fragment of an Analysis," 31, 32.

32. Evert Duyckinck and George Duyckinck, *Cyclopaedia of American Literature*, 2 vols. (Philadelphia: William Rutter, 1875).

33. Attempting to imitate its master, Humphreys' animal accidentally cuts its own throat (Poe, *Annotated Tales*, 197). Poe habitually associates hair, the sexualized body, and violence. The first thing discovered at the crime scene are "thick tresses—very thick tresses—of grey human hair . . . torn out by the roots," "perhaps half a million of hairs at a time" ("Murders in the Rue Morgue," *PT*, 422); and Marie Rôget's jilted paramour identifies her body by stroking her arms to see if they have her characteristically luxuriant hair.

34. Brooks, "Idea of a Psychoanalytic Literary Criticism," 13.

35. Sigmund Freud, "The Dynamics of the Transference," in Rieff, *Freud*, 114–15.

36. Lacan, "Agency of the Letter," 166.

37. Freud, "Analysis, Terminable and Interminable," 251.

38. *Webster's New Twentieth-Century Dictionary*, s.v. "stamen."

Chapter 4. Dark Fiber

1. William Rochfort, *A Treatise upon Arcanography; or, A New Method of Secret Writing, Defying Discovery or Detection, and Adapted for All Languages* (London, 1836); William Thompson, *A New Method for the Instruction of the Blind* (Nashville, Tenn., 1832).

2. James Swaim, *The Mural Diagraph; or, The Art of Conversing through a Wall* (Philadelphia, 1829).

3. Edgar Lind Morse, ed., *Samuel F. B. Morse: His Letters and Journals*, 2 vols. (Boston: Houghton Mifflin, 1914), 1:41 (emphasis added).

4. Kahn, *Codebreakers*, 111.

5. Limon, *Place of Fiction*, 20. Relatively little has been written on the relation of Poe's writing to technology. Robert H. Byer discusses Poe's response to the daguerreotype in "Mysteries of the City: A Reading of Poe's 'The Man of the Crowd,'" in *Ideology and Classic American Literature*, ed. Sacvan Bercovitch and Myra Jehlen (Cambridge: Cambridge University Press, 1986), 221–46; but the most useful material on the subject remains Walter Benjamin's references to Poe, urbanization, and technology in "The Storyteller," "The Work of Art in the Age of Mechanical Reproduction," and "On Some Motifs in Baudelaire." See Walter Benjamin, *Illuminations*, ed. Hannah Arendt (New York: Schocken, 1969), 83–110, 155–200, 217–52.

6. Quoted in William Sims Bainbridge, *Dimensions of Science Fiction* (Cambridge: Harvard University Press, 1986), 16. Both Jules Verne and H. G. Wells acknowledge Poe as an influence; Verne even continued Arthur Gordon Pym's adventures in *The Sphinx of the Ice Fields* (1897). Although Eric Rabkin and Robert Scholes describe Poe as one of the originators of science fiction, they are wrong to claim that "it is hard to think of anyone more different from Poe than Jules Verne." True, Verne is "the poet of hardware" who "loves to dilate on the technology of his adventures," "busy, busy, busy with material things." But Verne's materialism is derived from Crusoe, through Verne's unironic appropriation of the technological realism that orients the *Narrative of A. Gordon Pym*, "The Balloon-Hoax," and "Von Kempelen and His Discovery." See Robert Scholes and Eric S. Rabkin, *Science Fiction: History, Science, Vision* (New York: Oxford University Press, 1977), 9. Sam Moskowitz offers a detailed treatment of Verne's relation to Poe in *Explorers of the Infinite: Shapers of Science Fiction* (Cleveland: World Publishing, 1963), 46–61, 75–76.

7. Compare this to Mark Taylor's analysis of the cyborg, which

> is made possible by the gradual removal of the barriers separating interiority and exteriority, as well as public and private space. This collapse of differences proceeds in two directions at once: from outer to inner and, conversely, from inner to outer. On the one hand, the body itself is progressively colonized by prosthetic devices. . . . On the other hand, artificial wombs, test-tube babies, artificial intelligence, and computer literacy 'externalize' bodily and mental functions to such an extent that the outer is no more merely outer and the inner simply inner. . . . If, as contemporary biologists argue, physical organisms, human as well as nonhuman, are information machines created and

sustained by digital codes, the difference between the real and the hyperreal becomes obscure.

Taylor, "Terminal Space," 32.

8. Marshall McLuhan, *Understanding Media: The Extensions of Man* (New York: McGraw-Hill, 1964), 3; see Limon, *Place of Fiction*, 143.

9. Taylor, "Terminal Space," 7.

10. Nathaniel Hawthorne, *The House of Seven Gables* (Toronto: Bantam, 1981), 202.

11. Carleton Mabee, *American Leonardo: The Life of Samuel F. B. Morse* (New York: Octagon, 1969), 207.

12. Carolyn Mitchell, *When Old Technologies Were New: Thinking about Electric Communication in the Late Nineteenth Century* (New York: Oxford University Press, 1988), 3.

13. Ibid., 4.

14. James Beniger, *The Control Revolution: Technological and Economic Origins of the Information Society* (Cambridge: Harvard University Press, 1986), 7.

15. Mitchell, *When Old Technologies Were New*, 14.

16. Mabee, *American Leonardo*, 149. A former student of both Washington Allston and Benjamin West, and the first president of the National Academy of Art, Morse was one of the important American painters of his generation. Only his bitter failure as a history painter (due partly to his fervent anti-Catholicism) led him to forsake art in order to create the telegraph. In the midst of this decade-long pursuit (from 1833 to 1844), Morse, on a trip to secure funds in Europe, heard of Daguerre's new process, which he eagerly brought back to this country, thus earning the distinction of having introduced America to the two most revolutionary communication technologies of the nineteenth century. He may have taken the first daguerreotype made in America; almost certainly, he took the first portrait. Morse's career combines what are usually thought of as polar forms of representation: on the one hand, the iconic, "sensible" forms of painting and daguerreotypy; on the other, the noumenal code, reduced by Morse to a binary minimum.

17. See, for instance, the opening scenes of Aeschylus's *Agamemnon*.

18. A German version had been proposed as early as 1787. See Mabee, *American Leonardo*, 203.

19. Ibid., 207. In 1838, the year Morse submitted his request for a patent to Congress, four other telegraphic plans were also sent in; significantly, his was the only electrical system of record.

20. John R. Pierce, *An Introduction to Information Theory: Symbols, Signals, and Noise*, 2d rev. ed. (New York: Dover, 1980), 25.

21. Mabee, *American Leonardo*, 257.

22. Ibid., 258.

23. *PT*, 311. Poe is not necessarily referring to Morse's invention. The word was coined in 1792 by the French inventor Chappe, and was used to describe a semaphore system on poles that he invented, which achieved a minor success in England and France.

24. James Carey, "A Cultural Approach to Communications," in *Communication as Culture: Essays on Media and Society* (Boston: Unwin Hyman, 1989), 15. See

also Daniel J. Czitrom, *Media and the American Mind: From Morse to McLuhan* (Chapel Hill: University of North Carolina Press, 1982), 3–29, for a useful essay on the cultural meanings of the telegraph. As Stephen Rachman has observed, the association of telecommunications and space travel continues in the current telephone company gambit of awarding frequent-flier miles for long-distance calls.

25. Limon, *Place of Fiction*, 143.

26. Kahn, *Codebreakers*, 189.

27. The abbreviation of "cryptography" into "crypto" here reflects current usage.

28. Kahn, *Codebreakers*, 189.

29. See Robert H. Fowler, "Was Stanton behind Lincoln's Murder?" *Civil War Times* 3 (Aug. 1961): 4–23.

30. Jacob Bigelow, *The Elements of Technology*, 2d ed. (Boston: Hilliard, Gray, Little, and Wilkins, 1831), 61, 54. Limon describes Bigelow's influence in *Place of Fiction* (22), and offers an excellent comparative account of Hawthorne's literary negotiations with the telegraph, daguerreotype, and railroad in the chapter entitled "The Problems of Preemption," 135–50.

31. Bigelow, *Elements of Technology*, 54.

32. American painting has from the start been intimately tied to writing. Given space, one could trace a continuous line from the limner tradition of the seventeenth and eighteenth centuries, with its strong emphasis on outline and sign painting, through the text-based work of Edward Hicks and Thomas Eakins, to the reemergence of the sign in the pop art of the 1960s.

33. Both passages are cited in Richard Rudisill, *Mirror Image* (Albuquerque: University of New Mexico Press, 1971), 53, 54: *The Diary of Philip Hone, 1828–1851*, ed. Bayard Tuckerman (New York: Dodd, Mead, 1889), 1:391; "The Daguerreolite," *Cincinnati Daily Chronicle*, 17 Jan. 1840, 2.

34. Eighty years later, writers struggling to conceptualize the significance of film turned to the same metaphors of hieroglyphic inscription. "Abel Gance, for instance, compares the film with hieroglyphs: 'Here, by a remarkable regression, we have come back to the level of expression of the Egyptians'" (Benjamin, *Illuminations*, 227).

35. James Russell Lowell, "Our Contributors.—No. XVII," *Graham's Magazine* 27 (Feb. 1845): 52.

36. Dominique François Arago, "Report," in *Classic Essays on Photography*, ed. Alan Trachtenberg (New Haven: Leete's Island Books, 1980), 17.

37. *Webster's New Twentieth-Century Dictionary*, s.v. "information."

38. Edgar Allan Poe, "The Daguerreotype," *Alexander's Weekly Messenger*, 15 Jan. 1840; cited in Brigham, *Poe's Contributions*, 20–21.

39. Morse is quoted in Rudisill, *Mirror Image*, 57. Note, too, that Poe seems less interested in how this "most wonderful" of human inventions works than he is in the question of how one ought to spell and pronounce it: "This word is properly spelt *Daguerréotype*, and pronounced as if it were written *Dagairraioteep*. The inventor's name is Daguerre, but the French usage requires an accent on the second e, in the formation of the compound term" (Brigham, *Poe's Contributions*, 20). Again, Poe emphasizes linguistic structure as the key to comprehension.

40. On Poe's mathematization and formalization of concepts, see Leon Chai,

The Romantic Foundations of the American Renaissance (Ithaca: Cornell University Press, 1987), 103–19. Canguilhelm is quoted on 105–6.

41. "Marginalia," *ER*, 1318–19. Consider also Poe's insistence that "arithmetical or algebraical calculations are, from their very nature, fixed and determinate. Certain *data* being given, certain results necessarily and inevitably follow. These results have dependence upon nothing, and are influenced by nothing but the *data* originally given" ("Maelzel's Chess-Player," *ER*, 1255).

42. Lisa Cartwright, "Science and the Film Avant-Garde," *Cinematograph* 4 (1991): 15.

43. Ibid., 16.

44. Poe comically displays his mistrust of the senses in both "The Spectacles" and "The Sphinx" (*ER*, 618–42, 843–47).

45. Gabriel García Márquez, *One Hundred Years of Solitude*, trans. Gregory Rabassa (New York: Avon Books, 1968), 381.

46. Michael Davitt Bell, *The Development of American Romance: The Sacrifice of Relation* (Chicago: University of Chicago Press, 1980), 103.

47. The mind in question belonged to a rather acrobatic assistant, sequestered under the chess-table cabinet and in the Chess-Player's torso, who adjusted his position to remain invisible when Maelzel opened the cabinet doors.

48. In "The Thousand-and-Second Tale of Scheherazade," Poe describes, respectively, Maelzel's Chess-Player and Babbage's Calculating Machine as follows: "One of this nation of mighty conjurors created a man out of brass and wood, and leather, and endowed him with such ingenuity that he would have beaten at chess, all the race of mankind with the exception of the great Caliph, Haroun Alraschid. Another of these magi constructed (of like material) a creature that put to shame even the genius of him who made it; for so great were its reasoning powers that, in a second, it performed calculations of so vast an extent that they would have required the united labor of fifty thousand fleshly men for a year" (*PT*, 801). See the July 1846 "Marginalia" for additional references.

49. Robert H. Byer, "Secrecy, Authority, and Disfiguration: 'The Man that Was Used Up' and Jacksonian Politics" (manuscript, 1994).

50. Bell, *Development of American Romance*, 103.

51. N. Katherine Hayles argues that after 1945, "books, people, and societies ceased to exist as self-evident entities and became surfaces to be inscribed, amorphous constructions with shifting boundaries, structures of information." See Hayles, "Postmodern Parataxis: Embodied Texts, Weightless Information," *American Literary History* 2 (fall 1990): 396. Dozens of writers echo this emphasis on coding, including critics of American fiction (David Porush, *The Soft Machine: Cybernetic Fiction* [New York: Methuen, 1985]), philosophers (Michael Heim, *Electric Language: A Philosophical Study of Word Processing* [New Haven: Yale University Press, 1987]), and social theorists (Mark Poster, *The Mode of Information: Poststructuralism and Social Context* [Chicago: University of Chicago Press, 1990]).

52. Donna Haraway, "A Cyborg Manifesto: Science, Technology, and Socialist-Feminism in the Late Twentieth Century," in *Simians, Cyborgs, and Women* (New York: Routledge, 1991), 164. Simians, cyborgs, women: Haraway's title names some of the most prominent themes in Poe's cryptographic fiction.

53. Ibid., 161–62.

54. Terence Whalen, "Edgar Allan Poe and the Horrid Laws of Political Economy," *American Quarterly* 44, no. 3 (1992): 381–417. After the Panic of 1837, Poe's writing, Whalen argues, was "conditioned not only by the depression in the publishing industry, but also by the more catastrophic emergence of information, which systematically undermined all traditional standards of literary value" (384).

55. Whalen, "Horrid Laws of Political Economy," 392.

56. Almost all of the figures the General cites were, in fact, Philadelphia traders who specialized in false teeth, wigs, prosthetic legs, and the like. See *CW*, 2:391–92.

57. This in fact happened. Translated into English, "mellonta tauta" means "things to come." In 1904, H. G. Wells borrowed both Poe's title and elements of his plot in writing "A Story of the Days to Come." See *The Complete Short Stories of H. G. Wells* (London: Ernest Benn, 1966), 715–806.

58. The means by which Gibson and Sterling wrote *The Difference Engine* suggest how telecommunications have altered writing. According to the authors, no hard copy of the novel ever existed. Instead, the manuscript was exchanged electronically, through a descendant of the telegraph, with each author "free to add to and revise the text in any manner he saw fit. The other was also free to 'undo' such revisions at any time subject to the limitation of his own memory. Because no backup copies existed for reference, . . . after many exchanges, erasures, and addendums neither author could confidently point to a section of the text and claim exclusive authorship" (Bryan J. Malone, "Cyberpunk" [senior thesis, Williams College, 1993], 3:6). See William Gibson and Bruce Sterling, *The Difference Engine* (New York: Bantam, 1991).

59. John Perry Barlow, "Leaving the Physical World for the Conference on HyperNetworking, Oita, Japan," Internet document, Williams College, 1993.

60. Larry McCaffery, "An Interview with William Gibson," in *Storming the Reality Studio: A Casebook of Cyberpunk and Postmodern Fiction*, ed. Larry McCaffery (Durham: Duke University Press, 1992), 273.

61. Ibid., 270.

62. William Gibson, *Neuromancer* (Berkeley: Ace Books, 1984). *Neuromancer* is part of the *Cyberspace* trilogy, which also includes *Count Zero* (New York: Ace Books, 1987) and *Mona Lisa Overdrive* (New York: Bantam, 1988).

63. Cyberpunk fiction aims to eradicate "the difference between the organic and the synthetic by insisting that what had been perceived as difference was merely a function of a 'language' barrier, an interfacial or interlocutory deficiency." Cybernetics is thus an alchemical instrument akin to cryptography: it, too, is "a science of translation that aspires to a sorcery of control and True Naming" (Malone, "Cyberpunk," 3:9).

64. Defoe, *Robinson Crusoe*, 153–54.

65. Gibson, *Neuromancer*, 270–71.

Chapter 5. *Resurrexi*

1. Quinn, *French Face of Edgar Allan Poe*, 12.

2. See Ludwig [Rufus Wilmot Griswold], "Death of Edgar Allan Poe," *New York Daily Tribune*, 9 Oct. 1849, reprinted in *Edgar Allan Poe: The Critical Heritage*, ed. I. M. Walker (London: Routledge and Kegan Paul, 1986), 294–302, and

Harold Bloom, "Inescapable Poe," introduction to *Edgar Allan Poe*, ed. Harold Bloom (New York: Chelsea House, 1985), 1-14.

3. Quinn, *French Face of Edgar Allan Poe*, 4-5.

4. James Russell Lowell, "A Fable for Critics," in *The Poetical Works of James Russell Lowell* (Cambridge, Mass.: Houghton Mifflin, 1898), 141.

5. Shoshana Felman, "On Reading Poetry: Reflections on the Limits and Possibilities of Psychoanalytical Approaches," in Muller and Richardson, *Purloined Poe*, 133.

6. Quinn, *French Face of Edgar Allan Poe*, 4.

7. T. S. Eliot, "From Poe to Valéry," *Hudson Review* 2 (fall 1949): 333, 328.

8. Ibid., 327. John Pierce mentions Poe alone among writers in his *Introduction to Information Theory*, discussing both "The Gold-Bug" and cryptanalysis, and the relation of sound pattern to meaning in "The Bells," "Ulalume," and "The Raven" (64, 116-17).

9. "No American author has the fascinating appeal of Edgar Allan Poe. In fact, only Shakespeare and perhaps Charles Dickens have had as many films, musicals, and spoken-word recordings based on their work" (Ronald L. Smith, *Poe in the Media: Screen, Songs, and Spoken-Word Recordings* [New York: Garland, 1990], 7). One example: in 1928 two influential versions of "The Fall of the House of Usher" were produced: an important surrealist film by Jean Epstein, and an X-ray version by James Sibley Watson and Melville Webber, which may be said to have founded American experimental cinema.

10. Alfred Russel Wallace, *Edgar Allan Poe: A Series of Seventeen Letters Concerning Poe's Scientific Erudition in Eureka and the Authorship of Leonainie* (n.d.; reprint, New York: Haskell House, 1966), 6-7.

11. Ibid., 13.

12. Ibid., 6.

13. Jorge Luis Borges, *Borges at Eighty: Conversations*, ed. Willis Barnstone (Bloomington: Indiana University Press, 1982), 143.

14. Doten, *Poems from the Inner Life*, 40.

15. Howard Kerr, *Mediums, and Spirit-Rappers, and Roaring Radicals: Spiritualism in American Literature* (Urbana: University of Illinois Press, 1972), 4.

16. In her trances, Doten testified to the innate spiritual superiority of women, who were able to be in contact with "the divine Shekinah, the Holy of Holies," in whom "man shall recognize the image of his God, and kneel and adore" (Ann Braude, *Radical Spirits: Spiritualism and Women's Rights in Nineteenth-Century America* [Boston: Beacon Press, 1989], 86; for a closely related comparative view, see Alex Owen, *The Darkened Room: Women, Power, and Spiritualism in Late-Victorian England* [Philadelphia: University of Pennsylvania Press, 1991]). On literature and multiple-personality disorder, see Jeremy Hawthorn, *Multiple Personality and the Disintegration of Literary Character: From Oliver Goldsmith to Sylvia Plath* (New York: St. Martin's Press, 1983).

17. *Mysteries of the Unknown: Psychic Powers* (Alexandria, Va.: Time-Life Books, 1991), 42-43; Henry Hollen, *Clairaudient Transmission: A Metaphysical Interpretation of Genius, Inspiration, and the Creative Act, on the Basis of a Singular Experience* (Hollywood, Calif.: Keats Publications, 1931), 3. To Dr. Hollen, the thought that his wife was poetically gifted—a wife who even to his fond eyes had

"little of accomplishment in the sense of that deserving to be cited, even in the bulky annals of the commonplace"—seemed so unlikely that, after weighing the evidence, he concluded that she must be "informed and supported by an intelligence alien to herself" (28).

18. In addition to shorter pieces published in the *Banner of Light*, the *Spiritual Telegraph*, and elsewhere, Doten published four volumes of prose and verse: *Hesper the Home Spirit: A Story of Household Labor and Love* (Boston: William White, 1858); *Poems from the Inner Life* (Boston: William White, 1862); *Poems of Progress* (Boston: William White, 1871); and *My Affinity and Other Stories* (Boston: William White, 1871).

19. Good histories of spiritualism include Frank Podmore, *Modern Spiritualism: A History and a Criticism* (London: Methuen, 1902), and Ruth Brandon, *The Spiritualists: The Passion for the Occult in the Nineteenth and Twentieth Centuries* (Buffalo: Prometheus Books, 1983). The most detailed study of mesmerism and literature is Fred Kaplan, *Dickens and Mesmerism: The Hidden Springs of Fiction* (Princeton: Princeton University Press, 1975). See also Maria Tatar, *Spellbound: Studies on Mesmerism and Literature* (Princeton: Princeton University Press, 1978).

20. Kerr, *Mediums*, 16–21.

21. The introduction to *Mesmerism "in articulo mortis"* (a pamphlet translation of "The Facts in the Case of M. Valdemar") claims that although the narrative was "only a plain recital of facts," these were of "so extraordinary a nature as almost to surpass belief" (*CW*, 3:1024–26). This, of course, is precisely where Poe located much of his fiction, both seeking to defuse the reader's suspicions by anticipating them ("I now feel I have reached a point of this narrative at which every reader will be startled into positive disbelief" ["Facts in the Case of M. Valdemar," *PT*, 1240]) and dropping the occasional droll giveaway (speaking of Valdemar's fate as "this latter experiment" responsible for "so much of what I cannot help thinking unwarranted popular feeling" [*PT*, 1242]). My thinking here and throughout this chapter is indebted to Jonathan Elmer's wonderful essay "Terminate or Liquidate? Poe, Sensationalism, and the Sentimental Tradition," in *The American Face of Edgar Allan Poe*, ed. Shawn Rosenheim and Stephen Rachman (Baltimore: Johns Hopkins University Press, 1995), 91–120. As Elmer put it, in a sentence I have taken from an earlier draft of that essay, Poe's mesmeric fiction serves as a "model of the relation between author and reader, a relation that is, in its own way, marked by a social limit—the text itself."

22. Avital Ronell, *The Telephone Book: Technology—Schizophrenia—Electric Speech* (Lincoln: University of Nebraska Press, 1989), 341.

23. Taylor, "Terminal Space," 16.

24. Ronell, *Telephone Book*, 341.

25. N. P. Willis, *The Rag-Bag* (New York, 1855), 193.

26. Ibid.

27. Ibid., 194.

28. Braude, *Radical Spirits*, 5. Like its cousin, spiritualism, mesmerism was deeply indebted to technology: the mesmeric trance, for instance, was predicated on the operation of a universal electromagnetic fluid that, when activated by a "positive" mesmerist, would induce trance in a "negative" clairvoyant.

29. W. W. Aber, *A Guide to Mediumship* (1906), in *Spiritualism I: Spiritualist Thought*, ed. Gary L. Ward (New York: Garland, 1990), 22–23.

30. Ludwig [Rufus Wilmot Griswold], "Death of Edgar Allan Poe," 300. Compare also Baudelaire's 1852 comment that "all of Edgar Poe's stories are, so to speak, biographical" (Charles Baudelaire, *Baudelaire on Poe: Critical Papers*, trans. and ed. Lois Hyslop and Francis Hyslop [State College, Pa.: Bald Eagle Press, 1952], 43).

31. John Carl Miller, *Building Poe Biography* (Baton Rouge: Louisiana State University Press, 1977), 10. For a catalogue of Ingram's complete collection of Poe papers, see John Carl Miller, *John Henry Ingram's Poe Collection at the University of Virginia* (Charlottesville: University of Virginia Press, 1960).

32. Peggy Robbins, "Poe's Defamation," in *Edgar Allan Poe: The Creation of a Reputation* (Philadelphia: Eastern Acorn Press, 1983), 10.

33. "Every biographical account of Poe that has been published from 1874 to this date owes most of its contents to Ingram's discoveries and publications about Poe" (Miller, *Building Poe Biography*, xv).

34. Ibid., 11–12.

35. Walter Hamilton, *Parodies*, 2 vols. (London: Reeves and Turner, 1885), 2:6.

36. Miller, *Building Poe Biography*, 12. Identification with Poe extends across the bounds of gender: As Poe's one-time fiancée Sarah Hale Whitman wrote to Ingram, "once, during the spring of 1849, when my mother saw me in the dress of an Albanian chief, worn for a tableau, she was so appalled by my resemblance to Poe that she would not remain in the room or give me a second look. Everyone who had seen Poe remarked the resemblance. The aid of a burnt cork to the eyebrows & applied as a mustache on the upper lip, transformed me. The resemblance was magical" (John Carl Miller, ed., *Poe's Helen Remembers* [Charlottesville: University Press of Virginia, 1979], 191).

37. Don Felix de Salmanca [John Henry Ingram], *The Philosophy of Handwriting* (London: Chatto and Windus, 1879). Ingram also used a pseudonym when he published most of his verse: his one work of collected poems (1863) appeared under the name "Dalton Stone."

38. Silverman, *Edgar A. Poe*, 300.

39. For the argument that Poe was "Outis," see, for example, Burton Pollin, "Poe as Author of the 'Outis' letter and 'The Bird of the Dream,'" *Poe Studies* 20 (1987): 7–11. For evidence that Poe was also Walter G. Bowen, see *CW* 3:1377–78.

40. Like my first citation of Jonathan Elmer's "Terminate or Liquidate?" this sentence comes from an earlier draft of that essay and was subsequently revised out of the version published in Rosenheim and Rachman, *American Face of Edgar Allan Poe*. For the most complete version of Elmer's claims about these relations, see "Poe, Sensationalism, and the Sentimental Tradition," in Jonathan Elmer, *Reading at the Social Limit: Affect, Mass Culture, and Edgar Allan Poe* (Stanford: Stanford University Press, 1995), 93–125.

41. W. M. Lockwood, *Molecular Hypothesis of Nature* (1895), reprinted in Ward, *Spiritualism I*, 42.

42. Ibid., 21.

43. Ibid., 51.

44. Doten, *Poems from the Inner Life*, 104–5.

45. Ibid., 105–6.

46. "For a' That," in ibid., 97.

47. "Love," in ibid., 92.

48. Although skeptical of spiritualism, an anonymous writer for the *Springfield Republican* found himself puzzled by the existence of "Resurrexi." Doten liked his notice enough to include it as an epigraph to the poem:

> Whatever may be the truth about its production, the poem is, in several respects, a remarkable one. Miss Doten is, apparently, incapable of originating such a poem. If it was written for her by some one else, and merely committed to memory and recited by her, the poem is, nevertheless, wonderful as a reproduction of the singular music and alliteration of Poe's style, and as manifesting the same intensity of feeling. Whoever wrote the poem must have been exceedingly familiar with Poe, and deeply in sympathy with his spirit. But if Miss Doten is honest, and the poem originated as she said it did, it is unquestionably the most astonishing thing that Spiritualism has produced. It does not follow, necessarily, . . . that Poe himself made the poem—although we are asked to believe a great many spiritual things on less cogent evidence—but it is, in any view of it that may be taken, a very singular and mysterious production.

Doten, *Poems from the Inner Life*, 104.

49. Braude, *Radical Spirits*, 89.

50. Doten, *Poems from the Inner Life*, xii.

51. Ibid., 145.

52. Ibid., xxiii–xxiv.

53. The irony is that Poe always writes as if poetic composition were subject to cryptographic precision. "Poets in especial," he notes in "The Philosophy of Composition," "prefer having it understood that they compose by a species of fine frenzy—an ecstatic intuition—and would positively shudder at letting the public take a peep behind the scenes" (*ER*, 14). Writing as if he were immune to the emotional force of his own work, Poe claims of "The Raven" that "no one point in its composition is referable either to accident or intuition . . . the work proceeded, step by step, to its completion with the precision and rigid consequence of a mathematical problem" (*ER*, 14–15).

54. Doten, *Poems from the Inner Life*, 157.

55. Ibid., xxi–xxii.

56. Compare Oedipa Maas's experience in Thomas Pynchon, *The Crying of Lot 49* (New York: Harper and Row, 1966), where she finds herself in search of "the direct, epileptic Word, the cry that might abolish the night" (118).

57. Doten, *Poems from the Inner Life*, 150.

58. Baudelaire, *Baudelaire on Poe*, 86.

59. Ibid., 67, 31.   60. Ibid., 17–18.

61. Wallace, *Edgar Allan Poe*, 18.   62. Ibid., 14.

63. Stephen Rachman, "'Es Lässt Sich Nicht Schreiben': Plagiarism and 'The Man of the Crowd,'" in Rosenheim and Rachman, *American Face of Edgar Allan Poe*, 82.

64. Doten, *Poems from the Inner Life*, xvi.

65. See T. S. Eliot, "Note sur Mallarmé et Poe," *Nouvelle revue française* 14 (Nov. 1926): 524–26; "Edgar Poe et la France," *La table ronde*, Dec. 1948, 1973–92; and the introduction to Paul Valéry, *The Art of Poetry*, trans. Denise Folliot (New York: Pantheon, 1958), vii–xxiv.

66. Eliot, "From Poe to Valéry," 342.

67. Ibid., 327, 355.

68. Ibid., 331.

69. Ibid., 330–31.

70. Doten, *Poems from the Inner Life*, xi.

71. Eliot, "From Poe to Valéry," 341.

72. Ibid., 339.

73. Benjamin, *Illuminations*, 220.

74. Ibid., 217.

Chapter 6. Deciphering the Cold War

1. Silverman, *Edgar A. Poe*, 67.

2. Powers, *Gold Bug Variations*, 91.

3. Michael Rogin, " 'Make My Day!': Spectacle as Amnesia in Imperial Politics," *Representations* 29 (winter 1990): 99–123, 114.

4. On the Polish effort, see Wladyslaw Kazaczuk, *Enigma: How the German Machine Cipher Was Broken, and How It Was Read by the Allies in World War II*, ed. and trans. Christopher Kasparek (Frederick, Md.: University Publications of America, 1984), xii–xiii; *Friedman Legacy*, 51–74, especially 73.

5. Yardley also supported himself in his last years on the royalties from his classic playing manual, *The Education of a Poker Player*, thus linking cryptography to cards in the same manner as Poe had done a century earlier.

6. Friedman, "Edgar Allan Poe, Cryptographer," 266.

7. Clark, *Man Who Broke Purple*, 11.

8. Ibid., 11–12.

9. Kahn, *Codebreakers*, 392–93.

10. The words belong to the cryptographer Lou Kruh. See Meroke [Louis Kruh], "The Fabyan Forest Preserve," *Cryptogram* 60, no. 1 (1994): 8.

11. Clark, *Man Who Broke Purple*, 185–86. At the same time, Friedman became engaged to Elizebeth Smith, Gallup's chief assistant, who had run into Colonel Fabyan while working at the Newberry Library on the First Folio. Subsequently, she became a kind of shadow to Friedman, as well as an important cryptographer in her own right, building and breaking codes for the army, the Justice Department, and the World Bank.

12. Friedman distinguished himself especially through the solution of a book cipher used by a group of Hindus who were buying arms in America with which to stage a campaign for Indian independence. By taking advantage of contextual evidence and statistical clues, Friedman solved the cipher without ever discovering that the book used was Price Collier, *Germany and the Germans* (New York, 1913).

13. Kahn, *Codebreakers*, 48. It was still a year before Yardley would form MI8, the nation's first official cipher bureau. In 1992, the NSA placed a plaque in the

Riverbank Laboratories as a "long-delayed expression of appreciation on the part of the government." The text reads as follows:

TO THE MEMORY OF GEORGE FABYAN
FROM A GRATEFUL GOVERNMENT
In recognition of the voluntary and confidential service
rendered by Colonel Fabyan and his Riverbank
Laboratories in the sensitive areas of cryptanalysis and
cryptologic training
during a critical time of national need
on the eve of America's entry into World War I
Presented to mark the seventy-fifth anniversary
by the
National Security Agency
United States Department of Defense
1917–1992

14. Kahn, *Codebreakers*, 376.

15. Ibid.

16. Ibid., 376, 383–84.

17. As John Pierce points out, Zipf's law cannot be entirely correct in this form, because if word probabilities were inversely proportional to the rank of the word for all words, the sum of the probabilities of all words would be greater than unity. It does, however, strikingly illustrate the mathematical regularity of language. Indeed, according to Adrian Albert, "abstract cryptography *is identical with* abstract mathematics" (emphasis added). Albert is quoted in Kahn, *Codebreakers*, 737.

18. The actual frequency (based on an enormous sample of sixty million letters) is 17.9; a trivial difference, especially given that an average of the smaller samples gives a percentage of 18.0 (ibid., 743). In English, the order of letter frequency is as follows: *e t a o i n s r h l d c u m f w g y p b v k x j q z.*

19. James Bamford, *The Puzzle Palace: A Report on America's Most Secret Agency* (New York: Penguin, 1983), 46.

20. Ibid., 50.

21. The American use of cryptography goes back as far as the Revolutionary War. George Washington made extensive use of secret inks and ciphers during the Revolution, and Benedict Arnold's plans to hand over West Point to British major John André employed several different kinds of code, including a book code based on the *Universal Etymological English Dictionary* of Nathan Bailey (Kahn, *Codebreakers*, 177). However, it was not until 1917 that secret writing began to shape world history. In that year the British intercepted an enciphered telegram from the German minister Arthur Zimmermann to the Mexican government in which he offered Mexico the return of its "stolen" territory in Arizona, New Mexico, and Texas in exchange for wartime support. When the United States government released the contents of the telegram, public opinion in favor of intervention hardened overnight, hastening the American entrance into the war.

22. Kahn, *Codebreakers*, 338.

23. Bamford, *Puzzle Palace*, 53.

24. Kahn, *Codebreakers*, 277.

25. Ibid., 288.

26. *Time*, December 1945, quoted in Friedman, "Six Lectures on Cryptology," 9.

27. Kahn, *Codebreakers*, 389. The name Purple itself was meaningless, part of an American color code used to identify different classes of Japanese ciphers.

28. Ibid., 339. For decades, accounts of Allied cryptographic practice were subject to blackout and denial, and it is only in the last fifteen years that detailed accounts have come to press. See Edward J. Drea, *MacArthur's ULTRA: Codebreaking and the War against Japan, 1942–1945* (Lawrence: University Press of Kansas, 1992); Ronald Lewin, *The American Magic: Codes, Ciphers, and the Defeat of Japan* (New York: Farrar, Straus, and Giroux, 1982); and F. H. Hinsley and Alan Stripp, eds., *Codebreakers: The Inside Story of Bletchely Park* (Oxford: Oxford University Press, 1993). For a fascinating bit of social history, see Margaret T. Bixler, *Winds of Freedom: The Story of the Navajo Code Talkers of World War II* (Darien, Conn.: Two Bytes, 1992). The Allied decision to employ a large cadre of bilingual Navajos as radio operators was a brilliant stroke: by communicating only in their native tongue, these radio operators created a cheap and virtually uncrackable cipher that could be translated back into English in an instant.

29. Kahn, *Codebreakers*, 340. According to Admiral Chester Nimitz, commander in chief of the Pacific Fleet, cryptanalysis enabled the United States "to concentrate our limited forces to meet [the Japanese] naval advance on Midway when otherwise we almost certainly would have been some 3,000 miles out of place" (Kahn, *Codebreakers*, 573). Had the military chain of command been brought up to speed earlier in the war, the attack on Pearl Harbor would never have taken place; decrypted messages indirectly revealing the Japanese plans for attack languished in Washington, where their significance remained unrealized until the afternoon of 7 December. After the war, a committee appointed to investigate the failure to prevent the attack faulted military communication channels. But the same committee was extravagant in its praise for the effectiveness of wartime codebreaking. In the words of the Joint Congressional Investigation: "All witnesses familiar with *Magic* material throughout the war have testified that it contributed enormously to the defeat of the enemy, greatly shortened the war, and saved many thousands of lives" (quoted in Friedman, "Six Lectures on Cryptography," 11).

30. Standard War Department training literature "consisted of little more than Parker Hitt's *Manual*, a very brief paper by Captain Mauborgne" on the Wheatstone cipher, and "the two or three articles by Edgar Allan Poe" (Clark, *Man Who Broke Purple*, 117).

31. Bamford, *Puzzle Palace*, 154.

32. Lambros D. Callimahos, "The Legendary William F. Friedman," in *Friedman Legacy*, 241.

33. William F. Friedman, *Military Cryptanalysis: Parts I–IV* (Laguna Hills, Calif.: Aegean Park Press, 1979–93). The revised version of these works was published in two volumes as William F. Friedman and Lambros Callimahos, *Military Cryptanalytics: Parts 1 and 2* (Laguna Beach, Calif.: Aegean Park Press, 1985).

34. Bamford, *Puzzle Palace*, 154.

35. Kahn, *Codebreakers*, 154. And Friedman's work was used to train others besides American cryptographers. When Allied troops conquered Burgscheidungen Castle, the headquarters of German cryptography, they found photostats of a draft

of *Military Cryptanalysis*, which had been smuggled out of the United States and used to train German cryptanalysts (Clark, *Man Who Broke Purple*, 203).

36. Tom Bower, *The Red Web: MI6 and the KGB Master Coup* (London: Aurum Press, 1989); John Le Carré, *The Secret Pilgrim* (New York: Knopf, 1991); William Hood, "Safe House Fiction," *International Journal of Intelligence and Counterintelligence* 4, no. 4 (1990): 552. For a biographical sketch of Le Carré, see Alan Bold, introduction to *The Quest for Le Carré* (New York: St. Martin's Press, 1988), 9–24.

37. Victor C. Marchetti, *The Rope Dancer* (New York: Grosset and Dunlap, 1971); Victor C. Marchetti and John D. Marks, *The CIA and the Cult of Intelligence* (New York: Knopf, 1974).

38. W. Somerset Maugham, *Ashenden; or, The British Agent* (Garden City, N.Y.: Doubleday, 1941).

39. Hood, "Safe House Fiction," 553. For another wilderness of mirrors, see Ron Rosenbaum's essay "Kim Philby and the Age of Paranoia," in which Rosenbaum tracks down the library of the late Graham Greene, in search of marginal annotations (!) that might reveal whether or not Kim Philby had actually been a triple agent, faithful to the British Crown until death. See Rosenbaum, "Kim Philby and the Age of Paranoia," *New York Times Magazine*, 10 July 1994. Rosenbaum suggests that Greene's protagonist in *The Human Factor* is a portrait of Philby, noting that Greene sent the page proofs to Philby in Moscow for his comments.

40. See, for instance, William F. Friedman, "Jules Verne as Cryptographer," *Signal Corps Bulletin* 108 (Apr.–June 1940), reprinted in *Cryptography and Cryptanalysis Articles*, ed. William F. Friedman, 2 vols. (Laguna Hills, Calif.: Aegean Park Press, 1976), 2:281–315; and William F. Friedman and Elizebeth Friedman, "Acrostics, Anagrams, and Chaucer," *Philological Quarterly* 38, no. 1 (1959): 1–20.

41. Besides "Edgar Allan Poe, Cryptographer," Friedman's writing on Poe includes a long addendum to that essay: "Addendum," *Signal Corps Bulletin* 98 (Oct.–Dec. 1937): 54–75. In this pattern of essay and addendum, Friedman repeats Poe's own inability to leave cryptography behind in the addenda to "A Few Words on Secret Writing."

42. John Limon, conversation with author.

43. See, for instance, Jean Starobinski's study of Ferdinand de Saussure's compulsive search for anagrams in Latin verse: Starobinski, *Words upon Words: The Anagrams of Ferdinand de Saussure*, trans. Olivia Emmet (New Haven: Yale University Press, 1979).

44. Jorge Luis Borges, "The Library of Babel," in *Labyrinths: Selected Stories and Other Writings*, ed. Donald Yates and James Irby (New York: New Directions, 1962), 51.

45. Walter Begley, *Biblia anagrammatica* (London, 1904), 212. Technically, an anagram can be described as an unkeyed transposition cipher in which each letter is used once only, and in which no letters remain unused.

46. Clark, *Man Who Broke Purple*, 214. Compare Yardley's account of the *impossibility* of cryptanalytical error: "You can now see for yourself how utterly impossible it is for us to make an error in decipherment. Either we decipher a message or we do not. . . . In a case like this where a long telegram is completely

solved, it is utterly impossible to have anything but the correct solution" (Yardley, *American Black Chamber*, 327).

47. "The Vane Sisters" nicely illustrates how cryptographic approaches to reading polarize interpretation. To miss the code is in some sense to fail Nabokov's challenge, and while cracking the cipher does not end the process of interpretation (is this a ruse on the part of the narrator, a trap for credulous readers?), it includes one in the privileged company of analysts who possess the text's secret. In general, Nabokov's fiction produces an illusory sense that there exists only a single proper interpretation, a key that reveals the text's formal perfection. "Signs and Symbols" appears in Vladimir Nabokov, *Nabokov's Dozen* (New York: Avon, 1963), 52–58; "The Vane Sisters" is included in Vladimir Nabokov, *Tyrants Destroyed, and Other Stories* (New York: McGraw-Hill, 1975), 217–38.

48. Tony Tanner, *City of Words: American Fiction, 1950–1970* (London: Jonathan Cape, 1971), 174.

49. Ibid., 176.

50. Don DeLillo, *White Noise* (New York: Viking Penguin, 1986), 213.

51. Jack Grady, *Six Days of the Condor* (New York: Norton, 1974). In 1975, the book was made into the film *Three Days of the Condor*, directed by Sydney Pollack.

52. DeLillo, *White Noise*, 213.

53. Ibid., 38–39.

54. Henri Coulette, *The War of the Secret Agents and Other Poems* (New York: Scribner's, 1966): 53–90.

55. John Hollander, *Reflections on Espionage* (New York: Atheneum, 1976).

56. Ibid., epigraph.

57. Blunt was stripped of his title in 1979. On this period in British intelligence, see Peter Wright, *Spycatcher: The Candid Autobiography of a Senior Intelligence Officer* (New York: Viking, 1987). Wright is the former assistant director of MI5. Publication of the book is still forbidden within Great Britain.

58. Quoted in David C. Martin, *Wilderness of Mirrors* (New York: Harper and Row, 1980), 216; Robin Winks gives a "representative" list of fourteen novels in which Angleton prominently appears (*Cloak and Gown*, 539), including Aaron Latham, *Orchids for Mother* (Boston: Little Brown, 1977). *Orchids for Mother* offers a minilesson in the contamination of Cold War history by fiction. Since its publication, it has become common to claim, as John Leonard has recently, that Angleton's CIA code names included "Mother." But "Mother" is Latham's rather Hitchcockian invention, and was *never* used by Angleton. Leonard's mistake occurs in what is otherwise a very good article on the connections among literary modernism, espionage, and the Rick Ames case. See John Leonard, "C.I.A.—An Infinity of Mirrors," *Nation*, 28 Mar. 1994, 412–16. One of the more interesting Angleton novels is William S. Cohen and Gary Hart, *The Double Man* (New York: William Morrow, 1985). Cohen and Hart's title had earlier been used by Auden for his wartime book of poetry: W. H. Auden, *The Double Man* (New York: Random House, 1941).

59. Quoted in Tom Mangold, *Cold Warrior: James Jesus Angleton, the CIA's Master Spy Hunter* (New York: Simon and Schuster, 1991), 36.

60. Winks, *Cloak and Gown*, 300.

61. J. C. Masterman, *The Double-Cross System in the War of 1939 to 1945* (New Haven: Yale University Press, 1972). Norman Holmes Pearson makes his claim about the relation between Masterman's detective fiction and his recruitment in his preface to *Double-Cross System*, xi.

62. Winks, *Cloak and Gown*, 347.

63. Ibid., 408.

64. Indeed, in "Deciphering Eliot," Murray McArthur argues that Eliot's poetry is often based on an explicit cipher built around a repeating five-part structure and a variety of cryptonymic keys. Noting that scholars have often treated "Rhapsody on a Windy Night" as "some code or cipher," he claims that its organization is governed "by the necessities of the cipher itself," and says that the poem's success and "paradigmatic place in Eliot's work are to be found in the recovery and accounting of its cipher" (509).

65. Jerome Christensen, "From Rhetoric to Corporate Populism: A Romantic Critique of the Academy in an Age of High Gossip," *Critical Inquiry* 16 (winter 1990): 446. See also William Epstein's remarkable, if rather turgid, "Counter-Intelligence: Cold-War Criticism and Eighteenth-Century Studies," *English Literary History* 57 (1988): 63–99.

66. "Seminar on 'The Purloined Letter,'" 32.

67. Martin, *Wilderness of Mirrors*, 16.

68. On the ties among the OSS, the CIA, and academia, see Winks, *Cloak and Gown*.

69. Borges, *Labyrinths*, 76–87.

70. According to Theodore Draper, Weinberger's notes

had been deposited in the Library of Congress in two parts, classified and unclassified. Walsh's men assumed that the Iran-Contra material would have been placed in the classified section and went away empty-handed when nothing turned up. Only in 1991 was it discovered that the Iran-Contra material was available in the unclassified section. Why Weinberger should have put it in the unclassified section is not explained: the story is something like Edgar Allan Poe's "The Purloined Letter" . . . [Walsh] accused Weinberger outright of "lies" and complained that Weinberger deliberately "hid" his notes "where they shouldn't be."

Draper, "Walsh's Last Stand," *New York Review of Books*, 3 Mar. 1994, 26.

71. Meroke, "Fabyan Forest Preserve," 5.

72. ACA members contribute cryptograms or solutions to the magazine only under the guise of a pseudonym: "The use of noms allows a degree of anonymity; only cryptography being important" (*The ACA and You: A Handbook for Members of the American Cryptogram Association* [n.p.: American Cryptogram Association, 1988], 5). Such noms de plume are frequently derived from literature. Both Ahab and Kraken appear, along with the Ancient Mariner, Cuchulain, Dada, Daedalus, and, of course, the Gold Bug. In the palindromic nom de plume of another member, we are in a reversible realm of discovery or of foolishness, caught in a state of Yreka Fakery, in which the literary slips quickly into the occult; into Djinni, Mephisto, E.S.P., and Psi. In its vision of text and invisible context, of X. Act reading

and E.S.P., the list condenses within itself the paradox of the cryptograph, which is both scientifically precise and undeniably magic.

73. Martin, *Wilderness of Mirrors*, 36.

74. Ibid., 9.

75. As Stephen Rachman knows, I speak here from painful experience.

76. "Mathematics alone, however, was not enough. High intelligence, intuition, an inquiring mind, powers of precise analysis and patience were also needed. The work required complete dedication to the problem's solution and every ounce of mental and physical energy had to be exerted" (Jozef Garlinski, *The Enigma War* [New York: Scribner's, 1979], 23.

77. The skills required for cryptography and cryptanalysis are similarly dual. If cryptography is theoretical and abstract, cryptanalysis "is empirical and concrete"; the two are "twin or reciprocal sciences" that "mirror one another" in function (Kahn, *Codebreakers*, 436).

78. Martin, *Wilderness of Mirrors*, 43.

79. Admittedly, Dupin's analysis is based on dubious associations, which he tries to bolster through sheer assertion: "I knew that you could not say to yourself 'stereotomy' without being brought to think of atomies"; "you could not have forgotten"; "I was then sure that you reflected"; and so on—as if thought were mechanically produced through Lockean association.

80. Kahn, *Codebreakers*, 218.

81. Yardley, *American Black Chamber*, 28.

82. Clark, *Man Who Broke Purple*, 33.

83. Kahn, *Codebreakers*, 59.

84. In 1957, Friedman was ordered to undertake a secret operation to quell well-founded European suspicions that the Americans were reading the ciphered traffic of other NATO countries. Because Friedman's assignment entailed flights to England, Sweden, Switzerland, "and such other places as were necessary," a cover was needed. But how to obtain one? The answer was through *The Shakespearean Ciphers Examined*. Friedman arranged for a monthlong European tour of lunches and book signings (signing his name, that is, to a book on the problem of Shakespearean authorship) as a cover for his intelligence work, without telling even Elizebeth the real purpose of the trip (Clark, *Man Who Broke Purple*, 239).

85. Clark, *Man Who Broke Purple*, 37.

86. Ibid., 113. 87. Ibid., 158–59.

88. Ibid., 208. 89. Ibid., 221.

90. Ibid., 258–59. Such "floating anxiety" is a recurring motif in cryptographic biographies; as Yardley puts it, "cryptography steals into the blood stream and does curious things to people" (*American Black Chamber*, 231). Yardley tells of working so long with various Japanese ciphers that "every telegram, every line, even every code word was indelibly printed in my brain. I could lie awake in bed and in the darkness make my investigations." Sustained too long, cipherwork produces somatic disorders of the kind associated with Friedman, Angleton, and Eliot. Yardley's memoir is full of cryptanalysts unhinged by their work. One clerk asked to resign because she "dreamed constantly that a bulldog was loose in her room. For hours she chased it under and over the bed, behind the chair, under the dresser,

and finally when she caught it, she found written on its side the word *code*" (ibid., 221). Returning from a long vacation, Yardley found his most valuable assistant talking incoherently "with a strange light in his eyes." Noting dryly that "I myself had already had trouble in this respect" (he had been ordered to take a vacation to stave off a nervous breakdown), Yardley kept watch over him until "finally he came to me of his own accord and told me he was becoming afraid of himself. I told him to go away for a couple of months and try to forget codes and ciphers" (ibid., 321). For the cryptographer in the heat of analysis, nothing exists besides the cryptogram and the mind behind it. Even success can produce a feeling of terror. Awakening at night, like Kekulé, with the certainty of having cracked a code, Yardley experiences only a further alienation: "At last the great discovery! My heart stood still, and I dared not move. Was I dreaming? Was I awake? Was I losing my mind?" Compare this to Victor Sheymov's "seventh sense" of being watched: "Even if you don't have any objective indication of being under surveillance, sometimes you can somehow feel it. That is, if you can manage to distinguish it from simple paranoia" (Sheymov and Jellinek, *Tower of Secrets*, 302).

91. Clark, *Man Who Broke Purple*, 64.

92. Kahn, *Codebreakers*, 376.

93. Clark, *Man Who Broke Purple*, 136.

94. Friedman, "Shakespeare, Secret Intelligence, and Statecraft," 410.

95. Clark, *Man Who Broke Purple*, 251.

96. Ibid., 252. 97. Ibid., 249.

98. Ibid., 231. 99. Ibid., 250.

100. For Grady's most obvious debts to Poe, see *Six Days of the Condor*, 72, 99, 105–6.

101. Robert Dalzell (Ph.D. in American Studies, Yale, 1966), conversation with author.

102. Edward Weismiller, *The Serpent Sleeping* (New York, Putnam's Sons, 1962). In addition to *The Branch of Fire: Poems, 1949–1976* (Washington: Word Works, 1980), Weismiller published a chapbook on the novel. See *Serpent's Progress: The Writing of a Novel* (Middletown, Conn.: Wesleyan University Press, 1968).

103. The foreword to Grady's novel directed me to a passage in *The Invisible Government* by David Wise and Thomas Ross, which details the work of this CIA subdepartment. See Wise and Ross, *The Invisible Government* (New York: Random House, 1964), 224–25.

104. Rather like W. B. Tyler/Poe, Friedman concluded his final major piece of writing with a cipher whose content was to be revealed only after his death. His anagram read: "I put no trust in anagrammatic acrostic cyphers, for they are of little real value—a waste—and may prove nothing. Finis." Friedman's intended solution was that "the Voynich MSS was an early attempt to construct an artificial or universal language of the a priori type. Friedman." See Friedman and Friedman, "Acrostics, Anagrams, and Chaucer," 19.

105. Clark, *Man Who Broke Purple*, 237.

Chapter 7. Ciphering the Net

1. The export of cryptography is governed by the United States International Traffic in Arms Munition (ITAM) Act of 1943, which in its updated incarnation prohibits the export of any digital cryptokeys longer than forty bits.

2. For an introduction to the Internet, see Ed Krol, *The Whole Internet: User's Guide and Catalog* (Sebastopol, Calif.: O'Reilly and Associates, 1992), or Tracy Laquey, *The Internet Companion: A Beginner's Guide to Global Networking* (Reading, Mass.: Addison-Wesley, 1993).

3. John Seabrook, "My First Flame," *New Yorker*, 6 June 1994, 70–82.

4. Hawthorne, *House of Seven Gables*, 264.

5. Lawrence Detweiler, *Identity, Privacy, and Anonymity on the Internet*, an Internet FAQ, copyright © 1993, version 3.1. Excerpts from this work are hereafter cited as "FAQ," followed by the divisional heading. The FAQ emanated from *ld231782@longs.lance.colostate.edu*.

6. Ken Auletta, "Annals of Communication: Under the Wire," *New Yorker*, 17 Jan. 1994, 50.

7. The next day Joe responded: "Ah. I recalled his name as I was walking home. Yes, his life was indeed wrecked. He died lonely and an alcoholic, according to my teacher from high school." My quotations are excerpted from an exchange between Joe Dwight (*underdog@leland.stanford.edu*) and Natalie P. (*ndp102@psuvm.psu.edu*), posted on 11 and 13 Mar. 1993.

8. Donald Barlow Stauffer, "Poe in Etext," *PSA Newsletter* 21, no. 2 (1993): 4. To get a file via anonymous FTP, enter <ftp to wiretap.spies.com (IP [Internet protocol] address 130.43.43.43). Login as anonymous, then give your Internet address as the password. Change directory to /Library/ (<Library>), then to /Classic?, then to ?Poe?. Directory names are case-sensitive, so you must use capitalized words.

9. Julian Dibbel, "Code Warriors: Battling for the Keys to Privacy in the Info Age," *Village Voice*, 3 Aug. 1993, 33.

10. FAQs are written for hundreds of different newsgroups, sometimes by one author, sometimes by many. An author wishing to provide up-to-date information on, say, computer cryptography may issue a call for information, and then incorporate comments, illustrations, or bits of text from many different writers into the final document, which he or she can then "publish" with the stroke of a key. In their collaborative and revisionary nature, FAQs represent one more way in which electrical communications are revising print-based considerations concerning intellectual property and copyright.

11. Steven Levy, "Crypto Rebels," *Wired*, May–June 1993, 55.

12. Ibid.

13. Ibid., 56.

14. Ibid.

15. As Diffie told Levy, *The Codebreakers* "brought people out of the woodwork and I certainly was one of them. I probably read it more carefully than anyone had ever read it. By the end of 1973, I was thinking about nothing else" (Levy, "Crypto Rebels," 55).

16. The three MIT mathematicians behind RSA were Ronald Rivers, Adi Shamir, and Leonard Adleman.

17. Levy, "Crypto Rebels," 55.

18. Levy, "Crypto Rebels," 57. Anyone wishing to acquire a copy of PGP can obtain it electronically from the following Internet FTP site: In Finland: *nic.funet.fi* in *director/pub/unix/security/crypt*. Or one can download the program from the Grapevine BBS in Little Rock, Arkansas, at (501) 754-6859 (9600) baud, using this special login: for name, enter PGP USER, with the password PGP. My thanks to Sandy Sandfort for this information, from his article "Private Parts," *Future Sex* 1, no. 4 (1993): 8.

19. Christopher Lloyd, "Spymasters Order Redesign of 'Too Secure' Mobile Phones," *Sunday Times* (London), 31 Jan. 1993, main section (Home News), 12.

20. S. Steele, "BBS Legislative Watch: FBI Wiretapping Proposal Thwarted," *Boardwatch Magazine*, Feb. 1993, 19–22. From the proposed "Digital Telephony" act: "Providers of electronic communication services and private branch exchange operators shall provide within the United States capability and capacity for the government to intercept wire and electronic communications when authorized by law" (quoted in ibid., 21).

21. Levy, "Crypto Rebels," 55.

22. Ibid., 61.

23. Kuoppala's response came from *jkp@cs.hut.fi* on 12 Mar. 1993, 21:07:53 GMT.

24. Testimony given to the Subcommittee for Economic Policy, Trade, and the Environment, United States House of Representatives, 12 Oct. 1993. For the full text of Zimmermann's remarks, see the appendix.

25. Levy, "Crypto Rebels," 58.

26. *San Francisco Examiner*, 25 Nov. 1992. The books are published by the Aegean Park Press, a tiny publishing house devoted to cryptographic titles that is run by Friedman's friends and associates from the NSA.

27. There could be few odder signs of the social transformations at work in public-key cryptography than John Perry Barlow, cofounder of the Electronic Frontier Foundation, and regular lyricist for the Grateful Dead, being invited to address the NSA on the subject of privacy, cryptography, and communications. Arguing that "digitized information is very hard to stamp classified or keep contained," Barlow told NSA agents at the First International Symposium on National Security and National Competitiveness that "this stuff is incredibly leaky and volatile. It's almost a life form in its ability to self-propagate. If something hits the Net and it's something which people on there find interesting it will spread like a virus of the mind. I believe you must simply accept the idea that we are moving into an environment where any information which is at all interesting to people is going to get out. And there will be very little that you can do about it." Barlow spoke at McLean, Virginia, on 1 Dec. 1992.

28. Levy, "Crypto Rebels," 58.

29. Although the government will not mandate the use of Clipper or Capstone, it plans to pressure computer and telephone manufacturers into making them the de facto market standard, thereby squeezing out other encryption tech-

nologies. See Steven Levy, "Battle of the Clipper Chip," *New York Times Magazine*, 12 June 1994; for the NSA position, see Stewart A. Baker, "Don't Worry. Be Happy. Why Clipper Is Good for You," *Wired*, June 1994. Baker was the NSA's chief counsel.

30. John Markoff, "At AT&T, No Joy on Clipper Flaw," *New York Times*, 3 June 1994 (Business Day), sec. D. Although no mainstream press seemed to report the fact, Blaze periodically travels from New Jersey to California for cypherpunk meetings (Tim May, conversation with author, 14 June 1994).

31. Atul V. Salgaonkar (*avs20@ccc.amdahl.com*).

32. See Michael Warner, *Letters of the Republic: Publication and the Public Sphere in Eighteenth-Century America* (Cambridge: Harvard University Press, 1990), in particular 82–86 and 94–96.

33. Stuart P. Derby (*sderby@crick.ssctr.bcm.tmc.edu*).

34. Tarl Neustaedter (*tarl@sw.stratus.com*).

35. Consider Bill Gates's absorption in his first commercial code-writing experience, a version of BASIC created for the Altair 8000: "Bill and Paul [Allen] went on an eight-week code-writing binge, with Gates writing most of the code, often falling asleep at the keyboard, dreaming in code, waking up, and immediately starting to write code again, with no real transition between dreaming and waking—just code. ('It was the coolest program I ever wrote,' Gates later said)" (John Seabrook, "E-Mail from Bill," *New Yorker*, 10 Jan. 1994, 58).

36. Dr. Klaus Pommerening, of the Institut für Medizinische Statistik und Dokumentation der Johannes-Gutenberg-Universitaet, replied to my query on 3 Dec. 1993, 12:38:24 +0100.

37. Tim May, conversation with author, 14 June 1994.

38. Levy, "Crypto Rebels," 55.

39. Kahn, *Codebreakers*, 756.

40. Mike Cepek (*cepek@vixvax.mgi.com*) responded on 2 Dec. 1993, 15:50:08 CST. Paul Rubin posted on 2 Dec. 1993, 03:48:33 PST (*phr@netcom.com*). Lauren Hanson posted on 5 Dec. 1993, 12:30:52 CST, from *danica@wixer.bga.com*. Larry Lennhoff posted on 8 Dec. 1993, 17:59:58 GMT, from *llenn@atldbs.dbsoftware.com*. He added, "*Alvin's Secret Code* was my first introduction to the ideas of cryptography. I recently gave my 12-year-old niece a copy and spent a wonderful afternoon sending messages on scytales using simple substitution ciphers, etc. Her mom acted as the 'enemy agent' intercepting and (sometimes) decoding the messages." See Clifford B. Hicks, *Alvin's Secret Code* (New York: Holt, Rinehart, and Winston, 1963); Helen McCloy, *Panic* (New York: William Morrow, 1944).

41. From John K. Taber (*jktaber@netcom.com*), 1 Dec. 1993, 18:53:18 PST. See Helen Gaines, *Elementary Cryptanalysis* (New York: American Photographic Publishing, 1939). McCloy's *Panic* reveals once again the uneasy connection between murder and cryptography that has characterized detective fiction from the start.

42. From Karen Hunt (*vbm@mace.cc.purdue.edu*), 2 Dec. 1993, 09:48:12 EST.

43. From Carl Ellison (*cme@sw.stratus.com*), 4 Jan. 1994, 19:14:25 EST. In the same vein, another PGP user reports that his interest in cryptography "was sparked by finally getting annoyed enough at the government's attempts to know everything there is to know about me. So, I decided to empower myself to pro-

tect my mail—not because I have anything important or secret to say, but because my mail is between myself and the recipient, and no one else." Jeff Gostin (*jgostin@eternal.pha.pa.us*), 2 Dec. 1993, 17:36:13 EST.

44. For membership in the American Cryptogram Association, write to ACA Treasurer, P.O. Box 198, Vernon Hills, Ill., 60061-0198. Subscriptions to *Cryptologia* can be obtained from the Rose-Hulman Institute of Technology, Department of Mathematics, Terre Haute, Ind., 47803, (812) 877-8412. The cypherpunks list is run by Eric Hughes (*hughes@toad.com*). To be added to the list, send e-mail to *cypherpunks-request@toad.com*.

45. The exchanges between Kleinpaste and Helsingius are taken from Detweiler's FAQ. Kleinpaste's address is *Karl_Kleinpaste@cs.cmu.edu*.

46. Posted by *jash@kuhub.cc.ukans.edu* on 12 Mar. 1993. All further quotations from Anne are taken from this post.

47. Irwin, *American Hieroglyphics*, 159.

48. Rachman, "Es Lässt Sich Nicht Schreiben," 60–61.

49. This is an elaborate instance of the mechanical self-correspondence Peter Bachman describes when he writes of a friend "who lives by himself and who calls his own phone when he knows nobody is there. Who does he expect to answer? I theorize that he's calling to see if he himself picks up." Bachman (*pbachman@scott.skidmore.edu*), 8 Mar. 1993.

50. See, for instance, Whalen, "Horrid Laws of Political Economy," 381–417; and Meredith L. McGill, "Poe, Literary Nationalism, and Authorial Identity," in Rosenheim and Rachman, *American Face of Edgar Allan Poe*, 271–304.

51. Edgar Allan Poe, "Autography," *CW*, 2:259–91; "A Chapter on Autography," in *The Complete Works of Edgar Allan Poe*, 10 vols. (New York: Putnam's Sons, 1902), 10:77–161.

52. See Kent Ljunquist and Buford Jones, "The Identity of 'Outis': A Further Chapter in the Poe-Longfellow War," *American Literature* 60, no. 3 (1988): 402–15, for an argument against the identification of "Outis" and Poe. At any rate, it should be clear that cryptography is all about the process by which an author gets named "outis," or nobody, an invisible source for a visible text.

53. McGill, "Poe," 284.

54. Dwight Thomas and David K. Jackson, *The Poe Log* (Boston: G. K. Hall, 1987), 487.

55. Levy, "Crypto Rebels," 55.

56. The practice of exposing anonymous net posters recurs in a range of groups. In a post to *sci.astro* and *sci.space* about the Challenger disaster, *an8785* argued that anonymous posting in scientific discussions would constitute "a positive good," because it would prevent one from granting credibility to writers merely on the basis of their fame or power. By separating a text from the contextual "identity" of its author (pace Stanley Fish), both society and science would be better served. But he or she acknowledges that such postings "demand a lot from the readership" by requiring them to sift through responses that may be "incorrect, in poor taste or just plain dumb" (posted on 7 Mar. 1993, 14:24:48 GMT).

57. Baxter, *Greatest of All Literary Problems*, 489–520.

58. See Ginzburg, "Morelli, Freud, and Sherlock Holmes."

59. Paul Leyland, Oxford University Computing Service, 13 Banbury Road, Oxford, OX2 6NN, United Kingdom (posted on 12 Dec. 1993, 08:21:33 GMT).

60. Orson Scott Card, *Ender's Game* (New York: Tom Doherty Associates, 1991), 95.

61. This quotation is taken from an exceptionally detailed post by Detweiler entitled "The JOY of PSEUDOSPOOFING," posted on 26 Oct. 1993, 05:55:59 GMT. Detweiler polemically signs his message as follows: "Jim Riverman, Software Engineer, *jr@netcom.com*, (415) 941–4782 [work]." My calls to this number reached an answering machine owned by "Jamie Kelleher."

62. Lawrence Detweiler, "CRYPTOANARCHIST INFILTRATION ALERT" (posted on 6 Dec. 1993, 08:40:40 GMT).

63. From Timothy C. May (*tcmay@netcom.com*), "Re: CRYPTOANARCHIST INFILTRATION ALERT" (posted on 6 Dec. 1993, 20:21:41 GMT).

64. Perry E. Metzger (*pmetzger@snark.lehman.com*) posted his response to the "CRYPTOANARCHIST INFILTRATION ALERT" on 7 Dec. 1993, 02:21:45 GMT.

65. Detweiler, "JOY of PSEUDOSPOOFING."

66. He did, however, provide a forwarding e-mail address: *perry@gnu.mit.edu.*

67. Posted by Detweiler from *ld231782@LANCE.ColoState.edu* on 6 Dec. 1993, 08:40:40 GMT.

68. Jon Weiner, "Free Speech on the Internet," *Nation*, 13 June 1994, 826.

69. Pynchon, *Crying of Lot 49*, 11. Cranston's most famous role was, of course, as the Shadow, a living hieroglyph.

70. This is part of the signature block of Alexander M. Rosenberg (*alexr@apple.com*), 330 Waverley Street, Apt. B, Palo Alto, Calif., 94301. Speaking of a net conversation with another sysop (local network system operator), Clifford Stoll writes: "Systems managers post a lot of the messages, so you'll find notes like, 'We have a Foobar model 37 computer, and we're trying to hook up a Yoyodyne tape to it. Can anyone help?'" (Clifford Stoll, *The Cuckoo's Egg: Tracking a Spy through the Maze of Computer Espionage* [New York: Pocket Books, 1990], 152.

71. I have deleted May's telephone number and e-mail address out of respect for his privacy. Pynchon has had an enormous influence on science fiction and fantasy writers popular with computer jocks. Such authors include not only Gibson, but Orson Scott Card, Bruce Sterling, Robert Anton Wilson (he of the *Illuminati* trilogy), and Vernor Vinge, whom May cites as a catalyst for his thinking. See especially the title story in Vinge, *True Names . . . and Other Dangers* (New York: Baen Books, 1987), 47–143.

72. Tanner, *City of Words*, 167.   73. Ibid., 174.

74. Pynchon, *Crying of Lot 49*, 181.   75. Ibid., 53.

76. The Internet was born in 1969 as the ARPANET, a computer network of defense contractors established by the Defense Department to enhance the speed of military-related communication. By permitting scientists across the nation instantly to transmit data and images, the ARPANET was from the start a powerful scientific tool. In its place, Pynchon uses the telephone system as his figure for the "secular miracle of communication," in his revelation of squatters who spend the night "like caterpillars, swung among a web of telephone wires, living in the very copper rigging and secular miracle of communication, untroubled by the dumb

voltages flickering their miles, the night long," or of voices that "phoned at random," "searching ceaseless among the dial's ten million possibilities for that magical Other" (*Crying of Lot 49*, 180).

77. Dibbel, "Code Warriors," 34.

78. Ibid., 33–34. Nineteen forty-eight was also the year that the mathematician Norbert Wiener produced *Cybernetics; or, Control and Communication in the Animal and the Machine* (New York: John Wiley and Sons, 1948), the pioneering work on information systems that include feedback loops and servomechanisms.

79. In communication theory, entropy measures "the amount of information conveyed by a message from a source. The more we know about what message the source will produce, the less uncertainty, the less the entropy, and the less the information" (Pierce, *Introduction to Information Theory*, 23). See Claude Shannon, "A Mathematical Theory of Communication," *Bell System Technical Journal* 27, no. 3 (1948): 479–523, and Shannon, "Communication Theory of Secrecy Systems," *Bell System Technical Journal* 28, no. 4 (1949): 656–715. Friedman and Friedman address this essay in their discussion of cryptology as a science in F&F, 22.

80. Kahn, *Codebreakers*, 744.   81. Pynchon, *Crying of Lot 49*, 37.

82. Limon, *Place of Fiction*, 174–76.   83. Pynchon, *Crying of Lot 49*, 142.

84. Ibid., 17.   85. Ibid., 48.

86. For Limon's treatment, see "Polar Similarity" in *Place of Fiction* (167–81). Hanjo Berressem, too, has shown sustained allusions to "The Mask of the Red Death" and the *Narrative of A. Gordon Pym* in *V*. See "Godolphin, Goodolphin, Goodol'phin, Goodol'Pyn, Good ol' Pym: A Question of Integration," *Pynchon Notes* 10 (1982): 3–17.

87. At the height of the ball, they rush in, terrifying the other dancers, while Hop-Frog hooks their chain onto the movable chandelier. This he raises to the ceiling, while he proceeds to burn the court to death in front of the other guests. The scene reappears in *Crying of Lot 49* as follows: "While a battle rages in the streets outside the palace, Pasquale is locked up in his patrician hothouse, holding an orgy. Present at the merrymaking is a fierce black performing ape, brought back from a recent voyage to the Indies. Of course it is somebody in an ape suit, who at a signal leaps on Pasquale from a chandelier, at the same time as half a dozen female impersonators who have up to now been lounging around in the guise of dancing girls also move in on the usurper from all parts of the stage. For about ten minutes the vengeful crew proceed to maim, strangle, poison, burn, stomp, blind and otherwise have at Pasquale, while he describes intimately his varied sensations for our enjoyment" (69).

88. Ibid., 130.

89. Ibid., 131.

90. This opposition is actually too simple, for as Rachman shows, "The Man of the Crowd" is also about stolen texts. The unnamed crime at the center of Poe's story is plagiarism: long passages of the story are revised from "The Drunkard's Death" and "The Black Veil," two of Dickens's *Sketches by Boz*. Where alcoholism is the unnameable sin bedeviling Dickens's protagonist, Poe's is his own theft of Dickens: *that* is the crime that literally *lässt sich nicht lesen*. See Rachman, "Es Lässt Sich Nicht Schreiben," 70–82.

91. Pynchon, *Crying of Lot 49*, 128.

92. In a development that returns us to spiritualism, the Usenet discussion group *alt.para.channelling* is at times used as a space for channeling spirits directly from the ether.

93. Clark, *Man Who Broke Purple*, 233.

94. See Brandon, *Spiritualists*, 8–10.

95. Pynchon, *Crying of Lot 49*, 183.

Coda. Strange Loops and Talking Birds

1. Bamford, *Puzzle Palace*, 136.   2. Ibid., 429.

3. Ibid.   4. Ibid., 137.

5. As Romana Machado describes Stego, his Macintosh software program, computer steganography works by slightly altering pixel values. "Every computer graphics image is made up of an array of tiny dots of color, called pixels. The color of each pixel is determined by its pixel value, a number. Stego hides data by reading a data file one bit at a time, copying each bit to the least significant bit of each pixel value as it scans the image" (Net advertisement for Stego on *sci.crypt*, 12 Nov. 1993). Though visually undetectable, Stego does not provide cryptographic security, because anyone with a copy of Stego can retrieve data from a steganographized PICT file. (PICT is a Macintosh graphics program.) But Stego *can* be used as an "envelope" to hide a *previously encrypted* data file, making it much less likely to be detected. Stego is available via anonymous FTP from *ghost.dsi.unimi.it*, in the */pub/crypt* directory.

6. The encoded message in figure 17 is, however, only accessible to persons equipped with the full JPEG file and Photoshop software. My thanks to Chris Tweney and the Williams Center for Computing for helping me produce these files.

7. Lacan, "Agency of the Letter," 159.

8. Quoted in FAQ, 5.4.

9. Friedman's library is now housed separately at the General George C. Marshall Foundation, in Alexandria, Virginia, in a room that reproduces the labyrinthine filing system Friedman originally devised for it. According to Thomas Camden, the Friedman archivist, "The library is itself a kind of cipher" (conversation with author). My thanks to Mr. Camden and his staff for their kind assistance.

10. Clark, *Man Who Broke Purple*, 127–28.

11. Technically, the use of such a cipher would not violate the second law of classical theory, because although the cipher is received at once, the message cannot be deciphered until the key is sent by ordinary means at subluminal speeds.

12. William Wootters, conversation with author.

13. Tony Sudbery, "Quantum Mechanics: Instant Teleportation," *Nature*, 15 Apr. 1993, 586. Sudbery is glossing Charles Bennett et al., "Teleporting an Unknown Quantum State via Dual Classical and Einstein-Podolsky-Rosen Channels," *Physical Review Letters*, 29 Mar. 1993, 1895–99. In the words of their abstract:

> An unknown quantum state can be disassembled into, then later reconstructed from, purely classical information and purely nonclassical Einstein-Podolsky-Rosen (EPR) correlations. To do so, the sender, "Alice," and the receiver,

"Bob," must prearrange the sharing of an EPR-correlated pair of particles. Alice makes a joint measurement on her EPR particle and the unknown quantum system, and sends Bob the classical result of this measurement. Knowing this, Bob can convert the state of his EPR particle into an exact replica of the unknown state which Alice destroyed. (1895)

14. Sudbery, "Quantum Mechanics," 586; see W. K. Wootters and W. H. Zurek, "A Single Quantum Cannot Be Cloned," *Nature*, Oct. 1982, 802.

15. Sudbery, "Quantum Mechanics," 586. For more on Maxwell's Demon, see Harvey S. Leff and Andrew F. Rex, eds., *Maxwell's Demon: Entropy, Information, Computing* (Princeton: Princeton University Press, 1990).

16. Malone, "Cyberpunk," 2:18. His discussion follows from David Porush's essay "Frothing the Synaptic Bath," in McCaffery, *Storming the Reality Studio*, 331–33.

17. Limon adds: "I do not believe physics will find what it is looking for, but the most important fact of disciplinary relations is about to be the utter lack of sympathy of the philosophy most influential in the literary world for what physicists are, at any rate, brilliantly attempting. The antidisciplinarian age is ending as physics increasingly takes over territory abandoned by the humanities" (*Place of Fiction*, 180).

18. We can expect further negotiations between the human needs served by writing and the changing technological environment in which writing gets defined. One such negotiation occurred in 1992, with the "publication" of *Agrippa: A Book of the Dead*. *Agrippa* contains engravings by the artist Dennis Ashbaugh, and an on-disk semiautobiographical poem by William Gibson, whose consumption is designed to mimic its content: after one reading, *Agrippa* "literally enacts its comment on the ephemerality of memory." When the poem is called up from the disk, the text "scrolls by at a set rate once, and only once, before encrypting itself into random garbage according to a nearly irreversible algorithm. The accompanying holographic art was designed as a photosensitive palimpsest. Upon exposure to light, the image begins to decay only to reveal a more deeply etched image behind it, images dying into one another until nothing is left but the owner's memory" (Malone, "Cyberpunk," 3:7). But the punchline to this story of technological razzle-dazzle is that Gibson's subject in *Agrippa* is homely, an elegy for his Midwestern childhood and for his father that has none of the glamour of the cyberspace trilogy. At the outer edge of technological innovation, Gibson—who also released the text of *Agrippa* onto the Internet, where readers could download it for a one-time-only reading—returns to the most familiar reasons for writing. *Litera scripta manet*: even in an age of self-encrypting novels, the Horatian tag remains a promise that, though writing remains an unknown world, we shall always find ourselves written into its strange loops of self-reference. See William Gibson, *Agrippa (A Book of the Dead)* (New York: Kevin Begos, 1992).

19. Kahn, *Codebreakers*, 17. A comparable note of elegy is struck in the writings of the ACA. In one piece, "B. Natural" observes that "all too often when a cryptographer dies, his treasures fall into the hands of unappreciative persons and are either wasted or destroyed," thus depriving other members of access to cryptographic files and books of references of "inestimable value":

There was one instance in the past, a splendid library of cryptographic "finds" had been left, but it was impossible to induce the widow to part with a single item. In another case a member left his library to his sister who was non-cryptographic, and the articles were rescued from an outhouse where they were piled helter-skelter, a prey to mice and dampness, black with dust and grime. In view of such cases, a suggestion seems to be in order. All members of ACA who have accumulated files, books, and other items of value to other cryptographers should specify in *written directions* in their wills, as to what should become of these materials. Don't let these priceless books and files be sold for waste paper or used to start the furnace fires in a non-cryptographic household.

B. Natural [pseud.], "Who Will Get Your Cryptographic Treasures When You are Gone?" *ACA and You*, 63. For B. Natural there is an equivalence between the mode of cryptographic security and the value of the things enciphered. Adventure stories such as "The Gold-Bug" literalize this relation by having the decrypted cipher lead directly to the discovery of treasure. But for the members of the ACA, cryptography is a more rarefied thing; the "treasures" they seek are the tools that will permit them to continue enciphering and breaking codes. The value of the activity no longer lies in its telos in the world, but in the game of manipulating symbols, and the cracking of ciphers only leads to the making of ever more difficult codes.

20. Powers, *Gold Bug Variations*, 238.

21. Posting to *sci.crypt* from *altair.selu.edu*.

Black Chamber: America's first official cryptanalytic organization, designed to intercept and decrypt radio and telegraph transmissions from and to foreign governments. Founded in 1919, and headed by Herbert Yardley, it was dissolved in 1929 by Secretary of State Henry Stimson, with the lofty observation that "gentlemen do not read each other's mail." After its dissolution, Yardley wrote his best-selling account of his professional adventures, *The American Black Chamber*, which did much to popularize the idea of cryptography in this country. As David Kahn remembers: "When I was a boy, newly interested in the fascinating world of secret writing, Herbert O. Yardley's *The American Black Chamber* was my grail. . . . It was one of the most thrilling books I had read" (Kahn, *Codebreakers*, 361).

BBS: The electronic bulletin board system, a form of cyberspace community where participants, often using aliases, send public and private messages to each other on every topic imaginable. In addition, they may transfer software, play on-line games, download GIF or JPEG image files, and so on. Encryption and anonymous remailers are frequently used to disguise or limit information about the sender's identity and location.

Cipher: A text in which each letter of the plaintext is represented by a different symbol or combination of symbols. In a *transposition cipher*, the letters of the alphabet are jumbled according to a prearranged pattern: this is the type of cipher often used in decoder rings. In a simple *substitution cipher*, a given letter is replaced by any single letter, numeral, or character. To encipher a text, one merely substitutes the cipher letter for the desired plaintext letter. Substitution ciphers form the vast majority of amateur cryptographs; they are the type of codes used in fiction by Poe, Arthur Conan Doyle, and Jules Verne. They were also used by the Mexican government as late as World War I. In contrast to such *monoalphabetic ciphers* are the more complicated *polyalphabetic substitution ciphers*. A simple form of polyalphabetic substitution would be to add another cipher alphabet under the one given above and then to use the two in rotation, the first alphabet for the first plaintext letter, the second for the second, the first again for the third plaintext letter, the second for the fourth, and so on. Modern cipher machines produce polyalphabetic ciphers that employ millions of cipher alphabets.

Code: The set of words, phrases, letters, or syllables used to replace the words or phrases of the plaintext message. Code books sometimes run to one hundred thousand separate entries. In a *cipher*, by contrast, each letter or number in the plaintext is enciphered by its own figure (or set of figures). Speaking properly,

Poe only ciphered, although many cryptographic systems combine elements of codes and ciphers.

Cryptology: The science of codes, composed of two parts: *cryptography*, the art of making codes, and *cryptanalysis*, the art of breaking them. The term *cryptograph*, first used by Poe in "The Gold-Bug," refers to any encoded or enciphered text; it is now more common than its synonym, *cryptogram*. Although technically *cryptography* refers only to the art of *enciphering*, in lay usage the term refers to the whole range of activities grouped around secret writing. These include *deciphering*, in which one solves a text through the application of a known key or code, and *decryption* or *cryptanalysis*, terms that refer to the solution of a cipher or code without the key. Such an activity is sometimes known simply as *codebreaking*.

Cypherpunks: An influential band of computer scientists and cryptographers who believe that the unfettered existence of strong public-key cryptography is essential to the maintenance of First Amendment rights. Cypherpunks promote the development and use of a variety of digital encryption systems, including PGP and RSA. In the words of their charter, "those who want privacy must create it for themselves and not expect governments, corporations, or other large, faceless organizations to grant them privacy out of beneficence. Cypherpunks know that people have been creating their own privacy for centuries with whispers, envelopes, closed doors, and couriers." The cypherpunk charter is available from Eric Hughes (*hughes@toad.com*).

Detection theory: A subset of information theory, which concerns itself with determining the presence of a signal even when the signal is mixed with a specified amount of noise.

Encipherment: The act of putting plaintext into a cipher.

Enigma: A series of powerful codemaking machines used by the Axis powers from the 1920s through World War II. Developed by the German engineer Arthur Scherbius, Enigma's basic design involved two or more typewriterlike machines linked through multiple switchboards. Encryptions were performed by linking the switchboards in different combinations for different codes. Encryptions could be changed by rewiring the connections in the switchboards. Modified Enigma machines formed the basis for the top-secret German Ultra code, and for the Japanese diplomatic code Purple.

Entropy: A measure of the amount of disorder and randomness in a particular language. Information theorists calculate the entropy of a particular language (here synonymous with a transmission system) by knowing the number of constituent elements in that language correlated to the possibility of their occurrence in pairs, trigrams, four-letter groups, and so on. Technically, entropy is equal to the average number of binary digits per symbol that are needed in order to transmit messages produced by the source. In communication theory, entropy is interpreted as average uncertainty about what symbol the source will produce next.

Fingering: The use of an Internet program known as Finger. By fingering, any Internet user can discover the name and electronic address of every other user logged on at the same time. Conceptually, Finger is part of a larger pattern of metaphors used to link particular bodies to their electronic script. Other terms in this cluster include *digital signature, fingerprinting*, and *digital footprints*.

Frequency: How often one may expect to find a given letter in any given language. In English, the order of frequency is as follows:

e t a o i n s r h l d c u m f w g y p b v k x j q z

The frequency with which a given character appears in a cipher is often a clue to the language in which it is written. In German, for instance, the letter *e* makes up exactly 17.9 percent of the average German text. Although there are many ways to disguise these ratios, they form one of the cryptographer's most valuable tools.

Kasiski test: A "revolutionary" technique for solving polyalphabetic ciphers, based on the fact that repetitions in the key phrase combined with repetitions in the plaintext will produce identical encipherments. By using the Kasiski test, cryptanalysts can deduce the length of the key phrase. For example:

```
key        R U N R U N R U N R U N R U N R U N R U N R
plaintext  t o b e o r n o t t o b e t h a t i s t h e
ciphertext K I O V I E E I G K I O V N U R N V J N U V
```

In the instance above, the repetitions of *kiov* and *nu* in the ciphertext point to repetitions in the plaintext, which are often, as here, organized around such common words as *the, on*, and *to*. A Kasiski examination of the second cipher by W. B. Tyler found significant repetitions in the ciphertext, which indicates that it *is* a true cipher, rather than an illegible prank or hash.

Key: The system or pattern used to decipher cryptograms. Keys may take many forms, including the arrangement of letters within a cipher alphabet, the pattern of shuffling within a transposition, or the settings on a cipher machine. In *public-key cryptography*, a system pioneered in the 1970s by Whitfield Diffie and Martin Hellman, information secured through a pair of encrypting algorithms can travel over insecure channels without compromising security. In earlier systems of information transfer, the cryptographic key had to be transferred to the receiver along with the encrypted information, thus exposing it to interception. Any encrypted information could be decoded with the stolen key. Public-key cryptography solved this problem by providing each user with a pair of encrypting algorithms, one of which is public and widely distributed, and the other of which is private. The private key is kept secret by the sender. The public key is sent to others to allow them to encrypt or decrypt messages. A sender mails information by encrypting it in the receiver's public key; the receiver decodes it using his or her private key. The genius of public-key cryptography lies in its system of authentication; messages encoded with someone's private key can only be decoded using that person's public key.

Noise: Any undesired disturbance in a signaling system, such as random electric currents in a telephone system. Noise appears as static or hissing in radio receivers and as "snow" on television screens.

NSA: The National Security Agency, that branch of government responsible for the creation and maintenance of governmental and military ciphers, and for the interception and decryption of enciphered foreign communications. Formed in 1952 in near-complete secrecy, the NSA is an outgrowth of the Signal Intelligence Service (founded in 1930), which, in turn, had consolidated the various cryptologic and cryptanalytic services earlier provided by the War Department's Signal Service and by Yardley's American Black Chamber. The NSA is now one of the largest and most powerful government agencies, almost four times the size of the CIA, yet its membership, budget, and activities are all subject to federal blackout.

Plaintext: Any text—love letter, military strategy, private diary—to be encoded.

Quantum Cryptography: A form of cryptography in which, under certain experimental conditions, pairs of photons may be created that exert an influence over one another that cannot be explained by quantum mechanics. Measuring the polarization of one particle immediately and identically changes the spin on its antiparticle. Such polarization takes place regardless of the relative positions of the two particles in the universe, in a result that seems to violate the second law of classical theory. It is theoretically possible that a stream of such polarized photons could be used to encipher messages that could be sent over space in literally no time at all.

Steganography: Secret writing concealed within an apparently innocuous surface text. Such texts range from those written in invisible inks and the hidden microdot writings of spy novels to wholly literary forms. At the end of Vladimir Nabokov's "Vane Sisters," for instance, the first letters of each word in the last paragraph reveal an occulted message from two dead sisters: "Icicles by Cynthia, meter from me. Sybil." In contemporary forms of steganography, such as the Macintosh Stego program, encoded messages are hidden as almost-invisible noise in the code used to generate a binary image.

Vigenere table: The alphabet arranged in a series of twenty-six rows, with a letter slid over to the left for each row. These form the cipher alphabet. A horizontal alphabet running along the top represents the plaintext. Another alphabet, repeating the first vertical row, runs down the left side of the table. Armed with the keyword and the Vigenere table, one can encrypt messages encoded with the keyword by matching the coordinates of the key alphabet with the cipher alphabet to come up with the plaintext. The table was named after its sixteenth-century creator, Blaise de Vigenere. Forgotten in its own time, this auto-key system was rediscovered in the late nineteenth century and became the basis for later systems of cryptanalysis.

	a	b	c	d	e	f	g	h	i	j	k	l	m	n	o	p	q	r	s	t	u	v	w	x	y	z
A	a	b	c	d	e	f	g	h	i	j	k	l	m	n	o	p	q	r	s	t	u	v	w	x	y	z
B	b	c	d	e	f	g	h	i	j	k	l	m	n	o	p	q	r	s	t	u	v	w	x	y	z	a
C	c	d	e	f	g	h	i	j	k	l	m	n	o	p	q	r	s	t	u	v	w	x	y	z	a	b
D	d	e	f	g	h	i	j	k	l	m	n	o	p	q	r	s	t	u	v	w	x	y	z	a	b	c
E	e	f	g	h	i	j	k	l	m	n	o	p	q	r	s	t	u	v	w	x	y	z	a	b	c	d
F	f	g	h	i	j	k	l	m	n	o	p	q	r	s	t	u	v	w	x	y	z	a	b	c	d	e
G	g	h	i	j	k	l	m	n	o	p	q	r	s	t	u	v	w	x	y	z	a	b	c	d	e	f
H	h	i	j	k	l	m	n	o	p	q	r	s	t	u	v	w	x	y	z	a	b	c	d	e	f	g
I	i	j	k	l	m	n	o	p	q	r	s	t	u	v	w	x	y	z	a	b	c	d	e	f	g	h
J	j	k	l	m	n	o	p	q	r	s	t	u	v	w	x	y	z	a	b	c	d	e	f	g	h	i
K	k	l	m	n	o	p	q	r	s	t	u	v	w	x	y	z	a	b	c	d	e	f	g	h	i	j
L	l	m	n	o	p	q	r	s	t	u	v	w	x	y	z	a	b	c	d	e	f	g	h	i	j	k
M	m	n	o	p	q	r	s	t	u	v	w	x	y	z	a	b	c	d	e	f	g	h	i	j	k	l
N	n	o	p	q	r	s	t	u	v	w	x	y	z	a	b	c	d	e	f	g	h	i	j	k	l	m
O	o	p	q	r	s	t	u	v	w	x	y	z	a	b	c	d	e	f	g	h	i	j	k	l	m	n
P	p	q	r	s	t	u	v	w	x	y	z	a	b	c	d	e	f	g	h	i	j	k	l	m	n	o
Q	q	r	s	t	u	v	w	x	y	z	a	b	c	d	e	f	g	h	i	j	k	l	m	n	o	p
R	r	s	t	u	v	w	x	y	z	a	b	c	d	e	f	g	h	i	j	k	l	m	n	o	p	q
S	s	t	u	v	w	x	y	z	a	b	c	d	e	f	g	h	i	j	k	l	m	n	o	p	q	r
T	t	u	v	w	x	y	z	a	b	c	d	e	f	g	h	i	j	k	l	m	n	o	p	q	r	s
U	u	v	w	x	y	z	a	b	c	d	e	f	g	h	i	j	k	l	m	n	o	p	q	r	s	t
V	v	w	x	y	z	a	b	c	d	e	f	g	h	i	j	k	l	m	n	o	p	q	r	s	t	u
W	w	x	y	z	a	b	c	d	e	f	g	h	i	j	k	l	m	n	o	p	q	r	s	t	u	v
X	x	y	z	a	b	c	d	e	f	g	h	i	j	k	l	m	n	o	p	q	r	s	t	u	v	w
Y	y	z	a	b	c	d	e	f	g	h	i	j	k	l	m	n	o	p	q	r	s	t	u	v	w	x
Z	z	a	b	c	d	e	f	g	h	i	j	k	l	m	n	o	p	q	r	s	t	u	v	w	x	y

Index

Page references to tables and figures are printed in italic type.

Library of Congress Cataloging-in-Publication Data

Rosenheim, Shawn.

  The cryptographic imagination : secret writing from Edgar Poe to the Internet /
Shawn James Rosenheim.

    p.   cm. — (Parallax)

  Includes bibliographical references and index.

  ISBN 0-8018-5331-1 (hc : alk. paper). — ISBN 0-8018-5332-X (pbk. : alk. paper)

  1. Poe, Edgar Allan. 1809–1849—Knowledge—Cryptography.   2. Detective and mystery stories.
American—History and criticism.   3. American literature—History and criticism.   4. Poe, Edgar Allan,
1809–1849—Influence.   5. Modernism (Literature)—United States.   6. Influence (Literary, artistic, etc.)
7. World War, 1939–1945—Cryptography.   8. Cryptography in literature.   9. Internet (Computer
network)   10. Ciphers in literature.   11. Cold war.   I. Title.   II. Series: Parallax (Baltimore, Md.)
PS2642.C5R67   1997

818'.309—dc20   96-24761